S0-BAG-041

INDONESIA

page 304

Siargao
Lanuza
Tandag
Bislig

Surigao
Butuan
Davao
Mati
C. San Agustin

Gingoog
Tagum
Sarangani Is

Cagayan de Oro
Malaybalay
Davao
Digos
Samal
General Santos
Glan

Iligan
Marawi
Mindanao
Parang
Sultan Kudarat
Midsayap
Matalam
Mt Apo 2956
Koronadal
Maasim
Mt Busa 2083

Dapitan
Ozamis
Cotabato
Surallah

OroQuieta
Mt Malindang 2425
Pagadian
Olutanga

Dipolog
Sindangan
Moro Gulf

Zamboanga
Lamitan
Basilan

Sulu Archipelago

MINDANAO SEA

Samales Group

Jolo Group

Pangutaran Group

Tapul Group
Jolo
Siasi
Tawi-Tawi Group

Tawi-Tawi
Bambing

Sulu Strait

Cagayan de Tawi-Tawi

Sandakan
Lahad Datu

MALAYSIA
Sabah
Borneo
Crocker Range
Kudat

SULU SEA

Calamian Group
Coron
Busuanga
Culion

Linapacan

Cuyo West Passage

Cuyo Islands
Cuyo

San Jose de Buenavista

Dumaran

El Nido
Taytay
Roxas
Cleopatra's Needle 1593

Puerto Princesa

Palawan

Quezon
Brooke's Point
Bugsuk
Balabac

page 296

Balabac Strait
Banggi

Laoang
Oras
Catarman
Samar
Calbayog
Catbalogan
Catbalogan
Borongan
Guiuan
Homonhon

Tacloban
Burauen
Leyte Gulf

Masbate
Ticao
Masbate
Burias
Daanbantayan

Tablas
Romblon
Sibuyan
Sibuyan Sea

Sta Strait
Roxas

Semirara Islands

San Jose

Mindoro Strait
Bisanga

Panay
Kalibo
Ibajay
Roxas
Passi
Pototan
Iloilo
Miagao
Guimaras
Kabankalan
Sipalay

Boracay

Visayan Sea

Ormoc
Baybay
Danao
Cebu
Lapu-Lapu
page 257
Cebu
Toledo
Carcar
Argao
Bais
Tanjay
Sta Catalina

Sagay
Bacolod
San Car.
Bago
Guihulngan
Negros

page 240

Hilongos
Maasin
Kalibon
Baclayon
Tubigon
Bohol
Tagbilaran
Dauis
Dumaguete
Siquijor

Bohol Sea

Camiguin

Leyte

page 279

PHILIPPINES

APA PUBLICATIONS

Part of the Langenscheidt Publishing Group

INSIGHT GUIDE
PHILIPPINES

Editorial

Managing Editor
Francis Dorai
Editorial Director
Brian Bell

Distribution

UK & Ireland
GeoCenter International Ltd
Meridian House, Churchill Way West
Basingstoke, Hampshire RG21 6YR
Fax: (44) 1256-817988

United States
Langenscheidt Publishers, Inc.
36-36 33rd Street, 4th Floor
Long Island City, NY 11106
Fax: (1 718) 784-0640

Australia
Universal Publishers
1 Waterloo Road
Macquarie Park, NSW 2113
Fax: (61) 2 9888 9074

New Zealand
Hema Maps New Zealand Ltd (HNZ)
Unit D, 24 Ra ORA Drive
East Tamaki, Auckland
Fax: (64) 9 273 6479

Worldwide
**Apa Publications GmbH & Co.
Verlag KG (Singapore branch)**
38 Joo Koon Road, Singapore 628990
Tel: (65) 6865-1600. Fax: (65) 6861-6438

Printing

Insight Print Services (Pte) Ltd
38 Joo Koon Road, Singapore 628990
Tel: (65) 6865-1600. Fax: (65) 6861-6438

© 2008 Apa Publications GmbH & Co.
Verlag KG (Singapore branch)
All Rights Reserved

First Edition 1980
Eleventh Edition 2000
Updated 2008

ABOUT THIS BOOK

The first Insight Guide pioneered the use of creative full-colour pho-tography in travel guides in 1970. Since then, we have expanded our range to cater for our readers' need not only for reliable information about their chosen destination but also for a real understanding of that destina-tion. Now, when the Internet can sup-ply inexhaustible – but not always reliable – facts, our books marry text and pictures to provide those much more elusive qualities: knowledge and discernment. To achieve this, they rely heavily on the authority of locally based writers and photographers.

How to use this book

This book is care-fully structured to convey an under-standing of the Philippines and its culture, and to guide readers through its myriad sights and attractions:

◆ The **Features** section, indicated by a yellow bar at the top of each page, covers the history and culture of the country in a series of infor-mative essays.

◆ The main **Places** section, indi-cated by a blue bar, is a complete guide to all the sights and areas worth visiting. Places of special interest are cross-referenced by numbers to full-color maps.

◆ The **Travel Tips** listings, with an orange bar, provide a handy point of reference for information on travel, hotels, shops, restaurants and more.

The contributors

The challenge of stringing the

Map Legend

—— ·· —	International Boundary
————	Regional Boundary
— — — —	Province Boundary
—·—·—	National Park/Reserve
— — — —	Ferry Route
●	LRT (Light Rail) or MRT (Metro Rail)
✈ ✈	Airport: International/Regional
🚌	Bus Station
❶	Tourist Information
✉	Post Office
▯ † ♱	Church/Ruins
†	Monastery
☾	Mosque
✡	Synagogue
▯ ▯	Castle/Ruins
∴	Archaeological Site
∩	Cave
ⅼ	Statue/Monument
★	Place of Interest

7,107 islands that make up the Philippines into a coherent read was undertaken by **Francis Dorai**, Insight's Singapore-based managing editor. This 11th edition was completely restructured, building on the earlier edition put together by **Scott Rutherford**.

The stellar team of writers assembled for the update have done justice to a book whose first edition won the PATA (Pacific Area Travel Association) Award for Excellence in Travel Publishing in 1980.

The Features section was almost single-handedly updated by Filipino novelist and poet **Alfred Yuson**, who incidentally wrote a major portion of the 1980 edition. Yuson has at various times been a scriptwriter, film and music reviewer, and magazine editor. Adding authority to this section was eminent Filipino food critic

Doreen Fernandez, who wrote the essay on Filipino cuisine. And making sense of eclectic Philippine architecture was **Augusto Villalon**, who writes a weekly column on design and architectural issues for the *Philippine Daily Inquirer*.

The Places section update was the combined effort of three writers: the aforementioned Yuson covered the chapters on Central and Western Visayas and the Palawan Islands. Filipino journalist **Gina T. Mission** trudged through Northeastern Luzon, Bicol Peninsula, Luzon's Islands, Eastern Visayas, and Mindanao, where she grew up, for new material on these chapters. She also wrote the "Insight On" picture stories on Volcanoes, Handicrafts and The Living Seas. Finally, **Julie Gaw**, an American travel writer and editor with Chinese roots in the Philippines did the remaining groundwork. This included chapters on Manila, Manila's Environs, Central Plains, Ilocos Region and Central Cordillera. In addition, she wrote the chapter on Flora and Fauna, the "Insight On" picture story on Rice Terraces, and updated the Travel Tips section.

New photography was provided by **Patrick Lucero**, **Kevin Hamdorf** and **Mark Downey**, among others.

In 2007 Manila-based freelance writer **Chip Childers** updated this book under the supervision of **Low Jat Leng** at Insight Guides' Singapore office.

The current edition builds on the excellent foundations created by the writers of previous editions, most notably **Sylvia L. Mayuga**, **Elizabeth Reyes**, **Theon Banos Cross**, **Tony Wheeler**, **Catherine Daynos**, **Marcus Brooke** and **Bill Williams**.

The main places of interest in the Places section are coordinated by number with a full-color map (e.g. ❶), and a symbol at the top of every right-hand page tells you where to find the map.

INSIGHT GUIDE
PHILIPPINES

CONTENTS

Maps

Sun-ripened rice field
ready for harvesting in
Marinduque island, Luzon

Insight on ...

Information panels

Travel Tips

Places

THE BEST OF PHILIPPINES

The unique attractions of the Philippines, absorbing museums, dynamic culture, breathtaking landscapes, exciting adventure activities... here, at a glance, are our recommendations, plus some tips that even Filipinos won't always know

LEFT: National Museum in Manila.
BOTTOM RIGHT: army barrack ruins in Corregidor Island.
BOTTOM LEFT: the ubiquitous jeepney.

ONLY IN THE PHILIPPINES

● **Crucifixions, Pampanga.** The Catholic Church's condemnation hasn't stopped this yearly cavalcade of religious devotees and re-enactment of Christ's suffering, which sometimes takes on a surreal feeling. *Page 64*

● **Lights and Sounds of Rizal, Metro Manila.** National hero Jose Rizal's final hours before his execution are re-enacted in this open-air audio-visual presentation; this is a great way to learn about the country and its people. *Page 139*

● **Jeepneys.** A ride on this often brazenly embellished and garishly painted mode of transportation is *de rigeur* for any visitor to the Philippines. *Page 153*

● **Corregidor Island, Cavite.** Get a crash course on how the colonial militaries of Spain, America and Japan sought to defend the capital city. *Page 155*

● **Mt Banahaw, Laguna.** A mountain that has been held sacred since before recorded history, Banahaw draws throngs of dedicated worshippers during Holy Week in March/April. *Page 160*

PHILIPPINES FOR FAMILIES

● **National Museum, Metro Manila.** The best showcase for Philippine history and culture, with plenty of interactive fun for youngsters. *Pages 140–1*

● **Museo Pambata (Children's Museum), Metro Manila.** A must-visit for children, who can explore themes ranging from the environment and science to the human body. *Page 141*

● **Avilon Zoo, Rizal.** Northeast of Quezon City, this is one of the most highly acclaimed zoos in the country, with over 500 animal species. *Page 169*

● **Ocean Adventure, Subic Bay.** Marine theme park with dolphins, whales, sea lions and plenty of interaction to keep the family riveted. *Page 179*

● **Crocodile Park, Davao.** See Pangil, the 6-meter (19-ft) long star crocodile, snakes and other animals at this popular attraction. *Page 313*

TOP HISTORICAL SITES

● **Butuan, Agusan del Norte.** Considered by some to be the cradle of Philippine civilization; three museums here showcase the area's archeological importance. *Pages 23, 331*

● **Intramuros, Metro Manila.** In a city that was burned to the ground in World War II, one can still get a sense of Manila's rich and storied history. *Pages 136–8*

● **Vigan, Ilocos Sur.** Stroll among some of the country's best-preserved *calles* (streets) and houses from the Spanish era. *Page 187*

● **Fort San Pedro, Cebu.** Step inside its massive stone walls and back into the past, to an era where the "Pearl of the South" was under siege. *Page 258*

● **Silay, Negros Occidental.** Explore the now-peaceful streets of a city that used to be known as the bustling "Paris of Negros." *Page 273*

ABOVE: the 17th-century Fort San Pedro.
BELOW: massive caves at the Sohoton National Park.

BELOW: dioramas at the Ayala Museum bring Philippine history to life.

BEST CULTURAL EXPERIENCES

● **Metropolitan Museum of Manila, Metro Manila.** The fine works of Filipino master painters are displayed along with gold artifacts and pottery dating to the 8th century in this museum. *Page 143*

● **Ayala Museum, Metro Manila.** Recently refurbished museum whose historical and ethnographic exhibits and Philippine art collection make for an enriching day out. *Page 146*

● **Batanes.** Spend a night or two in one of the far-flung villages on the islands of Batanes – Batan, Sabtang and Itbayat – and experience one of the most isolated island cultures in the country. *Page 193*

● **Tinglayan, Kalinga.** Have the *barangay* captain of the quaint Luplupa village arrange a homestay on the banks of the Chico River. *Page 211*

BEST NATURAL ATTRACTIONS

● **Volcanoes.** In a country littered with soaring volcanic peaks such as Mayon, Pinatubo, Taal and Canlaon, rewarding treks up volcanoes are easy to find and hard to forget. *Pages 40–1, 158, 177, 220, 274*

● **Sierra Madre National Park, Aurora.** The largest national park with some of the most spectacular landscapes in the country and also home to endangered species such as the Philippine eagle and the cloud rat. *Page 199*

● **Sohoton Caves National Park, Western Samar.** Tour gigantic caves, underground rivers and natural arches; scenic outrigger trip up the Basey Golden River to the park entrance. *Page 247*

● **Boracay, Aklan.** Leave the cares of the world behind in this fabled paradise of pristine beaches, luxurious resorts and island adventures. *Pages 279–80*

● **Bacuit Archipelago, Palawan.** Take a *banca* cruise to enjoy the archipelago's jaw-dropping beauty formed by rugged karst outcrops, crystal-clear lagoons and white-sand beaches. *Pages 292–3*

● **Ultralight flight over Mt Arayat, Pampanga.** Take flight in an ultralight for a heart-stopping view of beautiful Mt Arayat and surrounds from the air. *Page 177*

● **Rice Terraces, Ifugao.** Often called the "Eighth Wonder of the World," these agricultural master-pieces were sculpted by Cordillera tribes some 2,000 years ago. *Pages 209, 212–3*

● **Chocolate Hills, Bohol.** The postcard-perfect sunrise over these hills, named for their confectionery-like appearance in summer, is an unforgettable sight. *Page 255*

● **Tops, Cebu.** From foothills high above, enjoy a view of the shimmering lights of Cebu city as you relax in this picnic-friendly park that is open till late. *Page 257*

● **Mt Luho View Deck, Boracay, Aklan.** Scramble up the tower and you'll have a near aerial view of the entire island of Boracay and environs. *Page 279*

BEST DIVING AND SNORKELING SITES

● **Tubbataha Reefs, Sulu Sea.** This UNESCO World Heritage Site is a favourite with seasoned divers for its steep coral walls and high diversity of marine species. *Pages 45, 47, 303*

● **Donsol, Sorsogon.** Swim with the world's biggest fish, the *butanding* (whale shark), in the waters right off the Bicol coast. *Pages 46, 222*

● **Apo Reef, Apo Island, Mindoro Occidental.** Stunning coral ecosystem in a 34-sq. km (13-sq. mile) reef, home to 400–500 coral species, that has rebounded from years of damage by dynamite fishing. *Pages 47, 226*

● **Panglao, Bohol.** A good base for exploring the "Visayas Dive Triangle" of Cebu, Bohol and Negros Oriental. *Page 253*

● **Busuanga Island, Palawan.** Dive in the north to see dugongs and rich marine life, or go south for the best wreck diving in the country. *Pages 289–90*

TOP: the rice terraces of Ifugao.
ABOVE RIGHT: butterfly fish in the pristine waters of the Tubbataha Reefs.
LEFT: the Philippines is home to some of the best diving sites in Asia.

BEST FESTIVALS AND EVENTS

● **Ati-Atihan, Kalibo, Aklan.** Probably the most famous and raucous of Philippine festivals, where the line between spectators and participants gets blurrier as the day gets longer. *Pages 77, 278*
● **Panagbenga (Flower Parade), Baguio, Benguet.** Watch a spectacle of marching bands and dance troupes during the "season for blossoming." *Page 205*
● **Kadaugan sa Mactan, Cebu.** Spanish explorer Ferdinand Magellan's fatal encounter with the first Filipino hero, Lapu-Lapu, is re-enacted on the waters off Mactan Island. *Pages 262–3*
● **Kadayawan, Davao.** Davao's incredible ethnic diversity is celebrated in a week of costumes, music, dance and traditional sports like horse fighting. *Pages 311, 383*
● **Fête de la Musique, Metro Manila.** One of the best parties of the year for music lovers, with over 100 talented Filipino musicians of all stripes performing on various stages at one venue. *Page 380*

BEST SHOPPING EXPERIENCES

● **Silahis Center, Metro Manila.** In the heart of Intramuros and chock-full of handicrafts and items from around the country. *Page 138*
● **Greenhills Shopping Center, Metro Manila.** The place to go to for freshwater and South China Sea pearls, and cheap electronic goods. *Page 147*
● **Divisoria, Metro Manila.** An intense shopping experience to be had at this bargain-basement flea market with thousands of stalls; get almost everything here. *Page 150*
● **Baguio City Market, Baguio, Benguet.** Get your weavings, carvings and produce not found anywhere else in the country at this crossroads of the Cordilleran mountain tribes. *Page 205*
● **Aldevinco Shopping Center, Davao.** Pick up ethnic and handmade wares from Muslim and tribal vendors. *Page 312*

TOP: tribal weavers from central Cordillera.
LEFT: Ati-Atihan parade in Kalibo.
RIGHT: indigenous woodcarving.

MONEY-SAVING TIPS

● **Take the Light Rail.** The LRT in Metro Manila is a cheap and time-saving mode of transportation. Use a multiple-ride, stored-value ticket, which at P100 gives you about eight rides. Each card gives one extra free ride at the end of its use.
● **Be assertive with taxi drivers.** By law, taxi drivers should take you to your destination for the metered fare, but many will try to give excuses for why they won't use the meter. When a driver quotes you a set price to a destination (*contrata*), it is usually around three times the normal fare. If insisting on the meter (*metro*) doesn't work, tell the driver you will add a tip. Start from around P20 on top of the metered fare and haggle up.
● **Be firm with touts.** Don't be pressured by touts at airports and bus and boat terminals. Be firm about your destination, agree on the price before you begin a journey, and keep in mind that any tout's first stated price is usually bloated to test how much he can get away with.
● **Haggle and negotiate.** Bargaining is often practised, but in some of the more rural parts, such as Sagada in Mountain Province, don't take it too far as it is not the way of doing business like in cities such as Manila and Cebu.

ASIA'S MAVERICK

Geographically part of Southeast Asia, yet far removed culturally,

the Philippines has a marked Latin temperament

Like lovely gems atop Asia's continental shelf, the Philippines lays where two tectonic plates had collided once upon a time to create its 7,107 islands. Its 90 million inhabitants, represented by 111 linguistic, cultural and racial groups, speak Pilipino, its national language based on Tagalog, while another 70 languages and dialects are also spoken. English, the other official language, is widely used.

Geographically, the country is a sprawl of half-drowned mountains, part of a great cordillera extending from the south of Japan to Indonesia. It stretches 1,840 km (1,140 miles) north to south, spanning 1,100 km (690 miles) at its widest. In land area, it is slightly larger than New Zealand.

Given the over three centuries of Spanish rule and 48 years of American government, it is not surprising if the Filipino seems more Latin than Asian to the visitor. Nearly everything belonging to the first settlers has persevered, including language and culture. To this foundation, add the endowments of the Spanish and Americans. "Three centuries in a convent followed by 50 years in Hollywood," goes an old saying. Threaded through both culture and lineage are also influences from China, India and Arabia.

The Philippines is the only predominantly Christian nation in Asia and has always been the odd man out. Even in matters of food, it seems out of place. Instead of fiery curries or spicy grilled meats, Filipino food tends to be a sedate mixture of an ascetic atoll diet, combining elements of Chinese imagination and Spanish conservatism, although there are a few areas where chillies come into their own.

For the past few decades, Philippines has been the sad butt of regional jokes, perceived as a country that can't quite get its act together. Having thrown off the yoke of the Marcos era, the country's reputation improved remarkably in the mid 1990s when former president Fidel Ramos used his own brand of military discipline and corporate elan to revitalize the economy. He was succeeded in 1998 by former action movie star Joseph Estrada and, not surprisingly, things took a turn for the worse. After two years in office, Estrada was removed amid allegations of corruption. His vice-president, Gloria Arroyo-Macapagal, took over in 2001. She won her re-election bid in 2004, and now things are looking up for the country, although changes for the better come slowly.

Despite the many hardships they have endured in their checkered past, the Filipinos have kept their equanimity, knowing that life is all about adapting to change. They are a friendly lot, as you'll discover when you experience the archipelago's many attractions, ranging from unspoilt beaches and serene countryside to exciting nightlife. ❑

PRECEDING PAGES: Cebu is famous for its locally produced guitars; water buffalo has right of way in Nueva Ecija. **LEFT:** Corregidor Island guide – with Filipino and American flags.

Decisive Dates

EARLY DAYS

Prehistory: Migrants cross land bridge from Asian mainland and settle in archipelago.

AD 900: Chinese establish coastal trading posts over the next 300 years.

1400: Muslim clergy start to bring Islam to the Philippines from Malaya.

1494: The Treaty of Tordesillas is signed between Portugal and Spain, dividing much of the world between the two colonial powers. Everything to the east of a line 370 leagues west of the Cape Verde Islands

belongs to Portugal, while everything to the west belongs to Spain.

EARLY COLONIAL INTRUSIONS

1521: Explorer Ferdinand Magellan lands on Cebu and claims region for Spain. Lapu Lapu (Rajah Cilapulapu), in defending his island of Mactan, slays Magellan, thus driving the expedition away.

1543: Next Spanish expedition led by Ruy de Villalobos lands in Mindanao. He names the archipelago "Filipinas," after Crown Prince Felipe II.

1565: Miguel Lopez de Legazpi sails from Mexico and gains a foothold in Cebu.

1571: Legazpi builds Spanish walled city of Intramuros. City is menaced from outset by enemies: Japanese *wako*, Dutch fleets, Chinese pirates and disgruntled Filipinos. The core of modern Manila begins to form outside of Intramuros.

1762: Late in the year, as a minor episode in the Seven Years' War with Spain, Intramuros is seized by England's General William Draper.

1764: End of the British occupation.

RISE OF NATIONALISM

1872: Uprising in Cavite, south of Manila. Spain executes Filipino priests Jose Burgos, Mariano Gomez and Jacinto Zamora, who quickly become martyrs to the cause of nationalism.

1892: Thinker Jose Rizal founds La Liga Filipina, is arrested and exiled to Dapitan, Mindanao. Andres Bonifacio founds the Katipunan with aim to revolt.

1896: Spanish colonists imprison and kill hundreds of Filipinos in Manila. Bonifacio and the Katipunan launch the Philippine revolution. Emilio Aguinaldo and rebel forces capture Cavite. Rizal is executed.

1898: The United States goes to war with Spain, defeats Spain. Treaty between the United States and Spain grants the US authority over the Philippines, along with Puerto Rico and Guam.

1899: War breaks out between the United States and the Philippines. Aguinaldo is inaugurated as president of the first Philippine republic.

1901: Aguinaldo captured after guerrilla war of resistance. He swears allegiance to the US. Scattered resistance continues throughout the decade.

1916: The US Congress authorizes the gradual independence of the Philippines.

1935: Manuel Quezon elected president. The Philippines is made an American commonwealth with the promise of independence in 1945; but World War II intervenes. General Douglas MacArthur takes charge of the Philippines' defense against Japan.

WORLD WAR II

1941: On December 22, Japanese land on Luzon.

1942: Japan overrun Manila. Quezon proposes and Roosevelt rejects Philippine neutrality. MacArthur retreats to Australia. Hukbalahap established with PKP member Luis Taruc in command. Quezon and Sergio Osmeña flee to the US, where they establish a government in exile.

1943: Japanese install puppet republic with Jose Laurel as president. Japanese rule is exceedingly brutal.

1944: Quezon dies. MacArthur and Osmeña land in Leyte, begins Allied effort to retake the archipelago.

1945: The Allies recapture Manila, declared an "open city" by the Allies and thus subject to unlimited bombardment. Much of the city is destroyed.

PROBLEMS AND OPPORTUNITIES

1946: Manuel Roxas defeats Osmeña for presidency. On July 4, the Philippines is granted independence. Elpidio Quirino succeeds Roxas who died while in office.

1951: US-Philippine mutual defense treaty signed.

1965: Ferdinand Marcos defeats Diosdado Macapagal in his bid for re-election to the presidency.

1969: Marcos is first president to be re-elected.

1970: Peso devaluation fuels price increases, food shortages, unemployment and unrest. Students stage a series of anti-Marcos, anti-US demonstrations. American senators accuse the Philippines of misusing funds supplied for Philippine forces in Vietnam. Marcos threatens to impose martial law.

1972–81: Martial law imposed. Marcos erects monuments to himself and accumulates a vast fortune. His wife, Imelda, dominates Manila government.

1981: Martial law lifted but Marcos keeps power to rule by decree. Marcos re-elected in contest boycotted by opposition.

1983: Leading opposition leader Benigno Aquino returns to Manila from US exile but is assassinated on arrival at the Manila airport. Circumstances point to government involvement.

1984: Legislative elections held. "Parliament of the street" holds frequent anti-Marcos demonstrations. Spiraling economic crises.

1985: General Fabian C. Ver and 25 others are charged with slaying Aquino, but are acquitted. Marcos announces a snap election. More than a million people petition Cory Aquino, widow of the assassinated Aquino, to run against Marcos.

1986: Violence escalates before elections, at least 30 killed on election day. Election rigging enrages Filipinos and millions join in uprising against Marcos regime. On February 26, Marcoses flee. Aquino elected to presidency. New constitution drafted. Labor leader Rolando Olalia murdered. Ceasefire with the New People's Army (NPA).

1987: Ceasefire breaks down, and the military kills 13 peasant demonstrators near presidential palace. Public ratifies constitution after third military mutiny put down. Concern about renewed human rights abuses. Pro-Aquino forces win majorities in House and Senate elections. Another bloody coup attempt fails.

1988: Provincial elections. The United States agrees to pay US$481 million a year for use of American military bases in the Philippines. Marcoses indicted by a US grand jury for fraud and embezzlement.

PREDEDING PAGES: 18th-century lithograph of local aristocrats and tribes. **LEFT:** Catholic baptism scene in Cebu, 1521. **RIGHT:** Gloria Macapagal-Arroyo.

1989: Ferdinand Marcos dies in Hawaii. A coup attempt splits the military; government calls on the United States for air support to help Aquino government.

1990: Cabinet revamped. Negotiations start on status of American military bases.

1991: Bilateral posturing regarding the US bases ends abruptly with dramatic eruption of Mount Pinatubo. Americans pack up and leave.

PRAGMATIC REVIVAL

1992: Fidel Ramos, Aquino's defense secretary and a strong ally who backed her during coup attempts, wins presidential election. His pragmatic leadership and problem-solving defy traditional perceptions of

inept Filipino government. Foreign investors return.

1998: Former action movie star Joseph Estrada is elected president.

2000: Impeachment proceedings begin against Estrada on charges of corruption; the economy is dealt a severe blow.

2001: Estrada's impeachment fails, and triggers massive street protests. After the military withdraws its support, Estrada is removed from office. His vice-president, Gloria Macapagal-Arroyo, takes over.

2002: US military joins the Philippines in large-scale exercises in the southern Philippines to rescue kidnapped American tourists.

2004: Arroyo narrowly defeats movie idol Fernando Poe Jr. in presidential election; peso hits all-time low. ❏

130   135   140   145   150

*Carte
des Isles*
**PHILIPPINES
CELEBES
ET MOLUQUES.**
Echelle de Cent Lieues Marines de France
Schaale van Honderd Zeemylen, 20 in een Gr.
20 20 30 40 50   100

Nota
Quoique cette Carte soit dressée avec
toute l'exactitude possible, on a suppri-
mé les noms de beaucoup de petites
Isles, pour éviter la confusion, n'ayant
besoin icy que de la position générale,
le detail viendra ensuite.

Hoewel dit Kaartje met alle moge-
lyke Naauwkeurigheid geschikt is,
echter heeft men 'er de Naamen van
veele klyne Eilandjes uitgelaaten, om
Verwarringe te myden: de Hoofd-
schikkinge is hier maar noodig, en
de Onderdeelinge zal volgen.

C. Bajador
Palinquin
C. Engano
LES   I. LU   **DE**
CONIA
ou
MANILLE
I. Polo
Baye
de Manille
Manille
I. Luban
I. Mindor
ISLES
I.s Calamines
Linapacan

C. du S. Esprit
I. Samar
FILIPPYNSE
I. Ley

I. de Paragoa
PHILIPPINES
I. Balaba
I. Panay
I. des Negres
Neger Eil.
Bojol
I. St. Jean
MINDANO
EILANDEN
I. Jolo
I. Moangis

Borneo
I. DE
I. Sanguir

LES
I. Morotai
I. Gilolo
DE
Ternate
Tidor

[Eiland van]
Equator

BORNEO
I. DE
CELEBES
ou
MAKASSAR
Detr. de [St. van] Makassar
Poulo Laut
ISLES
Sapelluia
Nulla
MOLUQUES
I. Ouby
MOLUKSE
N. Guinee
I. Ceram
I. Bouro
I. Amboina
I. Banda
EILANDEN
I. Madura
Makassar
I.
Balanga
I. Boaton
Lucaparos
I. du Volcan: Brandt Eiland
I. Seyer
JAVA
I. Lomboc
I. Laubana
Omba
'tHoog-Eiland
I. Haute
Bali
Combava
Ende ou de Flores
I. Solar
I. Timor
Ferro
Longitude de l'Isle de
Lengte van 't Eiland

130   135   140   145   150

J. V. Schley direx.
KAART van de FILIPPYNSE, CELEBES, en MOLUKSE-EILANDEN.

BORN OF FIRE AND WATER

When furious underwater action between vast tectonic plates threw up molten earth, the Philippine archipelago took form and came to life

I n the beginning, there were only the waters and a low-hanging sky. People had no place in the chaos, where all the elements of life floated in total confusion. In time, the bottom of the ancient ocean opened to spew up bits of earth. Islands rose precariously, threatened on every side by huge waves. They needed to be anchored, if people were to live on them.

There are echoes of this motif of unstable land in the creation myths still told by the indigenous tribes of the Philippines. A number of the archipelago's more than 7,100 islands continue to grow, while almost every year, typhoons threaten low shorelines and monsoon rains tear at mountain ranges in memory of the time when land first emerged.

Just recently, what is called a seamount by oceanographers and geologists was detected 12 km (7 miles) off the coastal town of Tabango in Leyte island. The underwater mass appeared in mariners' maps only from 1998. A mountain-like structure with a nearly perfect cone, it rises from depths of 300 meters (1,000 ft). Oceanographers have confirmed that the "Tabango Underwater Mountain" broke free of the sea's surface to grow 10 meters (33 ft) from 1992 to 1997. It is believed to be volcanic.

In the beginning

The Philippine archipelago was born out of huge, earthshaking movements. At the time, the Philippine tectonic plate sat squeezed between the vast Pacific and Asiatic plates. As the Pacific Plate, the world's largest, slid along its ever-moving northwest track, the smaller Philippine Plate buckled and was ground into the adjacent Asiatic Plate.

In a process called subduction, the much heavier Pacific Plate dived under the Philippine Plate and threw up vast amounts of molten material deep in the earth. When the Philippine Plate buckled, fissures formed and the trapped molten mass spewed forth in colossal volcanic eruptions

in over 200 known volcanoes in the archipelago.

Northern Luzon sits on the western edge of the Philippine Plate, while the remaining islands rest on the eastern edge of the Asiatic Plate. A narrow belt running southeast from Zambales Province to Legasi in Albay Province roughly follows the boundary

LEFT: a 17th-century Dutch-French map of Philippines.
RIGHT: 1968 eruption of Mayon Volcano.

BATTLE OF SEA AND SKY

All Filipinos have their own favorite creation myths which have nothing to do with geological theory.

One such story has it that several million years ago, there was a violent battle between the sea and sky. Their quarrel was started by a cunning bird who sowed discord in the hope of opening up dry land

The sea vented its might at the sky, hurling huge walls of water at it, and the sky spat down islands and rocks to quell its crashing waves. Bombarded by the sheer number and weight of the islands and rocks, the sea was forced to admit defeat and retreat. Thus, the bird achieved its purpose and the Philippine archipelago was born.

between the two plates. This belt contains the most vigorous of the Philippine's two dozen active volcanoes, including Pinatubo, Taal, Banahaw, Iriga and Mayon.

Unrelenting land building and tearing down is the legacy of the Philippines' geographic position. The earth's crust buckled under tectonic pressure to push up land masses, and volcanoes added their enormous debris. But persistent monsoon rains and ocean storms ripped at the land as it rose up from the depths. Volcanoes spit forth billions of cubic meters of ash and molten lava, and the winds and rains moulded them into vast plains in a process that

Russel Wallace (1823–1913), who first noted the zoological and geographical differences between the Asian and Australian continents.

The Wallace Line runs up the Lombok Strait between Indonesian islands Bali and Lombok. It continues north through the Makassar Strait that separates Borneo and Sulawesi, turns east into the Pacific and then back north again to encompass the Philippines. All animals to the east of the line, including those of the Philippines, owe their biological heritage to species originating in Asia. Those to the west owe their heritage to species originating in Australia.

However, when sea levels sank during the

continues to reshape the Philippine landscape.

About 2 million years ago, at the beginning of the Pleistocene epoch, the land was already formed. But events were taking shape in the earth's polar regions, causing three successive ice ages which lowered sea levels by 100 meters (330 ft). One large land area reached out into the Pacific Ocean from the Asian continent. Only the South China, Sulu and Celebes basins remained as seas.

Plant and animal beginnings

The so-called Wallace Line that defines most Philippine plants and animals is named after English naturalist, explorer and writer Alfred

last Ice Age, a series of land bridges cut through the shallow waters between Philippines' Palawan and Mindanao and Indonesia's Sulawesi and Borneo. Like the tentacles of a multiform octopus, these land bridges made possible a temporary alliance of flora and fauna, which led to adaptations and mutations in isolation when the land links sank again.

Sixty species of Bornean plants are found in the southern islands of Mindoro, Palawan and Mindanao. Flora identified with Sulawesi and Moluccas of Indonesia are widespread in the Philippines, mainly in the form of ferns, orchids and a great wood, the dipterocarp, which makes up the country's primary tracts of forests, as it also does in Thailand, Indochina and Indonesia.

In the wilds of Palawan and nearby Calamian islands, the same species of mousedeer, weasel, mongoose, porcupine, skunk, anteater and otter are found here and in Borneo's interior. Species of Palawan shrews, as well as a rare bat found in Mindanao, have kin in Sulawesi.

Fish in the waters of eastern Sumatra and western Borneo are like those in southwestern Philippines, as are the fish between Mindanao and Papua New Guinea. Many Malaysian and Bornean birds make their home in Palawan.

There is evidence of an even older land bridge that connected northern Philippines with Taiwan at a time when that island was itself connected to the Asian mainland. The remains of the stegodon, a pygmy elephant, have been dug up here as well as in Taiwan.

Early human survival

Early humans soon followed grazing herds onto the newly exposed grassy plains. Over thousands of years, bands of early hunters pushed farther out into the continental bulge. At times, the rising waters isolated them on islands for scores of generations. Necessity demanded that they adapted, or perished. Some took to the sea while others took to the mountains but both developed unique patterns of life as varied as the plants and animals they followed.

Much of early human history remains rooted in speculation, but in the Philippine archipelago, it is remarkably well-documented. Archeologists have dated humans in the Cagayan Valley, on northern Luzon, to more than 40,000 years ago. No human skeleton has yet to be found, but scientists agree that the flake and cobble tools unearthed in beds of stegodon, elephas, rhinoceros and bublalus fossils are proof of paleolithic human life. On Palawan, human skeletal remains have been dated to more than 20,000 years ago.

The domestication of animals and the beginnings of agriculture marked the neolithic period. A neolithic site in Dimolit, Cagayan, has yielded the earliest pottery in the Philippines, dating to 5,000 years ago. Another neolithic site is at Callo, in the Cagayan Valley, where stone tools and pottery were excavated and dated to 4,000 years ago. Even the fabled rice terraces of the Ifugao people have been

LEFT: rice cultivation dates back to 2,000–3,000 years ago. **RIGHT:** a Filipino tribal minority.

identified as being 2,000 to 3,000 years old.

Finds at the Butuan site in Agusan del Norte, Mindanao, and in caves on Palawan show that the early inhabitants were engaged in far-reaching trade. Ancient boats, gold ornaments, pottery and evidence of metalworking unearthed at Butuan point to long distance maritime commerce as early as the 10th century. Excavations on Palawan yielded burial jars, porcelain and stoneware of China's Sung dynasty (960–1279), indicating strong trade links with China as early as the 10th century. In addition, historians have uncovered accounts of trade missions to China. Chinese records show that several

tributary missions were made to China between the 10th and 15th centuries.

The claim to the most spectacular find belongs to a 5½-inch, 21-carat, solid gold figure weighing close to 1.8 kg (4 lbs), which suggests a link with Asian tradition as early as AD 1000–1300. Found on the banks of the Wawa River in Agusan del Norte in 1917, it bears little resemblance to the *anito* figures of native worship, but more to an Indo-Javanese queen or a deity in the Mahayana Buddhist or Hindu pantheon. The Golden Agusan image, now kept in the Field Museum of Natural History in Chicago, is proof that the Philippines was not isolated from its Asian neighbors. ❏

Le Petit Journal

Le Petit Journal
CHAQUE JOUR 5 CENTIMES

Le Supplément illustré
CHAQUE SEMAINE 5 CENTIMES

SUPPLÉMENT ILLUSTRÉ
Huit pages : CINQ centimes

ABONNEMENTS

	SIX MOIS	UN AN
SEINE ET SEINE-ET-OISE	2 fr.	3 fr. 5
DÉPARTEMENTS	2 fr.	4 fr.
ÉTRANGER	2 50	5 fr.

Douzième année   DIMANCHE 14 AVRIL 1901   Numéro 5

LA GUERRE AUX PHILIPPINES
Capture d'Aguinaldo

FOREIGN DOMINATION

After centuries of intrusion by Spanish, British, American and Japanese forces,
the Philippine call for freedom and independence was finally answered

Since prehistoric times, the islands have been populated by peoples of Malay origin. Most of them lived simply in scattered villages at river mouths. Their houses were made of bamboo and palm-thatch and they grew rice and fished for a living. Until 3,000 years ago, contact with the outside world was minimal. The following centuries saw arrivals by Chinese, Indian, Arab and Indonesian traders, who brought pottery, textiles, iron weapons, tools and jewelry to barter for pearls, coral and gold.

Unlike the Chinese settlers who exercised substantial commercial power but little political influence, the traders that came from the south 200 years later introduced Islam, an influence that swept through the Sulu Archipelago. The new faith consolidated groups that later vigorously resisted Spanish, American and, more recently, Philippine national rule.

The Spanish arrive

The archipelago's recorded history began half a world away in a small, dusty town in southwestern Spain. The Treaty of Tordesillas was inked in 1494, dividing between Spain and Portugal the yet-unexplored world. Everything to the east of a line 370 leagues west of the Cape Verde Islands in the Atlantic belonged to Portugal and everything west was Spain's.

The Portuguese set off to navigate Africa's Cape of Good Hope in search of the riches of the Spice Islands, while the Spanish headed across the vast Pacific. The captain of Spain's search was in fact a Portuguese who had taken up the flag of Castile and the Spanish name Hernando de Magallanes; to the English-speaking world, he is Ferdinand Magellan.

Magellan took 109 days to cross the Pacific Ocean and somehow managed to miss every island in this vast body of water, save the tiny atoll of Poka Puka and Guam. In 1521, he made landfall on the island of Homonhon, off the

southern tip of Samar. Calling the new lands Lazarus, after the saint's day on which he first sighted them, Magellan sailed on through the Gulf of Leyte to Limasawa island. There he celebrated the first mass in Philippines' history.

Six weeks later, Magellan was dead. He had sailed to the island of Cebu, where he Chris-

tianized the local *rajah* (king) and his followers. However, a chieftain of Mactan – the island where Cebu's international airport now sits – rebelled against the Rajah of Cebu and his foreign guests. Chieftain Lapu Lapu and his 2,000 men defended their island against 48 armorclad Spaniards in April 1521. A white obelisk marks the spot where Magellan was slain.

It was not until 1565 that Spain, under Miguel Lopez de Legazpi, gained a foothold in Cebu. Over the next few years, the Spanish pushed northward, defeating Muslim chieftain Sulayman and taking over his fortress of Maynilad, facing what is now Manila Bay. Here, in 1571, Legazpi built the Spanish walled city of Intramuros.

LEFT: rebel leader Emilio Aguinaldo is captured.
RIGHT: Spanish leaders Miguel Lopez de Legazpi and Ferdinand Magellan juxtaposed on an old engraving.

Bands of conquistadors, newly arrived from Mexico, fanned out from Intramuros to conquer Luzon and the Visayas. They met ineffectual opposition, and soon entrenched themselves as lords of great estates worked by the natives, called *indios*, in the manner as applied to Mexican "Indians." The friars who accompanied them rapidly converted the population, building churches, schools, roads and bridges while accumulating vast land holdings for the Catholic Church.

The Chinese community was vital to the welfare of Manila, as the city surrounding Intramuros came to be known. A great fleet of

strict sanctions and seasonal purges by the colonists who feared their numbers and skills.

Late in 1762, as a minor episode in the Seven Years' War with Spain, Intramuros was seized by England's Gen. William Draper, who collected almost 4 million pesos in exchange for sparing the city from razing. But his troops looted the city anyway, while civil governor Dawson Drake stripped the governor's palace of its lavish fittings and shipped them home in cases marked "Rice for Drake."

The Spanish retreated north of Manila to the province of Pampanga, where they set up a new seat of government. Due to a lack of reinforce-

Chinese junks converged here each year, carrying porcelain, silk, lacquer and enamel wares, paintings and a wealth of other products from Persia, India, Siam and Indonesia.

The Spanish colonists eagerly bought this merchandise for re-export to Mexico on the *Manila Galleon*; they received payment in Mexican silver carried by the vessel on its return. The 2,000-ton treasure ship sailed annually between Manila and Acapulco from 1572 until 1815, carrying cargo worth millions, in which each Spaniard had equity.

The Chinese who did settle were assigned to a particular district in Manila called Parian, outside Intramuros. They were often subjected to

ments, the British could not hold on to Intramuros, and were dislodged in early 1974.

In the late 18th and early 19th centuries, the Spanish introduced important political, economic and social reforms, allowing limited Filipino participation in government. They also introduced cash crops such as sugar, tobacco, indigo and hemp; at the same time, they put an end to the galleon monopoly on foreign commerce. But these reforms came too late.

By that time, the nationalist movement had taken root, led by the liberal clergy, professionals and a clique of Filipino students studying in Spain. A minor uprising sprang up in Cavite in 1872, causing the Spanish authorities to panic. Three well-known Filipino priests – Jose Burgos, Mariano Gomez and Jacinto Zamora – were garoted after being convicted of inspiring subversion.

Their deaths fanned the fire of nationalism during the last two decades of the 19th century. Three leaders emerged: Jose Rizal, Andres Bonifacio and Emilio Aguinaldo. Rizal led the Propaganda Movement to promote equality for the Filipinos. Bonifacio headed a secret society named Katipunan, which advocated armed insurrection, while Aguinaldo led the Philippines' first declaration of independence in 1898.

The Katipunan organized a major revolt in 1896. Many revolutionaries were captured and executed, including peace advocate Rizal, who was killed by a firing squad.

Revolutionary rivalry

With Rizal's death, the remaining revolutionaries were divided into two rival camps led by Bonifacio and General Aguinaldo, who was more skilled in battle. The latter had Bonifacio arrested, and under controversial circumstances, the Katipunan founder was executed.

This would have meant the end of the revolution had not the crafty Aguinaldo offered the Spanish a truce in return for his voluntary deportation to Hong Kong and some payment as well. Once in exile, the revolutionary leader formed a junta and purchased more arms, while seizing the opportunity to seek support from Asian neighbors such as Japan. In 1898, he returned to Manila and had himself inaugurated as president of the first Philippine republic. Independence was won – for a day – as the Filipino intelligensia gathered in Malolos, a town north of Manila, and wrote the charter for the first constitutional republic in Asia.

In the meantime, Spain and the United States had gone to war over Cuba. Admiral George Dewey sailed into Manila Bay and engaged the ageing Spanish fleet in what historians describe as a mock confrontation. Filipino revolutionary troops had already surrounded Manila and were preparing to march in and cap the victory when Aguinaldo hesitated, believing that their alliance with the Americans would seal the fate of Spain. Unknown to him, Dewey had allowed the Spanish admiral a face-saving gesture. In

return, the old colonists made way for the new. So the Americans took over and the revolutionaries were kept in their place.

Distrust of the Americans developed and grew, until the first exchange of fire between Filipino and American troops on the San Juan bridge on the outskirts of Manila on February 4, 1899. Hostilities erupted and ushered in guerrilla warfare that lasted until 1902, taking at least 300,000 civilian and military lives from both sides.

With the end of the Spanish-American War, Spain had ceded the Philippines, Puerto Rico and Guam to the United States, and paid an indemnity of US$20 million. Filipinos now

LEFT: early Filipino Catholic converts being baptised.
RIGHT: American troops torturing a Filipino native.

A TOAST TO INDEPENDENCE

General Emilio Aguinaldo and his revolutionaries celebrated the ratification of the declaration of Philippine independence with an elaborate French banquet at the Barasoain Church on September 29, 1898. Even the menu was in French. Two prominent chefs from Sulipan, a town celebrated for its French culinary excellence, served up a veritable feast which included crab, oysters, buttered prawns, salami *de Lyon* and salmon Hollandaise. These were washed down with fine wines and champagne, not to mention Chartreuse and Cognac. The revolutionaries may not have spoken French, but that day, they manifested great ability at eating French.

realized the Americans offered not independence but just another style of colonialism.

Aguinaldo's luck had run out, too. He found himself pursued by American troops all the way to the wilderness of northern Luzon, and was finally captured in Palanan, Isabela, on March 23, 1901. Aguinaldo ordered all revolutionaries to accept American rule, but the other generals refused and many were captured and executed.

Liberation at last

The Americans, defining their role as one of trusteeship and tutelage, promoted rapid political, economic and social development. "Benev-olent assimilation" was the policy announced by American President William McKinley, who spoke of a duty to "Christianize and civilize" the natives. Such words reflected his scant knowledge of the Filipinos, who had long been converted to Christianity. But America's rule did prove benevolent for the most part, imparting education in English and lessons in self-government. In 1935, the Philippines was made a commonwealth, with the promise of independence in 1945. However, World War II intervened.

On December 10, 1941, Japanese forces landed in the Philippines and fought its way down the Bataan Peninsula. Despite the heroic

THE MACARTHUR SUITE

The MacArthur Suite is one of the Manila Hotel's special attractions. It is a relatively recent feature within a new wing, however, and not anywhere near the rooms occupied by the General upon his triumphant retaking of Manila, which brought liberation to the Philippines. It was there he was known to have had a tryst with Filipina actress Elizabeth "Dimples" Cooper.

Some Catholics were scandalized over that episode, but by and large Manileños turned a blind eye, if not a buzzing lip, to the affair. The tryst was reportedly continued in Washington where the bedimpled *mestiza* followed the homecoming hero.

resistance of Gen. Douglas MacArthur's American and Filipino troops, the Japanese stormed the fortress island of Corregidor, occupied Manila, and eventually overran the whole archipelago.

On leaving Corregidor, MacArthur had pledged, "I shall return." He kept his word. In 1944, the American-Filipino troops fought their way back into Manila. The liberation of the Philippines may have cost enormous losses in lives and property but it was an event that Filipinos greeted with jubilation. ❏

ABOVE: General MacArthur and his forces land in Leyte in 1944. With the aid of Filipino-American troops, he storms through Manila and defeats the Japanese.

Hero for all Seasons

No self-respecting town in the country is without a statue of the man, or does not have a major street named after him. Reverence for thinker Dr Jose Rizal, who died a martyr's death at age 35 in the last years of Spanish rule, has spanned a century and spread to foreign lands.

Born on June 19, 1861, in the town of Calamba in Laguna Province, Rizal was to live a short but eventful life till his death in 1896. On the centennial of his death, a monument to him was unveiled in Madrid, the capital of the colonial government that had executed him by firing squad.

Rizal busts or markers can be seen in many places around the world: a plaza in Heidelberg, Germany, a residential building (No. 6 Gul Crescent) in London, in various cities across the United States where Filipino American communities have strong representation, and in Latin America.

In Jakarta, an international conference on Rizal was conducted in 1997, assembling scholars and historians. The moving spirit behind it, then Malaysian deputy Prime Minister Anwar Ibrahim, extolled him as "the pride of the Malay race."

Rizal was a scholar first and foremost, but there were many parts to him. He had studied ophthalmology to cure his mother's eye condition. He was also a physician, naturalist, botanist, engineer, linguist, sculptor, musician, composer, poet, dramatist, novelist, reformist, thinker and writer.

His two novels – *Noli Me Tangere* (Touch Me Not) and *El Filibusterismo* (The Filibusterer) – were written and published in Europe at the time he led the Propaganda Movement for political reforms. The novels were deemed incendiary by powerful friars.

On his return, he was exiled to Dapitan, Mindanao, where he set up a school, fixed up the waterworks, wrote music, walked the woods and discovered a unique lizard. The creature was sent to a European academy, which named it *Rizaliani Rizalii*. He also won the heart of Josephine Bracken, a beautiful young Irish woman who had accompanied her foster father to his eye operation. Rizal called her his "sweet stranger," and their brief seaside idyll was marred only by the event of a stillborn son.

Emissaries from Andres Bonifacio's Katipunan, which favored armed struggle, offered to help him escape so he could return to Manila to lead the revolution. He declined. Instead, he volunteered to

serve as a doctor for the war in Cuba and was actually allowed to sail away. But when his ship docked at the first port on the way to the Americas, a telegram came, ordering his return to Manila.

He was placed under arrest on the grounds of complicity in the revolution, and a quick trial sentenced him to death by musketry. In his cell in Fort Santiago, Jose Rizal composed a long poem in Spanish, *Mi Ultimo Adios* (My Last Farewell). He concealed it inside an oil lamp, which he handed to his sisters on the eve of his execution.

He walked calmly to his death at dawn on December 30, 1896, to a field by Manila Bay called Bagumbayan, later renamed Luneta for its crescent

shape. He protested against having to be shot in the back, for he was no traitor. As the shots rang out, he made a last attempt to twist his body to face the rising sun at the moment of death. His last words were "Consummatum est" – "It is finished."

His martyrdom set the country aflame. A revolution broke out, and soon Asia had its first independent republic, cut short though it was by the Americans' entry into the Pacific. The new colonial power recognized Rizal as the exemplar of his race, and installed him as the national hero.

Filipinos would not have it otherwise, for the poet and patriot clearly stood head and shoulders over everyone; he personified the romance of history, let alone the strength of ideas. ❏

RIGHT: portrait of Jose Rizal by Ben Cabrera (Bencab).

THE DEMOCRATIC ERA

Freed at last from colonialism, Filipinos had to live through the excesses of the Marcos years before Fidel Ramos was able to turn the country around

After the war, the American authorities devoted themselves first to desperately needed emergency relief, then to the Philippines' long-delayed independence – proclaimed on July 4, 1946 – and finally to the colossal task of rebuilding and development.

Manuel Roxas served as the first president of post-war, independent Philippines. Official records have him as the fifth Filipino president, following Gen. Emilio Aguinaldo, who was president of the first republic in 1899; Manuel Quezon, president of the commonwealth in 1935; Jose Laurel, who served as president of the so-called "puppet government" during the Japanese Occupation; and Sergio Osmeña, who became a leader-in-exile in the United States upon Quezon's death in 1944.

Roxas died before finishing his four-year term, and was succeeded by Elpidio Quirino, his vice-president. Quirino won the election in 1949 and served a full term. He initiated major steps in foreign relations, especially with east Asian neighbors, whose leaders he invited to a summit in Baguio City in 1950. But domestic problems dogged his administration and he lost in his re-election bid to Ramon Magsaysay.

Vice-President Carlos Garcia from Bohol succeeded the extremely popular Magsaysay who died in a plane crash. A proficient poet and chess player, Garcia was credited with initiating a "Filipino First" policy to stimulate local businesses and industry. But the problems inherited from a prostrate, post-war economy were gargantuan. He lost his re-election bid in 1961 to his own vice-president, Diosdado Macapagal of Lubao, Pampanga.

It was the convention that no Philippine president could ever get himself re-elected, as Manileño-led public opinion had a habit of turning oppositionist against whoever sat in that highest seat. Besides, politicians often made a mockery of the two-party system patterned after American democracy. The Nacionalista Party and the Liberal Party swapped leaders every so often, but mostly in time for elections, so that a tradition of turncoatism developed.

Macapagal's victory in 1961 ushered in serious efforts at instituting some measure of land reform. He led the way for the formation of Maphilindo, an alliance with Malaysia and

HELL OF A DEAL

Manuel Quezon, Sergio Osmeña and Manuel Roxas had all distinguished themselves by leading independence missions to the United States, to seek early sovereignty for their country. It was the fiery, eloquent (particularly in Spanish, and most notaby for expletives) Quezon who is credited with uttering the immortal line: "Better a government run like hell by Filipinos than one run like heaven by Americans."

To which, of course, generations of Filipinos, especially the many who lobbied for and who may still entertain notions of American statehood, have caustically replied: "Well, thanks to our Filipino leaders, we're still in hell."

LEFT: the Filipino flag is hoisted high. **RIGHT:** former president Diosdado Macapagal and his wife.

Indonesia, which led to the creation of ASEAN, the Association of Southeast Asian Nations.

Ferdinand Marcos changed parties to run against Macapagal in 1965. Once again, the rule of rotation prevailed and, in 1969, Marcos became the only Philippine president to gain re-election. He was the seventh president. That number was his lucky number too, and seven years after he became president, Marcos imposed martial law in 1972.

The official line given out was that the republic was in peril. Confronted with student unrest, Muslim revolts in Mindanao and a rural communist insurgency, Marcos faced little resistance from the opposition as well as the military, which he mollycoddled.

On September 23, 1972, the country awoke to an absence of media. No newspapers, radio nor TV broadcasts. But soon the word was out. Raids and arrests were made left and right by the military; all print and broadcast media had been blocked out. Hours later, a television station was allowed to transmit news from Malacañang Palace: Martial law was in effect and the executive order had already been signed two days earlier. A midnight to 4am curfew was in place. The slogan of the New Society would rule the day: *Sa ikauunlad ng bayan, disiplina*

ang kailangan (For the country to progress, what is needed is discipline). Marcos started ruling with an iron fist, erecting monuments to himself and accumulating a vast fortune for himself as well as his "cronies."

Marcos and his wife Imelda – called the Conjugal Dictatorship by disenchanted Filipinos – prospered until the 1983 assassination of the popular opposition leader, Benigno "Ninoy" Aquino, Jr. On his return to the Philippines after self-imposed exile in America, Aquino was shot dead under highly suspicious circumstances just after stepping off the plane at Manila Airport. The assassination fanned discontent. Faced with a restless populace, Marcos called a snap election in February 1986 to renew his mandate. Amid unsubtle election fraud, he was proclaimed the winner over Aquino's widow Corazon (Cory). But Marcos was losing ground; his political cronies began to jump ship and, in that same month, a four-day bloodless revolution climaxed with a standoff between Marcos's tanks and citizens at EDSA, a busy highway that ran between two military camps in Metro Manila.

Marcos and Imelda were bundled off in an American plane to Hawaii. Marcos died there in 1989. Imelda was later to return to the Philippines for an unsuccessful comeback bid.

The specter of the Marcos regime lingered

It was a massive task, made worse by continuing communist insurgency, political infighting, persistent undermining of her mandate by Marcos supporters, and deeply-embedded bureaucratic corruption. It was to her credit that Aquino managed to survive seven coup attempts – one of which she was forced to ask for American military assistance.

The woes of economic stagnation eventually dampened the initial exhilaration that accompanied Aquino's victory. Symbolic of the times were the daily electrical outages called brownouts in Manila.

But the most important signal of the end of

long after his departure. He left behind a depressed economy and an exhausted treasury.

Aquino's daunting task

The overthrow of Marcos was made complete by an event that would hitherto have been inconceivable: the inauguration of Corazon Aquino as president. She had her work cut out: overhaul the government and military, revive the economy, weed out corrupt bureaucratic practices and restore public trust – in essence, she had to rebuild the nation.

LEFT: Ferdinand Marcos was a gifted orator.
ABOVE: people power made Cory Aquino president.

NOT JULY 4, PLEASE

Sixth president Diosdado Macapagal excelled in foreign relations, but also gained the nationalists' nod by decreeing an end to the commemoration of Independence Day on July 4, the day Americans themselves celebrated their Independence Day. We can't celebrate our day of independence on the same day as our colonizer's, Macapagal seemed to say.

So he demoted July 4 to Philippine-American Friendship Day, and had the country revert to a distant day of self-won glory. Owing to Macapagal, June 12, the day Emilio Aguinaldo had proclaimed independence in 1899, now stands as the Philippines' Independence Day.

the post-Marcos era was the withdrawal of the American military. The US colonial presence at that time centered on Subic Bay Naval Base and Clark Air Force Base, both north of Manila. The bases were a significant factor in the economy and the Americans claimed the area's security depended on them, but as it also served US interests, the Filipinos felt the US should pay substantially more for the leases.

The bilateral posturing ended abruptly in 1991 with the eruption of Mount Pinatubo. Clark was covered in volcanic ash, so the Americans simply packed up and left. A year later, after the Senate decided against a new lease on Subic,

the Americans hauled up anchor and sailed away. Clark is now an industrial zone with the Diosdado Macapagal International Airport, while Subic is now a duty-free freeport zone with dozens of companies using its facilities.

Pragmatic revival

In the 1992 presidential election, Fidel Ramos, Aquino's defense secretary and a strong ally during the coup attempts, won a seven-way presidential election with just 24 percent of the vote. Ramos too faced numerous problems.

The Philippines has been sparring with China over a few small islands – including the Spratlys – in the South China Sea. The 51 almost non-existent islands sit astride potentially rich oil and natural gas fields, sufficient encouragement for China, Brunei, Taiwan, Malaysia, Vietnam and the Philippines to make claims on them. China's claim is that the waters of the South China Sea and beyond belong to it because of a brief period of naval power centuries ago. Since the late 1990s, military units have been periodically sent to the area to signal Manila's claim. Chinese construction of semi-permanent mini-barracks on one islet in 1999 did nothing to soothe nerves, nor does Taiwan's planned airport or Vietnam's tourist visits on various islands. Analysts have suggested the next significant threat to global peace could arise over these islands.

Besides a population that is increasing at a higher rate than even Thailand and Indonesia, the most immediate domestic problem has been the Muslim secessionist movement in Mindanao, which has claimed over 60,000 lives since the 1970s. Ramos successfully engineered peace and autonomy for the region with the

THE LEGEND OF FERDINAND MARCOS

The young Ferdinand Marcos was a dynamic orator from Ilocos Norte who billed himself a war hero and whose medals for valor was said to shame Audie Murphy's. (Like many of his claims, they were later proven to be fake.) On the political stage, he paraded a beautiful wife who could sing and charm the masses. For everything that has since been said about him, Marcos was a brilliant thinker and politician, driven to excel beyond everyone else's capacity for strategy, in-fighting, media handling, manipulation of the patronage system and corruption on a large scale.

He was a romantic figure to most. The son of an Ilocos congressman, he took up law studies at the University of the Philippines and became a champion orator, debater and sharpshooter. When his father was defeated in yet another local election, the rival enjoyed the fruits of his victory only for so long. Congressman Julio Nalundasan was brushing his teeth one night, by a window at home, in full view of anyone out in the street. A rifle shot rang out, and Nalundasan was dead.

The young Marcos was indicted for the crime, but while in prison he managed to continue reviewing for the bar exams, which he topped to become a lawyer. He defended his own case and argued so eloquently before a high court that he won acquittal. The Marcos legend had begun.

return to the political system of the majority of the Muslim rebels, including their primary leader. Many former guerrillas have become regulars in the national army, but radical splinter groups are still a threat.

During Ramos' single six-year term (a new Constitution written early in Aquino's watch had revised the presidential tenure to prevent a Marcos-type repeat), the future started looking better – and more certain – for Filipinos. Upon election, Ramos had promised to strengthen the econ-

PEOPLE'S PEP PILL

On hindsight, Aquino's transitional administration accomplished little, but at that time, it was an important symbol which helped boost the esteem of the country.

finally began to show signs of stability and improvement. One of Ramos' first tasks was to put Manila's lights back on – reliably – by having private industry build oil-burning power plants, eliminating the dreaded brownouts.

The turnaround

The new political stability and major economic reforms triggered a remarkable economic turnaround. Decades-old protectionism and state intervention gave way to economic liberalization and industry deregulation. The tele-

omy and enable the Philippines to share in the prosperity enjoyed by Pacific rivals such as Malaysia, Korea and Taiwan. He also promised improvements in electrical power supplies and in other areas of infrastructure, not to mention a general housecleaning of the corrupt political system. Such promises had often been heard but seldom kept. But a funny thing happened as Ramos set to work – he actually kept his word.

After years of institutional corruption and feuding, military putsches, rebel insurgences, earthquakes, volcanoes and typhoons, the Philippines

LEFT: former president Fidel Ramos tends to important matters. **ABOVE:** Makati extremes.

phone industry, which used to be a private monopoly, was opened to new players. Full deregulation of the petroleum industry was accomplished and the privatization drive included the public utilities.

The Philippines' strengths are its strategic location in the heart of the world's fastest-growing region, abundant natural resources, a working democracy, a high standard of urban living and a highly Westernized business environment. Add to this the large pool of educated, English-speaking managers and workers. In recent years, this advantage has made the Philippines one of the top bases for call centers outsourced from North America and Europe.

Although much of the economic activity is in Metro Manila, the recovery spawned dynamic growth centers elsewhere in the archipelago. North of the capital is the successfully transformed Subic Bay Freeport Zone. The one-time military base is now an economic zone with its own international airport, and offers generous investment incentives.

Modern industrial estates have sprouted south of Metro Manila. The provinces are being developed into an agro-industrial corridor to take up the excess from factories in the overcrowded capital. While the constitution prohibits foreigners from owning land, a new law now allows

land leases of up to 75 years, encouraging foreign investors from Japan and North America.

Unfortunately, much of the growth has been confined to industrial estates and financial centers, including three new central business districts – one adjacent to the financial district of Makati, one in the Ortigas area, and another in south Metro Manila. Agriculture has continued to be the economy's weak spot. Most farmers work as landless tenants and two-thirds of all poor families live in rural areas.

The high level of poverty has led a number of investors to underestimate the potential of the domestic market. In fact, there are intangibles that make for a more viable market than what the

numbers suggest. One finds that urban Filipino consumers are young, highly literate, live a Westernized lifestyle and have Western-lifestyle aspirations. Doubts on the potential of such a market are easily belied by the overwhelming success of new shopping malls, the growth of retail chains and the proliferation of fast-food outlets.

Visitors who have been to overcrowded shopping malls in Metro Manila and Cebu invariably wonder where the people's purchasing power comes from, given official statistics on poverty and unemployment. But such numbers miss two important facets of the Philippine economy: the informal economy and the number of Filipinos working overseas.

The real economy

A lot of business activity in the Philippines remains outside the scope of government monitoring – small businesses, direct-selling activities by people with other regular jobs, and personal services. Various estimates on the size of the informal sector range from a low of 25 percent to a high of 40 percent of the gross national product. With easily over 8 million Filipinos living or working abroad, dollar remittances have been a significant boost. From just a little over US$1 billion in 1990, dollar remittances are now almost US$13 billion annually, a trend expected to be sustained in the coming years.

Under Ramos, economic growth turned excellent, but in late 1997 the economy suffered from the Asian economic downturn.

The administration of Joseph Estrada, a former actor who was elected as president in 1998, was devastating for the economy. His presidency was plagued by corruption scandals from the very start, and in January 2001, he was forced out of office by massive street protests and the withdrawal of military support.

Already reeling from the Asian economic crisis, the currency and stock market plunged. His vice-president Gloria Macapagal-Arroyo, appointed as his successor, served the remaining four years of his term, and went on to win the next election in 2004. While initial hopes of an economic quick-fix proved a bit optimistic, Macapagal-Arroyo has targeted problematic areas such as corruption in government and inefficiencies in the infrastructure, and seems to have calmed investor fears to some extent. ❏

LEFT: the Philippine Stock Exchange in Makati.

"Imeldilfic" Imelda

Imelda Marcos threw two parties when she turned 70 on June 2, 1999. The first was in Rizal Park, attended by the usual motley gathering of so-called Marcos loyalists.

The second celebration involved a thousand bejeweled guests at a sit-down dinner at Manila Hotel. Madame Meldy showed up with a ruby-and-diamond tiara, necklace and bracelets.

Early on in Joseph Estrada's presidency, angry protest was generated by Imelda's insistence on having her late husband transferred from the Marcos crypt to the *Libingan ng mga Bayani* (Graveyard of Heroes), where past presidents and war heroes have been buried, in Metro Manila. Estrada was amenable to the idea, but had to backtrack in the face of a national outcry.

The continuing saga of the recovery of the fabled Marcos billions, reportedly stashed away in Swiss bank accounts, unfolds sporadically, raising hackles and destroying the reputation of government lawyers and alleged cronies.

The cry for justice over "the Marcos legacy" takes many forms and involves a welter of contenders. Ten thousand Filipino human rights victims who filed a class suit in a Honolulu court were awarded a legal victory but now have to contend with the Philippine government over the division of the token amounts recovered. Compromise solutions are ever in the works.

But this situation is probably how Imelda likes it. She confuses all, both enemies and protectors. Her penchant for making conflicting statements does not help her bid to return to the political limelight. One day, she would lament about her family's subsistence on the kindness of strangers; the next, she would boast that they practically own the entire country. All are public statements, for there, in the public eye, is where she thrives.

If anything, her only consistency is that she stands by her man. There has not been a single day when Imelda has failed to pull out a handkerchief and wipe a corner of her eye, while insisting that Ferdinand Marcos was not just a brilliant hero, but a practical man who had built his wealth before he turned dictator.

Born to poor relations of the landed Romualdez clan of Leyte province in the Visayas, she never managed to forget nor forgive her early station in

RIGHT: the inimitable Imelda Marcos.

life. She won a beauty contest once and, as Miss Manila, was swept off her feet by the dashing Marcos in a whirlwind seven-day courtship. Seven would be their lucky number in their rise to "a conjugal dictatorship." As a partner, she enhanced Marcos' political campaigns, singing onstage and providing glamor, or as how she describes herself, "the heart that gave the poor a glimpse of beauty."

As Marcos consolidated power, Imelda became Metro Manila Governor and Minister of Human Settlements. On the global stage, she was reported to have charmed Cuban president Fidel Castro and Libyan leader Mohammad Ghadaffi. Her love of the grand gesture prompted the building of cultural and

film centers to showcase "the good, the true and the beautiful." In 2004, the documentary film *Imelda* swept international film festivals. Imelda, despite having participated in its making, attempted to have its screening blocked in Philippine cimemas. The court ruling was overturned, however, and local viewers got a further glimpse into this controversial national enigma.

Now she is known the world over for having owned 3,000 pairs of shoes. "Imeldific" has become a generic catchword for ostentatious display and for global shopping. Thanks to no one but herself, she has become a much caricatured figure. But whatever she is, even her critics admit that she always makes good copy. ❑

FORCES OF NATURE: VOLATILE VOLCANOES

Volcanoes lying dormant for centuries have been known to suddenly turn active – spewing red-hot lava and causing widespread destruction

There is a good reason why the Philippines is called volcanic country. From the archipelago's 7,107 islands soar more than 200 volcanic peaks, 18 of which are active. Nestled among these volcanoes are marshlands, rolling highlands, tropical woodlands, rainforests, both cold and hot as well as mud springs, waterfalls, and extensive networks of caves and even subterranean rivers. An extensive variety of flora and fauna also thrive on these mountains.

Postcards of Mayon Volcano, both the most perfectly shaped volcano in the world and the most active in the country, continue to tickle the traveler's imagination. The rugged jungles that hug Mt Apo, Philippines' highest peak and a dormant volcano, remain to this day the greatest challenge for local climbers. Mystical Mt Makiling, another inactive volcano, according to local lore, is home to the fairy Maria Makiling. Taal Volcano, the world's smallest, awes the most jaded of tourists.

But volcanoes have a violent side: Mt Pinatubo's eruption in June 1991– now considered as the world's most violent and destructive ever – left 847 people dead and more than 1 million displaced. Devastation to land and property amounted to millions of dollars. Still, all was not lost. The ash and sand, called *lahar*, created a new and surreal landscape that is now a hot tourist destination. Entrepreneurs have also cashed in by creating tourist souvenirs made of *lahar*.

▽ **SMALL BUT HOT**
Taal Volcano, world's smallest and Philippines' most active volcano, is a popular trekking destination in the Philippines, with its smoldering lava fields and volcanic beaches.

▽ **LANDLUBBERS ONLY**
Swimming in Taal's Crater Lake is not recommended – its water is actually diluted sulfuric acid with a high concentration of minerals.

▷ **FLY LIGHT AND BRIGHT**
Mt Pinatubo's eruption gave rise to a spectacular *lahar* landscape that is best explored by foot or on an ultralight.

◁ **VOLCANIC WOES**
Eruptions wreak havoc on an agriculture-intensive country like the Philippines – this worker rues the damage to his plantation.

RICE FARMING

Rice farming is just one of the many good uses that volcanic areas in the Philippines have been put into. Their fertile slopes and surrounding plains, coupled by an usually abundant rainfall throughout the year, have made volcanic areas in the country agriculturally rich. Today, it is natural to find farms at the foothills of dormant volcanoes or in areas close to dormant volcanic mountains. Rice, the country's staple food, makes up the most common agricultural crop cultivated in upland volcanic areas. Although you will see rice fields everywhere in the Philippines, what is grown locally is often insufficient to sustain the ever growing population. The International Rice Research Institute in Los Baños constantly strives to develop new varieties of faster yielding rice and improvements in methods of cultivation to increase the country's rice output.

▽ **PLANTING RICE**
As more and more lowland rice fields give way to industry and golf courses, farmers find themselves planting rice, Philippines' staple food, on nutrient-rich volcanic areas.

△ **PERFECT CONE**
Mayon Volcano, widely regarded as the world's most perfectly shaped volcano, is a Philippine icon; its picture postcard grandeur leaves many visitors breathless.

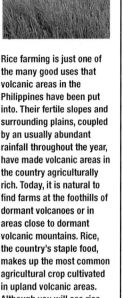

◁ **SEA CHANGE**
Frequent eruptions erode and change the surroundings considerably. New streams like this one are common.

▷ **PHILIPPINE EAGLE**
A possible sighting of the world's largest eagle, the monkey-eating *haribon*, adds to the excitement of climbing Mt Apo, Philippines' highest peak.

FLORA AND FAUNA

A rich and wild wonderland of diverse natural beauty awaits the visitor,
with many species endemic to the Philippines alone

Once linked by land bridges to Borneo and the Moluccas, the flora and fauna on the archipelago reflect closely that of its immediate neighbors. Philippine bio-diversity is seen in a wide range of habitats: from sandy beaches to mangrove swamps; cogon grass plains to towering mountains; and stands of commercial hardwood forests to mossy, misty forests where orchids thrive.

Botanists have discovered more than 12,000 different species of plants. Orchids thrive here, with more than 80 percent of them endemic. In addition, more than 1,000 species of fern and 30 species of mangrove inhabit the islands. A leisurely drive south of Manila to Tagaytay reveals hillsides of pampas grass, its silvery plumes a refuge for birds. Bamboo, rattan, vines and ferns are widespread, with mangroves and palm trees found near the coast.

More than 8,000 plant species flower, and these decorate the country with an array of colors and fragrant scents. Manila's street corners swarm with itinerant vendors selling garlands of *sampaguita*, the white, sweet-smelling national flower. The 1,000 orchid species include the popular *waling-waling* of western Mindanao. Frangipani, bougainvillea and hibiscus also abound.

Cogon grass is most prevalent in Luzon's Cagayan Valley, western Mindoro, Panay, Negros and Bukidnon. The locals use the rough grass as thatch for the roofs of their houses.

Trees are the most economically important of native Philippine plant species. Some 50 years ago, forests – conservatively valued at US$20 billion at the time – covered more than 53 percent of the islands. Hungry for foreign currency, commercial logging was a nationally prioritized industry from the 1950s to the 1970s. Although the government has banned commercial logging with decisive legislation –

especially after destructive landslides killed over 1,000 people in intensively logged areas of Aurora and Quezon provinces in late 2004 – more than 70 percent of the nation's original forests have already been destroyed. Vast tracts of hardwood stands however persist in the protected areas of Palawan and Mindanao.

More than 3,000 arboreal species attain a diameter of more than 30 cm (1 ft) and about two-thirds of those trees are dipterocarps: water-loving, tropical hardwoods reaching heights of 60 meters (200 ft). Philippine dipterocarps – often called Philippine mahoganies, though not true mahogany trees – include the red and white lauan, mayapis and ipil.

Dry forests, or molave forests, grow farther from the beach or mangrove forest. These small stands of heavy, highly-prized woods grow slowly, rarely exceeding 30 meters (100 ft) in height. Characteristic species include the molave – of the teak family – plus kamagong and ebony and the national tree, narra.

PRECEDING PAGES: lofty views from the Tagatay highlands in Luzon. **LEFT:** wild orchids in Coron, Palawan. **RIGHT:** traditional Igorot huts with roofs made of *cogon* grass.

On the wing

One-third of nearly 560 recognized bird species are endemic. Of these, 66 are "island-endemic," occurring on only one island. The majestic Philippine eagle, formerly called the "monkey-eating" eagle, is the national bird. Unfortunately, fewer than 100 remain in the wild.

Common birds include the brightly-colored Philippine flower pecker, bright yellow black-naped oriole, chestnut-headed bee eater and glossy starling. The white-collared kingfisher, with its iridescent coat of turquoise blue, makes itself at home near water. Among the rarer species – which tourists are unlikely to see – is the black shama, a shy, highly territorial forest bird endemic to Cebu. The endemic Palawan peacock pheasant – sought after for the male's brilliant feathers – lives on the ground in the untouched forests of Palawan. One of the most peculiar bird species is the Luzon bleeding heart dove, endemic to south-central Luzon and outlying Polillo Island. Grayish green on the back and upper mantle, the bird's white chest feathers are marred by a splotch of red, making it look as though it has just came from a fight.

Among the country's newest recognized bird species are Lina's sunbird and the Panay striped babbler. Ornithologist Robert Kennedy of the

PHILIPPINE EAGLE

The endangered *haribon*, or Philippine eagle, is the national bird of the Philippines, and is the second largest bird in the world, after the Californian Condor. Today, fewer than 100 *haribon* remain in the wild; they once soared freely over much of Luzon, Samar and Leyte. The Philippine eagle is thought to be monogamous, making the species' survival even more precarious. Its diet consists of a variety of small animals, including bats, snakes and flying lemurs.

The Philippine Eagle Nature Research Center in Malagos, Davao City, may be the eagle's last hope. The center has successfully bred two eagles in captivity, with the aim of reintroducing the young back to the wild.

Cincinnati Museum Center in the US, who has devoted his life to studying Philippine birds, has led countless research expeditions to the Philippines. In collaboration with Pedro Gonzales of the Philippine National Museum and Hector Miranda at the University of the Philippines at Los Baños, Kennedy first obtained specimens of the iridescent sunbird in the eastern mountains of Mindanao in 1993. He discovered and named the babbler in 1989.

Butterflies and moths are particularly abundant in Palawan, Mindanao and Sulu, numbering 850 different species. Palawan's endemic *Papilio trojano*, with bold black and green markings, has a wingspan of 18 cm (7 inches).

If you're lucky...

Few visitors will leave the Philippines without having seen some of the bird life described above, or the domesticated *carabao*, or water buffalo. Unfortunately, much of the remaining wildlife remains hidden from general view, unless the visitor heads to the local zoo.

Unique native wildlife, mostly limited to smaller creatures, includes 180 species of terrestrial mammals and 250 reptiles. The mammals include spotted deer or sambar – now an endangered species with limited distribution – plus leopard cats, Oriental small-clawed otters, civets and wild boar, the latter of which is a staple food for the local inhabitants.

The Asian bearcat, or *binturong*, is found in Palawan, Indonesia and Malaysia. The nocturnal creature is a cross between a raccoon and a furry bear, with retractable, hooking claws letting it climb trees, and a long tail. Despite its carnivorous teeth that helps it tear apart fish, birds and small rodents, the *binturong* prefers to munch on fruits and leaves.

The Panay cloudrunner, first described to science in 1996, is one of 15 new Philippine mammals found and classified in the past 25 years. Bearing the scientific name of *crateromys heaney,* the 1-kg (2-pound) gray, nocturnal rodent resembles the fox squirrel closely in looks. Little is known of its native existence in the mountains of Panay. Unfortunately, slash-and-burn agriculture is a very real threat to its wild existence.

You're more likely to see...

Native primates include the tarsier, flying lemurs and lorises of the tropical forests. The nocturnal tarsier, locally called *maomag* or *mago*, is the world's smallest primate, found in Bohol, Samar, Mindanao and elsewhere in Southeast Asia. Visitors may easily see these incredible creatures in their native habitat at the Philippine Tarsier Sanctuary in Corella, Bohol.

In Subic Bay, thousands of fruit bats with wingspans of 1.8 meters (6 ft) roost in the lauan trees of Cubi Point, heading off to feed nightly in northern Luzon around 8pm and returning by 5am. Most visitors to Subic will also see the long-tailed macaques walking the fence along the roadside, looking for a hand-out from visiting tourists – though feeding them is not recommended.

The Palawan Wildlife Rescue and Conservation Center (formerly known as the Crocodile Farming Institute) in Puerto Princesa is a favorite for viewing the endangered Philippine crocodile and other unique Palawan fauna such as the *binturong* (Asian bearcat) and peacock pheasant. The Davao Crocodile Park is another to see fearsome crocodiles and other rarely seen creatures such as pythons, raptors and reptiles from around the country.

Underwater life

With almost 36,300 km (22,500 miles) of coastline (twice that of the United States), the Philippine archipelago should rightly host a wealth of

underwater life with at least 488 species of coral and 1,000 different fish species exist here – including what is reputed to be the smallest fish in the world, the *sinarapan* of Lake Buhi, as well as the largest fish in the world, the whale shark.

Divers and snorkelers will be awed by the stunning colors of corals and tropical fish beneath the ocean waves. Octopus, cuttlefish and squid fascinate with their camouflage survival tactics, while close encounters with sea turtles (*pawikan*) are common. Manta rays and white- and black-tipped sharks frequent the waters of the open sea, such as those in Apo Reef and Tubbataha Reefs.

Commercial fish such as tuna, grouper, mackerel, round herring and sardines abound,

LEFT: the Philippine eagle. **RIGHT:** a flying lemur.

with shrimp, lobster, crab and mussels found in abundance. Pearls too are harvested in Philippine waters, from the natural South Sea pearls cultivated in the deep sea to the freshwater, cultivated pearls of Mindanao province.

At least some 20 species of dolphins and whales inhabit the waters of the Philippines, including the bottlenose, spinner and Risso's dolphin, as well as the melon-headed and pygmy sperm whale. Dolphin sightings are not unheard of on boat trips to Anilao and Puerto Galera, south of Manila. In the Tañon Strait off Dumaguete, Negros Oriental, are even more whale and dolphin watching opportunities.

Endangered species like the seagrass-eating dugong, or sea cow, live off the coast of Palawan in quiet waters. But perhaps the most unique underwater species is the massive whale shark or *butanding*, recently discovered in numbers larger than anywhere else on the planet. They congregate off the coast of Donsol, on the Bicol peninsula, from February to May every year. Despite its protected status, unscrupulous villagers have slaughtered several of the 20-meter (66-ft) long giants, selling the meat to traders en route to the lucrative Taiwan market.

The Philippines' biological heritage is threatened by development. Activities such as mining

MINDORO'S DWARF BUFFALO

Though visitors will see plenty of Tamaraw – Toyota's local version of a four-wheel drive "mega" taxi – cruising the streets of Manila, few will spot the endangered native tamaraw (*Bubulas mindorensis*), or dwarf buffalo, of Mindoro Island – the largest indigenous wild land animal. Hunting, shifting agriculture and cattle ranching have decimated the herds from 10,000 a century ago to only 260–300 tamaraw today, mostly in the grasslands of Mt Iglit – Baco National Park.

The government holds six animals in captivity in Rizal, Occidental Mindoro, with the hope of breeding more numbers under protection for release into the wild.

and clear-cut logging have denuded the land, while unsustainable fishing harms the sea, threatening the existence of the people of this predominantly fish-eating nation.

Worryingly, at least 130 species of Philippine fauna now stand on the United Nation's list of endangered and threatened species. In a promising move, the National Integrated Protected Areas System (NIPAS) was introduced in 1992 to protect the Philippines' natural heritage. At present, some 60 national parks, four marine parks, eight game refuges and bird sanctuaries and 10 wilderness areas are covered by NIPAS. ❑

ABOVE: a well-camouflaged lizardfish awaits its prey.

A Diver's Haven

"**A**sia's best kept secret" is how veteran Japanese diver Tokuji Ikeda describes diving in the Philippines. The vast potential of diving in Philippine reefs is only starting to be realized – the thrill of swimming with schools of massive groupers, seeing the sinuous grace of snappers, or photographing multicolored feather stars, jewel-encrusted coral gardens, schools of pelagic jacks and massive World War II wrecks. All of this comes with excellent visibility and at reasonable prices. The diving season is from November to June – though the waters may be at their clearest from March to June.

Luzon's most accessible dive area is Anilao in Batangas, a few hours' drive south of Manila. Facing severe environmental degradation 30 years ago, the locals banded together to protect their coral reefs. Looking healthier than ever, the rainbow of inhabitants in this macro photographer's paradise include nudibranches and bright clownfish guarding anemone homes.

Across the strait from Anilao is Puerto Galera in Mindoro, blessed with rewarding sports diving. Currents here can be swifter than in Anilao, encouraging tremendous coral growth and big fish but requiring planning and experienced guides. The Canyons is a perennial favorite, with spectacular corals, big sweetlips and rabbitfish. Early visitors might encounter white-tip sharks or the resident hawksbill turtle. An hour by *banca* (local pumpboat) leads to Verde Island, where strong ocean currents attract plenty of marine life to a great wall, awash with gorgonians, plus tropical fish and larger pelagics.

Once one of the best Philippine dive sites, Apo Reef, a 34 sq. km (13-sq. mile) atoll-like reef in Mindoro Strait, has suffered from dynamite fishing. Live-aboard dive boats allow divers access to the reef's sheer walls and drop-offs, breeding grounds of tuna, barracuda, manta rays and marine turtles. Apo also offers excellent opportunities to dive with harmless black-and-white-tipped sharks.

In northern Luzon, divers can visit several World War II wrecks in Subic Bay, though visibility tends to be hazy, even during the dry season (March to June). The famed 19th-century battleship USS *New York* lies in 27 meters (90 ft) of water, with *El Capitan*, a 130-meter-long (430-ft)

freighter, submerged just 12 meters (40 ft) below.

Balicasag Island, accessible from Panglao Island, is Bohol's best known dive site. Reef and pelagic fishes inhabit one of the archipelago's best walls, illuminated by glorious shafts of sunlight.

Partway up the western coast of Cebu lies Moalboal. A 35-meter (115-ft) wall drops right off the shores of Panagsama Beach, while a variety of dives await in Pescador Island Marine Park.

Coron Bay, off northern Palawan's Calamian Island, features some of the Philippines' best wrecks. The dozen accessible wrecks comprise a fleet of supply ships for Japanese Naval Admiral Kurita – torpedoed by US Admiral Haley's carrier air-

craft during the 1944 battle off Leyte Gulf.

By far, the Sulu Sea's Tubbataha Reefs offer the archipelago's best diving. Due to violent sea conditions during much of the year, live-aboard dive operators visit Tubbataha only from February to early June. Because of its open ocean location, pelagics of all sorts are commonplace, including white-tip and hammerhead sharks, marine turtles, manta rays and eagle rays. The sheer variety of species is unparalleled. Though evidence of dynamite fishing is apparent, the remoteness of the site – plus its designation as a UNESCO World Heritage Site and national marine park – helps to protect it. Because of the strong currents, diving with experienced guides is advised. ❑

RIGHT: a marine biologist monitoring coral growth in the waters of Apo Reef, Mindoro.

A GRACIOUS PEOPLE

The Filipino's desire to maintain smooth interpersonal relations at all times
stems from a wish to respect the other party's sensitivity

Filipinos are generally descended from a proto-Malay stock, preceded only by nomadic aborigines who crossed land bridges from mainland Asia before these were submerged to isolate the archipelago. Waves of migrants then came by boat – first the Indonesians between 3,000 and 500 BC, followed by arrivals from eastern India and south China. They settled in the mountains of northern Luzon and parts of Mindanao. Malays were the last migrants, arriving around 200 BC. They initially took over coastal areas to displace the aborigines, but eventually populated much of Luzon and Mindanao.

Creolization could not but result from the 333-year period of Spanish colonization. Many present-day Filipinos or Pinoys, as they call themselves, are of mixed heritage, known as Spanish *mestizo* or Chinese "Chinoys." This is true of urban areas, but even in the countryside it is not uncommon to come upon fair-skinned residents with obvious *mestizo* features.

Filipinos have a justifiable reputation as one of the most hospitable people in the world, especially in rural areas where traditional attitudes still survive. A foreign visitor lucky enough to have the name of a local resident is usually fed and shown around, if not offered a place to stay for free.

Filipinos are especially preoccupied with the notion of pride and self-esteem; public confrontation, criticism or arguments can lead to uncomfortable situations. Strong and fixed eye contact between males is considered aggressive and Filipinos often communicate with their eyes, lips and hands. Eyebrows raised with a smile are a silent "hello" or "yes" to a question. One might be pointed toward a direction with pursed lips. Polite language and gentle conversation are important.

While custom dictates a somewhat late arrival for social engagements, punctuality is expected for business meetings. Unlike some other places in Asia, women are on an equal footing in the Philippine business world.

Clannishness

An extended support system remains both the main strength of Filipino society as well as the

customary source of corruption. Kinship ties of both blood and marriage, often up to three generations removed, are kept well-defined and operative on all levels and facets of life. Clans operate as custodians of common experiences, and in memory of geographical and racial origins. They act as disciplinary mechanisms, placement agencies and informal social-security systems. When there is a marriage between two clans, it is as much an alliance as a binding of two individuals.

Within the sometimes tyrannical embrace of the clan, members of all ages find their place in an orderly world, where children are cared for by an array of helpful aunts, uncles, cousins and grandparents, and the elderly are given

---

PRECEDING PAGES: night comes alive at Bom Bom bar in Boracay. **LEFT:** a half-hidden smile from a *nipa* hut. **RIGHT:** mother-child bonding.

care and reverence through to their last days.

If foreign guests are invited to a Filipino home and find themselves at the receiving end of clan hospitality, it is considered good form to give special acknowledgement to family elders. It does not hurt to use the honorifics *lolo* and *lola* for the grandfather and grandmother and other elders of the clan. Greet them by putting their right hand to your forehead in a time-honored gesture of respect, which goes a long way in establishing relations.

Local sociologists have coined the phrase "smooth interpersonal relationships", or SIR for short, to indicate the key premise of human contact among Filipinos: the edges of face-to-face communication must be kept smooth at all times by gentle speech, no matter how unpleasant the message. Direct confrontation is generally avoided. When forced to deliver a negative message, Filipinos are fond of emissaries and subtle indirection, out of respect for the sensitivity of the other party.

Part of the SIR ritual are polite forms of address when conversing with strangers, especially older people and people of high social rank. The basic forms are the words *po* and *ho* to end sentences. Use *opo* and *oho* to say yes, and *hindi po* and *hindi ho* to say no. Even in face-to-face conver-

FILIPINO AMERICANS RETURN HOME

A recent phenomenon involves Fil-Ams, or Filipino Americans, from first- to third-generation migrants who are set to become the largest minority in the United States, outranking even the Chinese, in the 21st century. The official count stands at 2 million, but the figure may be higher, given the great number of illegals who maintain a TNT (for *tago ng tago*, or "always hiding") status.

There is now strong interaction between Filipino Americans and Filipinos, with the younger generation of American-bred Filipinos passionately retracing their roots. Nearly every family in the Philippines has relations or friends who have relocated to the Americas, so that the differences of culture, as well as the economic, are exposing new depths of filial ties. Fil-Am athletes and entertainers have started an influx, coming home to roost, bolstering professional basketball and the movie industry.

The half-breed Filipino, and the Filipino raised elsewhere but still subject to the pull of racial memory, cannot but help teach homegrown kin the way to a paradigm shift in terms of ambition, discipline, determination, professional conduct, and perhaps in the future, effective governance.

An eminent scholar has asked: "By defining themselves, could it be possible that the Filipino American will eventually define the Filipino?"

sation, one refers to a new acquaintance, an older person or a dignitary in the third person-plural *sila*. The intention is to maintain a respectful distance, beginning on the verbal level, from which to slowly establish a pleasant relationship.

Hiya, literally translated as shame but also defined as a delicacy of sensitivity to the feeling of others, prevents individuals from taking each other for granted. Related to *hiya* is *pakiramdaman,* or feeling each other out. Beyond words, Filipinos often intuit or divine what the other means to communicate.

A second, essential strand in the fabric of social relationships is *utang na loob,* or debt of gratitude. Favors long bestowed are never forgotten and always returned in an invisible bond of reciprocity. Of course, *utang na loob* (both individual and collective) has also been responsible for sluggish bureaucracies resistant to impersonal but rational management procedures, arguably the price of transition from tradition to modernity. To this day, it is a coarse individual who forgets *utang na loob.*

A third Filipino concept is *pakikisama*, which can be defined as "getting along" or submitting to group will. As with all cultural traits, this one has its negative applications. Positively applied, however, *pakikisama* has tremendous power to mobilize individual energies for collective goals.

Perhaps the crowning glory of local sociology is the Filipino expression traced to a linguistic root of *Bahala na,* or leave it to God. This is a typical Filipino reaction to crises and insoluble problems. Development experts have often decried *Bahala na as* passive and fatalist, the sole factor in the delayed maturity of the Filipino people. Some other students of the Filipino character, however, praise its philosophical origins. As proof, they point to how *Bahala na* at its best has supported Filipino morale through the trials of destiny.

Ethnic and minority groups

Ethnic groups weave a dazzling strain of color into the Philippine cultural fabric. Over 80 different ethnic groups are scattered in relative isolation about the islands. Some inhabit accessible villages, where visitors can catch glimpses of their native customs and lifestyles.

LEFT: women in Maria Clara dresses and men in *barong tagalog* shirts at a high-society *soiree*, Manila.
RIGHT: rural family in Iloilo Province.

Of the Philippine population, now approaching 90 million, some 10 percent are classified as cultural or ethnic minorities. Most of these people live outside the cultural mainstream of lowland Filipinos. Some 60 percent are made up of various Muslim groups living in Mindanao and the Sulu Archipelago. The remaining peoples – comprising mostly animists – inhabit the mountain provinces of northern and central Luzon, and the highland plains, rainforests and isolated seashores of Mindanao and Palawan. The ethnic groups include the following:

Mangyan: The sweet-potato-eating tribes of Mindoro island – Iraya, Tagaydan, Tatagnon,

Buid, Alangan and Hanunoo – are collectively known as Mangyan, a simple, reclusive people.

Tagbanua: The Tagbanua tribe of Palawan island has in recent years yielded their shores to intrusive outsiders, yet have managed to retain their own animist culture. They wear scanty dress, maintain a religion intimately joined with nature, and carve bamboo tubes with an old alphabet of Hindu origin. They are the first tribe in the Philippines to receive legal ownership of their land through new ancestral domain laws.

Negrito: The Aeta, Ati, Dumagat and Ita are collectively known as Negrito or the Philippines' Aborigines. Numbering some 40,000, these short, dark-skinned and kinky-haired people are now

The Filipina

Today's Filipina emerged from a checkered history. And she is still emerging, playing dual roles: at home a teacher, abroad a "Japayuki" dancing scantily in a Tokyo bar or a domestic helper inspiring the Greek neologism "Filipineza." The nurse and beauty queen, scholar and chambermaid, torch singer and ambassador trace their origins to a long line of priestesses.

Early tribes relied on the woman to perform sacred rites. Known as *Catalonan* to the Tagalog, or *babaylan* to the Bisaya – the priestess healed

with herbs and received the spirits in trance.

When the Spanish missionaries came, she sought to poison the cowled strangers and burn their altars. But she later became Christian, and proved to be the colonist's delight. She wound up helping him pacify warlike tribes and became an adopted waif to be melted in the Castilian mold. The friar, who was father figure to whole villages fancied her a naive child, tenderheartedly teaching her his alphabet. He gave her only enough to keep her serving and reverential, withholding higher education from her eager grasp.

Where once she worshipped nature and ancestral spirits, she now embraced Christian piety – praying endless rosaries and placing flowers on the altar. In her innocence, she proved too tempting a morsel for the friar fathers, and time and again, was seduced. Today's fourth generation after the Spanish counts many forebears who were mestizo *anak pare*, friar bastards.

Friar children, though illegitimate, enjoyed a slightly higher status as Castilian progeny. For mothers who adored fair-haired saints with blue eyes, the *anak pare* aroused special devotion. To be white was the subject of many silent prayers. To find a rich, handsome Spaniard to marry became the goal, and daughters were whipped when they played too long in the sun.

The Filipino male found his oppressed status even more galling when wife or daughter was raped by a powerful Spaniard. There was no recourse, except perhaps in drink, and many a young Filipina was torn between her own longing for a better life and her father's wounded pride.

The revolution against Spanish rule was a chance to gamble for freedom. Both *indio* and *india* sought to overthrow their common tyrant. He plodded and fought; she hid his arms, carried his secret documents, nursed his wounds and aided his escape. Brave widows, foremost among them Gabriela Silang of the Ilocos, took to the battlefield in place of slain husbands.

Later, with the same earnestness she had reserved for catechism, the Filipina worshipped at the American altar of formal education. The Yankee also prodded her into giddy new experiences – voting for the first time, shedding the *saya* (long skirt), bobbing long tresses, speaking her mind.

Her ambitions were awakened. Today, one encounters the Filipina in a great variety of professions, jockeying for public office, running modern corporations, sitting in international commissions, even governing the country.

New blandishments – Miss Universe and Miss International titles – have helped turn the Filipina's head, as paeans are sung to her combination of dusky Malay and fair Spanish beauty, with a touch of Chinese. Today, she graces fashion show and political stage with equal aplomb.

And yet her country's laws remind her of her former status as a friar ward. She still cannot sign contracts without her husband's consent, her adultery is punished more stiffly than his, and a separated wife is not given the same tax breaks. These inequities rankle, but yet the Filipina is told she shares equality with her man. ❑

LEFT: a 1939 portrait of demure Manila girls.

faced with cultural extinction. The Aeta live in the mountain jungles of Negros, Samar, and Leyte; in the rolling hills of Zambales, and Nueva Ecija on Luzon; and along the untamed shorelines of northern Luzon. The Ati group of Panay is probably the best known of the Negritos and are credited with welcoming history's first Malay *datus* from Borneo in the 14th century.

Mountain people: There are five major ethnic groups spread across the Cordillera highlands of northern Luzon: Ibaloi, Kankanaey, Ifugao, Kalinga and Apayao. Other indigenous groups here include the Bontoc and Tingguian.

These proud, unconquered tribes have evolved

blend American missionary teaching with their ancestral religion. Culturally, the Kankanaey are a highly individualistic tribe, raised within a community system of wards. The *ato* is the meeting place for village elders and the sleeping place for adolescent boys. The *ulog* is the dormitory for girls and unmarried women. In many parts of the Cordillera, the Ibaloi and Kankanaey coexist, with the former occupying the valleys and the latter the mountain ridges.

Ifugao: The Ifugao of the eastern and central Cordillera are the architects of the most famous rice terraces in the world; the Banaue rice terraces were first constructed 2,000 years ago and

robust indigenous cultures and traditions in highland seclusion, far removed from lowland colonial history. They live sedentary lives based on a highly-developed agricultural economy. They worship tribal ancestors or spirits of nature and are suspicious of "intruders" from the lowlands.

Ibaloi and Kankanaey: The Ibaloi tribes of the western and southern Cordillera grow rice, coffee and vegetables, and raise livestock on their terraced hillsides. They also mine precious metals like gold and copper in the upland region of Lepanto.

The Kankanaey of northwest Cordillera

ABOVE: a pair of Ifugao elders from Central Cordillera.

cover more than 260 sq. km (100 sq. miles) of steep mountainside in Ifugao Province.

Muslims: Considered as a whole, the Muslims of the south – also called Moros – constitute the largest cultural minority. Some claim Mindanao and the Sulu Archipelago farther to the south as their own holy land. The Muslims, fiercely independent and combative, are classified into five major groups: Tausug, Maranao, Maguindanao, Samal and Badjao.

The Tausug were the first tribe in the archipelago to be converted to Islam. They are, historically, the ruling people of the ancient Sultanate of Jolo, and regard themselves as superior to other Philippine Muslims. As a cultural group, the "people of the current," as they are known, lead a combative, "muscular" life, where violence is often a form of expression. The Tausug are traders, fishermen and artisans of fine Muslim textiles and metal works.

In contrast, the Maranao are the graceful "people of the lake" who live by Lake Lanao at 700 meters (2,300 ft) above sea level. In cool and aloof isolation, they continue to uphold their complex but vigorous sultanates.

The Maguindanao are the "people of the flood plain," inhabiting a less hospitable area in Cotabato Province, where land is periodically flooded by overflowing rivers. The largest

group of Muslims, the Maguindanao are a hardy clan, surviving on agriculture and fishing. They weave fine mats and baskets.

The Samal are the poorest and least independent of the major Muslim groups. They serve as the "loyal commoners" in the hierarchy of Muslim minorities. They live over the sea, in villages perched on stilts above coastal waters.

The Badjao are the "sea-gypsies," the true wanderers of the Sulu seas. They are born on the water, live upon their tiny craft for a lifetime – turning tawny and blonde in the sun and salt – and set foot on land only to die. The 20,000-strong Badjao are a superficially Islamic tribe.

CHINESE ASSIMILATION

Long before the Spanish conquest, the Chinese had been around, having traveled to and settled in the Philippines as independent traders, itinerants or pillaging corsairs. The legendary pirate Limahong attacked Pangasinan in northern Luzon in the 16th century and, when cornered by a Spanish expeditionary force, dug an extensive channel to escape to the gulf. Many of Limahong's men stayed to intermarry with the natives, thus producing the first Chinese *mestizo* in the Philippines.

Although occasionally made the butt of jokes, well-assimilated Chinese descendants never suffer from strong prejudice, let alone racist ire. Kidnap bands targeted

wealthy Chinese in the mid-1990s, but this was more an indication of ineffective policing than anything else. During that time, many well-to-do Chinese kept their heads down, for fear of attracting unnecessary envy or attention.

Former President Corazon Aquino and Cardinal Sin, the prime movers behind the People Power reaction against the Marcos dictatorship, are both descended from Chinese migrants from Fujian. Second- and third-generation "Chinoys" (a combination of Chinese and "Pinoy") are very much a part of the managerial pool of development-oriented Filipinos; in fact, many Chinese business leaders have become strong pillars of the economy.

A unique cultural group living on Basilan Island off Mindanao are the Yakan. A gentle people of partial Polynesian origin, with mixed Muslim and animist beliefs, they are the most skilled textile weavers of the southern archipelago. On backstrap looms they turn fine cottons and silks into geometric works of art.

The least study has been made of the non-Muslim ethnic tribes of the Mindanao highlands. The more than 10 tribes, among the most heavily costumed and most colorful, live in relative isolation in the Mindanao interior.

Of Malay stock, the Tiruray are a horse-riding hill people occupying the mountains of southwest Mindanao. The T'boli tribe of Lake Sebu in Cotabato have a wealth of crafts, elaborate ethnic costumes, and vivacious dances and music. They are also admired for their handsome brasswork, which finds its way into statues, belts, chains and tinkling anklets worn by heavily-ornamented tribal women.

The Bagobo live along the desolate eastern coast of the Gulf of Davao. In imitating the metal arts of the Moro (Muslim warriors), the tribe developed an ornate tradition in weaponry as well as inlaid, bell-bejangled metal boxes. The Subanon of western Lanao pioneered one of the country's strongest traditions of pottery. The 50,000-strong Bukidnon of east Lanao is a tribe of fiercely independent highlanders.

The modern Filipino

Manila is not the Philippines, a visitor is often told. The Manileño only represents one facet of the Filipinos. Out in the boondocks (a Tagalog word drawn into the American lexicon in the colonial years), daily existence is a far cry from the sophisticated, if often anarchic, features inherent in big city life.

The present-day Filipino covers the spectrum of cappuccino-sipping yuppie at a trendy cafe to the coconut sap gatherer shimmying up a tree. City folk are greatly Westernized, especially the upper classes and the gainfully employed. Still, there are many pockets in the metropolis where poverty dwells and the shanty dweller is seen as having degenerated into levels below country folk, since they eschew honorable work for a life of scavenging.

Propping up the national economy is the ever

growing number of Filipinos working overseas, whose common denominator is that they all send foreign currency home. There is the OCW for Overseas Contract Worker, since euphemized further into OFW for Overseas Filipino Worker. Legions leave their families for extended terms in the oil fields of the Middle East and factories in Taiwan and South Korea.

There are also Filipino seamen and domestic helpers, who include those who have left behind teaching positions in the Philippines to earn a steady income in Hong Kong, Singapore, Australia, America, and Europe.

"Cultural dancers" turn into servile, song-and-

dance "Japayukis" in Tokyo and Osaka. Roving bands of musicians dominate the bars in Asia. There are also the professionals — doctors, nurses, engineers, computer experts — who find greener pastures in the US and Europe.

The Filipino is everywhere. The extent of the diaspora nearly rivals that of the numerically superior Chinese. Altogether, these exiles number at least 8 million and are still growing. They enhance the local economy by an official count of US$13 billion annually. Most of them return, having saved enough to start small businesses, only to be replaced by the next generation of OFWs and adventurers who are convinced they can profit similarly from a spell abroad. ❏

LEFT: Maranao dance troop from Marawi, Mindanao.
RIGHT: a modern Filipina.

WITH FEAR AND FERVOR

*The mostly Catholic nation worships its faith in highly ritualistic display
and in forms which show a strong attachment to folk tradition*

The story is told that when Magellan landed in the thriving coastal kingdom of Cebu, it was not his sonorous promise of friendship with a white king, nor the gleam of Spanish cannons, nor the symbol of the cross that won the day. Rather, it was a local queen's first beguiled look at a statue of the Christ child. The idol was alien as could be, but before those lambent Castilian eyes, and the crown, scepter and tiny hand grasping all of the known world, the queen of a children-loving kingdom could hardly resist conversion to the new faith.

At the mass baptism that ensued, the queen (who was given the Christian name of Juana, while her husband, Rajah Humabon, was renamed Carlos) received the icon as a gift from Antonio de Pigafetta, chronicler of the expedition. Henceforth, promised the queen, the little one, Santo Niño of the Spanish, would replace the *anito* (idols) of her people.

The promise was not kept for very long; the records show a rapid return to animism after the conquistadors left. But through three centuries of conversion, the friars perfected that first encounter with astute psychology.

Kinship was the glue of indigeneous society, and in no time at all, the souls of departed ancestors, the spirits of nature and not a few mythical monsters were replaced by (and in many cases, incorporated with) an extended Christian family consisting of both the human and divine. God, of course, played the stern father, various saints were kindly aunts and uncles, the Virgin Mary was the merciful mother and her child, the darling of the family.

After the hardier business of conquest had subjugated the heads of families into paying tribute, pacification was pursued through the women and children. After generations of inculcation, women were convinced that true femininity lay in devotion, chastity and obedience, while children were to perfect their trust in the

Father. In lieu of visible divinities, the friars and governors did just as well as objects of these virtues. Depending on the temperamental and cultural quirks of the settlement, the focus varied between Mother, the Virgin Mary, and the Child Jesus. In the shrines and churches of Luzon, where women's equality with men had

RELIGIOUS COMPOSITION

The Philippines is predominantly Roman Catholic, with about 80 percent embracing the faith through traditional baptism as infants. The rest of the population may be divided into at least three other major religious groups: Islam (7 percent), practiced for centuries in Mindanao, the Aglipayan church (about 1 percent), and the Iglesia ni Cristo (Church of Christ) or INC (3 percent). There are also small numbers who are Buddhist, Taoist and animist.

INC, with 5 million members worldwide, has made strong inroads with its strait-laced collectivism and strict tithing practices. The church buildings can be recognised by their clean white or pastel facades and soaring Gothic spires.

PRECEDING PAGES: offerings of flowers at a religious celebration in Cebu. **LEFT:** Madonna and baby Jesus. **RIGHT:** intent on prayer.

long ago extended into roles of power as priestesses, Mary became the standard-bearer of Catholicism. In the Visayas of Queen Juana, where children to this day are indulged in extended childhood, the Santo Niño was king.

Propaganda was part and parcel of the missionary kit. Friars made sure that every important event was attributed to divine intervention. Thus Mary and her son (along with the various patron saints of particular places) became agents for fire prevention, earthquake-proofing (especially of churches), to ward off marauders' attacks, as well as deities of rain, fertility and the entire range of human needs.

have their own special image of the Virgin and Child: polished ivory by the classic skills of medieval European carvers; stained ebony fashioned by Mexican artisans; intricately carved in soft wood by Chinese sculptors (many displaying the almond eyes of their own immortals); or hewn from hardwoods by the persevering hands of local Filipino craftsmen.

Ubiquitous shrines

There is hardly a Catholic home without its own Virgin and Child enshrined, usually near the master bedroom. The Virgin is ever present in garden shrines – grottoes simulating her

Miraculous icons

In the mysterious mechanics of prayer and mass worship, it would seem that many of the wishes, pleas and heart-cries were indeed granted. Tradition continues to claim that in such a place and at such a time, crops were saved from destruction by locust and drought, floods were diverted, and brigands turned away by heavenly protectors.

All over the Philippines, at least 50 major icons of Mary and the Holy Child are associated with wondrous stories of miracles. Several of them, in fact, have been recognized by the Vatican as authentic miracle workers.

Practically all large Christian towns and cities

recorded apparitions in Fatima, Lourdes and Carmel. The usual spot is on a mound, hillock or mountainside that is carved out with hundreds of tortuous steps to the shrine.

Just a generation ago, it was standard practice to affix a Maria or a Jesus Maria to a Filipino child's given name. The practice is dying out. A striking aspect of the religious life of the Filipinos is their collective and deep devotion to the Blessed Virgin Mary, in all her forms.

Wealthy Filipinos often embark on extended pilgrimage tours to Lourdes, Jerusalem, or any new foreign site where a miraculous apparition has been reported, such as Medjugorje in the former Yugoslavia, or Naju in South Korea.

Closer to home, any news of a sighting or simulacrum (sometimes the shape of Our Lady is perceived to have appeared in a tree trunk or an otherwise greasy kitchen wall) instantly draws hordes of devotees, together with an equal legion of candle sellers and soft drink vendors.

The old folk still recall how rose petals with the image of Our Lady's face rained on the town of Lipa in Batangas way back in the 1950s, or how a decade later the Blessed Mother reportedly appeared to some children in the tiny island of Cabra north of Mindoro.

On December 8, the Feast of the Immaculate Conception, Catholic schoolchildren enjoy a holiday, while ritual-inclined parents flock to Intramuros, where a lengthy procession of *carrozas*, motor-driven and illuminated floats with rococo carvings, inch forward past an adulatory throng in a slow-moving display of richly dressed statues of the Virgin Mary.

> **POP PRELATE**
>
> As many as a million are attracted to the weekly extravaganzas of "Brother Mike" Velarde of El Shaddai. The brightly attired leader holds his Manila crowds in thrall.

Procession to the water

Marian processions take place in every city and town sometime or other during the year. And there are always any number of matrons or families who take care of dressing up hand-carved images that have been passed down through worshipful generations.

For sheer drama, no religious festival in the country can rival the Peñafrancia Festival held in September in Naga City. Drawing thousands of devotees and tourists, the 15-day celebration centers on the reputedly miraculous image of Our Lady of Peñafrancia, the Patroness of Bicolandia. Barefoot male devotees called *voyadores*, numbering in the hundreds, take turns carrying the 284-year-old image on their shoulders. This traditional ritual of transporting the icon from the Basilica Minore to the Metropolitan Cathedral is called the translacion. Eventually, the image is waterborne on an elaborately adorned pagoda atop a large boat. Cheering throngs gathered by the river banks witness its passage up the Naga River.

A similarly grandiose fluvial procession called Pagoda sa Wawa is staged yearly in

Hagonoy, Bulacan. Tragedies have marred these religious festivities, with boats catching fire and causing drownings. But the passion for tradition built on adoration of the Blessed Mother is never dampened. In the Marian Jubilee Year of 1999, a remarkably strong contingent that participated in a fluvial procession of Marian images down New York's Hudson River past Manhattan was that of Philippine-American representatives. They were shored up by Filipinos who flew in from Manila to be part of the fes-

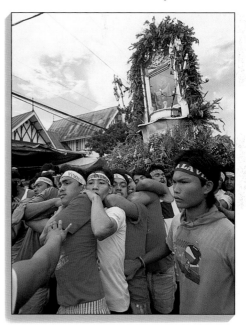

tivity, including media personalities who issued a live telecast to a Manila cable station.

One of the most enduring images of the People Power revolution staged on the busy highway of EDSA was the sight of a blue-robed icon that never left the side of the principal military rebel, Gen. Fidel Ramos, who would become president after Corazon Aquino. Noteworthy was the fact that Ramos was not Catholic but Protestant. A modern shrine to what is now named Our Lady of Edsa has since been erected by the historic highway, with a towering bronze statue of an Asian-looking Virgin Mary rising as religious counterpoint to a busy mall and soaring highway infrastructure.

LEFT: a collection of rare Santo Niño dolls.
RIGHT: penitents carrying the Virgin Mary aloft at the Peñafrancia festival in Naga City.

Offshoots

Aside from the mainstream Catholicism, there is the Aglipayan religion (officially called the Philippine Independent Church, started by Gregorio Aglipay early in this century as a breakaway, nationalistic faction of Catholicism), and the Iglesia ni Cristo (Church of Christ), or INC. The 5-million-strong INC is noted for hewing to a collective decision during elections, so that it has emerged as a powerful political bloc often courted by aspirants to national office.

The late 1980s saw the proliferation of various charismatic movements, preaching the importance of leading a Spirit-led and Spirit-filled life.

It started with a return to fundamentalism practiced by so-called born-again Christians. Soon every radio and television station had its own evangelist preaching versions of revivalism mixed with theatrical come-ons such as singing and dancing. The most successful televangelist to date is "Brother Mike" Velarde, a former radio broadcaster who found his true (and lucrative) calling by establishing the El Shaddai group, which counts millions among its followers. His extravaganzas, held every Saturday at various open-air fields in Metro Manila, can attract as many as a million people. Always smartly attired, Velarde holds his crowd in thrall,

VOLUNTARY CRUCIFIXION

On Good Friday, a spectacle is played out in various barrios in Pampanga and Tarlac, with sinners – mostly male – sacrificing themselves for the community by being literally crucified in a re-enactment of Christ's suffering. Hordes of local and foreign photographers descend on these sites, and the Department of Tourism markets the yearly rite as a tourist draw.

The Catholic Church occasionally frowns on such practices, but for the most part it remains content to have this folksy if gory devotion played out, perhaps to assure itself that the only predominantly Catholic nation in Asia stays that way for a long time to come.

sometimes for over 24 hours, with a curious mix of Bible sayings, rhetorical speeches, songs and prayerful importunings for grace. When Velarde asks his faithful to wave their handkerchiefs in the air, they need no second cue. Nor when he asks them to turn their umbrellas upside down to receive blessings from God.

El Shaddai is another bloc. The Catholic Church usually tolerated its activities as an extension of charismatic faith, but once sanctioned Velarde over allegations that he had been amassing personal wealth through tithing. ❑

ABOVE: brothers in arms – El Shaddai evangelists are led by their charismatic leader, Brother Mike Velarde.

Superstitions and Taboos

Another commanding force just as intense as Filipino devotion to folk Catholicism is the adherence to superstitions and taboos. Often associated with religious observance and festivities, these superstitions, commonly known as folk beliefs, typify a way of life that is animated by a sense of fatalism and fear of the unknown. Throughout life, certain practices, procedures and taboos haunt the Filipino. And nowhere are these more numerous than in procreation.

Thirty-six-year-old Emma Sacedon, mother of two children, for instance, has much to relate about her pregnancy, childbirth and child-rearing experiences. During her pregnancy, she was accorded not a few privileges, including the undertaking of only light housework, but at the same time, she had to heed a list of taboos on a daily basis, particularly during the first trimester.

Whatever food she desired was made available to her (even if she later decided not to eat it), so as to prevent miscarriage. But, she could not eat a twin banana lest she give birth to twins, nor consume soft drinks, which could increase the size of the fetus excessively. Nor could she stand by doors, which could cause difficult labor. Emma had to avoid looking at ugly pictures, which might make her baby ugly, or have her picture taken, which could cause a stillbirth. She confined her wardrobe to black, down to underwear, and slept with her legs tightly closed to repel bad spirits.

When her time finally came, both Emma's mother and mother-in-law hired a *herbolario* (quack doctor) who recited prayers to keep the spirits away while she was in labor. The older women believed the mere presence of the *herbolario* ensured easy delivery and that the baby would grow up obedient. During labor, Emma wore a medallion given by her mother. The medallion was believed to ensure an easy delivery and good health for both mother and daughter. While she did not entirely buy the medallion story, Emma did not want to be the first to defy it. Besides, what did it cost her to follow such a simple maternal wish?

After she gave birth, the expelled placenta was buried along with pen and paper, as it is Filipino

RIGHT: for believers, potions made by medicine men are far more effective than a doctor's prescription.

belief that it would make the baby smart. The baby's first feces was massaged onto its infant gums like toothpaste to ensure strong teeth. Emma used the baby's first urine on her own hair to prevent it from falling out when she grew old. To give her flawless skin, the baby had her first bath with water in which a ring had been soaked. Her first fingernail parings and hair strands were inserted between pages of the Bible to ensure she would grow up God-fearing and obedient, and in the pages of a mathematics book so that she would become a mathematics wizard. A triangular cloth used to tie the baby's navel tube was transferred, after the navel had healed, to the foundations of the family

home, along with that of her sibling, so that all the children would stay close to the family.

Emma did not immediately resume her normal life following delivery. She waited at least two weeks before taking a bath, using only water that had been mixed with a special herbal concoction to avoid future health complications. For a month, she only ate rice with chicken, beef or *til-ogon* (a deepwater fish), vegetables and fruits. Reading or watching television during those days was strictly forbidden, as doing so could cause blindness.

The litany of Filipino superstitions goes on. While modern Filipinos may not admit belief in them, most, however, would rather be safe than sorry in tempting fate. ❑

PSYCHIC PHYSICIANS

Public interest in the mystical practices of faith healers may be dwindling but the miracles claimed by their believers remain a challenge for the scientific mind

Manong Paul Bastawang lives in a shack on a low hillock among the pines of Baguio, north of Manila. His tiny yard is filled with old gasoline cans, rubber tires and giant fern stumps recycled into pots of plants.

Indoors, he disappears into a bedroom and emerges with several bottles of dried seeds, bark and leaves, all neatly labeled in his Igorot dialect. Laying them on a wooden table, he proceeds to explain their uses for curing cancer, malaria, snake bites, rheumatism, asthma and several other ills.

It is cold in the house and Manong Paul offers herbal tea to prevent stomach cramps. Sipping, the visitor notes a crude watercolour depiction of a flying saucer on the wall.

"Have you seen them, Manong Paul?"

"Yes," he answers quietly. "They like to hover directly over churches."

"Why do you suppose they do?"

"They could be recharging their batteries," he replies. "The watercolour is what I saw the other night. You see the lights surrounding it? It's like the light I see around plants that yield medicine."

He claims to pray every day. "When the right time has come, my Voice tells me to go to the forest. I am guided by white flowers that are friends of medicinal plants. They are very beautiful, glowing in different colors like the halos of the saints."

The second coming

Four o'clock on a Sunday afternoon at the prayer hall of the *Watawat ng Lahi* (Flag of the Race), an organization which believes that Philippine national Jose Rizal was a reincarnation of Christ and, as such, will come again. Their headquarters is perched on top of a hill called *burol na ginto*, hill of gold, near the town of Calamba, Rizal's birthplace in Laguna Province.

That afternoon, members are gathered for the

PRECEDING PAGES: the Ciudad Mistica women-only sect of Mt Banahaw. **LEFT:** a mystic healer in meditation. **RIGHT:** an Ifugao sacrificing chicken to appease spirits.

monthly meeting with the oldest and most respected Watawat associates – 16 dead Filipinos regarded as national heroes. Through a trance medium, some of them will speak in the *Banal na Tinig*, the holy voice of prophecy.

Everyone falls silent while resonant tones echo in the hall. The day, says the Voice, is not

long in coming when the new age shall be known in the Philippines by the building of a golden church and a golden palace, and the waving of a golden flag.

The subok

It is Good Friday in the lush hills of lakeside Tanay town in Rizal Province. High noon creeps in overhead. A gathering of men, hollow-eyed from fasting and overnight meditation, shuffle their feet around the courtyard of an old church. Creaking and groaning, a flower-decked *carroza* float emerges from the dim interiors, carrying the Santo Sepulcro, a wooden statue of the dead Christ. There is a rush toward it, then a scramble to insert objects in the folds of the robes, under the feet, in the hands.

The image – now loaded with handkerchiefs, bronze medals, pieces of paper inscribed with Latin phrases and images of Christ and the Virgin Mary, pebbles, tektites, bones, prayer books, crucifixes, catfish eyes – is encircled by a chain of linked hands. The procession moves on. Later, with the merciless sun beating a still afternoon into an oppressive silence, the same gathering of men appears at a nearby seafood restaurant. They share a meal, laugh, joke around. Then, as if by signal, they fall quiet again. There is a silent reaching for *anting-*

The men knit their brows in silent approval. One of them moves to touch the *anting-anting* in his open hand. He claims that it feels as hot as a kettle at boiling point. Held between thumb and index finger, the bronze medal spins with a life of its own.

The others step forward now. Lethal weapons are passed around – horse-hair whips, revolvers, more *bolo*. Throughout the rest of Good Friday afternoon and Holy Saturday, each person will test the efficacy of his own talisman – asking to be shot at, whipped, stabbed. Some get hurt. Others leave the *subok* unscathed, exuding a profound solemnity.

anting, the objects that had taken a ride with the Santo Sepulcro and thus have become talismans against death or physical harm. It is time to test their efficacy in the *subok*, the trial.

A man, in his forties, walks forward. He appears to be a fisherman, judging from the calluses on his thumb and index finger. He sharpens a long *bolo* knife in deliberate motions.

Satisfied that it is sharp enough, he then sits at a table, stretches his left arm with a fist tightly clasping his *anting-anting*. He raises a right arm with the *bolo*, brings it down suddenly, coolly hacking away at his stretched left arm. Neither cuts nor blood appear. Again, he strikes. Not the smallest scratch.

The magbabarang

On the island of Siquijor, off the island of Negros, lives the *magbabarang*. He collects special bees, beetles, and centipedes (collectively called *barang*), chosen because they all have an extra leg. The *magbabarang* keeps them inside a bamboo tube worn smooth.

On Fridays, the *magbabarang* performs a ritual from which his name derives. He takes a list of names and addresses, writes them on separate pieces of paper, and puts them in the bamboo tube. In a while, he opens the tube. If the papers have been torn to shreds, the insects are willing to attack the owners of the names. The ritual of vengeance begins.

The *magbabarang* proceeds to tie a white string on the extra legs of his assistants. He then lets them loose, with instructions to lodge themselves inside the victim's body, bite his internal organs and wreak havoc in his system until he dies. Then they go back to their master. If the strings are red with blood, the hex was successful. If clean, the victim was innocent after all and thus was able to resist the magic.

The Bolobolo

A woman arrives at the home of a *bolobolo* complaining of severe chest pains. The *bolobolo* diagnoses her, then produces a small

The ritual had taken three minutes. In three hours, the *bolobolo* says, the woman can move about normally. She offers to pay. The *bolobolo* refuses. That, says he, would be the loss of his God-given powers.

Truth or trick?

What to make of it all? Can these mostly unlettered Filipinos really be tuned in to power sources that people through the ages have been classified as divine? Or are they just a bunch of quacks, skilled at hypnosis and sleight of hand, unscrupulously trafficking in ignorance for personal gain? Or can there be, as the scales

bamboo tube from his pocket. An assistant hands him a glass half-filled with water, into which he carefully drops a moonstone. The *bolobolo* swallows some of the water, gargles and spits it out the window. He opens his mouth wide to show that it is empty. After praying in a low mumble, he dips one end of the bamboo tube into the glass, takes the other end of the reed into his mouth and begins to blow.

The water begins to darken to the color of mud. Soon, worms are wriggling in the glass. You are cured, the *bolobolo* tells the woman.

LEFT: herbal brews on sale at Manila's Quiapo Church.
ABOVE: a cult ritual in progress at Mt Banahaw.

balance delicately, some truth in-between?

Most of what is known in the West today, both good and bad, about the gray areas of the occult in the Philippines stems from the discovery of Pangasinan psychic surgery in the late 1940s by a few Americans. Details of the encounter are unclear. What is known is that a few diseased individuals received "miracle cures," unexplainable even by educated Filipinos who, though dimly aware of strange healing practices in the barrios of their childhood, had been schooled long enough in the rational, or Western, way of thought to dismiss them as superstition.

The first major healer encountered by the

Americans was a man called Eleuterio Terte, who began as a magnetic healer. His method was a simple laying on of hands, similar to the practice of any number of spiritual healers in Brazil, Hawaii, England and the southern United States. As reported, however, shortly after World War II, Terte suddenly noticed bodies opening spontaneously under his hands.

This is where the story of psychic healing in the Philippines began. By the mid-1960s, when Harold Sherman, an American psychic researcher, came to document psychic surgery, Terte had already trained 14 of the 30 surgeons now known the world over as Filipino faith

healers. A controversial bunch, they have been both praised and damned.

Psychic surgery is the most impressive example of spirit healing. Diagnosis is arrived at in meditation, and before the operation. During surgery, with short, cavalier slashes of the finger ½ meter away from the diseased part (sometimes a finger of an eyewitness held in the healer's hand is used), bodies appear to open up without a single knife stroke. Then a few gropes, turns, pulls, twists, and out comes a supposed organ, or an eyeball, followed by quick dabs of alcohol-soaked cotton on blood-drenched areas and finally, a closing up of the opening.

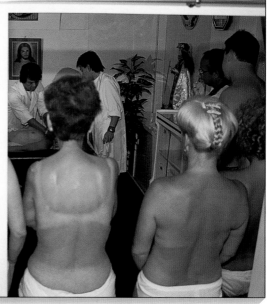

FAITH HEALER ALMOST MAKES MAYOR

Faith healing and excursions into the nether realm of the strange and powerful seems to have paled against a modern backdrop of mushrooming malls, laser surgery and high-tech activities such as video games and the Internet.

The only faith healing that occasionally gets attention is done at the basic level – the laying of hands – and this by Fr Corsi, a Catholic priest. And it is the Christian charismatic movement that gains from his practice.

The best-known psychic healer to emerge after Tony Agpaoa was Jun Labo, who maintained a successful clinic in Baguio funded by his second wife, a wealthy Japanese. It catered mostly to European and Japanese clients and

became lucrative. To cap his success, he ran for mayor and managed to win. But his opponent protested that he had at one time taken American citizenship. The protest was upheld, and Labo was prevented from assuming office. Meanwhile, scuttlebutt grew that Labo had degenerated into plain trickery, having lost his original power after turning too "commercial." He took his practice to Russia, where he had always had many adherents. But his run of bad luck had not yet eased. Officials clamped him in jail for allegedly conducting a scam. He managed to work for his release after a few months and returned to Baguio with a new and very young Russian wife.

When the parts removed are not thrown into a gory pail of organic material, they are deposited in bottles of alcohol, which then become the much-prized booty of visiting scientists and the scientific minded. More often than not, requests for these bottles have been refused. Those who have acquired them testify to one of three results. One, laboratory examinations show the contents to be genuine, diseased human tissue. Two, they turn out to be animal parts. Or three, that the contents have vanished – whether through evaporation, theft or "dematerialization" into the original "etheric" state.

To make the whole phenomenon even more baffling, sometimes what appears to emerge out of a patient's body are not even pig or chicken parts, but totally foreign material – including dried wax, twine and rusty razor blades.

The scientific response

There is little in scientific experience to explain this sort of impudence, and as the mind stutters in disbelief, it lets in the suggestion of a totally different sphere of reality. The healers churning up these objects from human bodies matter-of-factly call them witchcraft. Parallels to experiences in South America – where African spiritual rituals and Latin spiritualism combine in a manner similar to the Filipino's – have been drawn, making this explanation plausible.

But faith cannot evade aggressive empiricism. A few Filipino healers have been brought to the laboratories of Japanese, German, Swiss, and American scientists. They have been interviewed, nailed down on details of life histories and asked to enter their healing frame of mind at the precise moment when all the EEG, pulse rate, blood pressure and adrenalin-level measuring devices are turned on.

In the case of Antonio Agpaoa, possibly the most controversial Filipino healer, all the machines in the Tokyo laboratory of Dr Hiroshi Motoyama simply broke down. Dr Motoyama later outlines in his book, *Psychic Surgery in the Philippines,* that the first and most important condition for having the ability to heal is "to meet a god," followed by fasting, prayer and initiation to the "mission," and finally, constant contact with the god.

LEFT: psychic surgery is not for the squeamish.
RIGHT: the Supreme Pontiff of the Crusaders of the Divine Church claims the power to heal.

Link with ancient Polynesians

A recent theory purports that Filipino faith healers are descendants of the *kahuna*, the ancient healers of old Tahiti and Hawaii. Their shaman who made the distinction between a higher self of consciousness, a middle self of rationality and a lower self of age-old instinctive power, are said to have had the ability to dematerialize tissues and bones and then rematerialize them in perfect order.

The *kahuna* vanished with the coming of Christianity to Polynesia. Magic spells became prayers. Guardian spirits became a new pantheon of white saints.

However, psychic healers seem to have fallen out of favor in the past couple of decades, with no outstanding new names bruited about as worthy successors to the likes of Tony Agpaoa. The phenomenon that peaked in the 1970s does not seem to attract the same large number of foreigners any more. Neither do desperately afflicted Filipinos make a beeline to Pangasinan, once well-noted for its concentration of celebrated faith healers.

In its place, the new millennium may have refocused the people's interest on Christian prophecies and beliefs, some of which similarly, and quite ironically, require the suspension of scientific rationality. ❏

FIESTA FANTASTICA

Festivals take place all year round in the Philippines. Diversions range from re-enactments of Christ's crucifixion to greased-pig catching games

The present shape of the Filipino fiesta comes from the wisdom of old Spanish friars, who were disturbed by the early forced conversion to Catholicism by Filipinos. When natural calamity and tribal enemies threatened Christian settlements, the friars took the opportunity to lead everyone into church in quest of a "miracle." In time, the guardian spirits of harvest feasts were replaced by Christian saints, and as the tropical heat prompted ancient chants of fertility, the friars combed through their memories of Spain for songs and dances to woo a musical people into worship of the Virgin Mary.

January

Kalibo's Ati-Atihan festival, held in the third week of January, is the Philippines' most famous fiesta. *Ati-Atihan* means "making like Ati," and refers to the dark Negrito aborigines, the original inhabitants of Panay. In 1212, as legend has it, 10 Bornean lords escaping religious tyranny in the south fled northwards with their followers. Upon their arrival in Panay, they struck a deal with the local chieftain. The peace pact was later reinforced by a harvest feast prepared by the new arrivals for their Ati neighbors. Ever eager to please, the Bornean hosts made a merry welcome with gongs and cymbals, smeared soot on their faces and started dancing in the streets in merry imitation of their Ati guests. The Christ-child figure of Santo Niño was only introduced in later years.

Today, as column upon column of sooted Ati-garbed locals beat on drums and cymbals and march in syncopated rhythm, wild dancing breaks out everywhere. The unceasing and deafening Ati-Atihan beat overloads the senses, inducing everyone to end up joining in the madcap fun. The Ati-Atihan is so successful that it has been replicated in other parts of the Visayan Islands, albeit with various twists to reflect local historical associations. Also on the

island of Panay, in Iloilo City, a similar festival called Dinayang takes place on the fourth weekend of January.

February

The giant ring road encircling Metro Manila, Epifanio de los Santos Avenue, or EDSA, was

the focus for the bloodless February 1986 revolution that toppled former dictator Ferdinand Marcos. It was perhaps the Filipinos' finest hour in modern times. There was tension, of course, when the banners of revolt were first unfurled over Camp Crame. Nevertheless, despite their fears, hundreds of thousands of Filipinos converged on this road of resistance to form a protective human wall. There, confronted with tanks and troops, they brought their personal weapons of prayers, smiles, rosary beads and flowers to bear on the forces of discredited authority.

Since then, Filipinos have celebrated the anniversary of the EDSA People Power revolution

PRECEDING PAGES: revelers at the Dinayang festival, Iloilo City. **LEFT:** Ati-Atihan parade in Kalibo draws thousands every year. **RIGHT:** the face of Ati-Atihan.

with moving masses, stage shows, dancing, displays, singing and fireworks. Occupying centerstage of the celebration is the portion of EDSA between Camp Crame and Aguinaldo and the EDSA Shrine on Ortigas Avenue.

March and April

During the Lenten season, Holy Week turns into a colorful frenzy of celebration throughout the Philippines. Most notably, the heart-shaped island of Marinduque becomes a stage for a unique spectacle: the Moriones festival which re-enacts the Biblical story of Longinus and his miracle.

ater, Christ's resurrection is then dramatically re-enacted. Longinus reappears, now a convert.

The wrath of the Roman legionaries is immediately aroused. Longinus is pursued by the soldiers and brought to trial. He is thrown before Pontius Pilate, judged, and then ceremoniously beheaded. With his mask held high by a Roman soldier, Longinus' headless body is carried on a bamboo stretcher to the church, bringing an end to the Moriones festival.

May

The first of May is an important day throughout the Philippines as it heralds a merry month of

The drama unfolds as the villages of Boac, Gasan and Mogpog are converted into an immense stage. All-male participants don wooden masks carved from coral wood, to resemble Roman soldiers wearing perpetual scowls. On Ash Wednesday they roam the streets to terrorize – not for real, naturally – the locals. It is all good fun. On Good Friday, a stand-in for Jesus is crucified with the one-eyed Longinus' assistance. When he thrusts a spear into Jesus' side, the blood spurts into his blind eye and restores his full sight. By Easter Sunday, the Moriones (masked participants) and thousands of spectators crowd into an open-air arena alongside the Boac River. With great the-

fiestas, flowers, dainty maidens in pretty gowns, and the twin processions of the Flores de Mayo and the Santacruzan.

A riot of blooms attends the month-long tribute to the Queen of Heaven, or the Virgin Mary, which climaxes with a glittering parade of crowns and costumes on the last Sunday of May. Indeed, the celebration that was traditionally a religious affair has evolved into a paramount social one.

The Santacruzan is another Spanish legacy that commemorates the search for the True Cross of Christ. According to legend, Constantine the Great was converted to the Christian faith through the vision of a flaming cross in heaven, which is said to have led him to victory in battle. Queen Helena, the first Christian empress and who was canonized after her death, led a pilgrimage in search of the Cross, and claimed to have found it in Jerusalem in AD 324.

Throughout the archipelago, every town and barrio stages its own Santacruzan. The fiesta is managed by a *hermana* or *hermano mayor* (big sister or brother) or a *capitana* (lady-in-charge), who recruits pretty girls to be the *sagalas* (maidens) of the night. The procession that closes the Santacruzan is heady with romance, for it is the coming out of girls reaching adulthood. The last celebration before the monsoon rains of June, the Santacruzan is a puberty rite sublimated into a religious ceremony, leading young girls into adulthood and many young boys to their circumcision.

> **PIGS ON PARADE**
>
> The crispy roast pig is so prized among the Balayan and Batangas that during a local fiesta, the pigs go on parade surrounded by barbed wire to deter greedy hands.

June

At the centerpiece of any Filipino fiesta table, the *lechon*, or whole roast pig, is king. So revered is this succulent dish that the folks of Balayan in Batangas have highlighted the feast of their patron saint, St John, with a tribute to golden-red *lechon*. On the eve of the fiesta, an anniversary ball is held at the town plaza, where the *lechon* queen is crowned. Next morning, after mass at the Immaculate Conception Church, at least 50 *lechon* skewered on long bamboo poles are gathered in anticipation of the festivities.

The dress of each roast reflects the theme of the participating civic and social organizations. Medical associations, for instance, present their pig wearing a doctor's uniform, complete with stethoscope and mask.

The array of roasts is paraded and soon becomes the object of mischief. Pranksters hurl water or beer over the roast pigs, drenching the bearers and onlookers. A wet free-for-all ensues and the only objects left unscathed are the few *lechon* clad in raincoats. Till this day, the *Parada ng Lechon* remains one of the most riotous fiestas held in the Philippines.

After the parade, the *lechon* are taken to their respective home or club headquarters, where

the feasting and drinking begins in earnest. But true to the spirit of fiesta, some groups may surrender their prized roast to the crowds of merrymakers. Once again, it is free for all, only this time, everyone is busy stuffing themselves with the delicacy.

July

The festival of Santa Ana Kahimonan Abayan, held on July 27 in the northern Mindanao city of Butuan, is sourced to earlier times when human-eating crocodiles infested the Agusan River. Faced

with this common enemy, the townspeople implored their patron saint to give them bountiful harvests and safe passage across the river. Santa Ana heard their prayers and destroyed the creatures.

Today, the river-people honor their patron saint by staging a waterborne high mass celebrated by a line-up of priests. Hundreds of gaily-decorated boats are linked sideways to form a long platform spanning the river. The statue of Santa Ana is borne high on the shoulders of devotees and positioned in the middle of the floating platform. The ensuing mass is celebrated by several priests, sacristans and a choir. After the mass, the choir's chants and the

LEFT: masked Roman soldier at the Moriones festival.
RIGHT: the *lechon* gets a good roasting.

beating of drums fire the celebration into a frenzy. The Santa Ana Kahimonan Abayan festival also provides an opportunity for interaction among the various ethnic tribes, with the Tiruray, Manobo, Mandaya and Bukidnon people converging each year at Santa Ana to sell their wares and perform dances.

August

Four-meter-high (14-ft) papier-mâché *gigantes*, or giants, strut through the Quezon town of Lucban representing Juan Cruz, a farmer, his wife and their two children. They are also featured during the popular Pahiyas feast in mid-

peer through the second-floor windows of houses they pass along the way. Heightening the fun is the *toro*, an enormous papier-mâché bull painted bright red and rigged with firecrackers. Throughout the parade, the bull scampers around the town plaza, scattering spectators as fireworks shoot off from inside.

September

The tiny statue of Our Lady of Peñafrancia, patroness of the Bicol region in southern Luzon, is one of the most revered Marian images in the Philippines. Come September, thousands of devotees travel by any means to

May in honor of San Isidro de Labrador, the patron saint of farmers, when the town's houses are all decorated with colorful *kiping* (leaf-shaped rice wafers) and other farm produce. In August, a full-blown fiesta is dedicated to these symbolic, fun-loving *gigantes*.

Manning the *gigantes* on bamboo frames over the shoulders, especially while balancing on stilts, requires great discipline and involves considerable discomfort.

The men inside the figures have earlier vowed to perform the service in thanksgiving for an answered prayer. With much skill after months of practice, they can march, dance, curtsy and bow before the spectators, and even

catch a glimpse of her at the festival in Naga.

The religious observance begins on the second Friday of September, nine days before the actual feast day. From her shrine, the statue is carried on the shoulders of male devotees to the Metropolitan Cathedral. Thousands of eager arms stretch up from a sea of bodies desperate to touch the image, while shouts of *Viva la Virgen* fill the air. A nine-day *novena* is then held before the statue is returned to her shrine by way of the Naga River, escorted by a flotilla of outrigger canoes, bamboo rafts, and brightly-

LEFT: *gigantes* puppets and their smaller escorts.
RIGHT: a Sinulog fiesta dancer hams it up.

decorated motorboats. As dusk approaches, candles light the way, giving the river procession the magnificence of jewels against a backdrop of darkness.

October

Come hell or high water, crisis or no crisis, for a music- and laughter-filled week in October, Bacolod, the capital city of the sugar-producing province of Negros Occidental, hosts homecoming Negrenses and a horde of visitors for the big annual party called Masskara.

Masskara is coined from two words: *mass*, meaning crowd or many, and the Spanish word *cara*, or face; thus the double meaning for "mask" and "many faces." The Masskara festival was first conceived in 1980 to add color and gaiety to the city's celebration of its Charter Day anniversary, on October 19. The symbol of the festival – a smiling mask – was adopted by the organizers to dramatize the Negrenses' happy spirit, despite periodic economic downturns in the sugar industry.

Throughout the week, people from all over the Visayas, the grouping of islands in the central part of the Philippines, flock to the town plaza. They join Bacolodnons in the non-stop round of festivities, trying their luck in mask-

THE LONGEST CHRISTMAS

Filipinos pride themselves on celebrating the longest Christmas in the world. Officially, the religious observance starts on December 16, when almost everyone rises early for the first of the nine-day series of pre-dawn masses. It is in part a social event, with the focus as much on meeting friends, neighbors and relations, as on savoring the delicacies offered at churchside stalls. The climax is Midnight Mass on Christmas Eve. After this, families go home for the Media Noche, the post-midnight feasting, and only after which may presents be unwrapped. On Christmas Day, marked by day-long visiting, children are brought round to their godparents' for more gifts.

December 28 is Holy Innocents Day, commemorating the martyrdom of Christian infants mentioned vaguely in the Bible. This is the Yuletide version of April Fool's Day, when pranks abound. December 30 marks Dr Jose Rizal's martyrdom, followed by New Year's Eve and New Year's Day merrymaking. On the first Sunday of January, the Feast of the Three Kings, children awake to discover the shoes they have lined up the day before overflowing with goodies. These are mixed in with some dirt, which serves as evidence that while they were asleep, a camel, if not three, had actually entered the house like Santa. And with this, the official Christmas season ends.

making contests, greased-pig catching games, pole climbing, sack races, disco king and queen contests, coconut-milk drinking, and banana- and bread-eating competitions.

The more energetic and athletic sports aficionados compete in basketball, walkathons, cycling and motocross races. Throughout the week, too, rehearsals are held to make sure that everything runs smoothly at the culmination of the festival with the Sunday Masskara parade.

Masks rule at the parade, as brightly-costumed men and women dance and prance in the streets. Their faces are bedimpled, grinning or laughing in molded clay or papier-mâché.

Every group is represented: civic associations, commercial establishments, schools, even private and government organizations. They march out in enthusiastic bands wearing their painted masks and elaborate costumes.

November

Built in the 16th century, Manila's Intramuros district is a stellar example of a medieval fortress town. The heart of this Spanish-style city is Plaza Real, with its gardens, statues and fountains, around which are grouped a cathedral, the former governor-general's palace and government buildings. Today, in the quiet shady gardens and elegant colonial houses, visitors

can almost imagine carriages passing by, bearing *señoritas* and *caballeros*.

In November is a festival of regal revelry, when the walled city relives its colonial golden age. There are exhibitions of historical artifacts, cultural presentations at Fort Santiago and parades of Manila women clad in the traditional Maria Clara costume of the Spanish era.

The Casa Manila choral competition, called *Centar Villancios*, is held for visitors to enjoy the Spanish and Tagalog Christmas carols popular during the 18th century. It is a trip back into colonial times and a re-enactment of that elegant age. Manileños love it.

The Intramuros Festival goes on until December, when it culminates with the procession of the Feast of Our Lady of the Immaculate Conception, who is also the patroness of Intramuros. This is a parade of some 75 statues of the Blessed Virgin Mary brought from all over the country, many of which are believed to be miraculous. Glittering with gold and festooned with sampaguita, ilang-ilang and *dama de noche* flowers, the image-bearing floats are paraded at sunset from the old San Agustin Church to the Quirino Grandstand beside the bay in Rizal Park. It is a grand build-up to the festive Christmas season.

December

The scene is the town plaza of San Fernando, in the northern Philippine province of Pampanga. Three days before Christmas, at sunset, lanterns as big as 13 meters (40 ft) in diameter go on parade glow like phantasmagorical stars along the streets, illuminating the night. The air is cool and filled with the sound of Christmas carols. Through the streets, townspeople dance to the beat of a lively brass band. Children playing the traditional *pabitin* game scramble up a trellis to grab at candies.

The exhibits for the Christmas Lantern Festival are specimens of pyrotechnic splendor, representing the synergistic endeavor of every town barrio. The finest lanterns vie for the coveted Star of Bethlehem title. The cash prizes awarded are also nothing to sneer at.

Life for the housewives is turned upside down as visitors flock by to sample traditional Noche Buena – Christmas Eve – specialties of chicken *relleno*, roast pig, *bibingka* and other dishes. ❏

LEFT: Christmas decorations on sale.
RIGHT: painted boy warriors, Pinatados fiesta, Leyte.

A THRIVING ARTS SCENE

The Filipinos are the minstrels of Asia. But the country's other art forms, from theater and cinema to dance and painting, are also blossoming

Just as the Filipino may have a Spanish name, a distinctly Asian face and an American vocabulary, so Filipino art for the most part reflects the cultural accumulation of its people over the centuries.

Traditional arts have included pottery, weaving, woodcarving, indigenous music and poetry inscribed on bamboo tubes. Colonization introduced the new arts, unleashing a creative energy seldom matched in the rest of the Southeast Asian region. Numerous Filipino artists have done the country proud.

State and private support

Imelda Marcos built the Cultural Center of the Philippines (CCP) in 1970 and instituted the prestigious National Artist awards. Since its inception in 1973, over 50 Filipinos have been named National Artists in the fields of music, dance, theater, literature, visual arts, architecture and film. From time to time, awardees are picked and given an initial cash grant, a lifetime pension, a special car number plate bearing the title of National Artist, and in time, the honors of a state funeral.

The National Commission on Culture and the Arts was established during former President Corazon Aquino's administration, and has since become the governing agency for all cultural activities subsidized by government. It now coordinates with the CCP in the selection of National Artists. A new set of national awards are given to traditional arts practitioners, called *Gawad Manlilikha* or Craftsmanship Award. Recipients have included outstanding individuals regarded as living treasures for having mastered weaving, ethnic musical instruments and even boat-building. Both the NCCA and the CCP give grants to artists and cultural groups based on a meticulous selection process.

Regional outreach programs do their best to diminish the perception of a "Manila-centric"

bias toward cultural workers who may enjoy an advantage in location. For instance, the National High School for the Arts maintains a secluded campus on Mt Makiling in the Los Baños area of Laguna Province for rigorous training.

Annually, privately sponsored music, dance and theater groups conduct well-received world

tours, while in Manila and the more developed provincial cities, there is no lack of activity on the cultural front. On any given day, the calendar would be filled by exhibitions, book launchings, plays and concerts. And deep into the night, one may still chance on a crowded cafe where performance poetry in two languages is held before an enthralled young crowd.

Dance

A young woman moves slowly and confidently with a regal air, her head held high. She carries two large gilded fans. The opulence of her exquisite dress indicates that she is wealthy and privileged. She approaches attendants carrying

---

PRECEDING PAGES: graceful Bayanihan dancers.
LEFT: art on display at Vigan House, Nayong Filipino.
RIGHT: close-up of a Singkil dancer.

bamboo poles and begins to dance between the moving poles. The poles, crossed together on the floor, beat faster and louder, clacking furiously between her feet as she moves gracefully, her expression unchanging.

This dance is the Muslim *singkil*. It is a showpiece number often performed by professional folk dancers, and one such group, called the Bayanihan (literally, working together), has become an internationally-known troupe that aims to preserve and popularize traditional Filipino dance forms. Polished and professional, the Bayanihan promotes Filipino dance around the world. Traditional dance written and chore-ographed by Filipinos can also be seen in Manila, performed by lithe and talented interpreters. Popular companies are Ballet Philippines, Philippine Dance Company, Filipinescas and the Ramon Obusan Dance Company.

The best-known classical ballerina is Lisa Macuja, who made her name with the Kirov Ballet in Russia. Before her, the diminutive but masterful Maniya Barredo had performed outstandingly as a prima ballerina with the Atlanta City Ballet in the United States. Both would come home once a year to give their hometown Manila fans a special treat. Barredo retired recently, while Macuja resumed her career after

PRIVATE ARTS AWARDS

Private funding is responsible for the large part in keeping the Philippine arts scene alive and well. Since 1951, the Carlos Palanca Memorial Awards for Literature have been handing out cash prizes to winners of the annual literary competition. There are Filipino and English language divisions in categories including poetry, novel, essay and drama. A five-time top winner enters the Hall of Fame but reserves the right to compete anew.

Metrobank, as well as Philip Morris, sponsor annual painting contests that carry lucrative cash prizes. Other private companies extend regular funding for ballet and dance groups, orchestras and theater organizations.

marriage and childbirth, and is now based in Manila, where she heads Ballet Manila. A favorite among the new generation of ballerinas is Toni Lopez Gonzales, formerly based in Germany, and now with Ballet Philippines.

National Artist for Dance Leonor Orosa Goquingco was a traditional choreographer who built up her own company. Alice Reyes, a modern dancer and choreographer, was the pride of the Cultural Center of the Philippines' dance stage until the early 1980s. The best young choreographers are Denise Reyes and Agnes Locsin, both of whom fuse modernism with ethnic myths and legends.

Ballroom dancing has become such a phenomenon that open-air areas like a concrete section of Rizal Park are regular venues for this activity. And Filipinos are confident that they might yet make a mark in the Olympics if and when dance sport becomes an official event.

Music

They are the minstrels of Asia. Wherever one travels in the region, there are sure to be several Filipino bands performing in top hotels and nightclubs. From jazz to pop and from rock music to show band repertoires, Filipino singers and musicians are noted for their excellent covers of Western music. This copycat music occa-

tioal jazz circuit for his inimitably energetic assault on the piano. Another cult figure, Sugar Pie de Santos, has cut jazz albums in the US.

Over the past decades, the local music scene has matured, gaining confidence enough to include Filipino elements. There are the European and American pop tunes which have been translated into Tagalog or often sung in *Taglish* (a mixture of Tagalog and English). But more significantly, OPM, or Original Pilipino Music, has made such great strides that best-selling albums are now mostly original collections of Pilipino pop, rock and folk music.

One of the culture's most popular queens was

sionally alternates with uniquely styled versions, if not original compositions.

Internationally acclaimed performers include best-selling classical pianist Cecile Licad, West End and Broadway performer Lea Salonga, who spearheaded Filipino actor-singers in making the musical *Miss Saigon* a resounding success, and Paolo Montalban, who made a name for himself on American stage, film and television. Until his death a few years ago, Bobby Enriquez, known as "the Wildman" from Montreaux to Chicago, was toasted in the interna-

Nora Aunor, who started as a warbler peddling soft drinks to stopover passengers at the whistle-stop train station of Iriga, Albay, in Bicol. However, from the moment the little 14-year-old hit Manila in *Tawag ng Tanghalan*, the country's most popular amateur contest, she was on her way to becoming the 1960s' biggest success story, with a TV show and movie production company of her own. Some measure of her success has been replicated by other singers who competed in amateur competitions before making it to popular variety programs on television.

Other big names in the local music scene include Ryan Cayabyab, a composer, music arranger and director, pianist and vocalist;

LEFT: Ballet Philippines often draws inspiration from its ethnic roots. **ABOVE:** making music from bamboo.

megastar singer Sharon Cuneta; pop diva Pops Fernandez; chanteuse Kuh Ledesma; folk-ethnic rock singer-composer Joey Ayala; folk singer and composer Gary Granada; and the rock band Eraserheads. Bands like Rivermaya and Parokya Ni Edgar have played successful tours of the United States.

Folk music is best sampled at Malate's Hobbit House on A. Mabini Street, where the legendary Freddie Aguilar, who is known all over Asia for his monster hit ballad *Anak* (Child), has performed regularly over the years. His *Bayan Ko* (My Country) became the anthem of the anti-Marcos movement in the 1980s.

Spanish-influenced passion plays. These plays developed into street theater under the broader term of fiesta. Indeed, the fiesta is the ultimate street theater, complete with drama, religious passion and revelrous audience participation.

Filipino theater is generally coupled with dance and music. Within the traditional fiesta, the comedy or *Moro-moro* is often performed. This folksy form always tells of the historical conflict between Christians and non-believers with music and dance. In cosmopolitan Manila, the *zarzuela*, a musical comedy form seemingly adapted from the Italian opera, enjoys an occasional revival.

Traditional music prevails as well. Classical composers produce marches, suites, chamber music, chorales and sonatas, and the best-known performers are the Philippine Philharmonic Orchestra, the Manila Symphony Orchestra and the Philippine Madrigal Singers. The ethnic music of indigenous and Muslim groups uses gongs and other brass or bamboo percussion instruments, the Jew's harp and even fiddles with human hair for strings.

Theater

There is much to see in the theater scene. Another Western tradition, the stage play was eagerly assimilated by Filipinos, especially the

As natural performers, Filipinos hold the theater sacred. Every college or university has its own stage, and Western drama flourishes. Contemporary playwrights write in Pilipino and produce fiery comedies and dramas.

Undoubtedly, the biggest Filipino name to date in theater is the actress and singer Lea Salonga, who became an international star after her captivating performance as Kim in the musical *Miss Saigon*. The best-known full-length play written in English is *Portrait of the Artist as Filipino* by the late National Artist for Literature Nick Joaquin. It enjoys frequent restagings and has also been made into a film. A Pilipino version has also been well-received.

Cinema

Filipinos saw their first moving pictures in Manila in 1904. For the most part, they were European films with Spanish subtitles. The first Filipino-made film – about a virtuous country girl – was produced in 1919 and set the tone of the art for the next 30 years.

Filipino cinema has not been particularly distinguished in any way, except for a love of sentimentality and overacting. In recent decades, movies have digressed into flesh-and-blood flicks and the usual action genre.

More recently, however, there are signs that Filipino cinema is moving on. Film director Lino Brocka is possibly the Philippines' most interesting cinema personality. His first non-commercial film, *Tinimbang Ka Ngunit Kulang* (You Were Weighed But Found Wanting), which tells of a small town's outcasts seen through a young man's eyes, drew rave reviews and shook the local industry. He went on to make several films with a political message, including *Bayan Ko* (My Country), an anti-Marcos film, and *Fight for Us*, a story of a former priest and political detainee whose post-EDSA revolution optimism fades as he witnesses the violence of vigilante groups. Brocka died in a car accident at the peak of a career that saw him lionized by critics in foreign countries, France in particular. He was posthumously declared a National Artist for Film.

Another excellent film director was Ishmael Bernal, whose gritty films of social realism have also been hailed by film circles abroad. One of his most acclaimed works was *Himala* (Miracle), which starred the former singer turned drama queen Nora Aunor. Like Brocka, with whom he became a champion of Philippine cinema as well as political activism, he passed away in the early 1990s, cutting short a career forged during the golden age of Philippine cinema. This era began in the early 1980s when Marcos' daughter Imee founded the influential Experimental Cinema of the Philippines.

Other outstanding contemporary directors are Mike de Leon, Peque Gallaga, Tikoy Aguiluz, and Marilou Diaz Abaya, whose spectacular production of *Rizal*, the nth film on the national hero, was a hit during the Philippine Centennial year of 1998. The films of these directors often make the rounds of prestigious film festivals abroad. Independent films are also very much alive and well in Manila, with directors Kidlat Tahimik, Briccio Santos, Nick Deocampo and Raymond Red making significant inroads into the cultist European market.

Literature

Before the arrival of the Spanish, the indigenous people had a distinct oral tradition that included creation myths, native legends and folk tales. Proto-historic peoples even used a syllabic writing system called alibata.

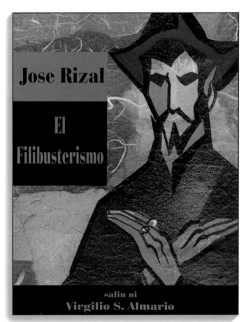

The first printed book, *Doctrina Christiana*, written in Spanish, appeared in the 16th century. For almost 300 years in the archipelago, the printed word was mostly Spanish, and typically related to religious themes, except for a few works in the native Tagalog language.

National hero Jose Rizal set the standard for prose and poetry with his pre-revolutionary *Noli Me Tangere* and *El Filibusterismo*, which he wrote in Spanish. After 1930, there was little Filipino writing in Spanish because of the widespread use of English, and also the increasing use of Tagalog as a medium of literary expression. During American rule, the short story was a popular form among writers.

LEFT: Lea Salonga and co-star in the Broadway musical *Miss Saigon*. **RIGHT:** national hero Jose Rizal wrote the landmark *El Filibusterismo* in Spanish.

Until his passing in 2004, Nick Joaquin remained a lion in Manila literary circles. Essayist, poet, playwright, short story-writer and novelist, his pen spanned the worlds of both *belles-lettres* and journalism. Jose Garcia Villa, also named a National Artist and often regarded as the country's greatest, if most eccentric poet, called himself "Doveglion" – a contraction of dove, eagle and lion. A period of self-exile in the US in the 1930s led to a collection of poems that has been hailed by American critics for

ARTS DOYEN

The first Filipino artist to achieve international recognition was Juan Luna. He received the gold medal at the Exposicion Nacional de Bellas Artes in Madrid in 1884.

their startling lyric power. He remained in New York City, conducting private poetry workshops with a coterie of admirers, until he passed away in the mid-1990s.

Arguably the best-known Filipino novelist abroad, F. Sionil Jose heads the Philippines chapter of PEN (Poets, Essayists and Novelists) International. He owns the Solidaridad Bookshop on Padre Faura Street in Manila, and continues to publish the regional journal *Solidarity*. His short stories and an epic series of novels about the people of the land, both in Manila and in the countryside, have been translated into many languages and was recently published by Random House.

National Artists for Literature include English-language fiction writers Francisco Arcellana and N.V.M. Gonzalez. Poet, novelist and critic Edith L. Tiempo, together with her husband and fellow novelist Edilberto K. Tiempo, established the National Writers Workshop in Dumaguete City in 1962. The workshop continues to train young writers under the direction of the widow Edith, who in 1999 was the first Filipina writer to be named National Artist.

Contemporary Filipino literature is written in Pilipino and English, the former becoming increasingly popular as the search for national identity becomes more distinct. But writing in English continues to thrive, its dynamism recently enhanced by the success of Filipino American writers such as Jessica Hagedorn, Bino Realuyo, Eric Gamalinda and Eugene Gloria, who won the much-coveted US National Poetry Award in 1999.

Painting and sculpture

As early as 1821, a Filipino Academy of Painting was established. Throughout the 19th century, painting in the Philippines was heavily influenced by Spanish trends. Both Juan Luna and Felix Resureccion Hidalgo achieved international fame when they won prizes at the Madrid Exposition of 1884.

Luna painted epics and scenes of social significance, while Hidalgo was best known for his neo-Impressionist scenes. Among the great painters who have had much influence since the 1930s were Fernando Amorsolo, Cesar Legaspi, Hernando Ocampo, Fernando Manansala and Jose Joya.

Contemporary Filipino artists are among the most productive in Asia, with their sculptural works adorning lobbies of hotels and corporate buildings. An oil painting by Anita Magsaysay Ho was purchased for a record US$400,000 at a recent auction in Singapore. Other major artists are sculptors Napoleon Abueva, Ed Castrillo, Imelda Pilapil, Renato Rocha and Ramon Orlina, and painters Arturo Luz, Victorio Edades, Diosdado Lorenzo, Malang and Bencab. ❑

LEFT: noted artist Arturo Luz takes a break.
RIGHT: a close-up of *Resting by the Ricefield*, a 1956 oil painting by Fernando Amorsolo.

INDIGENOUS ARTS AND HANDICRAFTS

Traditional arts and crafts from villages have found new life as esoteric art forms and decor accessories in modern Manila homes

There is no doubt that Filipinos are a supremely artistic people. Historical facts show that the simple tools and weapons used by the early nomadic people were artistically designed. Effigies of the early people of the Philippines' 110 indigenous tribes have men and women donning a variety of headdresses, earrings, anklets, belly rings, bracelets, and necklaces that were no doubt the height of fashion in those times. Such artistic expressions, influenced by their religious beliefs and cultural practices, reached an apogee in the early Iron Age when people of Malay descent migrated in droves to the country.

Soon, visual art forms expanded to include wood carvings, weaving and pottery. Creative artisans seeing the wealth of natural materials available – bamboo, rattan, nipa palm, *pina* and *abaca* (pineapple and hemp fibres), seashells and marble, to name a few – soon fashioned a range of handicrafts. Today, the selection of ethnic arts and crafts is mind-boggling. Wherever you go in the Philippines, you'll see brilliant weaves, intricate beadwork, silver tribal jewelry, rustic wood figurines and dishes, handsome ceramic pots, jewel-colored capiz shell chandeliers, earthy *pandan* leaf mats and coasters, delicate *pina* embroidery, rattan basketry or shiny brassware.

The best range of crafts is found in Manila – in Ermita, Makati and the Quiapo area, and also in specialty shops or malls. However, the major cities of Cebu, Davao and Zamboanga will also yield sufficient reward for the inveterate shopper.

▷ **VIGAN POTTERY**
Vigan, apart from being one of the best preserved Spanish cities in the Philippines, is also well known for its rustic ceramic pottery called *burnay*.

▷ **BAG LADY**
Hats and bags made of rattan or bamboo are popular handicrafts in this tropical country. Hats are especially useful at beaches in keeping the sun out of your eyes.

△ **IFUGAO ART**
A classic example of how religion and culture have influenced the arts – wood carvings of Ifugao gods are popular souvenir items in Central Cordillera, north Luzon.

△ **BIG BUSINESS**
Instantly recognised as being Filipino all over the world, much of Cebu's rattan and wicker furniture is exported.

THE ART OF T'BOLI WEAVING

In the southernmost part of Mindanao is the spectacular Lake Sebu, surrounded by rolling highlands and mountains. This is where the T'boli people, the Philippines' most visually colorful tribe live and produce the much sought-after *t'nalak* cloth, said to be made of dreams woven into the cloth. Made from pounded bark, the weave is a striking blend of primary colors. When sewn into traditional attire, the cloth is a perfect foil for the beautiful ethnic accessories worn by T'boli women. For modern Manileños, however, the cloth is prized for its use as table cloths, bed covers and scarves. In the old days, T'boli women could weave *t'nalak* even with their eyes closed. But as the big cities beckon, young tribal people, including T'boli women, are lured by urban jobs and lifestyles. As a result, age-old traditions like *t'nalak* weaving *are* in danger of becoming vanquished.

▽ **PASTIMES THAT PAY**
Filipinas are putting to good use their creative skills – such as this factory worker in a garment factory producing embroidery work for export.

△ **SHELL SAVVY**
Give a Filipina flowers or shells and she'll produce beautiful garlands and shell necklaces in an instant, accompanied by a warm smile and a Mabuhay!

◁ **BACK TO BASICS**
Sadada women of the Central Cordillera are known for their beautiful weaving. Completely handmade, it's a craft that has been honed to near perfection through the generations.

▷ **WEAVE-A-MAT**
Brightly colored mats of Tawi-Tawi, Philippines southernmost province, have proven to be a hit with interior designers both in Manila and abroad. The range now includes other decor items.

CROSS-CULTURAL CUISINE

Filipino food cannot be easily pinned down as any one dish. It is instead a flighty
marinade of the different influences of Chinese, Spanish and American cuisines

What is Philippine food? This is a question even Filipinos ask. Is it chicken *tinola*, with ginger, young papaya and pepper leaves? *Pancit*, the noodle dish of many variants and flavors? Or chicken *relleno*, a capon stuffed with Spanish olives and sausages? Or *leche flan*, crème caramel made with coconut milk and flavored with the rind of local limes? It is, thanks to land, history and society, all of the above.

Indigenous food

Philippine cuisine starts from its variegated land and sea-scape. The natural ingredients found in the different terrains of its 7,100 islands and their surrounding waters, tempered by a tropical climate, have shaped the multi-textured cuisine which nutritionists describe as one of the healthiest in the world. Filipinos eat a lot of rice, vegetables and fish, while consuming minimal amount of meat.

Native Filipino food belongs mainly to an Austronesian matrix, with resonances of the food of its Southeast Asian neighbors. *Sinigang*, the quintessential one-dish meal, has meat, fish or prawns and vegetables stewed with tamarind, green mangoes, *bilimbi* or other sour fruits or leaves. As in the soups of Thailand and Indonesia, its sourness is not only "cooling" but also has healing effects.

Rice is the staple, as it is in Vietnam and Malaysia – countries with a major influence on Filipino food. To complement the wholesome but plain taste of rice, its accompanying dishes should be sweet, sour or spicy. The variety of rice ranges from the prized tiny-grained *milagrosa* to the *malagkit, or* glutinous rice that features in leaf-wrapped cakes known as *bibingka, puto, suman* and *kutsinta*.

The coconut, as in any other Pacific Rim country, is king here. Its mature flesh can be grated or squeezed out as coconut cream or milk. The water and flesh of the young, green nut can be drunk or made into sweets. The sap is fermented into toddy (*tuba*) or distilled into the potent *lambanog*. The leaves are used to wrap rice cakes or meats for baking or grilling. The crunchy heart of the palm gives a piquant flavor to spring rolls and salads.

A TASTE OF FILIPINO

Food historian Monina A. Mercado describes Filipino food thus: "Drawing origins from various cultures but displaying regional characteristics, Filipino food was prepared by Malay settlers, spiced by Chinese traders, stewed in 300 years of Spanish rule, and hamburgered by American influence in the Philippine way of life. The multi-racial features of the Filipino – a Chinese-Malayan face, a Spanish name and an American nickname – make up Philippine cuisine, producing dishes of oriental and occidental extraction."

Understanding the origins of Filipino cuisine is perhaps the best possible introduction to Philippine culture.

PRECEDING PAGES: seafood figures prominently in Filipino cuisine. **LEFT:** a colorful array of indigenous vegetables and fruits. **RIGHT:** rice is a must-have staple.

The different Filipino peoples have different signature dishes, according to what ingredients are available in their local terrain.

The Bicol have *laing*, a dish cooked with fish, taro leaves, chilli and coconut milk; the Ilonggo, *binakol*, which is chicken with young coconut (traditionally, cooked in a coconut shell); the Ilocano, *pinakbet*, a vegetable stew of bitter melon, okra, tomatoes and eggplant steamed with an anchovy sauce; the Tagalog, *sinampalukang manok*, chicken flavored with green tamarind pods and tendrils.

Certainly one of the oldest dishes is *kinilaw*, fish or shrimp flavored with ginger, onions and sauce, so much so that it no longer resembles the original Spanish dish.

With such an abundance of fresh fruits, vegetables and seafood available in the Philippines, only the lightest of cooking methods will do justice to the food.

As such, there is boiled meat with vegetables, steamed crab and shrimp, chicken steamed directly over rock salt (*pinaupong manok*), fish cooked in vinegar and ginger (*paksiw*) or stuffed with tomatoes, onions and black pepper and grilled over burning coals.

Compared to surrounding Asian lands with their hot curries and spicy grilled meats, Fil-

chili and dressed briefly in vinegar or lime juice to the point when it reaches a still-fresh translucence. It is "cooked" by the sourness rather than by fire. *Kinilaw* is a very old dish – an archeological site in Mindanao had some *kinilaw* remnants which were carbon-dated to at least 1,000 years old. The name *kinilaw* also applies to any local sour salads.

Adobo is a common meat dish. It features pork or chicken, or a combination of both, cooked with vinegar, bay leaf, peppercorns and garlic. The name derives from the Spanish dish *adobado*. However, Filipinos have totally transformed the dish, using shellfish and vegetables and a variety of sauces including soy and liver

ipino dishes might seem bland. But Filipino food is really a blend of the foreign cultures that have shaped the country. The resulting taste is perhaps more sedate and fit for more sensitive tastebuds.

Chinese noodles

From the Chinese merchants, who since the 11th century had been trading silk and pottery for sea and forest products such as beeswax and birds' nests, come the dishes now known as *comida China*. Many dishes have been a part of local cuisine for so long that most Filipinos do not even realize they are foreign. *Pancit* is one such example. It is comprised of rice, mung bean, egg and any type of noodle cooked with meat, seafood and vegetables. Every region, town and home has its own version of *pancit*, with different ingredients added. In the fishing town of Malabon, squid, shrimp and oyster are added, while another town uses Chinese sausage and white gourd, and yet another adds flaked smoked fish and crumbled pork crackling. The cook's creativity is an important factor that shapes the final result.

Chinese rice porridge has been adapted as *arroz caldo,* which is soft rice with chicken or tripe flavored with *kasubha,* a spice less potent than saffron, and sprinkled with lime juice and roasted garlic.

The ancient Chinese traders lived among the ordinary people, so their food was introduced to Filipino society at that level. Intermarriage also created a large Chinese minority which integrated harmoniously into the mainstream culture. Dumplings (*siomai*), stuffed buns (*siopao*) and noodle soups (*mami, lomi*) are found at street stalls, in cafeterias, homes and restaurants. Eateries offering Chinese dishes were the first restaurants set up and they served dishes bearing Spanish names for the sake of the clientele: *sopa de nido* is bird's nest soup, *morisqueta tostada* is fried rice and *pescado en salsa agrio-dulce* is sweet-sour fish.

Spanish paella

Three hundred years of Spanish colonization have been imprinted, not just on everyday menus, but more especially on feasts and celebrations. Since Spanish cuisine called for ingredients not available in the tropics, like olive oil, saffron, blood and pork sausages, the dishes took on an exclusive value and were found mainly on tables of the elite class.

Paella, for example, which in Spain is a common dish cooked in the field, with meat such as rabbit or seafood, is in the Philippines a fiesta dish, for which are gathered sausages, ham, clams, crabs, chicken, pork, pimientos, saffron, olive oil and wine.

With the introduction of Christianity came dishes associated with the celebration of Christmas: Sugared brioches (*ensaymada*) dipped in thick hot chocolate, sliced Edam cheese, apples and oranges, chestnuts and walnuts, stuffed

LEFT: street vendors at Intramuros, Manila.
RIGHT: desserts from the southern island of Mindanao.

turkey or capon, ox tongue with mushrooms or stuffed beef rolls with lardoons (*mechado*). The desserts were *leche flan, mazapan, turrones* and *membrillo.* These dishes were eventually made with local ingredients. For example, cashew nuts substituted for almonds and mangoes for quince.

Naturally, the Philippines has the best Spanish restaurants in all of Asia.

American steaks

A visitor here may mistakenly think that America is the dominant foreign influence in Philippine cuisine. American-style fast-food restaurants are highly visible. Today, the young

carry sandwiches rather than rice cakes in their backpacks. While some hotel restaurants may offer *adobo,* you will be able to find steaks, chops, salads, cakes or pies in any or all of them.

While Chinese influence can perhaps be found at the most basic level in Filipino cuisine, the Spanish, in fine dining, it is American food that has gained the most prominence. Convenience is its strength: it comes pre-packed or pre-cooked for quick, easy meals that are easy to take home as well.

And which dish is Filipino?

It is not easy to pin down a dish which is wholly Filipino. Generally, Filipinos have adapted the different foreign cuisines and transformed them such that they have become Filipino dishes. You will not find the same food cooked quite the same way in the original countries. Spanish dishes such as *pochero* come with an accompanying eggplant-and-garlic relish while American steaks and chops come smothered local marinades.

The input of Filipino culture really comes in in the sauces and dips, which makes a single meal accessible to different tastes. The cook may create a *sinigang* with what he considers the absolutely right degree of sourness. The diner, however, is free to fine-tune this to his own taste with different relishes or dipping sauces. There is *patis* (fish sauce) or *bagoong* (shrimp paste) with chopped onions, tomatoes and cilantro. Thus, while a social group partakes of the same food; each individual may come away with a different experience, depending on which dip he chooses.

This communality is the hallmark of Philippine culture. Folk dramas are written, scored, directed, acted and staged by whole communities. Similarly, the food is grown by some and harvested by others, while cooked by yet others. And the resulting dishes are shared by all, sometimes even the entire village.

FIESTA FEASTING

Throughout the islands, patron saints' feast days are celebrated with food, prayer and appropriate ritual. Lucban town remembers San Isidro, the patron saint of farmers, on May 15 with food decorations: fruits, vegetables, breads, whole roast pigs, as well as brilliantly colored leaf-shaped rice wafers called *kiping* fashioned into chandeliers and windows. During the afternoon procession, all these decorations are stripped from the houses and given to friends and passers-by to consume.

Lakeside Angono honors San Clemente on November 24 with a fluvial procession on the lake, while bands play and the fish pens are blessed. All then return to the church and along the way are doused by water hoses and pistols in commemoration of blessings from the lake and the rain which are gifts given to Man.

San Dionisio town stages a *komedya*, a full-length play in verse, in the belief that the saint would be displeased otherwise and would bring on the rains.

And there is always the feasting: family, neighbors and visitors from other towns partake of the fiesta food. In the old days, doors were open to both friend and stranger, because the fiesta – masses, processions, theater and games, ritual and feasting – was a way of thanking God and one another for the year's bounty.

Specialty restaurants

You can find indigenous cuisines in the homes, in the streets at barbecue stands, pushcarts and strolling vendors who peel fruit and offer it in flower-like sections, and in transportation centers and markets. Here, cooked food is laid out on trays while customers point to their choices – thus the name *turo-turo,* "point-point."

There are also regional specialty restaurants where one is faced with an array of fresh fish, crustaceans and rarities such as the coconut crab whose coconut diet accounts for the taste of its flesh. You can sample, for example, the chilli-hot food of Bicol or the exotic cuisine of Pampanga which features stuffed frog and coconut milk desserts. There are also grill outlets known as *ihaw-ihaw* which specialize in *pulutan,* food for drinking sessions. Some specialty restaurants serve *ante bellum* cuisine that would have been found on the tables of the 19th-century elite.

Chinese eateries range from simple bicycle carts offering salty, sweet or sour nuts, fruits and tidbits and street corner *panciterias* that serve up *lumpia* (spring roll) and noodles, to luxurious restaurants that serve 12-course meals including a whole suckling pig, Peking duck, freshly-killed steamed fish (which was swimming in a tank only minutes before), Hunan ham and Hong Kong scallops.

The Spanish restaurants and homes of the elite offer Asia's best Iberian cuisine. The aperitif vocabulary in Manila starts with *gambas al ajillo* (shrimps in olive oil and garlic), *almejas o mejillones al horno* (baked clams or mussels), and *champinones adobados* (marinated mushrooms). Family reunions generally feature such dishes as *callos a la Madrilena* (tripe), *bacalao a la Vizcaina* (codfish) and *zarzuela de mariscos* (a seafood medley).

Also available here are cuisines imported from other shores. Japanese businessmen and joint ventures have made sushi and sashimi familiar (especially to those fond of *kinilaw*), and put tempura and sukiyaki into the lexicon. Italian restaurants proliferate because pasta is akin to *pancit,* and the pizza that American chains taught the young Filipino to love has acquired local toppings such as local sausages, farmer's cheese and salted egg.

Thai, Vietnamese and Korean restaurants are popular because the foods taste familiarly Asian, even though they operate on a higher chilli register. Even the food brought in by traders and overseas workers from the Middle East, like *shawarma,* is becoming indigenized – chicken and beef instead of lamb. The many bakeries offer not only sweet Chinese cakes and Spanish *churros* and *bocaditos* but also European pastries and *baklava.*

Filipino food thus starts with the indigenous and the indigenized and, because of travel, education, business and trade, now also embraces imported dishes in their original forms. ❑

MANGO, MANGOSTEEN AND MORE

The Philippine mango, heart-shaped and golden, is one of the land's glories. Its sweet and firm flesh – celebrated in verse and song – is eaten fresh, juiced, dried, cooked in syrup or made into jam or added to crepes, salads, savories and desserts. Less known is the brown-skinned lanzones that are pinched open to reveal white sweet-sour sections within. Durian is famous for "tasting like heaven" to the initiate and "smelling like hell" to the alien. One tempers its richness by turning to its neighbor, the sweet mangosteen, encased in a hard, russet husk.

Other delightful fruits are the pineapple, guava, star fruit, soursop, custard apple and rambutan.

LEFT: food galore at a wedding party in Puerto Galera.
RIGHT: *lumpia*, or spring rolls, is Chinese-inspired.

THE SPORTING LIFE

Filipinos are enthusiastic about many sports, most notably basketball and boxing,
but it's in billiards and bowling that they excel internationally

Unexpectedly for the outsider, basketball is the national passion. Indeed, inch for inch, Filipinos are among the best players in the world, and the sport is marked by year-round amateur and professional tournaments.

Manila was the first Asian city to establish a professional league in 1976 with the birth of the Philippine Basketball Association or PBA. It has since become the mother league that transforms erstwhile unknowns into household names. Basketball players become much-loved celebrities, and often double as movie or television icons. Two such players have even managed to have themselves elected to the Senate. Imports (American pros, mostly black) reinforce PBA teams in two of the three conferences held every year, with the last reserved as the All-Filipino Conference. Teams are owned by companies which profit from the media exposure the whole year round from live television coverage of doubleheaders thrice a week.

Simplicity of equipment lies at the root of basketball fever, and every town plaza sports a basketball court across the church and town hall. Young boys go through their paces using a makeshift basket. At one time or another, nearly every Filipino male tries his hand at the game. Like his professional counterpart, the backstreet jock revels in showy creativity. He does not just pass the ball, but indulges in hangtime before executing a behind-the-back feed that, for want of accuracy, ensures a torrid scramble. If he lays emphasis on a feint, it's a sterling performance. The longer he holds the ball, the more he hogs the limelight. Not always effective basketball, to be sure, but a thrill for the spirit.

Boxing

Next only to basketball in popularity is boxing. Not only does it provide an opportunity for destitutes from distant provinces to rise in economic stature, it is also one sport where the Filipino has proven himself to be world-class.

Legendary boxers include Pancho Villa who lorded it in the flyweight division in the 1930s. He campaigned successfully in the United States, where he lived it up by posing with such Hollywood personalities as Mae West.

Flash Elorde was the world's junior lightweight champion for all of seven years in the 1960s.

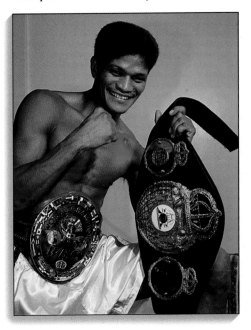

Current champions and top-class contenders include Luisito Espinosa, Gerry Peñalosa, and Manny Pacquiao. The latter is the reigning WBC International Super Featherweight defending champion, and his fights are watched by millions the globe over. The Philippines' best showing in an Olympic event has been a couple of silver medals in boxing's lighter weight divisions.

Billiards

Billiards is the one sport where the Filipino has proven himself a global champion. The current nine-ball world champion is Efren "Bata" Reyes, whose exploits in the professional pool rooms in the United States and Europe, glorified through

LEFT: basketball is played everywhere, even in this church yard. **RIGHT:** Luisito Espinosa, boxing champion.

global sports television, have made him an endearing hero. He started playing as a nine-year-old who worked as a "spotter" in his uncle's parlor in Manila, where he slept nightly on a pool table. Filipino cue artists are known to rule the game with such superiority that at one time, the top three finishers in the annual US pro circuit were all Filipino campaigners. It is also often acknowledged that at any given time, at least four of the top 10 players in the world would be carrying Philippine colors. Other feared billiards masters have been "Amang" Parica, whom Reyes beat a decade ago, and Francisco "Django" Bustamante, who operates from Germany as the

part is Bong Coo. Both still compete internationally, but may be past their prime.

Chess

Since the postwar period, Filipino chess players have been some of Asia's best representatives. But not until Eugene Torre (whose name appropriately means "rook") became the first Asian grandmaster in 1973 did there seem enough justification for the thousands of chess aficionados battling in clubs, corner stores, barber shops and under mango trees. The traditional approach has been similar to that in basketball; tactical genius is given a premium in favor of

top-ranked nine-ball competitor the world over.

Such is Reyes' mastery of the game that when he was fielded into the national team for the Southeast Asian Games, he took only a few hours to familarize himself with the larger balls and table used in snooker, and still came away with the gold medal. Filipinos are hoping billiards becomes an official Olympic event, confident it is where they stand the best chance of bagging that elusive and first Olympic gold.

Bowling

Rafael "Paeng" Nepomuceno has won the world bowling championships a record six times since the late 1980s. His female counter-

safe, solid strategy. The idea has been to attack, and to create romantic situations of cut-and-thrust in the manner of Mikhail Tahl's precarious but inventive games.

Beneath this overlay, Torre inserted serious book study and single-mindedness to emerge national champion at age 18. He then represented Asia in high-rating tournaments, in the process winning over some of the world's chess superstars. For the legion of chess fanatics in the country, Torre's ascendancy only confirmed the remarkable national affinity for the game. The Philippine national team, led by Torre, placed a record-high seventh in the Chess Olympics held in Greece in the late 1970s.

Torre is now semi-retired, occasionally serving as a coach for national teams. Taking over as the country's top player is Joey Antonio, the country's latest grandmaster. Asian tournaments used to be ruled by the Philippines until China started looming large of late. But it remains a tight contest between the two countries for Asian supremacy. And it is still safe to say that somewhere out there, astride a *carabao* perhaps, some 10-year-old has already set his sights on Antonio's crown. If he is disciplined enough to attract the necessary backing, he will certainly make it. It is as good an assumption as saying that in these romance-happy isles, chess has found a more-then-willing mate.

CHESS MASTER

Florencio Campomanes, who was a renowned national master in his younger days, headed FIDE, the world's top chess body, for well over a decade. He retired in 1997.

Jai alai

Brought to the Philippines decades ago from the Basque area of Spain, *jai alai* is believed to have been invented by the Mayan Indians and imported into Spain. Even in distant Manila, many of the *pelotaris* (players) are still Basques, or have some Basque lineage.

What makes the game a remarkable and exciting spectacle is the shattering speed at which the ball is thrown and returned. Players leap around the court with astonishing agility, clambering up the side wall or the wire netting separating the *fronton* (court) from the spectators to return a difficult ball.

The granite blocks of the former Manila *fronton* on Taft Avenue were imported from Shanghai – where the stadium had been dismantled by the Chinese government as being part of the decadent past. Its Philippines inauguration in 1940 by President Manuel Quezon was billed as the most elaborate sporting and social event in the history of Manila.

Cebu City set up its own *fronton* in the 1970s. With Marcos' downfall, *jai alai* was mothballed due to its reputed links with "crony" operators. It took over a decade before the Philippine Amusement and Gaming Corporation, or Pagcor, a government agency, managed to reopen the franchise in Manila against objections from Church leaders.

Armed with renewed vigor, games were played every afternoon at the new *fronton* behind Harrison Plaza off Roxas Boulevard in Manila. These rowdy affairs with noisy spectators often reached fever pitch as betting was both legal and frantic.

Not surprisingly, *jai alai* was once again closed down – this time by the Arroyo-Macapagal administration in August 2001. Prior to its ban, it was estimated that more than half a million bets were placed daily, involving 20 percent of the capital's population.

Given its long history, the game could stage a

comeback. Some say it is still played illegally, but for the time being the *frontons* remain dark.

Cockfighting

Banned in most countries, cockfighting has had a long tradition in the Philippines. No self-respecting town will do without a cockpit (*sabungan*) and, every Sunday or public holiday, the galleries around the central pits are packed with raucous crowds seated in tiers reaching the roof.

The pre-fight shouting is directed at the bookmakers (*kristo*), since their arms are always stretched out like Christ as they acknowledge bets. The *kristo* are minor attractions in them-

---

LEFT: chess players in Rizal Park. **RIGHT:** originating from Spain, *jai alai* is a game of shattering speed.

selves for their uncanny ability to absorb all the bets and odds without writing anything down. Thousands of pesos change hands at each bloody duel; even houses, land titles and car registrations have been placed as bets.

Combat proper begins after the arbiter has unsheathed the razor-sharp spur attached to both cocks' right legs and allowed each combatant a sharp peck at the other's neck. Thus teased and aroused into a fighting mood, the cocks are let loose, and the dance of death begins. With hackles up, the duelists fix each other with a chilly stare and in the next instance lunge at each other, their talons taut with intent to destroy. In mid-air, the combatants do a swift combination of pecking, clawing and stabbing with their miniature scimitars. The loser scurries to one end of the arena, where it crumples into an ungainly heap.

The game is over, and the betters are already counting their chances at the next match.

Horseracing

The race track of the Philippine capital is on Felix Huertas Street, in the district of Santa Cruz. It is known to the locals as San Lazaro. In the cool of the early morning, the horses come prancing across the sands from the nearby sta-

COCKFIGHTING DERBY

About twice a year, a "Super Derby" is held at the capacious Araneta Coliseum in Cubao, Quezon City, which has a seating capacity of 25,000.

An army of American breeders from Texas plane in with their champions, to pit against homegrown "Texas" cocks that have been the result of cross-breeding with imported stock.

A common joke is that a Filipino cocker would sooner save his favorite gamecock, in the event of a fire, than his spouse. The sight of men lovingly fondling their potential champions, common all over the countryside, certainly adds credence to this claim.

bles. The jockeys sit high-kneed but relaxed in the lightweight English saddles.

Horseracing in the Philippines has come a long way from the 1860s, when fashionable races organized by the Manila Jockey Club-Manila were held twice a year at the Hippodrome. At that time, fans arrived in flamboyant carriages, the women in flowing skirts with parasols and the men with buttoned coats and Ascot ties. After the races, the gentlemen and their ladies would repair to a ball held at the same site.

Today, jockeys in colorful silks mount thoroughbred horses bred from imported stock. There are electronic totalizers, computers and photo-finish cameras, and air-conditioned booths with push-buttons that summon club personnel to place bets on the horses, plus cocktail lounges and bars. Racing in Manila is undeniably big business.

At the start of the day's races, fans gather in the compound fronting the grandstand beside the paddock. The small but spunky Philippine ponies make their entry, breathing gently, some skittish, kicking and throwing their heads in the air, ears laid back, eyes rolling and tugging at the reins held by trainers who talk soothingly, reassuring and calming the animals.

It is a race track scene one might find anywhere in the world. And yet it is unique. A Philippine race track is different from anything that horseracing enthusiasts will have seen in Europe or America. There is no green turf (the track is of sand), no ridiculous hats, elaborate dresses, checkered suits or other paraphernalia that have grown alongside the sport elsewhere. Horseracing in the Philippines is in its purest form, where enjoyment is derived from seeing the animals in motion.

The track on Felix Huertas Street is a near-perfect oval – its immensity telescoped by the tricky light of the early morning. It measures 1,300 meters (6 furlongs) around the track, which is made of sea sand over a soft rock and charcoal base. Encircling the outer track are dozens of stables, on top of which perch a number of stable lads, all eagerly monitoring the progress of their charges.

As the horses come down from the stables, their hooves kick up the fine sand and it hangs around them, softening the shining beauty of their coats as if one is looking at them through gossamer. Then the jockeys are weighed complete with whips and saddles. Everything is ready for the start.

There is some fine, honest racing around San Lazaro, the horses running smoothly and with a dull thunder on the packed sand track. You can see the muscles smoothly moving beneath the soft shine of their coats, moving magnificently, stretching out, heads forward, and tails high. As the race draws to a close, the excited crowd breaks into a loud cheer, and lucky bettors rush off to collect their winnings.

While the Gran Copa Cup is the main event of the racing year, other highlights at San Lazaro are the Founders Cup, the Presidential Cup and the National Grand Derby. Acknowledged as the Philippine version of the English Derby race held at Epsom Downs, the National Grand Derby has become one of the most colorful spectacles of local racing.

Martial arts

Most visitors to the Philippines have heard of or seen demonstrations of karate, kung-fu or other forms of Asian martial arts, but few people anywhere have heard of, and fewer have seen, *arnis de mano*, Filipino stick fighting. The sport

is so old that it was first banned by the conquering Spanish. The origin of *arnis* was the defense of the traveler from robbers. The art is played with a 1-meter-long hardwood stick, or *tungkod*. Opponents armed with two *tungkod* swing and parry at each other. Out of the movements of *arnis* evolved *eskrima*, a martial art that substituted the wooden sticks of *arnis* for bladed weapons.

The decline of these practices came as a result of their ineffectiveness against Spanish guns. More complicated movements characteristic of *arnis* were later added in an approximation of dance and spectacle. *Arnis* is played regularly by aficionados in Manila. ❏

LEFT: a boy and his prize cockfighter.
RIGHT: horse racing at San Lazaro, Manila.

AN ARCHITECTURAL PASTICHE

*Filipino architecture is a rich mix of its native and foreign influences. A visit to
the historical towns of Vigan and Taal allows glimpses into a lost world*

Philippine architecture reflects the country's historical blend of influences from the Austronesian, Malay, Chinese, Hindu, Muslim, Spanish and American cultures. While the spectrum of styles is broad, including fusion examples, one can discern three main eras: the early native huts of wood, bamboo, *nipa* and grass, then, arising in stark contrast, the massive Spanish baroque churches and colonial townhouses made of wood and stone, and lately, the modern concrete-and-glass structures of the cities.

Before the arrival of the Spanish, people lived in small villages along seacoasts or riverbanks. In its pre-Intramuros days, Manila was a riverside fort safeguarded by wooden palisades that protected settlements loosely strung along the Pasig River and the shores of Manila Bay. The bamboo and wood huts in the settlements were usually huts covered by *nipa* palm.

Construction of rural traditional huts has changed little over time. Designs vary by region, but common features include a steep roof over a one- or two-room living area raised on stilts. Floors may be of split bamboo to allow dirt and food scraps to fall through to pigs and poultry. Its elevation provides protection from seasonal monsoon floods and the multipurpose space beneath the house is used as a shelter for animals or an additional room for the family. Quite often, the lightweight structure, called *bahay na nipa*, would collapse with earthquakes, burnt quickly or was blown away easily by typhoon winds. However, this type of house could be swiftly rebuilt with the abundant local materials.

Modern twist to stilt huts

When the early settlements became towns during the colonial era, houses became sturdier as residents grew more affluent. These urban dwellings are modified variations of the simple hut, typically two-story structures rein-

forced with concrete and an iron roof. During the 19th century, wealthy Filipinos built some fine houses, usually with solid stone or brick lower walls, an overhanging wooden upper story with balustrades and *capiz* shell sliding windows and a tiled roof. Family quarters remained on the second story and were con-

BAROQUE AND BULLETS

The old church in the town of Morong, once a Spanish center, is today considered one of the finest examples of tropical baroque architecture. Built in 1615 by Chinese craftsmen, the building is noted for its exquisitely carved three-story facade and four-story octagonal bell tower.

These two features were redesigned by a wealthy citizen of the woodcarving town of Paete two centuries after construction. At the time, the baroque movement swept Europe, throwing echoes to the colonies, where the clergy was motivated to refurbish older structures.

Note the bullet holes in the side walls, where captured Katipunero rebels were shot by the Spanish.

PRECEDING PAGES: San Augustin Church, Manila.
LEFT: the Manila Hotel where Gen. MacArthur based his headquarters. **RIGHT:** Makati skyline at night.

structed completely out of wood; they were expanded to include a living room, at least two bedrooms and an open porch behind the cooking area. The open area under the house was enclosed with stone or brick walls, with windows covered with heavy iron grilles. Rows of individual houses stood one after the other at the edge of narrow streets that were laid out in a *cuadricula,* a grid arrangement.

Foreign influences

The Spanish spent 3½ centuries establishing cities and firmly entrenching Christianity by stringing the coastline with massive fortress-

Makati architecture, whether recently constructed or dating back to the area's 1960s origins, has always borne the International style without reference to local traditions – unlike the Oriental roofs on buildings posing as "asianized" high-rises in other Asian cities. Even the individually designed single family residences clustered around the business center are international in character. These are affluent communities where the tree-shaded streets follow the classic 1950s American suburban model. Makati's architecture bears out its identity as the Philippines' window to the world.

The other direction from the airport leads to

churches and convents. A change into American hands in 1898 introduced new nuances. In a matter of decades, modern and mundane International style buildings with their industrial materials of concrete and glass began to appear in Manila.

The drive from Manila airport into the city branches into two directions and affords glimpses into various eras and styles of Filipino architecture. One way leads to the high-rise canyons of Makati, a once sleepy suburb that is now the nerve center of business and finance. With its swanky shopping malls and glass-clad skyscrapers, one could be in the downtown area of any modern city in the world.

an older, more historic Manila through Roxas Boulevard, a palm-fringed parkway along the shores of Manila Bay.

Here, rows of new highrises stand next to uneventful concrete medium-rises of 1970s vintage that overpower the few surviving International style structures and Art Deco examples from the 1930s. On the boulevard, the sweeping vista of the landmark Cultural Center of the Philippines (1969) is notable. This is the Manila developed during the American colonial era (1898–1946).

Roxas Boulevard, originally named Dewey Boulevard after Admiral Dewey of the United States who defeated the Spanish, leads to the

Rizal (previously called Luneta), Manila's principal park beside Intramuros, the Spanish colonial walled city. Roxas Boulevard, Rizal Park and Intramuros are key elements in the 1904 Master Plan for Manila by Daniel Burnham, the American urban planner, who after a short stay in Manila, established himself as one of the founders of modern American architecture in Chicago.

Burnham designed a Parisian system of parks, avenues and waterways radiating from Intramuros. This has been retained as a monu-

> **CHESSBOARD STREETS**
>
> Towns in the Spanish empire were built in a *cuadricula*, a chessboard of streets. At the center was a Plaza Mayor in which the cathedral stood opposite the government office.

and the Elks Club (now the Children's Museum). Across the park, the green roofs of the Manila Hotel are visible: the hotel is one of the earliest examples of traditional architecture which has been updated into a pseudo California mission-type style.

Rizal Park, conceptualized as a tropical version of the expansive Mall in Washington DC, is a vast green lung sweeping inland from Manila Bay to Taft Avenue. Taft Avenue was once a grand tree-lined way where the most imposing neo-classical government

ment although the moat has been filled in and it is now a golf course in the heart of the city.

Two architectural styles are evident here. One is the neo-classical Beaux Arts style of colonnades and porticos fashionable in the early 1900s. The second simplified and expanded upon the traditional Philippine-Spanish two-story wood and stone houses.

At the bayfront section of Rizal Park are two neo-classical examples built a few years after the completion of the Burnham Plan, the Army and Navy Club (now the Manila City Museum)

LEFT: native huts made from bamboo and *nipa* palm in 19th-century Luzon. **ABOVE:** Intramuros, Manila.

buildings were erected 75 years ago. These include the Manila Post Office, the Manila City Hall and a complex of three government buildings, two of which have become the National Museum, and the third is the Department of Tourism. The National Museum, worth visiting for the quality of its collection, is housed in two of the most architecturally outstanding buildings in the country.

Further along are the Philippine Normal School and Philippine General Hospital, both built by American architects in the early 20th century. Both retain the tiled roofs, wide windows and arcades of traditional Philippine architecture. Taft Avenue shifted the focus away from Spanish churches and plazas and established the American footprint in Manila.

Keeping 19th-century styles

While World War II bombs flattened most of Manila, the 1587 San Agustin, the country's oldest stone church, is the only structure left intact in Intramuros. Its carved altars, choir loft and *trompe l'oeil* ceilings are outstanding. Within its one-block Renaissance-style complex are the country's premier museum of religious relics, a monastery, cloisters and a botanical garden.

The Intramuros restoration program now

Spanish friars thought local structures of bamboo and thatch were improper for worship, so they directed Filipino and Chinese artisans to build large stone churches, vaguely following the baroque style of Spain. Façades rising to a tip fronted rectangular churches and buttresses reinforced thick stone walls against earthquakes. Bell towers stood separately.

San Agustín (Intramuros, Manila), San Agustín (Paoay, Ilocos Norte province); Santa María de la Asunción (Santa María, Ilocos Sur province) and Santo Tomás de Villanueva (Miag-ao, Iloilo province) are all on the prestigious UNESCO World Heritage List.

requires all new structures to follow the traditional architecture of the late 19th century. The best example is Plaza San Luís, a series of new structures built in the old-style, interconnected by courtyards that open into a museum, shops, restaurants and a small hotel.

Casa Manila, in Plaza San Luís, recreates the 19th-century home of an affluent Manileño. Its collection of art, period furniture, and decorative details is a mix of Philippine, Chinese and Spanish traits, and is the best example of the eclectic taste and the east-west fusion style of the era. Still standing are the ruins of the Ayuntamiento, the seat of the Spanish government and the Intendencia, the customs house that was the eastern terminus of the Manila-Acapulco galleon route. Walking on top of the restored walls and fortifications of Intramuros offers views of Manila Bay, the Pasig River and Fort Santiago. The Intramuros gates had drawbridges that were raised every night in order to keep undesirables from crossing the moat.

Although Intramuros is a glorious taste of the past, with its *cuadricula* of streets bounded by fortifications and a moat, no less, the town of Vigan (eight hours' drive north of Manila) is considered the best surviving example of a 19th century Spanish colonial town.

A grid of streets pierces the entire historical district in Vigan framing broad views towards the plaza with rows of well-preserved houses built in the 18th and 19th centuries. The majestic Vigan Cathedral and Archbishop's Residence at Plaza Salcedo, the main plaza of the town, are magnificent examples of architecture from the Spanish colonial era. On the opposite side of the plaza, the Ilocos Sur Provincial Capitol, a graceful porticoed central structure flanked by side wings in the classic Palladian manner, is an excellent example of American-built civic buildings of the early 20th century.

The museums that offer glimpses into the lifestyles of the Vigan of old are the Ayala Museum behind the Provincial Capitol, the Museum at the Archbishop's Residence, and the Crisologo Museum. Vigan art and antiques may be purchased in shops on the ground floor of stately homes on Crisologo Street.

Taal, two hours' drive south of Manila, is another town with well-preserved 19th-century

LEFT: Vigan Cathedral. **RIGHT:** old Spanish-style stone houses in Laoag, Ilocos Norte.

houses. The grand Basilica of Saint Martin crowns the hill that the town is built on and is an imposing sight visible from any point in the town. Unlike flat Vigan, Taal topography cascades a grid of streets towards the sea. Two typical *bahay na bato* houses are open to the public: the Agoncillo residence and the Apacile residence. The latter is noteworthy for its fine Art Deco detailing, a radical departure from the usual florid decoration.

Unlike Vigan and Taal, most other towns have not preserved the old Spanish ambience, preferring instead to replace heritage architecture with nondescript modern buildings.

Ingenious rice terraces

The most outstanding architectural monument in the Philippines, however, is a landscape: the magnificent rice terraces (*see page 203*) that lay out paddyfields in giant steps up the steep slopes of the Philippine Cordilleras. They are a powerful statement of the enduring interaction between man and nature. Traditions are kept alive: from the maintenance of the terrace walls to the skilful engineering that allows constant irrigation. Small villages dot the terraced areas where age-old harvest rituals persist. The terraces are the only "living cultural landscape" on the UNESCO World Heritage List. ❑

THE EVOLUTION OF PHILIPPINE HOUSES

The *bahay na nipa* is a single-room dwelling, cradled above the ground on poles, and built of bamboo, rattan and *nipa* palms. It resembles a large life-sheltering basket. The structure, built from the natural materials that grow in the surrounding area, responds perfectly to the tropical island environment, a lightweight, pliant structure that cannot withstand strong typhoons and sways with earthquakes.

Evolving into the Spanish colonial townhouse, its lower floor was walled with stone while the second level family quarters was supported by tree trunks, built of the best hardwood, embellished with carving and handcrafted furniture, and enclosed by two sets of sliding windows, a

set of wide wooden windows covered with *capiz* (Placuna placenta) shells and another set of wooden shutters. A steep roof of terracotta tiles capped the house.

In the early 20th century, concrete replaced stone. Houses became smaller, with a single floor raised off the ground by a few feet for ventilation, but windows remained large to allow maximum air circulation.

And after a long fascination with Western styles, the traditional house is now going through a revival. Many new houses recycle material from demolished old structures, recreating a Philippine setting and returning to the kind of dwellings that used to proliferate in pre-colonial eras.

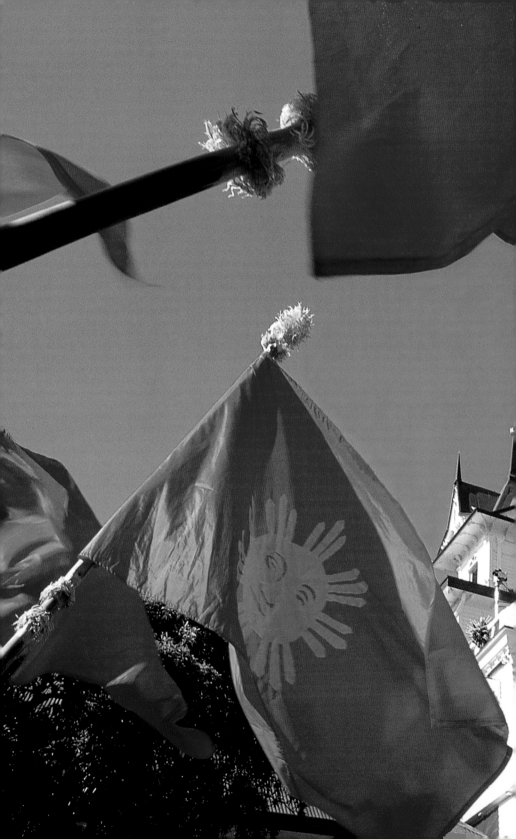

PLACES

*A detailed guide to the entire country, with principal sites
clearly cross-referenced by number to the maps*

Manila, the in-your-face capital of the archipelago's 7,107 islands, is the usual starting point for most journeys in the Philippines. Increasingly, however, with the opening up of the skies, visitors may enter through other gateways, such as Cebu City, Davao, Zamboanga or Laoag.

The first-time traveler from Europe or North America may find Manila intimidating in its chaos and frenetic energy. Worry not, for aside from the predictable scam artists, Manila holds merit for the traveler. It is an old city, with history that lingers in the architecture of Malacañang Palace, the thick stone walls of Intramuros and the faces and bustle of Chinatown. Day trips beyond Manila lead the curious to active volcanoes like Taal and Pinatubo, to beach resorts and scuba diving in Batangas, to mountainside worshippers on Mt Banahaw and to the rainforest river rapids of Pagsanjan.

Manila is on the southern part of Luzon, the largest island, located at the northern end of the archipelago. North of Manila are the lofty highlands of Baguio and Banaue, where cascading rice terraces spill over as far as the eye can see, and the refined Ilocos region, home to jewels such as the well-preserved Spanish city of Vigan.

South of Luzon are the Visayas, a smattering of variously shaped islands that can keep travelers engaged for years. Increasingly, adventure tours are moving into such untouched locations as Samar and Leyte in the eastern Visayas. Central to the whole Visayas region is the island, and city, of Cebu, not only the gateway to resorts and coral reefs, but also a growing entrepreneurial city – noted, too, for its guitars. Boracay, off the northern tip of Panay, is a national showcase, with fabulous white sand beaches.

The Palawan archipelago, west of the Visayas, consists of roughly 1,700 minuscule islands, some harboring a single village, if that. Palawan is best known for its remote beach locations, difficulties of road travel, and exotic wildlife, including such rare species as the sea turtle, Palawan peacock pheasant, scaly anteater and Palawan bearcat, or *binturong*. Like many of the archipelago's islands, Palawan invites exploration by curious, but patient tourists.

Mindanao is in the deepest south. On its sunny shores and cool mountains exist cultures quite diverse from the northern islands, including various Muslim groups, distinctive tribes and Badjao sea gypsies, who spend almost all their lives on the water. Mindanao has seen the kidnapping of tourists and fierce fighting between rebel groups and the government in recent years, and its southwestern areas are not recommended for even the most adventurous travelers. But many of its cities, such as Davao and Cagayan De Oro, remain accessible.   ❏

PRECEDING PAGES: sculptured Banaue rice terraces of Ifugao Province; Mayon is the most active volcano in the Philippines; Independence Day celebrations in Cavite.
LEFT: the translucent blue-green waters of Apo Island in Negros.

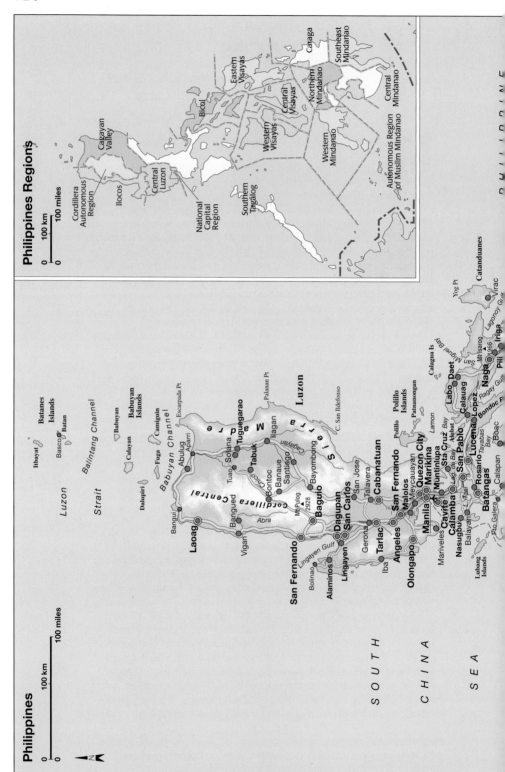

Philippines

100 km

100 miles

N

SOUTH CHINA SEA

Luzon Strait

Batanes Islands

Balintang Channel

Babuyan Channel

Babuyan Islands

Ibayat
Basco
Batan
Babuyan
Calayan
Fuga
Camiguin
Dalupiri

Bangui
Laoag

Vigan
Bangued
Abra
Cordillera Central
Mt Pulog
2928
Baguio
Dagupan
San Carlos

San Fernando
Lingayen Gulf
Lingayen
Alaminos
Bolinao
Iba
Gerona
Tarlac
Angeles
Olongapo
Mariveles

Abulug
Aparri
Escarpada Pt
Tuao
Solana
Tuguegarao
Tabuk
Bontoc
Banaue
Chico
Santiago
Ilagan
Cagayan
Bayombong
San Jose
Talavera
Cabanatuan
San Fernando
Malolos
Meycauayan
Quezon City
Manila
Marikina
Muntinlupa
Cavite
Calamba
Nasugbu
Balayan
Taal
Batangas
Rosario
Balayan Bay
Pto Galera
Lubang Islands

Sierra Madre

Luzon

Palanan Pt
C. San Ildefonso

Polillo
Polillo Islands
Patnanongan
Lamon
Lamon Bay
Sta Cruz
San Pablo
Lucena
Bondoc P
Tayabas Bay
Boac
Calapan
Ragay Gulf

Labo
Daet
Calauag
Naga
Pili
Iriga
Virac
Catanduanes
Calagua Is
San Miguel Bay
Yog Pt
Lagonoy Gulf
Mt Isarog
1966

PHILIPPINE

Philippines Regions

100 km

100 miles

Cordillera Autonomous Region
Ilocos
Cagayan Valley
Central Luzon
National Capital Region
Southern Tagalog
Bicol
Western Visayas
Central Visayas
Eastern Visayas
Caraga
Northern Mindanao
Southeast Mindanao
Central Mindanao
Western Mindanao
Autonomous Region of Muslim Mindanao

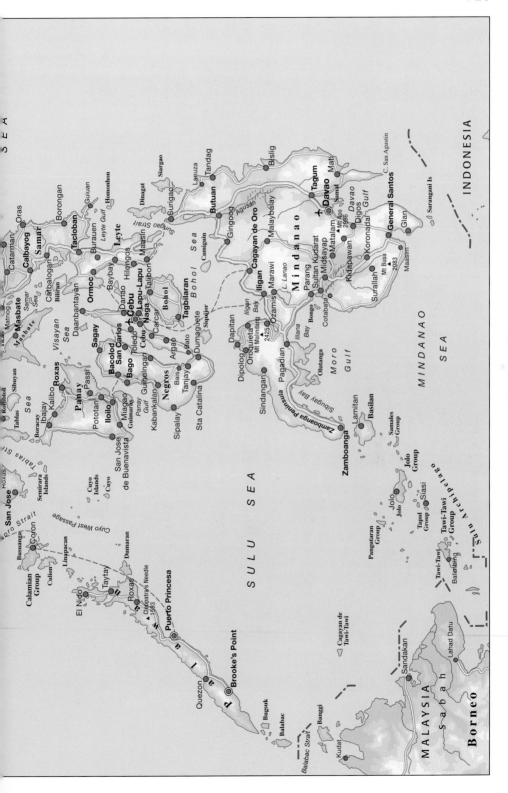

LUZON

*Spanish heritage, simple farming and fishing communities,
moody volcanoes and the vibrant capital city: Luzon has it all*

Luzon, at 104,688 sq. km (40,410 sq. miles), is the largest island in the archipelago, occupying 35 percent of the nation's total land area and home to half the country's population.

Relatively mountainous, Luzon rises to a peak of 2,928 meters (9,606 ft) at Mt Pulog, in Benguet province. However, the broad, flat Central Plains fill the nation's rice basket, and rivers flowing from the uplands water the rich soil of the agricultural lowlands, where sugar cane, coconuts, corn and tobacco are also important crops.

Key to the success of Luzon throughout the centuries has been Manila's strategic location at the mouth of the Pasig river, on the shores of Manila Bay. Wending 23 km (14 miles) inland, the Pasig opens into the 900-sq. km (350-sq. mile) Laguna de Bay, the Philippines' largest lake. At the same time, Manila's prime geographic location has transformed the city into the most developed and polluted area in the country. The sprawling metropolis produces textiles, chemicals and metal products, and assembles electronics such as computer components for export.

From a historical standpoint, Luzon holds the distinction of having two of the first three cities founded by the Spanish invaders in the late 1500s. After gaining a foothold in Cebu in 1565, Miguel Lopez de Legazpi seized Manila – then known as "Maynilad" – in 1571, building the thick stone walls around Intramuros. By 1572, the Spanish conquistadors had founded their third city on the northwestern Ilocos coast at Vigan. Here, the Spanish flavor and tradition is best preserved in the former Chinese and mestizo districts.

Manila serves as the main gateway to a land rich with opportunities – including mountainous rice terraces in Ifugao province, and beach communities where fishing is a way of life and coral illuminates the underwater world. Nearby is Laguna de Bay, home of Tagalog culture, where skilled handicrafts still flourish today. Further south, Quezon hosts some of the nation's outstanding indigenous wildlife in forests now somewhat denuded by loggers.

Historical sites in this northern portion of the archipelago range from the island fortress of Corregidor to the war-torn peninsula of Bataan. Volcanoes of all sorts abound, including the small and deadly Taal, and Mt Pinatubo – which angrily awoke from its 450-year slumber in 1991. The windswept Batanes Islands off the northern tip of Luzon offer remote hiking experiences, while the islands off the southern coast have their own distinctive events, including an annual rodeo. Northeastern Luzon features a wealth of caves for exploring, plus the Cagayan river – the longest in the Philippines. ❑

PRECEDING PAGES: overview of old Manila, with Rizal Park on the left.
LEFT: garishly colored jeepneys are found everywhere in the Philippines.

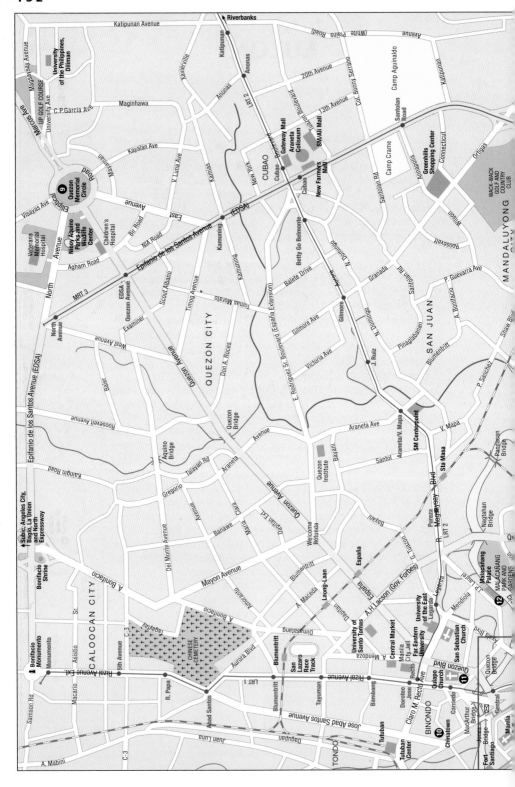

Manila

1000 m
1000 yds
0
0

N

MANILA

PASIG CITY

Lanuza Ave

Pasig Blvd

Ninoy Aquino Stadium

San Miguel Corporation

Doña Julia Vargas Avenue

Marisco

Ave

San

Boulevard

Shanuan

Pioneer

J. P. Rizal Extension

Ortigas Center ⑧
SM Megamall

EDSA -
Shaw Boulevard

(EDSA)

Shaw

Boni

Guadalupe
Bridge

Guadalupe

GUADALUPE

MacArthur

Ave

Fort Bonifacio
Global City

Fort
Bonifacio
Entertainment
Center

Carlos P. Garcia Ave

(C-5)

PATEROS

TAGUIG

AMERICAN
MEMORIAL
CEMETERY ⑦

Lawton Ave

Bayani Road

LIBINGAN NG MGA BAYANI
(GRAVEYARD OF HEROES)

Nichols-McKinley Road

Mandaluyong
City Hall

Boni

Avenue

Barangka Drive

Pasig

Estrella

Coronado

Power Plant
Mall

Rockwell
Center

NORTH
FORBES
PARK

MAKATI CITY

MANILA
McKINLEY
GOLF CLUB

MANILA
POLO
CLUB

Kalayaan Ave

Buendia

SOUTH
FORBES
PARK

A. S. Arnaiz Ave

Bayani Road

Muntinlupa City

PARAÑAQUE

VILLAMOR
GOLF COURSE

Andrew

Avenue

Manila
Domestic
Airport

Sta Ana
Race Track

J. P. Rizal

Avenue

Kalayaan

MANILA
SOUTH
CEMETERY

N. Garcia St. (Reposo)

SALCEDO
VILLAGE

Makati
Avenue

Paseo de Roxas

Ayala
Center

MRT 3

Ayala Avenue -
Pasay Road

Palm Ave

Paseo de Roxas

Ayala

(Buendia)

LEGASPI
VILLAGE

Makati Stock
Exchange

Ayala Museum ⑥
Greenbelt
Mall

A. S. Arnaiz Ave
(Pasay Road)

Amorsolo

EDSA

Pasong Tamo

Pasong Tamo Ext.

Magallanes

Avenue

Chino Roces

Sampaloc

Del Pan

A. Francisco

Pasig Line

Buendia

Sen. G. Puyat

South

Superhighway

EDSA - (EDSA)

Bridge

New Panaderos

Vito Cruz

Chino Roces

Kamagong

Pasay
Road

PASAY
CITY

EDSA -
Taft Avenue

Magallanes

Epifanio de los Santos Avenue

Ninoy Aquino
International Airport

Redemptorist
Church

Airport Ave

Quirino Ave

Badaran

Mia Road

F. B. Harrison

Libertad

Aurora Blvd

Park Avenue

LRT 1

Libertad

Metropoint
Mall

Gil Puyat (Buendia)

Leveriza

Tramo

Line

Pres. Quirino

Pedro Gil/Paco

Pedro

Gil

Pedro

Quirino Avenue

Andres

Arellano Ave

Taft

Vito
Cruz

Avenue

Vito
Cruz

St. Vito Cruz

M. Adriatico

Pablo Ocampo

Boulevard

World
Trade Center

Land Reclamation

Mall of Asia

Manila Bay

ERMITA

MANILA

PACO
PARK ①

National

United
Nations

Avenue

United

Pedre Faura

RIZAL
PARK

Padre Burgos

National

Mabini

Kalaw

Roxas

A. Mabini

San

Remedios
Circle

Philippine
General Hospital

Rizal
Memorial
Stadium

MANILA
ZOOLOGICAL
AND
BOTANICAL
GARDENS

Metropolitan
Museum
of Manila

Malate ②
Church

Folk Arts
Theater

Cultural Center ④
of the Philippines

Coconut Palace ⑤

Sofitel
Philippine Plaza

Manila
Film Center

Philippine
International
Convention Center

③

National
Library

Rizio Dr.

p.136

METROPOLITAN MANILA

Map on pages 132–33

Bustling Manila has powerful reminders of the Philippine past, along with attractive parks, fine museums, exhilarating nightlife and rapidly developing business suburbs

A city of contrasts, Manila is a hodgepodge of cultures, merging together the influences of its many foreign visitors and colonizers over the years. A city built by the Pasig river, Manila – originally "Maynilad" – takes its name from the *nilad*, a white flowering plant that once grew along the river's banks. Hence, embark upon a trip through the place "where the *nilad* grows."

Foreign powers rule

On both sides of the river's mouth, trading communities formed as early as the 5th century, with merchants from all over the known world paying visits. By the mid-16th century, Muslims with ancestry in Borneo had entrenched themselves here. Spanish conquistador Miguel Lopez de Legazpi arrived in 1571 and constructed the city fortress, Intramuros. The native *indios* were put to work, and slowly converted to Catholicism. Gradually, however, when increased maritime trade saw an influx of people and ideas from around the globe, the liberal attitudes of English and American traders, among others, helped raise the city onto a truly cosmopolitan plane. It was just a matter of time before the Castilian sword and cross fell.

LEFT: Intramuros, with Manila Cathedral in the background. **BELOW:** a 1940s illustration of Manila.

Revolutionary rumblings came to a head in the 19th century, when Jose Rizal clearly defined Filipino-Spanish relations in his 1886 novel, *Noli Me Tangere*. Taking his cue in 1892, Andres Bonifacio founded the Katipunan, a secret society promoting complete independence from Spain. Four years later, he led the first armed insurrection. After two years of guerrilla war against the Spanish, the revolutionaries found themselves beaten with the capture of their capital by the United States, which was, itself, at war with Spain. Four more years of struggle against the Americans followed, until the last rebel capitulated. From 1902 to 1946, the people of the islands lived under another period of colonial, albeit benevolent, rule. The Americans left a useful legacy: an education system, democratic government, infrastructure lessons in technology and Western mores.

In 1941, Japanese bombers gave Manileños a brief foretaste of yet another foreign power. Manila quickly surrendered. Except for a few monuments and buildings, Manila was practically levelled during the war. Some families evacuated the city, while their young men allied themselves with the Americans against the Japanese, and did so with outstanding valor. The US repaid the gesture by granting the Philippines independence in 1946, a year after retaking the islands.

The nerve center

Metro Manila today continues to be a bustle of people and traffic, racing against time to catch up with the

Filipinos are well known for their artistic and musical abilities. Many of the lounge acts and bar bands encountered throughout Asia and beyond are Filipino.

21st century. With an estimated population of 12 million, it has become the much-too-large heart of a country whose many other parts are sorely lacking in progress and development. As the one massive nerve center, Manila's heaving pulse has always been an indicator of the strengths or weaknesses that characterize the Philippine people as a whole.

Of course, Manila is not the Philippines, though countless tourists leave Manila with what they think is an image of the Philippines: happily Westernized Asians on the move and in the know, flashing their best hospitality smiles. It is a shallow impression, and false, too. To go beyond the facade for a deeper understanding of Philippine people and history, start in Old Manila.

Intramuros: a city "Within Walls"

For its small space and relatively out-of-the-way location, **Fort Santiago** Ⓐ (open daily 8am–6pm; entrance fee) has become a popular promenade for lovers and artists. Within Fort Santiago is the **Rizal Museum** (open Tues–Sat

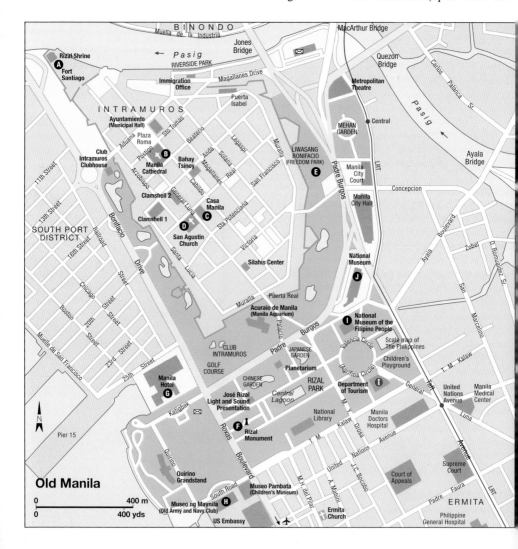

Old Manila

0 — 400 m
0 — 400 yds

8am–noon and 1–5pm; free with fort entrance), housing memorabilia of Philippine national hero Dr Jose Rizal. On another end of the quadrangle is Rizal's cell, where he wrote his last legacy of poetry to the Filipino people.

From Fort Santiago, cross over to **Manila Cathedral ⑧**, an imposing Romanesque structure constructed of adobe. A plaque on its facade reveals a relentless history, beginning in 1571, of reconstruction after the repeated ravages of fire, typhoon, earthquake and war. Statues by Italian artists, of the saints to whom Manileños owe special devotion, grace the facade. Among them are St Andrew the Apostle, on whose feast day in 1574 the Spanish repulsed Chinese invaders, and Santiago Matamoros (St James the Greater), patron saint of Spain and the Philippines. Fronting the cathedral is Plaza Roma, so-called since 1961 when Rome renamed one of its squares Piazza Manila, to commemorate the elevation of the first Filipino cardinal, Rufino J. Santos.

Although Intramuros was laid out as a pentagon, its uneven sides more approximate a triangle. The old western wall fronted the sea before reclamation began a century ago, but is now flanked by Bonifacio Drive, which runs south to Roxas Boulevard. The perimeter of Intramuros measures nearly 4.5 km (3 miles). Inside, following Legazpi's blueprint for the capital, succeeding Spanish governors built 18 churches, chapels, convents, schools, a hospital, printing press, university (in as early as 1611), palaces for the governor-general and the archbishop, soldiers' barracks, and houses for the assorted elite. Though Intramuros is a far cry from the bustling Spanish city it once was, it has come a long way from the ravages of wartime. Once a jumble of broken buildings, portions of the old city have been restored, including the *Ayuntamiento* (Municipal Hall), once the grandest structure here.

Map on page 136

Manila's coat-of-arms detail from Fort Santiago – the key defence site of the Spanish walled city of Intramuros.

BELOW:
Fort Santiago.

Wealthy Spanish merchants who lived in houses like Casa Manila had all the modern conveniences of 100 years ago, including grand bathtubs and side-by-side toilets, plus an ice chest in the kitchen.

Part of the continuing restoration plan is to replicate eight houses to illustrate different styles and periods through which local architecture has evolved. A few are already open to the public, including the splendid **Casa Manila** 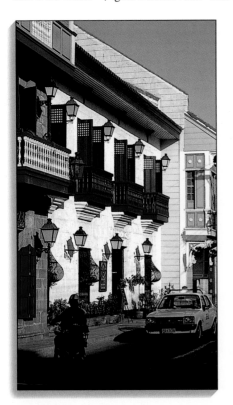 (open Tues–Sun 9am–6pm; entrance fee) in the extensive Plaza San Luis. This restored Spanish merchant's house from the late 1800s features beautiful hardwoods throughout, plus *capiz* shell sliding windows. Down General Luna Street is the three-story El Amanecer Complex, a reproduction of a 19th-century town home that now houses **Silahis Center** (open daily 10am–7pm; tel: 02-527 2111; www.silahis.com), Manila's one-stop destination for handicrafts shopping.

Further south, at the intersection of General Luna and Calle Real, incongruous Chinese *fu* dogs carved of granite guard the entrance to the courtyard of **San Agustin Church** (open daily 8am–noon and 1–6pm; entrance fee), the only structure in Intramuros not bombed in World War II. The church facade is notable for its combination of styles – with Doric lower and Corinthian upper columns – and the absence of one of its original twin towers, a victim of earthquakes in 1863 and 1889. The remarkable main door is carved *molave*, a Philippine hardwood, its panels depicting St Augustine and his mother, St Monica. Adjoining the church is a magnificent monastery-museum containing a treasure trove of Philippine artifacts, religious art and Chinese, Spanish and Mexican pottery. The cloister gallery exhibits fine paintings of the life of St Augustine and portraits of notable Augustinian friars, including Fr. Manuel Blanco, who produced the classic *Flora de Filipinas*.

Around the stone walls of the old walled city is **Club Intramuros** (open Mon noon–8pm, Tues–Sat 5.30am–8pm, Sun 5.30am–noon), with an 18-hole golf course. Also visit the excellent **Bahay Tsinoy** (open Tues–Sun 8am–5pm; entrance fee; tel: 02-526 6798; www.kaisa.ph/museum) on Cabildo Street, a museum of the Chinese in Philippine life.

Pasig river

From San Agustin Church, turn right at Calle Real to prowl the remains of Intramuros to Muralla Street on the east. Follow the walls or pass through one of the restored gates leading back to the Pasig river, or into a plaza, **Liwasang Bonifacio** (Freedom Park). On this busy square is a statue of revolutionary leader Andres Bonifacio, with the Central Post Office just to the north. To the east stands the art-deco Metropolitan Theater and Mehan Garden. Intersecting these landmarks is a complex sprawl of highway taking much of Manila's traffic north across the Pasig river. The Pasig may not be the cleanest river to relax next to, but projects by Manila Mayor Lito Atienza have been impressively effective in cleaning up the areas next to the river, and creating several pocket parks and restaurant rows along its banks.

Rizal Park

Formerly known as Luneta, **Rizal Park** is a large field with an elevated strolling ground, bounded by Roxas Boulevard and ending at the sea wall facing Manila Bay. On this section is Quirino Grandstand, from where officials preside over Independence Day

BELOW: restored Casa Manila dates back to the 1800s.

parades and where religious congregations converge. In the early morning, some Chinese practice *tai chi* here. In 1995, Pope John Paul II held mass to an estimated 4.5 million admiring worshippers here, earning a spot in the Guinness World Record as the "largest Papal gathering."

In the central portion of Rizal Park stands **Rizal Monument ⑦**, a guarded memorial to the national hero. This spot also has the distinction of being Kilometer Zero, the point of reference for all road distances throughout the largest Philippine island, Luzon. Behind the monument is a series of plaques inscribed with Rizal's poem *Mi Ultimo Adios* (My Last Farewell). A marble slab highlights the spot where Rizal met his martyr's death by firing squad, while an obelisk marks the site of the earlier executions of Filipino priests Gomez, Burgos and Zamora. To the north side, along Burgos Street, are the Chinese garden, planetarium, Japanese garden and orchidarium (small entrance fee for each). Within the orchidarium is a restaurant called Lush Life. There is also an open area, used for wedding receptions and other intimate gatherings.

On the northern side of the park, at the exact spot where Rizal was executed for treason by the Spaniards, is the **Lights and Sounds of Rizal** – a 30-minute audio-visual presentation in an open-air theater setting, dramatizing the most poignant moments of Rizal's final hours before his execution for treason (open Wed–Sun 7am–7.30pm [Tagalog]; 8am–8.30pm [English]; entrance fee).

Northwest of the park, located next to Quirino Restaurant Grandstand, is **Manila Hotel ⑥**; this was once the most exclusive address in the Pacific. Although her charm and glamor have faded somewhat since 1912, the site of General Douglas MacArthur's former headquarters still has its allure. Along the Kalaw Street side of Rizal Park is where the National Library can be found.

Map on page 136

Rizal Monument at Manila's Rizal Park is a tribute to Philippine hero Jose Rizal.

BELOW: San Agustin Church by day.

Near the park's Central Lagoon, a group of speaking- and hearing-impaired people run a food kiosk, offering a cool spot from which to people-watch. Alternatively, head to the tried-and-true Harbor View Restaurant or the SeaFood Wharf Restaurant, in the old Army-Navy Club compound, for a beer and *pulutan* (cocktail snacks Filipino-style) while watching the sunset over Manila Bay.

Museum district

TIP

If museum hopping, avoid Sunday and Monday, when most city museums are closed.

Try to visit the **Museo ng Maynila** (City Museum; open Tues–Sat 9am–6pm; free), housed in the century-old Army and Navy Club building at the southwestern corner of Rizal Park. The displays provide details of the city's historical development, and guided tours usually leave on the hour.

The park's eastern section, across Orosa Street, offers two impressive, Greek-style buildings: the **Department of Tourism** (DOT; tel: 02-524 2345) and the Department of Finance, home to the **National Museum of the Filipino People** ❶ (open Tues–Sun 9am–5pm; entrance fee; tel: 02-527 0278). Visit the DOT for travel information, or view one of the ethnographic displays in the front lobby. The Museum of the Filipino People offers comprehensive exhibits, ranging from ethnographic displays and prehistoric burial jars to artifacts recovered from the Spanish trade galleon *San Diego*.

Between here and Taft Avenue, which runs along the eastern side of the park, sprawls a topographic map of the Philippines (try viewing it from the light rail system) and a children's playground, featuring gigantic prehistoric beasts cast in cement. Burgos Street, on the park's northern side, leads past the Old Congress Building, which once hosted the Philippine Senate and now houses the **National Museum** ❶ (open Wed–Sun 10am–4pm; entrance fee; tel: 02-522

BELOW: National Museum.

5846). The museum mainly showcases paintings by National Artist Juan Luna, and renovation and administrative changes will eventually see the remainder of the collection move to the DOT building. Northward is Manila City Hall, and beyond, Liwasang Bonifacio, from where three bridges head over the Pasig. From this point, a number of jeepneys and buses, starting from across the river, follow Taft Avenue to all points south.

This south-of-the-river section of the city is quite easy to get around in. On the westernmost side is Roxas Boulevard, running from Rizal Park to Parañaque, near the airport. Just south of the park, abutting the Roxas Boulevard seawall, are the sprawling grounds of the US Embassy. Next door is the impressive **Museo Pambata** (Children's Museum; open Tues–Sat 8am–5pm, Sun 1–5pm; entrance fee; tel: 02-523 1797; www.museopambata.org), which offers superb entertainment and interactive displays for children of all ages.

Ermita and Malate

From Taft, turn right at any of the streets beginning with United Nations Avenue, where the Manila Pavilion stands; this will lead to Ermita. The other side of Taft offers little except **Paco Park ❶** (open Mon–Thur 8am–5pm, Fri–Sun 8am–7pm; entrance fee), a peaceful, circular promenade, originally a Spanish cemetery in the 1820s. Ermita is an unusual district in many respects, its tourist reputation built on its proximity to Rizal Park, the seawall along Manila Bay and many government buildings, including the Supreme Court on Padre Faura Street. Ermita offers many hotels, plus a conglomeration of eateries, nightspots, boutiques, antique shops, handicraft and curio stalls, and travel agency offices.

When the Spanish arrived, Ermita was a seaside village called Laygo, whose

Map on pages 132/136

Ermita's handicraft shops sell delicate capiz shell artifacts – including chandeliers.

BELOW: Roxas Boulevard and Manila Bay sunset.

Ermita was a hot night spot for foreign men, second in Asia only to Bangkok, until Mayor Alfred Lim closed the bars and strip joints in the early 1990s. Ermita and Malate have since reinvented themselves, revising the arts and offering some of Manila's best nightlife.

residents venerated a small female icon carved out of dark wood, set atop a clump of pandanus by the seashore. Although stupefied at the statue's pre-Christian look, Legazpi's men turned the image to their advantage, telling the villagers that the image's name was *Nuestra Señora de Guia* (Our Lady of Guidance), and that it had been brought by angels. They installed it in a wooden chapel not far from the spot where it was found. Ermita Church – reconstructed eight times – still stands at the original site on M.H. del Pilar Street.

Legend holds that a Mexican hermit made the small seaside village his retreat in 1591. Four years later, an Augustinian priest founded the hermitage dedicated to the Virgin, and the name Ermita (hermitage) stuck. By the 19th century, the district had become an aristocratic suburb.

In line with the bohemian lifestyle of its younger residents and visitors, Ermita has given birth to a group called the Mabini painters, named after the street where their tiny galleries compete with stalls hawking cheap cultural souvenirs. Artists, writers, musicians and dancers make themselves at home here, adding to the city's eclectic mix. Near these galleries is Cortada Street, a tiny quarter for crafts and brassware from Muslim Mindanao in the south.

During daylight hours, Mabini and del Pilar offer an assortment of antique shops where pottery, religious icons, ethnic ware, old bottles and assorted junk command varying prices. By night, the area buzzes as locals make their way to Remedios Circle and Julio Nakpil Street for fine dining. The selection on Nakpil ranges from delectable Spanish cuisine at Casa Armas to modern European food at refined Sala. The same area boasts thriving nightlife, from drag shows to a number of dance clubs for all persuasions along Nakpil and Orosa streets. Irresistible, too, is the swinging Latin scene at Café Havana in Remedios Circle.

BELOW: Nakpil Street night owls showing off tatoos.

West of Remedios Circle stands **Malate Church** ➋ dedicated to Nuestra Señora de los Remedios (Our Lady of Remedies), patron saint of women in childbirth. Her image, brought from Spain in 1624, is still venerated on the main altar. In front of the church, bronze statues of Our Lady, and Rajah Sulayman – ruler of Manila until ousted by Legazpi in 1571 – make an odd couple as they confront the sunset.

Further south, along Roxas Boulevard at Quirino Avenue, the Manila Yacht Club and Philippine Navy Headquarters stand on reclaimed land, intruding on the sea view. On the land side is a government complex that includes the Manila Hospital, the **Metropolitan Museum of Manila** ➌ (open Mon–Sat 10am–6pm; entrance fee; tel: 02-521 1517; www.metmuseum.ph), with displays of old masters, a collection of pre-Hispanic gold artifacts, and more, and the Central Bank of the Philippines which houses the **Money Museum** (open Mon–Fri 9am–noon and 1–4pm; free; tel: 02-524 7011), a comprehensive collection of Philippine money and other currencies from around the world. Behind the hospital on Adriatico Street are the **Manila Zoological and Botanical Gardens** (open daily 7am–6pm; entrance fee; tel: 02-525 8157).

A relaxing way to see Manila Bay is to stroll along the wide avenue between Roxas Boulevard and the ocean. Fondly referred to as "Baywalk", it is most spectacular at sunset but becomes livelier as the evening progresses, with food kiosks and open-air restaurants enticing with refreshments and live entertainment.

Cultural Complex

Past the Navy Headquarters, on the seaward side of Roxas Boulevard, is the immense **Cultural Center of the Philippines** ➍, the centerpiece of reclaimed land called the CCP Complex.

Map on pages 132–33

Although Manila's zoo in Adriatico Street (open daily 7am–6pm; entrance fee) features some fascinating local endangered species, it does not have a great reputation for animal welfare – something travelers may wish to consider before making a visit.

BELOW: stately Malate Church sits incongruously in the nightlife area.

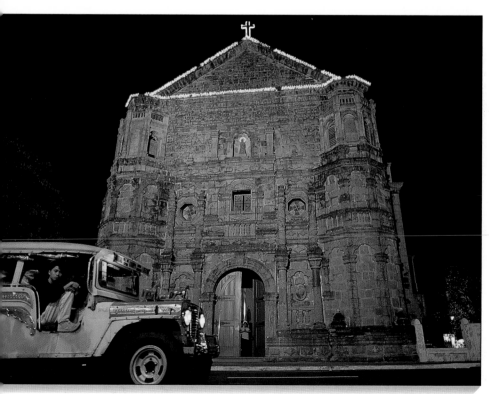

The main building houses three theaters, two art galleries, a library and a museum. The rest of the complex includes the Folk Arts Theater, the Design Center of the Philippines, Philippine Center for Industrial and Trade Exhibits (Philcite), Philippine International Convention Center (PICC) and the World Trade Center. Architecturally, the Government Services Insurance System (GSIS) building to the southwest is the most interesting. It houses the Philippine Senate, a theater and the **GSIS Museo ng Sining** (open Tues–Sat 8.45–11am and 1–4pm; free; tel: 02-551 1301), featuring contemporary Filipino art by painters like Fernando Amorsolo and Hernando Ocampo.

Coconut Palace was specially built for the 1981 visit of Pope John Paul II. The good Pope however suggested that Mrs Marcos spend her money more wisely – and stayed elsewhere.

In the northwest corner is a former Marcos guesthouse, the **Coconut Palace ❺** (open Tues–Sun 9–11.30am and 1–4.30pm; tel: 02-832 0223; entrance fee). Built entirely from indigenous materials such as narra and molave hardwoods, coconut wood and husks, the palace was built to host Pope John Paul II during his 1981 visit. Today's visitors can ogle at guest rooms such as the Visayas Room, showcasing thousands of shells; the Mountain Province Room, executed in the bold red and black colors of the highland people; and the Ilocos Room, with its priceless mother-of-pearl furniture. The Coconut Palace is available for private rentals, often hosting lavish parties for Manila's rich and famous. Although guided tours are available, call in advance to avoid a private event.

Directly south of the Coconut Palace is the Sofitel Philippine Plaza (formerly the Westin), with comfortable restaurants in the lobby atrium – a welcome escape from the city bustle and traffic.

BELOW: Sofitel Philippine Plaza.
RIGHT: Coconut Palace.

Palm-fringed Roxas Boulevard continues to dominate the crescent of the bay, leading from the airport, just beyond its southern end, into the heart of the city. Hotels, restaurants and nightclubs fill the area. Although much of Manila Bay

has been reclaimed for future development, the landfill sits empty, save for the gingerbread house effect of a lone Iglesia ni Cristo church in the distance.

Map on pages 132–33

Pasay and Parañaque

Past the CCP is **Star City**, an amusement park with rides and theme areas that change seasonally. Roxas Boulevard then approaches Senator Gil Puyat Avenue, still called by its old name, Buendia. On the bayside is the **World Trade Center**, used as a trade and exhibit hall, convention center, and concert venue. Nearby is the **SM Mall of Asia**, built in Pasay at the end of the **Epifanio de los Santos Avenue** (EDSA). Opened in mid 2006, this is the largest shopping mall in the Philippines and the sixth largest in the world, occupying 20 hectares (50 acres) of reclaimed land on Manila Bay.

A left turn under the Buendia flyover leads straight to Manila's business center, Makati. Down from the flyover is the Cuneta Astrodome, an inappropriately named box structure where professional basketball is played. Close to the end of the boulevard is Redemptorist Road, forking left to Baclaran, an area on the Pasay-Parañaque boundary famous for the *lechon* (roast suckling pig) stalls that fringe the **Redemptorist Church**.

NAIA Avenue, at the boulevard's end, turns left to **Ninoy Aquino International Airport**, as well as **Philippine Airlines' Centennial Terminal** and the domestic flight terminals. From NAIA Avenue, turn right at narrow Quirino Avenue and go past Parañaque to Las Piñas Church, which has a historic bamboo organ. Where Roxas Boulevard ends, the coastal road begins, curving around the bay towards the historical attractions of Cavite. An hour or so from this point takes you to **Tagaytay Ridge**, the viewing point overlooking Taal Lake and its Volcano Island.

TIP

The LRT (Light Rail Transit) and MRT – 2 and 3 (Metropolitan Rail Transit) are fast ways to move around the city, particularly during the rain, when flooded roads can cause huge traffic jams in the city.

BELOW: the Redemptorist Church in Baclaran.

Makati

From NAIA Avenue, take a short bus or taxi ride to Makati via **Epifanio de los Santos Avenue** (EDSA), one of Manila's main thoroughfares. Another **Makati** main street, **Ayala Avenue**, has been dubbed the Philippine Wall Street, as it is the financial hub. Much of what Makati is today – tall skyscrapers, walled-in, residential "villages" for the more well-to-do, modern shopping centers, first-class restaurants and international hotels – can be traced to the development foresight of the Zobel de Ayalas, an old family of Spanish descent. Owners of a vast tract of swampland, the family initially sold off the land haphazardly. The triangle of Ayala and Makati avenues and Paseo de Roxas actually served as runways for Manila Airport for decades. In the 1950s, the Ayalas hit on the idea of developing the area called Makati as the new residential and business capital of the Philippines, first building Forbes Park as the premier enclave for themselves and other exclusive residents. Businesses followed, gradually relocating from north-of-the-Pasig Escolta.

The Ayala family continues to lead urban development, building even more world-class hotels, international restaurants and modern shopping complexes in the business district, such as **Ayala Center**'s Glorietta and Greenbelt shopping malls. Rows of glit-

BELOW: the Makati
business district
with colorful
jeepneys.

tering boutiques have sprung up in this area in recent years, tempting shoppers with fashion's best-known names. More restaurants have even begun to infiltrate residential areas, such as Legaspi and Salcedo Village, making Makati more of a walking-friendly neighborhood.

Near Greenbelt, on Makati Avenue, the **Ayala Museum** ❻ (open Tues–Fri 9am–6pm, Sat–Sun 10am–7pm; entrance fee; tel: 02-757 7117; www.ayala museum.com) offers an impressive collection of Philippine art from various historical periods, as well as the Fernando Amorsolo Gallery, a noted Filipino painter.

From Ayala Avenue's end at EDSA, cross the highway to McKinley Road to enter the high-class neighborhood of **Forbes Park**. The first planned residential community in Makati, this gated neighborhood is the premier housing area for business tycoons, expats and embassies. Long-term visitors may want to visit the Manila Polo Club or Manila Golf Club, among the most exclusive country clubs in the Philippines.

Beyond McKinley is the **Fort Bonifacio Global City** development, where the **Fort Bonifacio Entertainment Center** – nicknamed The Fort – stands. Many good restaurants and fun nightclubs can be found here. Nearby **Serendra** has fashionable bars, restaurants and good shopping. On the northeast corner of Makati is the **Power Plant Mall** at the Rockwell Center, a respite from Glorietta's and Greenbelt's hustle and bustle.

Nearby is the peaceful, park-like **Manila American Memorial Cemetery** ❼ (open daily 6.30am–5pm), where the remains of 17,200 Allied dead rest below rows of white crosses and stars of David. The **Libingan ng Mga Bayani** (Graveyard of Heroes) is close by, its eternal flame burning by the Tomb of the Unknown Soldier.

From Fort Bonifacio, it is easy to access the C-5 Expressway, planned years ago and finally built to ease a little of Manila's omnipresent congestion. C-5 connects to the South Superhighway, running to the lakeshore towns of Laguna de Bay.

Northwest along EDSA, Makati ends at Guadalupe Bridge. A right turn before the bridge, along the winding J. P. Rizal Extension, leads to the riverside town of **Pateros**, center of the *balut* duck egg industry. The sandy soil of the area provides the local Pateros duck with an abundance of snails. A unique Filipino delicacy, *balut* is an embryonic duck boiled in its shell. *Balut* vendors sell their wares at night, their raucous cries of "bah-LOOOOT" carrying through to anyone hungry enough to feast on them. Filipinos often wager on the number of *balut* that can be eaten at one sitting, but a *balut*-eating mêlée frequently turns into a beer drinking contest, and no one remembers to count. Just don't try to eat *balut* on an empty stomach, warn the experienced ones.

Ortigas Center and Greenhills

Beyond the Pasig river, northeast of Makati, spread Pasig City and Mandaluyong City. Straddling them is **Ortigas Center ❽**, a serious rival to Makati as the country's premier business district. The **San Miguel Corporation** and **Asian Development Bank (ADB)** are based in Ortigas, as is **SM Megamall**, one of the country's biggest shopping centers. Plenty of malls, eateries and upscale hotels dot the area. Northwest of the Ortigas Center sprawls the impressive park-like landscape of the exclusive Wack-Wack Golf and Country Club. Further northwest along Ortigas Avenue one comes to Greenhills Shopping Center, a haunt for those seeking to buy freshwater and South China Sea pearls, and good-quality knock-offs of designer labels and popular brand names.

Map on pages 132–33

Dioramas at the Ayala Museum in Makati bring Philippine history to life.

BELOW: armed guard at a mansion in Forbes Park.

Quezon City

Heading north on EDSA leads to **Cubao**, Quezon City's commercial center, from where jeepneys and buses run to all parts of the city. Although a popular place, some people deride Cubao as a crude, traffic-infested jungle of shops and supermarkets that don't quite make the grade. This image is being revamped with the opening of **Gateway Mall**, the Araneta family's current project. Cubao landmark, the **Araneta Coliseum**, was billed as the world's largest domed coliseum in the 1960s.

West of Cubao, Rodriguez Boulevard (España Extension) leads to the Welcome Rotunda, where España becomes Quezon Avenue. Quezon, crossing EDSA, runs directly into **Quezon City**, the country's official capital before its integration into Metro Manila. Though a few non-governmental organizations and several universities are based here, Quezon City serves only nominally as the capital, with government institutions firmly vested in downtown Manila.

Despite the traffic, the area surrounding the 27-hectare (67-acre) **Quezon Memorial Circle** ❾ has a fair bit of greenery, with an orchid farm, the Manila Seedling Bank and the Ninoy Aquino Parks and Wildlife Center nearby. A 66-meter (215-ft) high tower in the circle, which offers excellent views, honors late president Manuel Quezon. Northeast of the circle, closer to Katipunan Avenue (part of C-5) in **Diliman**, is another university belt consisting of the University of the Philippines, Ateneo University and Miriam College.

North of the Pasig

Across from Intramuros lie the districts of **Binondo** and **Tondo**, once villages that were contemporary with Sulayman's original Maynilad. These areas, now

Araneta Coliseum was host to the "Thrilla in Manila" – the 1974 heavyweight championship fight between Mohammed Ali and Joe Frasier. The mall next to the coliseum – Ali Mall – was named after the winner of that famous bout.

BELOW: slum area near Manila's Chinatown.

heavily congested, are characterized by small shops and cramped residential quarters. Chinatown, which occupies most of Binondo, may be reached by crossing over Jones Bridge from Liwasang Bonifacio. At the foot of the bridge is a small street, Escolta, formerly Manila's major commercial street.

Thanks to their largely Chinese community and proximity to the river, Binondo and Santa Cruz became the city's richest mercantile borough at the height of the Manila–Acapulco galleon run. (Manila still has one of the world's major overseas Chinese populations – estimated at more than 1 million, and predominantly from nearby Fujian Province.) Evidence of past grandeur may be seen in the old colonial houses that are now threatened by the encroachment of modern concrete buildings. Their sad, decaying look fails to obscure features once marking an era's resplendence – arched wooden windows, fancy wrought-iron grillwork on balconies, massive wooden doors and brick walls. Such eloquence is also visible in the Carriedo Fountain in front of Santa Cruz Church.

Manila's **Chinatown** ❿ is a maze of such eclectic arrangements, the Spanish having granted the land for perpetual use to the Christian Chinese in 1594. The traditional Chinese apothecary selling dried seahorses and ginseng tea huddles close to a modern bank outfitted with automatic doors and shotgun-toting guards – of which there are many throughout the city. Chinese restaurants exist next to Italian furniture shops, while illegal Chinese immigrants hawk cheap wares on the street. And down the choked grid of narrow streets still bearing Iberian names clip-clop the *calesas*, horse-drawn carriages that are sometimes still the preferred mode of transport in this part of the city.

In traditional Chinese style, certain streets are known for selling a particular item. Ongpin Street is the king of gold and jade jewelry, while Nueva Street

Map on pages 132–33

Chinese stone lions placed near entrances are supposed to repel bad luck.

BELOW: burnt offerings and horse-drawn *calesa* in Chinatown.

offers office supplies. Head to Pinpin Street for furniture, and tiny Carvajal Street for the busy wet market and lunchtime *dim sum* with the locals.

Binondo is bounded on the north by Recto Avenue (Azacarraga), beyond which is Tondo, a district once the spawning ground of revolutionaries during Spanish times. Close to the harbor's piers and densely populated, Tondo once qualified as the largest slum in Southeast Asia, and still isn't the safest place in town.

Divisoria

Towards the western end of C. M. Recto Avenue, between Tondo and San Nicolas, is **Divisoria**, Manila's wild bargain basement. Sprawling over several blocks, this flea market is a mad emporium for shoppers of all economic levels. Fruits, handicrafts, hardware and more are peddled in a thousand stalls, above which the drunken ghost of *caveat emptor* hangs in a blissful state of abandon. Mall fans can visit the neoclassical Tutuban Center, founded in 1993 in the original Tutuban Railway Station – constructed in 1891 and closely linked to the activities of the revolutionary Katipunan.

Just north of Tutuban Center is the Philippine National Railway Station. From here, one can take a train – though it's not generally recommended – through Manila and south all the way to Legaspi City.

An important, insanely busy thoroughfare, Recto Avenue crosses through the city's most populous five districts, and is commonly a jam of jeepneys full of college students. The southern end is marked by a heavy concentration of cinemas, department and hardware stores, magazine stands, and sidewalk vendors retailing everything from cheap clothing, toys, sunglasses and watches to playing cards and *Playboy* magazines. This juncture of Recto and Rizal Avenue (Avenida Rizal) competes with the Quiapo Church area for the distinction of bearing the highest pedestrian traffic in Manila.

BELOW:
herb and tonic
vendor in Quiapo.

Quiapo and San Miguel

Past Avenida Rizal, Recto Avenue is marked by a stretch of small shops selling new and second-hand books for the university belt, an area that begins right after Recto Avenue's juncture with Quezon Boulevard. Turning left at Quezon leads you to **Central Market**, really a textile emporium, and eventually to España, which runs to the residential and governmental area of Quezon City. Turning right at Quezon Boulevard from Recto Avenue will take you to **Quiapo Church ⓫**, at the foot of Quezon Bridge. The area beside the church is the terminus for most public road transport plying north-south routes in the city. A boisterous quarter of the city, it has long been considered the heart – some say armpit – of downtown Manila.

Outside the church patio are Quiapo's fabled herb sellers. Ills of all kinds, from menstrual cramps to a lackluster love life, find an answer in these vendors' organic cornucopia of leaves, seeds and oils culled from local plants. In case of a sudden rise in national health standards, they double as sellers of amulets, candles, religious calendars and lottery tickets for the hopeful.

Viscous devotion

The church interior is laden with the appropriate ambience for the Filipinos' peculiarly viscous form of devotion, being dark, dank and heavily peopled at all hours. Down the length of the aisle, old women walk on their knees in fervent prayer. Men wipe their handkerchiefs on the icons and touch these to their lips, applying a second dab to the brows of their children. And a third is a final accord with spiritual power, the token of which is then folded with solemn contentment and placed into the pocket close to the heaving chest.

Quiapo Church is the devotional arena for Friday novenas, and perhaps more importantly, home of the Black Nazarene, a life-sized Christ statue kneeling and bearing a huge cross on his shoulder. Every January 9, the image is borne forth in a frenzied all-male procession leading a massed throng of barefoot devotees down the back streets of the district. It is believed that whoever touches the Christ image shall be purged of their sins.

Around the corner from the church stands a gem of a *bahay na bato* (stone house) on Bautista Street, the 1914 **Bahay Nakpil Bautista** (open Mon–Fri 9am–5pm, Sat 9am–noon; donations welcome), once home of four Filipino freedom fighters. In front of Quiapo Church is Plaza Miranda, where the public mood is assessed come political kite-flying time. Bounding this plaza are numerous markets, including one in the area under Quezon Bridge, where jeepneys heading northwards make their U-turns. This cheap handicrafts market is known simply as **Ilalim ng Tulay** (Under the Bridge).

North along Quezon Boulevard towards Recto Avenue is another conglomeration of army surplus stores, pawnshops, restaurants, hole-in-the-wall palmists and astrologers, martial arts schools, and movie houses. A right turn on Recto

Map
on pages
132–33

BELOW:
one of Quiapo's
many religious
processions.

Map on pages 132–33

Clocktower at the University of Santo Tomas.

BELOW: Malacañang Palace – office and residence of the President.

Avenue leads to the university belt, where colleges and universities disgorge tens of thousands of students to add to downtown Manila's transport problems. The University of the East, for instance, lays claim to having the largest enrolment in Asia, with its more than 60,000 students. Near where Recto Avenue becomes Mendiola Street is **San Sebastian Church**, reputedly the only prefabricated steel church in the world. Every single piece of its structure was fabricated in Belgium and shipped here for assembly at the end of the 19th century.

Malacañang Palace

Mendiola Street threads past private colleges to **Malacañang Palace ⓬**, the office-cum-residence of most Philippine presidents and previous rulers. The building now houses the **Malacañang Museum** (open Mon–Fri 9am–4pm by appointment made at least one week in advance only; entrance fee; tel: 02-736 4662; www.op.gov.ph/museum), showcasing memorabilia of past Philippines presidents.

Originally a country estate owned by a Spanish nobleman, Malacañang became the summer residence of Spanish governor-generals in the mid-1800s. Nineteen Spanish executives took turns ruling the country from Malacañang before it was turned over to the first of what would become 14 American governor-generals. Following Independence Day in 1946, nine Filipino chief executives set up shop in the Presidential Palace, the last being Ferdinand Marcos. Corazon Aquino broke with tradition by operating from the adjacent Guest House. Gloria Macapagal-Arroyo became the first president since Marcos to both live and work in the Palace proper. North of Malacañang, at the corner of Lacson (Governor Forbes) and España, is the **University of Santo Tomas (UST)**, founded by Dominicans in 1611 and the oldest university in Asia.   ❑

Jeepneys

Garishly colored jeepneys are as essential and ubiquitous in the Philippines as double-decker buses are in London. The jeepney gets you everywhere you want to go. Though the colors and banners have mellowed somewhat in recent years, public transport by jeepneys continues to be *de rigueur*, as it has for the past half-century.

What began as the sensible recycling of surplus US army jeeps left behind after World War II has grown into an institution of folk and pop art on wheels. No self-respecting jeepney driver would allow his beloved vehicle to crawl naked through the streets of Manila: a full dressing up is of utmost importance. The chrome bodies, either buffed to a shine or painted in vibrant colors, exhibit a wealth of brazen embellishments, from small nickel stallions on the hood-and-chrome embellishments – homage to the horse-drawn, tin crafted *calesas* – to non-functional antennae festooned with plastic streamers. Religious slogans and graffiti decorate the exterior, but, almost surprisingly, jeepneys have yet to become popular as billboards for anything beyond their owners' whimsy. Each one, without fail, lists its destination (and sometimes the route) on the vehicle's front and side. For all intents and purposes, there are no rules dictating where the driver can and cannot stop. Tying up traffic in the middle of the road to pick up passengers is a simple fact of life, except in areas where traffic enforcement is taken seriously.

Depending on the driver, a strand of sweet-smelling *sampaguita* flowers may hang from the rear view mirror, while Snow White and her seven dwarves jangle above the dashboard, where a statue of the Virgin Mary or the Sto. Niño often occupies a place of importance, next to the sign imploring "God Bless our Trip."

The back of the jeepney – almost invariably open-air – extends longer than a normal jeep, with a row of padded seats on each side. Passengers crowd into the tight space, knees knocking, and ready handkerchiefs to shield nose and mouth from the diesel fumes. Outside, the jeepney's sleek rear end offers a glistening series of handrails and supports, for those who prefer to take their chances standing up. Such accoutrements are also necessary when the driver decides not to stop while picking up a passenger, and he must literally jump aboard. For anyone considering a ride, note that jeepneys sometimes depart not when full, but when completely overloaded.

Ever since the supply of surplus army jeeps ran out, the ingenious Filipinos have been building these machines from scratch. Sarao was the leading manufacturer but closed due to competition from other jeep assemblers. The metal body is hammered into shape; workers carefully pad seats with fiber from coconut husks; while others prepare motors. Willy's Jeep in Detroit initially supplied the engines, but after costs rocketed in the 1970s, Sarao had to look elsewhere. Today, second-hand, reconditioned Japanese motors keep jeepneys plying the streets.

Etymologically speaking, *jeepney* combines *jeep* with *jitney* to offer low-cost, high-pollution public transit. ❏

RIGHT: adding an important finishing touch to a colorful jeepney.

MANILA'S ENVIRONS

Map on pages 170–71

The volcanic hinterland of Manila embodies a revolutionary past and teems with natural attractions, from spectacular waterfalls to glorious beaches, its people still practicing ancient crafts

Cavite Province, south of Manila, proved pivotal to the Philippine Revolution of 1896, yielding countless revolutionary heroes devoted to overthrowing three centuries of Spanish rule. Fifty years later, Filipino and American forces on Cavite's Corregidor Island battled valiantly to regain Philippine freedom from the Japanese.

Corregidor Island

That famed sunset over Manila Bay does not always sink into a watery horizon. Rather, it may fall behind faint mountains. These vague, dull-blue contours outline the elongated peninsula of Bataan, an infamous World War II battleground and the last Allied holdout in the Pacific. Off the southern tip is **Corregidor Island ❶**, hallowed ground for veterans.

A small rocky island 48 km (30 miles) west of **Manila ❷**, at the mouth of Manila Bay, Corregidor – "the Rock" – has come a long way from the devastation of World War II. Today, ruined barracks, 100-year-old mortars and deep memories peek out from a now forested island. Corregidor stands as a memorial to peace, valor and international understanding, recalling the drama of World War II in the Pacific, when Filipino and American troops bravely held their ground, even as the US was unable to send help. Two monuments have been erected on the island. Through one, a domed white-marble memorial, the sun shines onto an altar built to honor those killed during the 1942 Japanese invasion. The second, an upward-reaching modern steel sculpture made from melted cannons, represents the flame of freedom.

Corregidor Island is 1 hour from downtown Manila, via jetboat (daily at 8am) from the CCP Complex on Roxas Boulevard. On the island, streetcars ferry visitors on a half-day, guided tour (fee), visiting MacArthur's headquarters in Malinta Tunnel, the mile-long barracks, military structures and the Japanese Garden of Peace. A small museum displays photographs of pre-war Corregidor, plus identification tags and personal effects of those who lost their lives here. Even for children, or those not enamoured by military history, Corregidor Island is worth the visit.

Las Piñas and beyond

South of Manila, visit **San Jose Church** in **Las Piñas** to see the world's only bamboo organ, built in 1821 and refurbished in 1975. Its pipes – 832 bamboo and 122 metal – reverberate each Sunday, and during February's Bamboo Organ Festival.

The crowded towns in northern Cavite – **Zapote** and **Bacoor** – seem an extension of Manila's traffic and chaos, littered by factories, refineries and neon

LEFT: army barrack ruins in Corregidor Island.
BELOW: bamboo organ, San Jose Church in Las Piñas.

Monument to Emilio Aguinaldo at his birthplace in Kawit. Aguinaldo's declaration of Philippines' independence in 1898 – amid war between Spain and the US – was not recognized by the American forces.

BELOW:
Aguinaldo House Museum in Kawit.

lights. Further south, beach resorts in one-time shipbuilding towns – Noveleta, Rosario and Tanza – cater to Manileño weekenders, though their proximity to industry has made their waters less than inviting.

Cavite takes its name from the hook shape of its old population center – *kawit*, Tagalog for hook. At the hook's tip is **Cavite City**, until recently the provincial capital. Here the Spanish outfitted galleons for the Manila–Acapulco run, as well as small boats to fend off the marauding Moros. During a Dutch attack in 1647, a stone fort was damaged: its ruins still stand at Porta Vaga.

In the 1870s, a mutiny by Filipino dock workers gave the Spanish government good excuse to punish the leaders of an increasingly incendiary movement. The ensuing martyrdom of *indio* priests Gornez, Burgos, and Zamora ignited the sparks of revolution. Though the revolution nearly proved successful, the US aborted the foundation of a new republic after winning the 1898 Spanish-American War. Cavite then housed a US colonial naval installation at Sangley Point until the late 1960s, at which time the Philippines Navy and Air Force took over the base.

Kawit

Emilio Aguinaldo, general of Cavite's revolutionary forces and president of the first but short-lived Philippine Republic, was born in **Kawit ❸**. Long after the revolution in Manila had collapsed from disorganization, Aguinaldo planned and implemented his strategy in Kawit, building a solid southern front to resist the Spanish. On June 12, 1898, revolutionaries hoisted the Philippine flag from his house, to a battle hymn that eventually became the national anthem.

Preserved as a shrine to the revolution is the **Aguinaldo Shrine and Museum** (open Tues–Sun 8am–5pm; free), an architectural achievement of late colonial

vintage, with an impressive interpretive display of revolutionary Philippine history. The elaborate house, with its secret escape tunnels, is among the country's finest old Spanish-style homes (*bahay na bato*).

South of Kawit, in General Trias's out-of-the-way Gateway Business Park, stands the outstanding **GBR Museum** (open Wed–Sat 9am–5pm by appointment only; entrance fee), so named for its owner, businessman Geronimo B. de los Reyes. Featured in five galleries are brilliant photographs of an almost unrecognizable Philippines from 1860–1930, archival photos of the Philippine-American War, a collection of rare books and maps, and perhaps the world's finest collection of Chinese imperial yellow Peking glassware.

Traveling southwest along the coast, the old Jesuit town of **Maragondon** offers one of the loveliest churches in the archipelago, with its ornately carved door and rococo interior. Trumpeting angels on the altar and friezes on the pulpit conjure up images of the rattling swords and whizzing bullets of a revolution that overflowed into this church. Andres Bonifacio, head of the revolutionary Katipunan, was imprisoned here for trying to divide and rule the struggle in Cavite, and was later bludgeoned to death in the hills of Maragondon.

Tagaytay Ridge

South of Cavite, toward the Batangas border, is **Tagaytay Ridge**, with magnificent views over Taal volcano and its massive crater lake. Many Mileños escape the heat on weekends by heading to the cooling relaxation of 600-meter (1,970-ft) high **Tagaytay City**, where pineapple, papaya and other tropical fruits abound. There are a number of viewpoint restaurants on Aguinaldo Highway, along the ridge. Further east, the ruins of Marcos country mansion atop the

Map on pages 170–71

Because of their industriousness, the Spaniards called the Chinese seng-li, or sangley – "business" or "trader" in the dialect of the Chinese from Fujian, who originally made up most of the Chinese immigrants. Sangley Point in Cavite was an important Chinese trading port in the 13th century.

LEFT:
Tagatay highlands.
BELOW: horse
riding at Tagatay.

highest mountain in the area is now a public area called **People's Park**, where visitors can enjoy mountain breezes and spectacular views.

South to Batangas

Some of the oldest ancestors of Tagalog culture can be linked to Batangas Province. Archeologists have traced human habitation here, around the southwestern coastline of Balayan Bay, to 250,000 years ago. Years later, fleeing Bornean chieftains came to the southern coast of Luzon, traversing the Pansipit river to settle on the shores of Lake Taal, later controlling much of southern Luzon and Bicol. Archeological finds at graves in Calatagan and Lemery show that the people of this region, called Bombon, conducted a lively trade with Arab, Chinese and Indian merchants over the centuries.

West of Tagatay City (tel: 0917-532 9097) is Sonia's Secret Garden, where you can dine on delicious food amid lush gardens. Call ahead as Sonia does not open for fewer than eight people.

BELOW: Batangas is known for its coffee.

Upon the arrival of *conquistadores* Juan de Salcedo and Martin Goiti in 1570, the Bombon inhabitants were easily subdued. As Jose Rizal pointed out, "The people, accustomed to the yoke, did not defend their chiefs from the invader... The nobles, accustomed to tyrannize by force, had to accept foreign tyranny when it showed itself stronger than their own." Delighted by the rivers and "excellent meadows," the Spanish soon granted tracts of lands (*encomienda*) to individuals and used Catholicism to spread their cause. A century and a half would pass before the locals, annoyed that Augustinians and Jesuits had snatched their land, began taking up arms against the class-conscious Spaniards.

From the 18th century, Batangas enjoyed rapid economic growth, spurred on by the introduction of the coffee bean. Coffee thrived in the rich volcanic soil, fueling the rise of the Taaleño middle class and leading exports during the mid-19th century. However, a coffee blight destroyed plantations in the late 19th century, and the industry has never fully recovered.

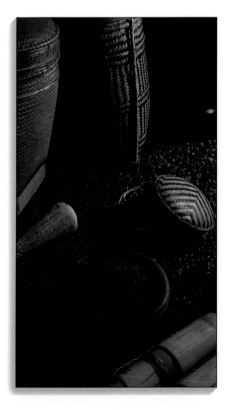

Batangas Province, for visitors, can be divided into two parts – around Lake Taal, and along the irregular coastline. The jagged coast of Batangas has one of the archipelago's most interesting collections of bays, coves and peninsulas. In the northwest, the towns of **Nasugbu**, **Lian** and **Matabungkay** lead to beach strips with a range of beachfront accommodation, from bamboo cottages to upscale resorts.

The **Calatagan Peninsula** in the southwest– once the playground of the wealthy Zobel-Ayala family – offers a relatively unspoiled strip of white sand beach.

Lake Taal and Taal City

Two hours' drive south from Manila is the 300-meter (1,000-ft) high **Taal Volcano ❹**, a crater within a lake. As one of the smallest, most active volcanoes in the world, it smolders and occasionally rumbles, always presenting a dramatic sight. Since its first known eruption in 1572, Taal has erupted over 40 times. A *banca* (pumpboat) can be hired from Talisay to cross the lake and hike up the crater, though it is advisable to take a guide. In 1999, the volcano churned ominously enough for geologists to warn trekkers against climbing it.

Taal City ❺, southwest of Taal lake and along the Pansipit river that flows into Balayan Bay, is one of the most culturally preserved sites of the Spanish colonial era. The **Basilica of St Martin de Tours**, part of the Taal Heritage Village, cannot help but impress: it is one of the largest Catholic churches in Asia. From the belfry, take in the sweeping vista: waving fields of sugar cane, the meanderings of the Pansipit river, and present-day television antennas sprouting like a newly laid bamboo grove on the rooftops of century-old houses. Nearby stands the Shrine of Our Lady of Caysaysay, miraculous for the statue's supposed ability to return to this same spot whenever it is relocated.

Local specialties

A Taal original is the flip-open, butterfly knife (*balisong*) sold at roadsides. Also indigenous are the delicious *tawilis* and *maliputo*, two species of fish found only in Taal lake. Drying in the sun in the public market are frames of bleached *piña* – woven from pineapple fibers – awaiting embroidery. A tradition of the provinces near Laguna de Bay, this detailed needlework distinguishes the *barong Tagalog*, or traditional Filipino man's dress shirt.

Perhaps it was needlework that gave Marcela Agoncillo of Taal a whole page of Philippine history – she sewed the first Filipino flag, which was unfurled from Aguinaldo's Kawit house in 1898. Learn more about this lady at the restored Agoncillo Museum, and take the opportunity of visiting a beautifully restored ancestral house at the **Leon Apacible Historical Landmark** (open daily 8am–noon and 1–5pm; entrance fee) on Taal's Marcela Agoncillo Street.

The small town of **Anilao**, in southern Batangas, is a popular haven for scuba divers. Although the beaches are rocky and not particularly suited to swimming, Anilao offers some of the best macro diving in the Philippines, with close-up glimpses of a variety of tropical fish. Other dive sites, such as Bonito

Map on pages 170–71

TIP

Before climbing any volcano – especially unpredictable Taal and Mayon in the Bicol region – be sure to check conditions with the Philippine Institute of Volcanology and Seismology (tel: 02-426 1468; www.phivocs.dost.gov.ph).

LEFT: fishing at Lake Taal. **BELOW:** embroidering on *piña*, a cloth made from pineapple fiber.

Island, are accessible via **Mabini**. Farther east, off Batangas Bay in the municipality of **Lobo**, isolated white sand beaches can be found. Verde Island, best accessed from Puerto Galera in Mindoro, is another top dive site.

East of Taal lake, **Lipa City** has an interesting collection of old ancestral homes, flower gardens and coffee plantations. In the center of town sits **Casa de Segunda**, a typical Spanish-colonial *bahay na bato*, built in "stone house" style and lovingly restored to its original grandeur.

Laguna Province

Traversing the South Superhighway from Manila, visitors come to the province of **Laguna**, which hugs the southern shores of Laguna de Bay. In Laguna, the 400-year-old marriage between *conquista* and the insular Malay settlements is still tangible in polite forms of address, sweets and neat window flower boxes.

Beyond Santa Rosa, home of the Enchanted Kingdom amusement park, the first town of interest to tourists is **Calamba ❻**, birthplace of Jose Rizal. The old Rizal house on main street is now a national shrine, landscaped with fruit trees from all across Asia. It is a treat to wander this garden, fragrant with giant *mabolo*, *santol* and mango, and then stroll indoors to the high-quality appointments of a home typical of Laguna gentry. Rice harvested from private fields was stored in huge grain baskets, coffee was ground in the kitchen, and reading was done by the light of kerosene lamps.

Just beyond Calamba, Los Baños is home to the **International Rice Research Institute** (IRRI), funded since 1960 by the Rockefeller and Ford foundations and dedicated to developing new varieties of rice to feed a growing world population. The **Riceworld Museum** (open Mon–Fri 8am–5pm; free; tel: 02-844 3351) in the main complex offers an introduction to the history and science of rice cultivation.

On the southern slope of extinct volcano Mt Makiling, beyond Los Baños, lies Hidden Valley Springs, in **Alaminos**. This mountain hideaway is a pleasant private resort – albeit pricey – where several springs are channeled into specially constructed bathing pools. Paths lead through a jungle of fruit trees, giant ferns and wild orchids to the gurgling pools.

The stature of holy mountains Makiling and Banahaw dominates life in Laguna. On the periphery of these two extinct volcanoes, sulfur springs gush forth with a force as strong as the mountain myths and legends that haunt the imagination of the people. **Mt Makiling** is said to be the home of goddess Maria, a beautiful siren and guardian of the forest. To **Mt Banahaw**, her male counterpart, must the stout-of-heart travel to gain strength and wisdom. Nature lovers and birdwatchers alike take to the slopes of Makiling, while in the foothills of Banahaw live spiritual sects and faith healers, practicing all sorts of soothsaying. They claim to draw their insight and power from the towering, mystical mountain, where fairies and nymphs are said to roam.

Eastward stands **San Pablo**, the provincial capital and commercial center given over to the mundane concerns of trade. January is the time to dine here, when an abundance of fish teem near the lakeshores –

The towns surrounding Laguna de Bay are renowned for their sweets, from lengua de gato (melt-in-your-mouth butter shortbread) to the stickier rice concoctions. Indulge while you can!

BELOW: Jose Rizal's house in Calamba.

driven there by the rising sulfuric content of the waters in what are thought to be the craters of extinct volcanoes. From San Pablo, the road leads southward to Quezon and Bicol.

Intriguing cemetery

Past San Pablo's seven lakes, in the east, lies **Nagcarlan**, a gem of history in Laguna province, with its church and fascinating underground cemetery counted as national treasures. Baroque, Moorish and Javanese styles add a mystifying touch to these two structures. Glazed blue ceramic tiles decorate parts of the church and a wall of the cemetery's underground crypt. On the landing leading to the underground tombs – now sealed off – are faded epigraphs in Spanish, too blurred to translate. In 1896, a cemetery crypt provided a clandestine meeting place for the Katipunan, the secret revolutionary society.

Nearby **Liliw** has a remarkable church located right at the end of a road that seems to head straight into Mt Banahaw. This town is known for its high-quality, handmade footwear – though larger, Western sizes are often unavailable.

Out of Liliw, the road runs eastward to **Majayjay**, the oldest settlement in the area. It has a Brigadoon-like quality, laid over a series of small hills with roads twisting and curving to reveal one colonial treasure after another. Majestic Mt Banahaw stands beyond. White-haired grandmothers contemplate travelers from the ground floors of squat stone houses, while children in the plaza stop to stare. As elsewhere in the Philippines, everything converges on the church at the center of town, but there is added drama to Majayjay's elevated structure, which has been reconstructed many times and has walls three layers thick.

The church retains much of Majayjay's troubled history, marked by ongoing

Map on pages 170–71

TIP

Thermal activity beneath Mt Makiling feeds a number of resorts in Pansol, near Calamba, with steaming spring water. Visit them on a weekday to avoid the throng of weekender Manileños.

BELOW: Mt Banahaw is home to many sects and faith healers.

On the southern shores of Laguna de Bay is an old Spanish trading town – Laguna's first capital, simply called Bay. This helps to explain the Spanish name "Laguna de Bay," or, simply, Lake of (the settlement called) Bay.

tension between Franciscan missionaries and the locals forced to labor on its construction for years. The people of Majayjay had voted with their feet, erecting huts outside the town boundaries, only to have them torched by friars in need of labor to support their infrastructure. Not surprisingly, the people of Majayjay had little choice but to participate enthusiastically in the revolution of 1896.

Northeast in **Luisiana**, groves of giant pandanus trees grow thickly in the swampy soil along the road. Once the leaves are dried, they are woven into mats and bags, now the envy of fashion connoisseurs worldwide. Continue past Luisiana's cemetery, north and west through Cavinti to Pagsanjan.

Pagsanjan and points north

Pagsanjan ❼ (pronounced *pag-san-han*) awaits along the Magdapio river, or Pagsanjan river, offering classic whitewater experiences. At **Pagsanjan Falls**, visitors change into swimsuits or shorts and travel upriver in small *banca*. Often the boatman has to push, or lift, the *banca* over shallows or other obstructions. The return journey, however, is thrilling, as the boats negotiate the rapids.

Before coming to the falls, the *banca* slides into a picturesque gorge, glistening with small cascades, vibrant moss and lichen. The walls rise nearly 100 meters (330 ft), the air still and softly humming with forest sounds. Finally, the waterfalls are reached. At the second falls, passengers from the *banca* transfer onto bamboo rafts, guided by long ropes from the shore into the mouth of a cave beyond the falls, drenching the visitor with refreshingly cool water. Francis Ford Coppola filmed this river for parts of his 1979 movie, *Apocalypse Now*. By spending the night in Pagsanjan, visitors can make the most of their trip, waking early to be the first on the river. Weekdays are best, to avoid crowds.

BELOW:
Pagsanjan Falls.

SPLASHING OUT ON PAGSANJAN

Pagsanjan Falls is one of those frustrating places to visit, its spectacular scenery marred by overzealous boatmen and shockingly high, non-negotiable prices.

Visitors should arrange a trip to the falls through one of the hotels in Pagsanjan, where prices are fixed and journeys are guaranteed. The set rate is P580 a person, plus P100 for the mandatory life jacket and seat cushion. The minimum charge, however, is P1,160 per boat, with a maximum of three guests to any one boat.

An increasing number of touts roam the streets outside city limits, stopping private cars and hustling unsuspecting tourists onto overpriced, unregulated boats. Resist these touts at all costs, as they will request additional fees halfway down the river, refusing to budge further.

Be aware that boatmen may play on your good nature and con you into paying for additional items – a cold drink for such hard work, or a barbecued snack somewhere along the way.

The scenery is indeed beautiful, but, if you're not up to the haggling and the hassle, you may prefer to give Pagsanjan a miss. The local government is still working to eradicate these annoying problems that have confronted tourists here for years.

The next destination towards Laguna de Bay is the provincial capital, **Santa Cruz**. Like Pagsanjan, the provincial capital 1688–1858, this old town is laid out in grander colonial style than smaller settlements by the lake, with lovely old Spanish-style houses. Santa Cruz makes *quesong puti*, an excellent white cheese from *carabao* (water buffalo) milk, and has cornered the market in antique Chinese pottery excavated from old graves in the surrounding coconut plantations. Those interested in the more scholarly value of these items can visit a small museum in **Pila**, south of Santa Cruz.

Map on pages 170–71

The road northeast of Pagsanjan heads into the hills to **Lake Caliraya**, a reservoir dug by the Americans in the 1930s. Facilities here are limited, though the lake is a haven for windsurfers escaping Manila for the weekend. The Lagos del Sol Resort has good amenities and a nearby golf course is planned.

Further north, Paete, Pakil and Pangil offer miniature snippets of colonial Spanish style. Approached from the highway, their narrow streets and tiny houses, with carved balusters and scroll-worked eaves, take on an elfin quality. The exemplary churches in these towns are as tiny as they are exquisite, the most outstanding being the Santiago de Apostol Church in **Paete**, dating to 1645. A long woodcarving tradition is evident on its facade, as St James, the town's patron, rides off to battle the Moors, surrounded by a cornucopia of palms and blossoms characterizing Filipino baroque. Likewise, a tradition of papier-mâché (*taka*) flourishes in Paete; wander the narrow streets to see rows of reindeer forms being prepared for export. **Pakil** to the north is noted for its delicate filigree wood shaving art – *pahiyas tambag*. The delicate toothpicks topped by fanned peacock's tails, butterflies or spiraling trees found in Manila's hotels come from Pakil. Ask for Ms Dominga Pasang on Gonzales Street to witness her filigree work.

BELOW: making papier-mâché decorations in Paete.

At the northern boundary of Laguna Province is **Mabitac** in the foothills of the Sierra Madre. Here stands a magnificent 17th-century church built on a hilltop to prevent mountain flood waters pouring in.

Quezon Province

Named after native son and former Commonwealth President Manuel L. Quezon and his First Lady, **Quezon Province** stretches like a narrow belt along the eastern coast of Luzon.

Geography is destiny here; people live concentrated along the western, sheltered side of the Sierra Madre mountains and in secluded inland valleys. The small, relatively flat area to the south has an ample road network, while the mountainous four-fifths of northern Quezon remains practically inaccessible by land. Much of its forested terrain is home to nomadic people and wildlife – and, until tree felling was banned in 1999, also to loggers. East of the Sierra Madre, the flat coastline – in places falling sharply from 30-meter (100-ft) high cliffs – encourages a scattering of isolated villages that live off coastal waters.

Despite this natural beauty, Quezon witnessed bloody encounters between the Japanese and American forces during World War II. And, as if the war was not enough, the province has become a haven for communist guerillas. The history of Quezon is one of bombings and killings, of land problems and milita-

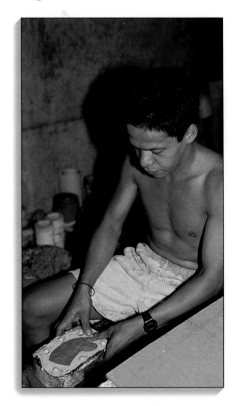

Quezon Province now aims to become the food basket of southern Luzon, pushing agriculture to the forefront and increasing milkfish production.

BELOW: tranquil Villa Escudero.

rization, of the rebellion of its people in an attempt to right a wrong. In 1985, Marxist rebels in their heyday invited a photographer to take shots of a bloody daylight ambush in the municipality of Gumaca. That photo, splashed in newspapers around the world, introduced Quezon to the global community as the impoverished host to a stubborn guerilla force. Although unrest is intermittent, and concentrated mostly in the deep south of the province, travelers should check the conditions with the local tourism authorities before heading in.

Exploring Quezon

The better known, southern portion of Quezon is in many ways a continuation of Laguna Province, though more deeply marked by the coconut industry, from which it once garnered a large percentage of agricultural revenue. The strongly Hispanicized lordly classes of yesteryear – horse-riding gentry resting secure on the income from their coconut plantations – have left tangible relics of their lifestyle throughout the area, beginning in **Tiaong** on Laguna's southwestern boundary. Barely past the art-deco angels gracing the arch of the provincial boundary marker lies **Villa Escudero**, a working coconut plantation of 800 hectares (2,000 acres). Reputed to be one of the best managed in the country, this plantation is a self-contained community of some 300 interrelated families, many of them third-generation laborers. A lush resort on the plantation grounds has an impressive museum of ecclesiastical and other artifacts.

Sariaya, 12 km (8 miles) east, is a prosperous trading town, marketing heirloom pastries and fruit candies. Antique houses loom over narrow streets, the highest overlooking the dome of Sariaya's church, a hush of stained-glass windows displaying an unusually bloody, crucified Christ.

Isolated splendor

Southeast is **Lucena**, provincial capital of Quezon, and, to its north, the quiet, hilly town of Tayabas. Further north is **Lucban**, a provincial border town where isolation has ripened an exotic fruit to fullness. It could have been only yesterday that the Spanish came and left here. The church bells still peal at four in the morning, shaking a sleepy old town from dreams of moss and mountain pools. Mt Banahaw looms like a forbidding parent over this tropical Gothic outpost. Up north, along a rickety road, is coastal **Mauban**. While the scenery is outstanding – even around a power plant – few visitors reach this far.

Come mid-May, Lucban, like Sariaya, springs alive to the festival of *pahiyas*, literally the "enjewelment," when all homes are decorated with the summer's rich harvest plus rainbow-colored sheets of *kiping* – leaf impressions made of rice flour. Giant *carabaos* and scarecrows of papier-mâché dance jubilantly past the courtyard of Lucban's 400-year-old church, all for the feast day of San Isidro Labrador, patron saint of the farmer and worker. If there is only one Philippine festival a tourist is able to attend, this memorable fiesta – magically created by the Franciscans – should rank high on the list.

Quezon's long coastline plunges into rich, relatively untouched fishing waters. These waters, in turn, lap the shores of some of the finest beaches in the country, rimming both mainland and offshore islands. East of Lucena is the coastal town of Padre Burgos, a jumping-off point to **Pagbilao Grande** and **Pagbilao Chico** islands in Tayabas Bay. Connected by a sandy isthmus, these islands are actually a million-year-old coral reef, riddled with hundreds of coves and caves. According to sentimental islanders, this geographical evolution transpired to accommodate the well-loved legend of Bulaklak and Hangin.

Map on pages 170–71

BELOW: in Lucban, *kiping* decorations are strung up to celebrate the harvest festival of Pahiyas.

Legendary lovers

The already-betrothed god Hangin (meaning *wind*) once wandered the earth. One day, his eye hit on Bulaklak (*flower*), a mortal woman of haunting beauty. They fell in love, but torn by divine edict and mortal law, they were left no choice but suicide. Afterwards, their bodies were turned into the islands Pagbilao Grande and Pagbilao Chico, forever linked by a bridge of white sand. Local people say that on this sand each May, Bulaklak and Hangin cause a child to drown, joining them as offspring in the other world. The legend is carried with you as you walk through wildly overgrown patches of tropical forest and crescent-shaped coves of staggering variety. It could well be Hangin himself whistling on Estamper Point, a cave lookout on the top of Pagbilao Chico. From this peak, locals say, hundreds of Japanese sailors, whose ships had been sunk by American submarines, hurled themselves to death, to avoid capture.

North of Pagbilao Grande, via the town of **Pagbilao**, lies 1,000-hectare (2,500-acre) **Quezon National Park**, a short detour from the main highway. Check in with the park warden upon arrival. In two hours, you can hike to the 360-meter (1,180-ft) high peak through moist vegetation for a fine view. Birds twitter among large trees and writhing ancient vines and roots. Doves, orioles, woodpeckers and red-crested royal *kalaw* birds alight here in droves. This is one of the best places to do bird-watching.

Northern Quezon

Northern Quezon, composed of Real, Infanta, Gen. Nakar, and the Polillo islands, is best accessed from Siniloan and Mabitac, on the northeastern tip of Laguna de Bay. The winding road northeast comes first to Real, then Infanta.

Quezon National Park attracts numerous bird watchers. This particular species is the black-billed coleto.

BELOW: the day's catch for this fisherman in Tayabas Bay.

Though this area once saw a phenomenal amount of logging, government bans have at least slowed the felling of trees. But unrest remains rampant.

The terrain is generally rugged to mountainous, with most of the *barangay* (the smallest socio-political unit) situated along the coastline. The climate is classified as having no pronounced dry season with maximum rainfall occurring October–January. The people are fishers, loggers and farmers, and two minority ethnic groups, the Dumagats and Negritos, live nomadically in the hinterlands of Infanta, Gen. Nakar and other forested parts. Commercial set-ups are also present, but are mostly situated in the town centers.

Real ❽, a northern municipality with its coastline facing Lamon Bay, is bounded on the north by Infanta and Gen. Nakar towns, on the south by Mauban and on the west by the Sierra Madre mountain range. The wealth of virgin natural areas in this district provides plenty of outdoor activity for nature lovers. Trekking and mountaineering sites abound. Balgbag Falls in Barangay Mapalad is majestic, with 30 meters (100 ft) of cascading water. Off the coast of Real is Baluti Island, covering an area of about 23 hectares (57 acres). A wide river separates the island from the mainland. Mostly covered with pine trees instead of coconut trees, it has a good swimming beach, with clear water and gray sand.

A smooth drive from Real is **Infanta**, where the long, wide Libjo Beach, a popular picnic area, is located. Further on is the town of **Gen. Nakar**, which has a few fine beaches with beautiful rock formations and a verdant forest. The fine-sanded Pamplona Beach has a cold spring. However, the ultimate nature treat, at least for Northern Quezon, are the **Polillo Islands ❾**. Polillo Coral Reef, measuring 5 km long by 2 km wide (3 miles by 1 mile) is located just before the entrance to the cove of Polillo town and is perfect for snorkeling and diving.

Map on pages 170–71

BELOW: a fiesta celebration in Real.

On the eastern coast is **Burdeos**, home to Bakaw-Bakaw Island, filled with mangrove trees and shrubs, and the Burdeos Coral Area, one of the richest marine areas in Quezon. There are also small caves nearby, and isolated beaches which are good for swimming. Binombombonan Island is an uninhabited white sand island perfect for snorkeling and diving, while Ikulong Island has a pearl farm run by a Japanese businessman. Anilon Island looks like a long stretch of sand bridge during low tide, and the white sand of Minasawa, a game refuge and bird sanctuary, is covered with broken shells.

Balesin Island , south of Polillo, is world class and idyllic, with fine resort facilities and opportunities for snorkeling and scuba diving in one of the richest and least explored fishing grounds in the archipelago.

Rizal Province

Long before the Spanish laid eyes on **Laguna de Bay**, the archipelago's largest lake, the heart-shaped body of water already cradled a thriving community. The waters spread over 90,000 hectares (222,000 acres), with the Sierra Madre range to the east, and Mt Makiling and Mt Banahaw to the south. Farmers grew rice on the surrounding plain, fishermen harvested the abundant waters, and traders shipped goods to lakeside towns aboard gliding *bancas*. Large *cascos*, or barges, roofed with bamboo mats, sailed to Laguna's northwest shores and down Pasig River. This 27-km (16-mile) long waterway, connecting the lake to Manila Bay, flowed heavy with goods for sale to the Taga-Ilog people in old Maynilad.

In 1901, two years after Spain ceded the Philippines to America, Rizal Province was created from 19 towns belonging to the old Spanish province of Manila (excluding the city proper, but including Makati), and 14 towns of

Some historians contend that the US named Rizal Province after Jose Rizal in a canny public relations move – soothing inflamed local sentiment about the aborted 1890s revolution with a bow to the national hero, and discouraging future dissent.

BELOW: prawn fishing at Laguna de Bay.

the former political and military district of Morong, northwest of the lake.

Three routes lead from Manila to the Rizal countryside. The northern road runs from Caloocan to Marikina; the middle route runs from EDSA to Pasig; and the southern road passes Parañaque. The road between Marikina and Pasig forks 20 km (12 miles) from Manila. To the east lie **Cainta** and **Taytay**, the first towns that the Spanish subjugated and, more recently, the first to succumb to creeping industrialization. In Cainta, many inhabitants are said to be descendants of British soldiers who invaded the lakeshore in 1762. Traditionally, these people are called *sepoy*, for their bronze-colored skin.

The **Avilon Zoo** (open daily 8am–5pm; entrance fee; tel: 02-941 8393; avilon zoo.com.ph) in Rodriguez (Montalban) is one of the newest and most acclaimed zoos in the country. About an hour northeast of Quezon City, it has over 500 species of animals on display, half of which are indigenous to the Philippines.

Just beyond Taytay lies hilly **Antipolo** ⓫, celebrated in song and legend as the home of the icon of Our Lady of Peace and Good Voyage (*Nuestra Señora de la Paz y Buen Viaje*). This dark icon, carved by a Mexican craftsman, first gained stature by safely crossing a turbulent Pacific Ocean in 1626. Ever since, Antipolo has enjoyed many pilgrimages, as no trips should be taken without a visit first to Nuestra Señora. She is enshrined atop a hill, surrounded by a bedlam of carnival crowds and peddlers of candles, medallions and *sampaguita* flowers. For a view of the Manila skyline and a brilliant sunset, follow the Sumulong Highway to the crest of the mountain in Antipolo.

Artists' Village

From Cainta, the road leads southeast to **Angono**, home of the **Angono Artists' Village**, one of the top art centers in the Philippines. In the early 1990s, ancient petroglyphs dating back 5,000 years were discovered on a cave wall just outside town. In Doña Justa Village, visit the **Nemiranda Arthouse** (entrance fee; tel: 02-651 3867; www.nemiranda.com), featuring the whimsical sculptures and naked female forms favored by one of the top contemporary artists in the country. Down the street, the Balaw-Balaw Restaurant offers an eclectic collection of culinary treats such as monitor lizard and wild boar in addition to an art gallery that includes the town's papier-mâché *gigantes* used in festivals. Visit on Friday to see painter/owner Perdigon Vocalan and his students in full swing. The **Blanco Family Museum** (open daily 9–11am and 1–5pm; entrance fee), started in the mid-1960s, features hundreds of works by the family's nine artists.

Past Angono, along the lakeshore, sits the fishing town of **Cardona**, the balconies of its houses hanging over the lapping waters of the lake, where a milkfish industry prospers. Just beyond Cardona lies the old Spanish center of **Morong**. The dome and belfry of its church rise over a sea of green fields. The exquisitely carved facade is one of the finest examples of tropical baroque architecture in the Philippines. Further along the lakeshore lies **Tanay** and its lovely waterfalls. From Tanay, through Pililla and on into Laguna Province runs a 20-km (13-mile) stretch of winding mountain road. Laguna de Bay gleams murky blue below. ❏

Map on pages 170–71

BELOW: Jose Blanco, owner of the Blanco Family Museum, teaches his son to paint.

Luzon

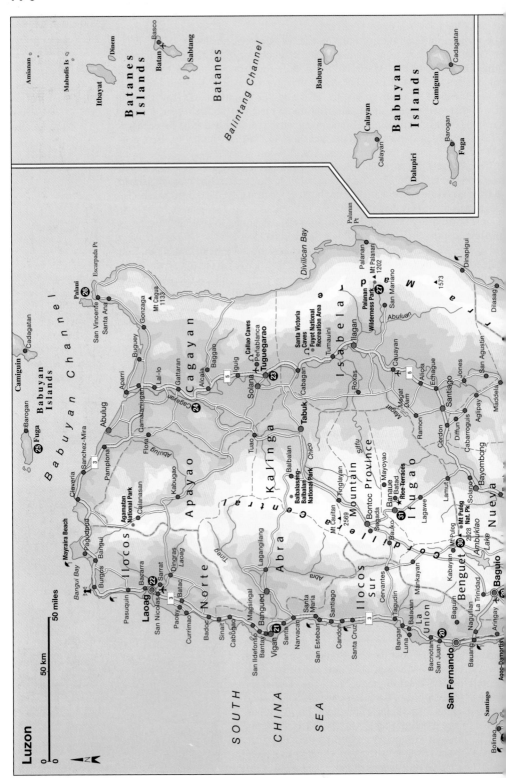

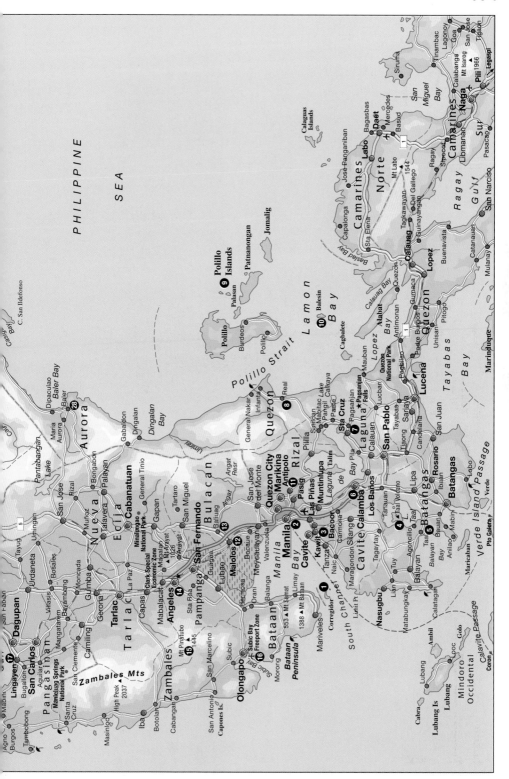

THE CENTRAL PLAINS

Map
on pages
170-71

The sheltered agricultural region north of Manila benefits from plentiful rivers and rich volcanic soil, its past marked not only by political achievement but also by the miseries of war

When Filipinos speak of Tagalog culture, they are referring to the culture that sprang forth on the central plains of Luzon: a culture nurtured in rich alluvial soil and suckled by plentiful rivers and monsoon rains. North from the urban sprawl of Metro Manila, the scene is nothing but rice fields – muddy during the dry season, and becoming green during the rainy season, when two crops are planted and harvested. Farther north, the rice gives way to vast fields of sugar cane, which in turn give way to corn.

The region of the Central Plains covers the largest contiguous lowlands in the Philippines. To the east, the Sierra Madre mountain range shelters it from fierce ocean typhoons whipping off the Philippine Sea. The Zambales range, to the west, cuts it off from the South China Sea, with the rugged Cordillera mountain range to the north. These mountain ranges serve as spawning grounds for the rivers that water the fertile soil of the Central Plains.

Officially, Bulacan, Pampanga, Tarlac, Nueva Ecija, Bataan and Zambales provinces make up the Central Plains of Luzon, though the latter two are undeniably mountainous. The main artery through this sea of rice, sugar and corn is the Pan-Philippine Friendship Highway. The tollway portion, about 85 km (50 miles) from Manila to Mabalacat in northern Pampanga, is known as the North Expressway, or National Highway.

LEFT: separating rice grains from the lighter chaff.
BELOW: planting rice seedlings.

Bulacan

Metro Manila gives way to **Bulacan Province** in a continuous industrial sprawl. The first Bulacan town of **Valenzuela**, along the National Highway, is noted for its factories and the San Miguel Brewery.

Fishing folk settled in Bulacan sometime before the 1st century. They initially lived along the shore of Manila Bay, but soon discovered that the interior's rich soil was well drained by rivers and streams. They quickly pushed inland, turning to farming.

The Bulacanos sided with their long-time trading partners in Maynilad against the invading Spanish, but were soundly defeated at the Battle of Bangkusay Channel in 1570. For the next three centuries, Bulacanos lived under Spanish rule, but not without wit.

Bulacan writers developed a unique Spanish-Tagalog jargon that allowed them to flatter the Spanish on one hand, while coyly criticizing them on the other. Francisco "Balagtas" Baltazar was the foremost Bulacan wit in the late 1700s. Like other aspiring poets, Balagtas labored under strict friar supervision of his Spanish meter and metaphor, but he slipped Tagalog into his works to protest against Spanish tyranny. The friars thought that his celebrated poem *Florante at Laura* was about dueling Christians and Moors, but it really criticized Spanish forced labor, exorbitant taxes

Bulacan derives its name from the kapuk tree – locally called bulak – which once grew profusely in the area, producing vast amounts of tradable kapok, or Java cotton.

and the capriciousness of the friars. In the 1890s, Marcelo H. del Pilar of Bulacan went a step further, lampooning with a cartoon pen the religious pamphlets regularly churned out by the friars. His sharply tuned epigrams soon became rallying cries for revolution throughout the islands.

Off the North Expressway, on the old highway, sit **Meycauayan**, famed for its leather crafts, and **Marilao**, noted for its pig farms and poultry production. The tanning carabao hides and manure exacerbate the smell, so hold your nose.

If it is the first Sunday in July, pull off the expressway into **Bocaue**. The river festival here honors the 300-year-old Holy Cross of Wawa, said to have once saved an old woman from drowning. However, the crucifix lapsed its protective duties in 1993, when 269 people died in a festival tragedy involving an overloaded boat ferrying residents and their patron saint down the river. The festival resumed only in 1999, after local fishermen urged officials to revive the celebrations. Without it, they claimed, their nets were nearly empty.

Asia's first democracy

Up the road from Bocaue, **Balagtas** (Bigaa) has a monument to the father of Tagalog poetry, Francisco Baltazar. One of the oldest known tiled-roof houses in Bulacan also sits here, *Bahay na Tisa*, built in 1849. Further on is **Malolos ⑫**, the provincial capital, the leading historical site in the province. Here, on September 15, 1898, Emilio Aguinaldo convened the first Filipino legislative assembly, the Malolos Congress, which framed the Malolos Constitution. This was the first democratic constitution ever undertaken by a former colonial subject, and unique for Asia in splitting the roles of church and state. The Malolos Congress met in **Barasoain Church**, where former president Joseph Estrada took

BELOW: rice winnowing.

his oath of office in 1998. The **Barasoain Museum** (open Mon–Fri 8am–3.30pm; free) stands on church grounds.

The revolutionary delegates' printing press stands along architecturally significant Parancillo Street, inside **Museo ng Casa Real** (open daily 8am–noon and 1–5pm; free), the historic town hall dating back to 1580, though the present structure dates from 1980. Around the corner is the private, ancestral Bautista House, with sculptures of Greek maidens on its facade.

Blessed water buffalo

On May 15, the town of **Pulilan**, northeast of Malolos, beyond Plaridel, celebrates the Carabao Festival. Like all fiestas in the region at this time of year, Pulilan's is dedicated to San Isidro Labrador, patron saint of farmers. Uniquely, though, this one stars the *carabao*, or water buffalo. Thousands of *carabao*, adorned with flowers, parade to church where they kneel to be blessed.

Northeast is **Baliuag** (or Baliwag) **⑬**, a town once famous for its *buntal* (a type of reed) hats and furniture inlaid with *carabao* bone. The **Baliuag Museum** (open Mon–Fri 8am–5pm; free), opened in 1998, is something of a disappointment. The beautiful 110-year-old Castilian house, once the Municipal Hall, offers little by way of interpretive history. More interesting is **San Agustin Church**, a faithfully restored stone and brick structure, with a tall bell tower.

Thirty km (20 miles) north, **Madlum** and **Aguinaldo caves**, plus a mountain redoubt, Biak-na-Bato, served as hideouts for revolutionaries in the 1890s. The nearby resort of **Sibul** is famed for the medicinal effects of its waters. In the eastern portion of Bulacan stands the **Angat Reservoir**, providing approximately 80 percent of the water supply for Metropolitan Manila.

Map on pages 170–71

Rice harvest dance in Luzon's Central Plains gives thanks to yet another fruitful year.

BELOW: merry-making at Pulilan's Carabao Festival.

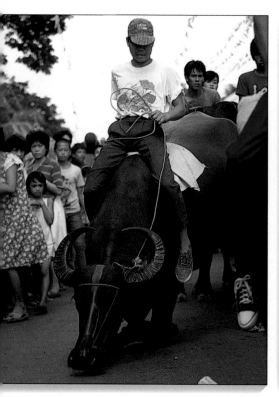

Pampanga

One of the best ways to explore the stark moon-like volcanic terrain of Mt Pinatubo in Pampanga is by an ultralight.

Crossing from Bulacan into **Pampanga Province**, one cannot help but notice the increasing prevalence of *lahar* (volcanic mud) – an ashen reminder of Mt Pinatubo's forceful eruption in 1991. In Pampanga's low-lying areas, residents wage a constant battle against mudflows during the rainy season, when floods carry *lahar* down the mountains at phenomenal speeds, taking lives and threatening property. Even the **FVR Megadike** – named for former president Fidel V. Ramos – faces continual reconstruction in its efforts to contain *lahar* flows.

Culturally, Pampanga is a world apart from the other provinces of the Central Plains. The local inhabitants, called Kapampangans, are not Tagalog like their neighbors. The first Pampanga settlers arrived in Manila Bay from Sumatra, Indonesia, around 1,700 years ago. Encountering an established population along the bay's shoreline, the Sumatrans moved up the Rio Grande de Pampanga and Rio Chico rivers to the vast open plains. Soon, they had established large farming communities along the riverbanks, becoming known as the Dwellers of the River Banks, or *Taga-Pampang*. Spanish records attest to the tight community which met them with curiosity and great intelligence. Spanish firepower impressed the Kapampangan leaders, who, in exchange for privileges, chose to support the new leaders against the invading Chinese, Moros, Dutch and British.

By the 18th century, a large *mestizo* Chinese community was well entrenched in Pampanga, descended from the Chinese who had fled the 17th-century massacres in Manila. The Chinese gradually took over large tracts of sugar cane and rice lands from the Kapampangan elite, growing their wealth into the 18th century as Manila opened up to international trade.

Driving along the North Expressway, the silver dome of **Apalit Church** is

visible to the west. Pampanga's capital lies 66 km (40 miles) north of Manila in **San Fernando**, noted in history as once being the country's capital. Today, it is largely a commercial town, and one of three places where Chinese settled in large numbers. It is best visited during Christmas for the Lantern Festival.

Southwest of San Fernando is **Bacolor**, temporary capital of the Philippines after the 1762 British invasion and devastated by Pinatubo's eruption. Climb the Church of St William's belfry – half buried by *lahar* – for a view of the ashen landscape. Along the Megadike is **Betis** and the beautiful interior of the Church of St James, reflecting the local Kapampangan woodcarving tradition. It is sometimes called the "Sistine Chapel of the Philippines" for its ceiling murals.

Fifteen km (9 miles) northeast of San Fernando are Candaba and mountainous Arayat. **Candaba's swamps** are noted for their scenic beauty and the ducks from China that winter here. The 1,100-meter (3,500-ft) **Mt Arayat** in Barrio Bano, 15 minutes from Angeles City, is 2 km (1½ miles) from **Arayat** proper. The national park offers swimming holes and trekking and cycling trails.

Near the end of the Northern Expressway are Angeles City and Clark Field. **Angeles City** 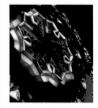 is home to a large nightlife district along Fields Avenue. The area is also filled with good restaurants, cheap motorcycle rentals, and a host of other attractions for those not interested in the clubs. The **Angeles City Flying Club** (tel: 045-865 1356; www.angelesflying.com), for example, offers ultralight flights around the Mt Arayat and Clark areas. Its private airstrip and 8½-hectare (21-acre) facility at Magalang are about half an hour away from Angeles City.

Clark Field, a major US military air base until its devastation by Mount Pinatubo in 1991, has been transformed into the **Clark Special Economic Zone**. It is home to resorts and golf courses, a casino and giant duty-free stores that are more like malls and sell everything from imported US grocery items to sporting goods. The **Clark International Airport**, also known as **Diosdado Macapagal International Airport**, is located here.

Although 1,445-meter (4,740-ft) **Mt Pinatubo** 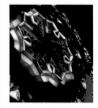 stands on the eastern edge of Zambales Province, many treks and tours to the volcano originate in Angeles. Visitors can hike through the *lahar* areas or to the crater with a guide during the dry season, or fly over the crater on clear days with Omni Aviation. Because of the unpredictability of flash floods and *lahar* flows, the military enforces a 16-km (10-mile) off-limits area around Pinatubo during the wet season, which is from July–October. Check with the local tourism office (DOT Region III; tel: 045-961 2665/2612) before departing.

The Christmas Lanterns of San Fernando go on parade on December 22. Spectacularly lit, some of these span 3 metres (10 ft) in diameter.

BELOW: a casino in Angeles City.

Tarlac Province

The Northern Expressway ends in Pampanga, but the National Highway continues on through **Tarlac**. A latecomer to the central plains, Tarlac was carved from Pampanga and Pangasinan in 1873, its population being a cross-section of Ilocanos, Pampangos, Pangasinenes and Tagalogs. Although it is the region's major sugar-producing area, the province is best known for the infamous World War II Bataan Death March, which claimed the lives of thousands of Allied prisoners of war.

Near **Capas** lies San Miguel, with Luisita Mall – a development by the family of Corazon Aquino. Here

is the statue of Ninoy Aquino, staggering on the airplane ladder (where he was shot) that used to be on Ayala Avenue in Makati.

To the east of Tarlac, **Nueva Ecija** is the largest Central Plains province, sheltered by mountains to the north and east. Farmers migrated here from Bulacan when farmland grew scarce in the south. More than 60 percent of the population is Tagalog, the rest is descended from Ilocano migrants.

Four rivers irrigate the rich agricultural lands of Nueva Ecija, which is second to none in the region for rice production. As a tourist destination, it has little to offer except **Minalungao National Park** in General Tinio, overlooking the narrow, penetrating Penaranda river, lined with sheer limestone cliffs, and offering dense forests and unexplored caves for the adventurer.

The average rice-farming family of four produces some 100 bags of rice. After paying fertilizer and irrigation costs, rent and taxes, the family is lucky to realize US$1,000 for one season's efforts.

BELOW: farmhouse in Nueva Ecija.

Bataan and Coastal Zambales

The laying of wreaths takes place year-round at **Mt Samat** on the Bataan Peninsula, site of a fierce battle in 1942 before Filipino-American forces eventually surrendered to the Japanese. Near the summit is a giant cross and the memorial Shrine of Valor. Once a quiet fishing port on the peninsula's southern tip, **Mariveles** has slowly become industrialized. Several beach resorts are located between Orani and Mariveles, but the ones along Bataan's west coast are far better.

North of Bataan lies **Zambales Province**, noted for its rugged mountain range and picturesque coastline. Just north of **Olongapo City**, on the coastal road, is **Barrio Barretto**, where many of the retired US Navy veterans who once were stationed at Subic now run an eclectic batch of restaurants and seaside bars. Further north, along the coast to Alaminos, Pangasinan, is one of the most relaxing, scenic routes in the country, over fine roads with little traffic.

DEATH MARCH UNDER THE SUN

On the peninsula of Bataan, zero-point kilometer markers are found in the towns of Mariveles and Bagac, the starting points of the dreadful Death March in World War II.

In 1942, more than 75,000 Filipino and American prisoners – already weakened from lack of food and water – were forced to hike 100 km (60 miles) up the peninsula under relentlessly miserable conditions to Japanese concentration camps in Tarlac.

The punishing march took a heavier toll among the Allied prisoners than the actual fighting itself. One tenth of the marchers perished along the road, suffering beneath the blistering April sun. Their route is now marked along Bataan's eastern coast.

Three km (2 miles) before Capas, near the southern border of Tarlac province, there stands a monument to the thousands of Filipino and American soldiers who died during the march.

A distance of 12 km (7½ miles) west of Capas is Camp O'Donnell, the concentration camp that was the ultimate destination of the forced marchers, and which housed those who remarkably somehow managed to survive this horrific ordeal.

Together with Bataan, Zambales was among the first provinces in Luzon to be brought under Spanish rule, when Juan de Salcedo plundered the region's western coast in 1572. He encountered a fierce and proud mountain people, the Zambal, who gave him such trouble that he mounted a punitive expedition to eradicate them. Today, Tagalogs have resettled southern Zambales, with Ilocanos in the central region. The indigenous Zambals have been pushed north, near Pangasinan, where in the mountain areas there were once government reservations for Aeta Negritos. Owing to the destruction of Mt Pinatubo, however, many of the Aetas have been forced to relocate elsewhere.

Subic Bay

Next to Olongapo sits the **Subic Bay Freeport Zone** ⑯, a former US Navy base that has been transformed into one of the country's most successful industrial and tourism centers. International charter flights connect Subic to various cities, bringing in foreign tourists who mingle comfortably with the car loads of people from Manila who visit on the weekends. The freeport offers jungle tours, secure beaches, a casino, duty-free shopping and the **Ocean Adventure** marine theme park (open daily 9am–6pm; entrance fee; tel: 047-252 9000; www.ocean adventure.com.ph) offers interactions with three types of dolphins, false killer whales and sea lions. Drive around the Binictican housing area to see a replica of a suburban American neighborhood built by the US Navy to house the families of sailors. It is now home to many expatriate investors in the freeport.

Driving west to San Marcelino and San Antonio, visitors may stop at Pundaquit, a jump-off point for tiny Capones Island. Northwards, beach resorts dot the coastline, although the beaches are better further on in southern Pangasinan. ❑

Magsaysay Avenue, the road into Olongapo City from the Subic freeport, was lined with nightclubs during the days of the US Navy. Today, it is home to restaurants, money-changers and interesting little shops selling navy mementos.

BELOW: canopy walk, Subic Bay rainforest.

Map on pages 170–71

ILOCOS REGION

A wild, rugged coastline offering diving, surfing and superlative seafood vies for attention with the Spanish colonial treasures of Vigan city in the part of the Philippines Marcos called home

Map on pages 170–71

There is a rugged symmetry to Ilocos that sets it and its people apart from others in the Philippines. Perched on a narrow ledge along the rugged northwestern coast of Luzon, it is a wild place, but with many charms. Here the coast rises from the South China Sea to rocky bluffs and rolling sand dunes, with a narrow strip of arable land tucked into the Cordillera Mountains. Here lie the Ilocano provinces of Pangasinan, La Union, Ilocos Sur (South) and Ilocos Norte (North) – a region once renowned for its gold deposits.

Sometime after the 1st century, waves of migration swelled from Borneo to the northern Philippine coast. The seafarers flooded the coves (*looc*) along the jagged coast, around which they built their communities (*ylocos*). With superior numbers and metal weapons, the immigrants soon pushed local tribes, such as the Tingguian (Itneg) headhunters, high into the bordering mountains.

Exploring Pangasinan

Three rivers flow west from the Cordillera, bringing life-giving waters to the rice, tobacco and sugar cane fields of **Pangasinan** province, second only to Nueva Ecija as the country's most prolific rice-growing area. Along the western shoreline of the Lingayen Gulf, from Dagupan to Bolinao, fishing is a way of life, with Pangasinan *bangus* (milkfish) famous throughout the country. In summer, locals protect the *bangus*, which come ashore to lay eggs. It was along this coast, thousands of years ago, that the first Pangasinan settlements developed. Their main industry, the extraction of salt from sea water by solar evaporation, provided the province's name: *asin* is the local word for salt, and *pang-asin-an* means "where salt is made."

Pangasinan's Lingayen Gulf has stood as a regional trading center since earliest times. Tattooed Zambals and mountain Igorots came to barter gold nuggets for pigs, *carabao* (water buffalo) and rice, with Ilocanos gradually descending from the northern coast to trade, and finally settle, in Pangasinan. Later, the Chinese and Japanese arrived, exchanging silk, metals, ceramics and mirrors for local indigo, fibers, sugar cane, beeswax, deerskin and civet musk.

In the late 16th century, the Chinese corsair Limahong made his way to Pangasinan, followed shortly by the Spanish conquistadors. Fighting side-by-side against the Chinese did little to improve relations between the Pangasinans and Spaniards, the former retreating to the mountains, escaping the clenched fist of Spanish rule. The Spaniards mounted expeditions against the escaped heathens, with gold-hungry soldiers raping and looting as they progressed.

The main route through Pangasinan is the National Highway, running from Tarlac to Sison, near the La

LEFT: goofing around at a Pangasinan beach. **BELOW:** fishing nets put out to dry at Bolinao.

Union border. A second route, the Romulo Highway, runs from Tarlac northwest past Lingayen to Alaminos. The least traveled route, along the Zambales coast, is one of the loveliest highways in the country.

On the highways

The National Highway passes through **Urdaneta City**, which has a strip of fast food eateries and is known for producing much of the nation's dried fish. *Bagoong* is also sold here – the muddy-colored, pungent Pinoy version of caviar that lends its flavor to most Ilocano dishes. Beyond Urdaneta, a turn-off leads 12 km (7½ miles) toward the coast, to the Shrine of Our Lady of Manaoag, where the devout have seen the Virgin Mary. Faith healing, too, is alive and kicking.

The Romulo Highway enters Pangasinan just after the Tarlac town of **San Clemente**, and passes on to Mangatarem. Near Mangatarem is the **Manleluag Springs National Park**, with a hot spring nestled in the foothills of the Zambales Mountains. The next two towns, Aguilar and Bugallon, paint a picture of old Pangasinan with their churches. The facade of Aguilar Church is pink from the ancient Chinese redbrick showing through the modern whitewash.

The right fork in Bugallon leads to **Lingayen** ⓱, the sprawling old capital by the sea with two distinct sections, architecturally and culturally different from each other. The older section, built inland by the Spanish in their particular style, has all buildings facing the town plaza. Market day is a portrait in small-town trade, with some hard bargaining among the vendors under their large *buri* fans, which are used as sun screens. The Americans built the newer part of Lingayen by the sea, a choice of obvious intelligence. Today, although this section is a bit down-at-the-heel, its spread of wide-crowned flame trees can be a

BELOW: an oversized *buri* fan.
RIGHT: fish market in Lingayen.

startling first sight. The provincial capital building is modeled on early American colonial architecture, with marble columns and a golden eagle.

Between Lingayen and **Dagupan** lie many World War II beaches with memorials recording where the Japanese landed in December 1941, and where Americans came ashore in January 1945. From Lingayen, a 40-km (25-mile) coast road leads west to **Alaminos**.

Hundred Islands

At Alaminos, signs lead to Lucap, where numerous *banca* wait at the pier to ferry travelers to the **Hundred Islands National Recreation Area ⓲** (actually 124 volcanic islands). **Quezon Island**, the largest, has a nice beach, pavilions, toilets and viewing decks, while Children's Island is for campers. **Governor's Island** is more secluded, particularly the small beach at the back. With a little urging, boat operators also offer tours of the lesser known islands like the one named after former first lady Imelda Marcos. There are no diving facilities on the islands, and some underwater explorers bring their own equipment.

Few venture beyond Alaminos to **Bolinao ⓳**, just an hour away. It is regrettable, because the old town and its *barangay* and islands are where Pangasinan's heritage maintains its ancient patterns. Scenic Cape Bolinao is an emerging beach area with a string of comfortable resorts along the coast. The **Bolinao Museum** (open Mon–Sat 9am–4.30pm; donation) stands as the cultural link, displaying some important archaeological finds from backyards and beaches, including gold bracelets from under coconut trees and ceramic shards washed up by floods. Even as a lack of funds keeps excavations to a minimum, pot-hunters have turned up Tang, Song and Ming porcelain, as well as skeletal remains

Map on pages 170–71

TIP

If visiting one of the isolated beaches in the Hundred Islands, be sure to pack lunch. Bring plenty of drinking water (it is very hot) and shoes or slippers to wear in the water to avoid getting cut by the sharp coral.

BELOW:

one of 124 islands in the Hundred Islands National Recreation Area.

adorned with gold earrings and necklaces. All of these are considered significant links in 7th–15th-century Philippine history – though many of the finds have ended up in private collections, or have been spirited out of the country.

One Bolinao treasure that has not lent itself to cultural piracy is the **Church of St James**, in the center of town. Built in 1609 by the Augustine Recollects, it stands in old stone grandeur. The niches on both sides of the facade still have ancient wooden santos, aged by wind and sun, their features blurred by time. Generations of Bolinao have lived unchanged lifestyles in this quiet spot, still speaking a dialect distinct from their Pangasinan neighbors.

To the port of Bolinao, and the surrounding islands of Silaqui, Santiago and Dewey, have come Chinese corsairs, English and Dutch freebooters and Moro pirates. **Santiago Island** has been home to more than its share of fugitives, many of them escaped slaves. Today, Santiago is a haven for scuba divers and features the spectacular, coral-laden Fourteen-Mile Reef.

Along the South China Sea coast to the south are other interesting spots. Dendro Beach is a golden-sand beach near the Piedra Point lighthouse. In Agno, Umbrella Rocks dot the mouth of the Balincaguing river, looking more like toadstools than umbrellas. Farther south, **Tambobong**'s White Beach is accessible through Burgos. In the center of the Cape Bolinao peninsula, **Bani** and **Mabini**, offer excellent cave exploring.

La Union Province

Just north of Pangasinan is La Union, carved from Pangasinan, Ilocos Sur and the Cordilleras in 1854. After World War II, La Union became administrative center of the Ilocos region, with San Fernando as the capital, located 270 km (170 miles)

Map
on pages
170–71

from Manila – a four-hour drive. If traveling on a Partas or Maria de Leon bus, be sure to request San Fernando, La Union, not San Fernando, Pampanga.

As you enter La Union, the sea begins to glint behind the palms, where creamy sand beaches await. **Rosario** boasts roadside stalls selling dried fish 24 hours a day, as night travel is frequent here. **Santo Tomas**, the first coastal town in La Union, has the freshest, cheapest oysters in the country. Wood carving trade also thrives along the highway. The Agoo–Damortis National Seashore Park sits on a hooking point in Lingayen Gulf, near **Agoo**. The Shrine of Our Lady of Charity in the baroque-styled Agoo Basilica attracts visitors on Good Friday, when patron saints are paraded through the city's streets. Opposite, the **Museo de Iloko** (open Mon–Fri 9am–4.30pm; donation), in the old Presidencia of Agoo, houses artifacts of Ilocos culture.

Further north, **Bauang Beach**, with fine grayish sand, is one long strip of resorts. Water sports, mountain-biking, cultural events and a water parade cap the Rambak Festival here on Easter Sunday. Along the road, stalls sell sweet green grapes. Just inland is **Naguilian**, the *basi*-making capital of the Ilocos region.

Although La Union's capital at **San Fernando** produces loud bursts of sound and an array of colors on market day, the region is better explored from one of the nearby resorts. All the same, an impressive dragon-encrusted Chinese temple called Macho overlooks San Fernando. In the second week of September, the local Filipino-Chinese community travels south to Taal, in Batangas, to fetch the statue of the Virgin of Caysaysay to celebrate her feast day.

Basi, the local Ilocano wine, is a fermented sugar-cane concoction colored with duhat bark. It is quite good, sometimes tasting like port. But the taste differs from maker to maker, so sample first.

Seafood and surf

The **La Union Botanical Gardens** lie 8 km (5 miles) east of San Fernando, and the region's best medical facility, Lorma Hospital, is just north of town. Out on the nearby beach are quieter cottages and small resorts. While here, try the fresh seafood, including a dish known as Jumping Salad – chucks of raw fish cured in a light vinegar, spiced with garlic and chilies.

Six km (4 miles) north of San Fernando, along Monaliza Beach in **San Juan ⑳**, runs the best surf on the Ilocos coast. Beginners can try the sandy beach break fronting La Union Surf Resort, while the more experienced can handle the rockier point in front of Monaliza. Typhoon swells bring the waves in as early as July, but the best season is November–February, when competitions are held. Beyond surfing, San Juan is a pottery-making town, with a century-old church and an even older Moro watchtower.

In **Bacnotan**, watch local silk production at the Don Mariano Marcos Memorial State University. In the mountains to the east, around **Bagulin**, trails along the Bagulin-Naguilian river offer limited trekking, although hiking is better in the Cordillera Mountains.

Balaoan, along the National Highway, features a sprawling treehouse that can be seen from the main road. The church of St Catherine, in **Luna**, houses an image of Our Lady of Namacpacan, patroness of Ilocano travelers, while **Bangar**, just before the Ilocos Sur border, is a known center for making native *bolo* knives and the labor-intensive weaving of wide blankets.

BELOW:
beachside vendor
at Bauang Beach.

*Woodcarver at work
in Vigan, Ilocos
Sur Province.*

Ilocos Sur Province

The province of **Ilocos Sur** twists along the coast as the narrowest Ilocano province, with the Cordilleras nearly reaching the water's edge in some places. The mountains are almost bare of timber and the soil is sandy; principal crops are tobacco, rice and corn. To augment the deficiencies of the soil, most Ilocanos have turned to trade and handicrafts. Each town in the region seems to have its own specialty. Towns along the coast extract salt from seawater. In San Esteban, locals quarry rock to make mortars and grindstones. San Vicente, Vigan and San Ildefonso specialize in woodcarving, importing raw materials from the mountain provinces. Skilled silversmiths work in Bantay. Other towns make saddles, harness, slippers, mats, brooms and hats.

The first town in Ilocos Sur, along the National Highway, is **Tagudin**, where a functioning sundial built by the Spanish in 1848 sits in front of the Municipal Hall. Farther north in Santa Lucia, an 18th-century "miraculous" statue of the Dark Virgin of Santa Lucia graces the church. **Candon** has a beach complex with a huge swimming pool, and a thriving nightlife. Just beyond Candon – and totally unrelated to the nightlife – roadside stalls sell *itak*, the local *bolo* knife.

Santiago has a short stretch of golden sand, while the next town, **San Esteban**, has rocky Apatot Beach and a Spanish stone tower built to keep watch for marauding Moro pirates. Now a national landmark, a centuries-old church that served as a fortress during the 1986 revolution stands in **Santa Maria**. Near Santa Maria is **Pinsal Falls**, a setting for many films, and home of the legendary footprints of the Ilocano giant, Angalo. A road from **Narvacan** leads to Abra Province, an easier route than the road from the Cordillera.

On entering **Santa**, a small picturesque church with a pure-white facade and

BELOW:
Bantay's Santa
Maria Church.

slight greenish tint stands by the sea. *Carabaos* (water buffaloes) wander on the beach, and fishermen drag their nets in waist-deep water by the shoreline. Farther north, Bantay's elevated **Santa Maria Church**, one of four baroque churches in the country designated as UNESCO World Heritage Sites, offers a good view of the area. The nearby belltower was built to call the faithful to prayer and to serve as a lookout for Moro pirates.

Maps:
Area 170
City 188

Historic Vigan

Juan de Salcedo entered Vigan, Ilocos Sur, in the late 16th century, convincing the Ilocanos that a Spanish garrison might be useful against the headhunting neighbors they had earlier displaced. Besides, the Spanish crown had awarded him the entire Ilocos region as his *encomienda*, or fiefdom. Before long, the Spanish introduced corn, cocoa, tobacco and Christianity, building churches, convents, fortifications, schools and missions. A Spanish friar from the Augustinian order was appointed as the agricultural officer, financial adviser, teacher and architect. However, the Ilocanos remained rebellious.

Compulsory native labor and hired Chinese artisans produced Spain's most lasting landmarks in the Ilocos – the megalithic churches, like the grand cathedral of Vigan. Chinese masons concocted a special mix of coral, limestone and sugar for the bricks used in these massive structures. Nicknamed "earthquake baroque" by Filipino historians, these were built both to dramatize the power of the Old World god and to withstand natural disasters.

The 17th and 18th centuries subsequently saw a flowering of European baroque that filtered into the Philippines, now most evident in the historic quarter of Vigan, with its grandiloquent plastered brick houses complete with hardwood floors,

BELOW: restored interior of an old Spanish villa in Vigan.

capiz shell windows and intricate grille work. These are now the ancestral homes of once-wealthy Chinese, Spanish and *mestizo* merchants and artisans in Vigan.

Vigan ㉑, the provincial capital of Ilocos Sur, was built by the Spaniards in 1572, their third settlement on the islands after Cebu and Intramuros in modern-day Manila. It remains everything that Intramuros should be: a living, breathing repository of Spanish architecture and Filipino culture.

The **Cathedral of St Paul Ⓐ**, built in 1641, stands in the center of Vigan. In 1758, a royal decree transferred the northern Luzon Diocese of Nueva Segovia to St Paul's, making it the ecclesiastical center of the whole area. Augustinian-built, this grandiose stone structure 86 meters (280 ft) long, and supported by buttresses, cannot help but impress. Stretching out in front of St Paul's is the elliptical **Plaza Salcedo**, with a belltower separate from the church, as is the style here in earthquake country. Revolutionary Gabriela Silang, the first woman to lead a revolt against the Spanish, was hanged in the plaza in 1763.

North of Plaza Salcedo is the **Archbishop's Palace Ⓑ** (open Mon–Fri by appointment only; free), displaying sliding *capiz* shell windows, floral motifs, gardens and a priceless collection of ecclesiastical artifacts. Like other local buildings, it served as a garrison for US forces under Colonel James Parker in 1899.

Museum and jail

West of the plaza stands **Ayala Museum Ⓒ** (open Tues–Sat 8.30–11.30am and 1.30–4.30pm; entrance fee), also called Burgos House and the birthplace of martyr Father Jose Burgos. The best repository of Ilocano culture in the region, the well-maintained house features a fine collection of antiques, icons and a library. Perhaps equally interesting is the **Ilocos Sur Provincial Jail Ⓓ**, to the

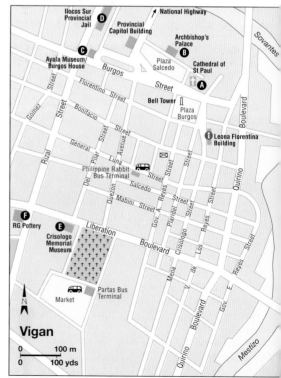

north of Burgos House, directly behind the Provincial Capitol Building. The present colonial structure dates from 1855, although a jail was first built on this site in 1657. The open atmosphere of the prison is a refreshing change. Few are confined to solitary cells, families live inside the walls on weekends, and inmates make handicrafts, and study auto mechanics and cosmetology. More significantly, former Philippine president Elpidio Quirino was born in the small room up the wooden stairway on November 16, 1890, when his father was warden of the prison.

Heritage Village

Looping back to the south of Plaza Salcedo and St Paul's, one finds the best street food in town – crispy *empanadas* dipped in *basi* vinegar – at **Plaza Burgos**. From here, the cobblestoned Mena Crisologo Street stretches southward along Vigan's most famous attraction, the old ancestral houses of the former Mestizo District, now called the **Vigan Heritage Village**. The well-ventilated brick structures with red-tiled roofs and *capiz* shell windows served as homes to the wealthy, who made their money trading indigo dyes, *abel* (woven) fabrics, gold and tobacco. Today, horse-drawn carriages ferry visitors through the lovingly preserved area that now houses antique shops, bakeries, craft shops, hotels and a few funeral parlors with impressive, antique hearses. UNESCO has contributed funds to maintain and renovate the village.

Hand-rolled local cigars in Vigan.

Other Vigan attractions include the **Crisologo Memorial Museum ❸** (open Sun–Fri 8.30–11.30am and 1.30–4.30pm; free; tel: 077-722 8520), on Liberation Boulevard. Upstairs original furnishings of a typical ancestral home are on show, while the first floor features odd family memorabilia, including graphic photographs of Congressman Floro Crisologo after he was assassinated in Vigan Cathedral in 1970. Don't miss **RG Pottery ❻** at the western end of Liberation Boulevard, where the famous Ilocano jars, or *burnay*, are made for storing vinegar, *bagoong* (local fermented fish paste) and the local wine, *basi*. Walk back into the kiln area and you will see one of the best examples of a Chinese dragon kiln. Built by the owner's grandfather, the kiln attests to Chinese influences in the Ilocos.

BELOW:
a fiesta participant.

The local fiesta falls on January 25, honoring the conversion of St Paul, while Viva Vigan, a cultural festival, occurs during the first week in May. This is a good chance to see all of Ilocano culture on parade, in song, dance and drama. For more information, visit the tourist office in the historic **Leona Florentina Building**, at the northern end of Mena Crisologo Street.

Near Vigan, the church in **Bantay** features Philippine earthquake baroque with Gothic influences. Its belfry, a few meters from the church, was used as a lookout for Moro pirates. Further north, in **Magsingal**, the **Museum of Ilocano Culture and Artifacts** has a collection of early trade porcelains, neolithic tools, weaponry, baskets, agricultural implements and old Ilocano beadwear.

A guesthouse and picnic huts can be found along the white sands of Pug-os Beach, in **Cabugao**, just 30 minutes north of Vigan, while the last town in Ilocos

San Nicolas' church in Laoag was the first stone-and-brick church in the Ilocos region.

Sur, **Sinait**, has a century-old church where the Black Nazarene, found floating in a casket off the coast in the 17th century, is enshrined and feted in early May.

Ilocos Norte

Unlike its poorer cousin to the south, Ilocos Norte stands rich in timber, minerals, fisheries and agriculture. Garlic, the principal cash crop, gives the province its flavor and aroma. It is also noted as the home province of the Philippines' longest-serving president, Ferdinand Marcos, who came from Sarrat.

The first town in Ilocos Norte is **Badoc**. Exhibited at **Luna House** (open Tues–Sat 9am–5pm; donation), are reproductions of works by the l9th-century master Filipino painter, Juan Luna. The Badoc Church also warrants a visit. Beyond, at the kilometer 460 junction, turn left for **Currimao**, once host to a thriving tobacco monopoly. Today, tourists enjoy the beach here, with its rocky outcrops of coral formation.

From Currimao, a side road leads to **Paoay**. A UNESCO World Heritage Site, Paoay Church is a real stunner, successfully wedding the strong features of earthquake baroque – such as massive lateral buttresses – with an exotic oriental quality, reminiscent of Javanese temples. Built of coral blocks at the turn of the 18th century, its belltower served as an observation post during the Philippine revolution and was occupied by guerrillas during the Japanese occupation.

Just north of the town is **Lake Paoay**. Here, loom weaving is a major activity, producing textiles with ethnic Ilocano designs. Marcos once made himself at home at **Balay Ti Amianan** (Malacañang of the North; open Tues–Sat 9am–5pm; free), built in 1976 as a 60th birthday present from Imelda, in Ilocos Norte's *barangay* Suba.

BELOW: Paoay Church, blending oriental and baroque styles.

San Nicolas, on the south bank of the Laoag river, is the pottery capital of the Ilocos and here, the first church in the region, made of stone and brick, was built in 1591. There is also an old Spanish house near the plaza that is a copy of the Rizal House in Calamba, Laguna. Today, the town is the province's industrial center. South, down the National Highway, is the Marcos Mausoleum in **Batac**.

A road leads east from San Nicolas to **Sarrat**, birthplace of Ferdinand Marcos and where the **Marcos Museum** (open Tues–Sat 9am–5pm; free) houses family memorabilia, including the grand four-poster bed where this famous Ilocano was born, the clock beside it set to the time of his birth. Even today, the Marcos influence is felt in Ilocos Norte, where his only son Ferdinand "Bong Bong" Marcos Jr serves as governor, and daughter Imee is a congresswoman. Sarrat's **Santa Monica Church and Convent**, which are connected by a massive bridge-staircase across a river, are well-preserved specimens of colonial architecture. Further inland, in **Dingras**, are some church ruins and an old Spanish well.

Sinking belltower

Across the Don Mariano Marcos Bridge (named after Marcos' father) from San Nicolas is the capital of Ilocos Norte, **Laoag** ㉒, the Sunshine City, nearly two hours north of Vigan. **St William's Cathedral**, dating from the 16th century, is another notable example of earthquake baroque. Over 85 meters (93 yards) from the cathedral stands the incredible Sinking Belltower, having noticeably mired itself in the sandy soil.

In the center of the plaza, the Tobacco Monopoly Monument commemorates the lifting in 1881 of the century-long Spanish tobacco monopoly, which forced locals to grow tobacco solely for delivery to the government. The Ilocandia

Map on pages 170–71

Most visitors to the Marcos Mausoleum in Batac think the waxy body on display of the former president looks too perfect to be real. Till this day, it is unclear where exactly Imelda has laid her late husband's body to rest.

BELOW: savoring an Ilocano cigar.

Map
on pages
170–71

The stones in the Bacarra River reputedly possess healing powers. Do not be alarmed to see older people rubbing them onto their skins.

Museum of Traditional Costumes is housed in the old Tabacalera or Camarin de Tabaco, where tobacco was once stored before being shipped to Manila. In Aurora Park, the fountain sculpture shows the Ilocano ideal of the perfect woman: her arms draped in garlic bulbs and tobacco leaves.

Laoag International Airport is the third-busiest airport in the country, with flights to and from Manila a few times a week. Laoag is also the transfer point for the Batanes Islands north of Luzon, and it receives flights from Taiwan and Hong Kong, for those keen to play the tables of the Spanish-styled Fort Ilocandia Resort and Casino. The nearby **La Paz Sand Dunes** have long been a favorite setting with Philippine film directors and 8 km (5 miles) north of Laoag sits **Bacarra**, one of the only two places in the country where the 17-stringed wooden harp is still carved and played. Bacarra is also known for its quake-damaged belltower, whose facade has suffered from restorative zeal.

Into the far northwest

One of the most scenic drives in the country is on the coast north of Laoag. Salt making prevails in **Pasuquin**, not far from the phonetically funny Seksi Beach. Cape Bojeador lighthouse, near **Burgos**, the tallest in the country, rewards a climb up a narrow, iron spiral staircase with a dramatic view of the northern coast. A short drive east, the visitor can enjoy an even loftier view from the viewing deck in **Bangui**. Here, the coves and golden sand beaches of Bangui Bay spread out on the vista, with Pagudpud in the distance.

Pagudpud on Bangui Bay is known for its fresh lobsters and has excellent coral reefs and beaches. The reef off Mayraira Beach is virtually untouched. From here, there's a sweeping ocean vista along the Patapat Viaduct. ❑

BELOW:
La Paz Sand Dunes.

Remote Batanes

Beyond the northern tip of Luzon is the country's smallest province, mountainous **Batanes** – Home of the Winds. The Ivatan people, of Malay stock, and émigré Ilocanos inhabit these 10 isolated islands, 160 km (100 miles) above Luzon and 75 km (45 miles) below Taiwan.

The islands came under Spanish control only in 1788, when the locals were persuaded (under threat of force) to move to the lowlands and adopt Western dress and Christianity. The US took over from the Spanish in 1899, introducing a public school and improving local infrastructure. Today, the 230-sq. km (90-sq. mile) islands are noted for their unspoiled marine environment and natural beauty – often compared to that of New Zealand and the Scottish Highlands, and the signature all-weather headgear of the Ivatans, known as *vakul*. Another defining icon of Batanes are the nearly impenetrable stone and limestone block buildings and churches, with thick walls and thatched roofs to withstand windy conditions and typhoons.

To survive, the Ivatans must be self-sufficient, farming the green hills. Garlic, the leading export, is harvested from February to April. Schoolchildren lead the family's livestock out to graze early in the morning, spend the day at school and later fetch the animals, heading home in the evening. The Ivatans are noted fishermen, constantly building new rounded-bottom boats to replace those lost to the rough seas.

The capital, Basco, is a one-hour flight from Laoag, Ilocos Norte, and Tuguegarao, Cagayan. The dry season is from April to June, when the winds are calm and the sea smooth. Between July and September, the islands are hit by typhoons quite frequently. December–February is the next best time to visit, with some rain, and temperatures dipping to 7°C (41°F). Transportation and communications are generally unreliable, so visitors should be adventurous and not be on a tight schedule. A few jeepneys ply the island roads, with *carabao* (water buffalo) carriages heading into the farmlands. Boats travel between islands on no set schedule; trips will be cancelled altogether in rough weather. There is however better cell phone coverage and more regular flights from Luzon, as well as a commuter flight to Itbayat Island now.

Batan, Sabtang and Itbayat are the main islands. Their towns are anchored by old Catholic churches, roughly 200 years old, built in the baroque style characteristic of the Ilocos. Local cottage industries include making ropes, doormats, baskets and hats, building boats and crafting fishing nets.

Few people live on the remoter islands of Dequey, Siayan, Mabudis, Ibuhos, Diogo, North and Y'ami. Batanes has a population of only 17,000. With such a small population, there is no need for formality. Most inhabitants even leave their doors and windows wide open.

For more information on tours and travel in the islands, contact the Batanes Eco-cultural Tourism Cooperative at cell tel: 0919-369 5341; e-mail: batanestourism@yahoo.com.❑

RIGHT: Batanes woman wearing the quaint *vakul* headgear.

NORTHEAST LUZON

Isolated Cagayan Valley and its surrounding territories may be wild and windy, but they are also archeologically rich and a destination for spectacular caving, trekking and surfing

Map on pages 170–71

Amongst the most windswept of Philippine regions, Northeast Luzon begins with Nueva Vizcaya and Quirino in the south, Isabela in the middle, Cagayan Valley at the northeastern corner, and the Batanes and Babuyan groups leading the way towards neighboring Taiwan. Except for Nueva Vizcaya, almost the entire region is characterized by sweeping vistas, rolling hills, secret beaches, and dramatic drops into the rolling Pacific Ocean.

This "hidden" valley is a structural depression, located between tributaries of the Cagayan river flowing from the Cordillera Central mountains in the west, the thickly forested Sierra Madre mountains towering over the Philippine Sea in the east, and the Caraballo mountains in the south. Such isolation, coupled with a long history of fierce colonial struggle that impoverished most of its people, has kept the region rural and remote. But beneath the valley's slow pace of life is an exciting world that its original settlers largely ignored, a world which can only be described as wet, windy and wild.

Cagayan

In contrast to the economic condition of most of its people, Cagayan is rich. The province has it all, from being the historic setting of Pleistocene elephants, rhinoceroses, cobble tools and seafaring Neolithic Ybanag villagers, to harboring a Spanish legacy, apparent in grand, old Catholic churches. Through Cagayan flows the country's longest river, and here is one of the richest archeological sites. Naturally, the region has the Philippines' largest remaining lowland forest and longest cave system, plus healthy agricultural and mineral resources.

Tuguegarao **㉓**, the capital, is an hour's flight from Manila. Bus lines also ply the Manila–Tuguegarao route. Getting around is by tricycle, jeepney, or on foot. There are a few modest places to stay in town.

To learn more of the province's colorful history, visit the **Cagayan Museum and Historical Research Center** (open Mon–Fri 8am–noon and 1–5pm; free). This is home to an extensive collection of fossils, iron-age pottery, china from the Ming and Song dynasties, and liturgical collections. To see Cagayan's natural grandeur, go to the Provincial Capitol Compound and gush at the scenic view of rolling hills, the Cagayan river and Sierra Madre mountains.

St Peter's Cathedral, built in 1761, is evidence of Cagayan's link with Spain. Nearby, San Jacinto Chapel was the first chapel in Tuguegarao, built in 1724. At the southern edge of the town is the Tuguegarao Horno, where old Spanish kiln bricks, used to construct the cathedral and chapel, were baked.

To begin explorations, head east to **Peñablanca**

LEFT: lush Cagayan Valley.
BELOW: St Peter's Cathedral in Tuguegarao.

town, home to **Callao Caves**, the longest, second-deepest and most awe-inspiring in the Philippines. While no one knows the exact number of caves, best estimates top 300, only 30 of which have been mapped. The small village of Callao serves as the gateway to these underground treasures.

Caving here caters for all levels of ability. For the novice, there are easy passages leading to rock formations, stalagmites and stalactites. For the hardcore caver, rarer gems such as calcite rafts, crystalline waterfalls, and even mud and gypsum formations await in shining glory, after hours of negotiating subterranean rivers, rappel drops and other challenges.

Inside the Callao Caves Park is a spot called Mororan, known for its continuous rain shower. Jump off the natural limestone diving boards and swim the clear waters flowing from the Pinacanauan river. Also in Peñablanca are the equally incredible underground treasures of Sierra Cave and the Odessa Cave System, the technically challenging Lhoret Cave, and Don Don, with its roller coaster crawls.

The best time to go caving is March–May. Since Callao Caves are protected, permission from the Department of Environment and Natural Resources (tel: 078-844 1621) is required. It is mandatory to hire an accredited guide who will arrange for the permit and escort you through the caves. Guides are found at the park entrance.

Longest river

Rio Grande de Cagayan , the longest river in the Philippines, bisects Cagayan Valley from north to south. It is also home to various fish, including *lurung*, considered the rarest and most delicious in the country. It is traversed by the impressive Bunton Bridge – the second longest in the Philippines.

On 11 hectares (27 acres) of rolling terrain overlooking the river can be found **Iguig Calvary Hills**, duplicating in life-sized concrete structures the Fourteen Stations of the Cross, amidst a cluster of Spanish relics like a brick stairway, a three-centuries-old well and Dominican convent ruins.

North to the coast

At the northern end of the valley, past **Gattaran**, home of the majestic Tanlagan Falls, is **Camalaniugan**, where the Bell of Antiquity, probably the oldest church bell in the Philippines (brought to Manila in 1638), is located.

On the coast, **Aparri** is considered one of the best big game fishing ports for marlin and sailfish in the Philippines. Around town, the coastline spreads out into a run of beaches, tangled estuaries and swamps. Here, ancient tribes once wove cloth, baked clay, and fashioned fishing and hunting implements from the bamboo that grew in their forests.

Buguey, east of Aparri, is the oldest Spanish foothold on this coast and one of the last places in the Philippines where one can still find older locals playing 19th-century wooden harps. West of Aparri, bamboo craft is alive and well in **Sanchez-Mira**.

Fuga Island 25, northwest of Aparri, is a ravishing islet where stunning beaches glow pink with pulverized coral and attract visitors for scuba diving and snorkeling. Delicious wild honey gathered from the interior forests, and an ancient church in the old town are the most rewarding fringe benefits.

White herons flock to the rice fields on the periphery of many towns along the northern coast of Cagayan. These herons keep travelers company on the 1½-hr drive to the northeastern tip of the province at Port San Vicente.

Map on pages 170–71

The communal spirit is strong in most rural provinces – as seen in these men moving an outhouse across paddy fields.

BELOW:
game fishermen at Aparri, Cagayan.

Unlike the churches of Cagayan, which were built in the earlier colonial baroque style, Isabela's, strung out in squat dignity along the National Highway, show a simpler antique Spanish architecture, with unrestored red-brick work.

Off this coast is **Palaui Island** , home to Cape Engano. Its white beaches, steep, rugged cliffs and the surrounding Babuyan Channel are refreshingly rugged and remote. Wave-polished corals, seashells and beautiful rock formations sprouting like mushrooms make a haven for snorkeling, scuba diving, shell collecting, fishing, swimming and forest exploration. Every year, national and international game fishing competitions are held here. Climb up the old Spanish lighthouse and take in the unlimited view of the **Don Hermanas Islands**, jutting out of the South China Sea.

Isabela

This second largest province in the Philippines, named after Queen Isabella of Spain, is tobacco country. The rich mountain soil of **Isabela's** grassy plains and forests is also good for rice and ideal for grazing. **Ilagan**, the capital, lies at the junction of the Cagayan and Abuluan rivers, and is accessible by land and air from Manila. Around town are a few modest hotels and pension houses. **Santa Victoria Caves**, located at Fuyot National Recreation Area, is a multi-chambered cave with a natural swimming pool, ideal for caving and bird-watching.

The prime attraction of **Tumauini** town, north of Ilagan, is a century-old church, which has a round bell tower with decorated friezes. Southeast of the capital is **San Mariano**, gateway to the 200,000-hectare (500,000-acre) **Palanan Wilderness Park** . Palanan's forests make up 10 percent of the country's remaining primary rainforest, and the park is also noted for its biological diversity, home of the Philippine eagle and numerous endemic species of flora and fauna. Palanan and the surrounding area are some of the last places where the Agta Negritoes still live in their traditional manner.

BELOW: church ruins in Isabela.

The town of **Cauayan** houses the Isabela Hotel and Resort, site of the only Casino Filipino in the region. The resort features amenities like water slides, horseback riding, cycling and skating lanes. The airstrip here serves short flights to Palanan, which are the only means of access to the Sierra Madre mountains. At the southern entrance of **Santiago**, to the southwest, is a picturesque view of rice fields against an urban backdrop of buildings and housing.

Elsewhere in Isabela, the beach of **Dinapigue** is popular for its white sands and crystal waters. It is the end of the coastal road and the gateway to **Sierra Madre National Park**. **Magat Dam**, a multi-billion-peso complex, located in Baligatan, Ramon, is the biggest dam in Asia.

Quirino

In the upper Cagayan River Basin, **Quirino** stands ringed by the peaks of the Sierra Madre and Mamparang ranges. Generally mountainous, the province, like most of the region, is largely agricultural. Its ruggedness, however, has kept its landscapes – considered some of the country's best – in pristine form. **Cabarroguis**, the provincial capital, is accessible via a seven-hour bus journey from Manila to Isabela, from where jeepneys run to the town.

Love of the unknown, unpredictable and untamable are all reasons to come to Quirino Province. Populated by waves of people drawn here by its vast natural resources, the province was until the 20th century occupied mostly by Dumagats or Negritos, the aboriginal inhabitants of the Philippines, who can still be found living around the Sierra Madres. Roads are, due to river crossings, only for the truly prepared, but the scenery and dramatic nature of the jagged mountains are worth the journey. Ask about conditions before heading into the jungle.

Those on a cultural pilgrimage should visit **Bugkalot Ethnic Community**, the tribal village home of once-fierce headhunters in the upper reaches of Nagtipunan. The tribe's constant interaction with the lowlanders, however, has changed their culture, and headhunting is no longer practiced.

Explore the Nagbukel Caves in **Diffun**, or just picnic and hike around. Cool yourself at **Bisangal Falls**, some 35 km (21 miles) from Cabarroguis, sitting in a virgin forest that serves as a wildlife sanctuary for endangered species such as the Philippine eagle. Nearby **Aglipay Caves**, a series of 38 inter-linking caves, features well-preserved stalagmites and stalactites.

The surrounding rolling hills and verdant forest offer good opportunities for trekking. **Maddela**, accessible from San Agustin, Isabela, offers some of the best whitewater (check www.whitewater.ph) in the archipelago, while **Governor Rapids** has a gigantic perpendicular wall and deep bluish water.

Nueva Vizcaya

West of Quirino is the agricultural province of **Nueva Vizacaya**, four hours by bus from Manila. At **Santa Fe**, the entry into Nueva Vizcaya is marked by a gradual ascent into the brown foothills of the Caraballo Mountains. On a zigzagging road through the 915-meter (3,000-ft) high **Dalton Pass**, history records a long and bloody battle between Philippine-American

Map on pages 170–71

Don Hermanas Islands, in legend, were two sisters who bade goodbye to their husbands and were left waiting hundreds of years for their return.

BELOW: whitewater kayaking.

troops and the rear guard of the Japanese army towards the end of World War II.

On the lonely pass now, with a memorial on a hill, there are only the rumblings of huge trucks hauling timber, and smaller ones groaning under sacks of rice and sweet potatoes. Scattered all along the road are stalls selling woven bamboo baskets of all shapes, executed in unvarnished strips and ornamented with a few lines of earthen colors. Sold alongside are lush sweet peppers and potatoes grown in the surrounding foothills. The baskets have caught the attention of wholesale exporters and are increasingly appearing in markets abroad.

Reaching **Aritao**, St Dominic Cathedral shows vestiges of the grandeur of this old town, but there is little else to see. Beyond lies **Bambang**, a dusty 15 km (9 miles) with a geographical curiosity – the snow-like salt hill of Salinas Salt Springs, which spews salty water into the mountain air.

After Bambang, at the 260-km marker, sits the Villa Margarita Mountain Resort, with spring-fed pools set in a citrus plantation. **Bayombong**, the provincial capital, lies just beyond. It does not offer much, unless it is the August fiesta, when Aetas come down from the nearby mountains to dance in front of a century-old church. If you dare, try crossing the **Hanging Footbridge of Ambaguio**, an 80-meter-long (260-ft), 20-meter-high (65-ft) wood, vine and rope bridge.

Aurora

Finally, at the southernmost tip of Cagayan Valley is the long, narrow, and coastal province of **Aurora**, known for its relaxed country charm, which is obscured only by the wild and wet surf at **Baler ㉘**, the capital city. Sitting on the fertile delta formed by the San Luis and Aguag rivers, Baler enjoys most of the provincial tourist action. It is accessible via a four- to five-hour bus trip

James Gilmore, commander of the US gunboat Yorktown, was captured with all his men when he came to Baler in April 1899 to relieve Spanish soldiers besieged in the city's church.

BELOW: Aeta child.
RIGHT: Santa Fe is famous for its handwoven bamboo baskets.

from Manila. Once in the city, hire a tricycle or walk around the *poblacion*.

The centuries-old **Baler Catholic Church**, with its simple, plain façade, stood witness to the last Spanish garrison of four officers and 50 men captured by Filipino insurgents. The La Campana de Baler, a quality ancient bell, is stored as a relic at the church.

Across the way is the Lt Commander James Gilmore Marker and nearby is the Quezon Memorial Park, created in memory of the late President Manuel L. Quezon, a native of Baler. Nearby is the Aurora Quezon Marker, built in honor of his wife, and the Quezon Resthouse, the family dwelling.

Surf city

Outside the town proper are numerous white sand beaches adorned with sea shells, corals and rock formations. Ideal for swimming, snorkeling, boating and scuba diving, these beaches transform themselves into surf areas during the northeast monsoon in October–March.

Sabang Beach is the most popular surf spot, while Charlie's Point 10 minutes north really swells during typhoons. This is where Francis Coppola filmed the "Charlie don't surf" scene of the movie *Apocalypse Now*. A 15-minute walk away from Sabang is the best break in Baler, inappropriately named Secret Spot.

The sea around Baler teems with islets – including Aniao, Lukso-Lukso and Dimadimalangat – which are simply too alluring to skip. Elsewhere in Aurora Province, primordial wilderness blankets a good part of the territory, with forest cover, rivers and endless beaches awaiting your footprints. The spectacular Ditumabo Falls, Banyu Springs, Cunayan Falls, Dibut Bay, Dilasag Coast and Lamao Caves should not be missed. ❑

Map on pages 170–71

TIP

The coasts stretching in either direction from Baler offer a variety of waves reachable by road or by boat. The friendly local surfers, known as the "Baler Boys," might just share their secret wave riding spots with you, if you charm them enough.

BELOW: surf time at Baler.

CENTRAL CORDILLERA

Luzon's mountainous land-locked provinces are still the home of distinct ethnic groups, practicing ancient rituals and farming the astonishingly spectacular rice terraces

Map on pages 170–71

A morning mist hangs low over a tightly knit community of 30 small huts, made of cogon thatch. An old man winds his way through the vegetable beds tucked around the village (*ili*), stopping at the council house (*ato*), where his peers are waiting for him. Dressed scantily, despite the cold mountain air, the men squat around a low fire, puffing on tiny pipes of carved hardwood and cast bronze. The council house is made of pine, blackened by age and soot. Its roof is a bulky, round thatch of cogon grass; the spirits of visiting forefathers would not appreciate an iron roof resounding under the rain. An approaching storm threatens the rice harvest: to placate the gods, a chicken is being sacrificed at the sacred tree, which, with the *ato*, is the center of life in the highland community.

Perhaps, one day, this will be a rare scene in the **Cordillera Autonomous Region** (CAR), encompassing all the land-locked provinces of the Cordillera mountains. The highlands account for 7 percent of the total land area of the Philippines, though they are home to less than 2 percent of the country's population. Created to preserve the cultural uniqueness of the highlands, the CAR is composed of Benguet, Ifugao, Mountain Province, Abra, Kalinga, and Apayao provinces.

Three main roads lead from the lowlands to the Cordillera. The famous Kennon Road, built by the Americans in 1903, zig-zags north from Sison, Pangasinan to Baguio, Benguet. From La Union province, the Marcos Highway branches off from the National Highway in Agoo, reaching Baguio in less than two hours. Quirino Highway (Naguilian Road) leads in from Naguilian, further north. To the east is a road from Nueva Vizcaya to Banaue, Ifugao.

LEFT: Batad village and rice terraces.
BELOW: tatooed Ifugao woman.

Ethnic groups

Igorot, literally "people of the mountains," is a blanket term invented by the Spanish. The people of the region prefer to be called by the name of their own distinct ethnic groups – the Kankanaey and Ibaloi of Benguet; the Ifugao of Ifugao Province; the Kalinga, and the Isneg of Apayao; and the Bontoc, Balangao, Gaddang and Bayyo of Mountain Province.

The Kankanaey and Ibaloi, long exposed to the lowlands, are regarded as the most sophisticated. The Bontoc are the proudest and most warlike, whose men maintain a deep territorial imperative. Codes of conduct and legal matters are associated with the hardworking Ifugao, who also take their rituals seriously, employing as many as 15 *mumbaki*, or priests for a ceremony. For the Kalinga, the major preoccupations are oratory skills and a unique system of peace pacts, *bodong*, which culminate in grand celebrations.

The Spanish, whose occupation of the lowlands involved only a modicum of effort, encountered stiff opposition in the mountains from these "restless and

warlike tribes." Even Spanish missions failed in these mountains. Headhunting by certain tribes particularly infuriated the Spanish, who mounted many punitive expeditions but never pacified the mountain peoples. It was not until American occupation and the opening of the highlands by army engineers that the tribes were finally mollified, American Episcopalian missions meeting more success than the Spanish ones.

Today, Christianity is well-established in the region, with mission schools omnipresent and English usage phenomenal. Many of the mountain people have adopted Christian first names – Clifford and Kathleen, for instance – while retaining tribal surnames like Kinaw-od and Killip. Yet many still cling to ancient tribal customs, as at a highland funeral. On such an occasion, a feast lasts for 3 days. The deceased sits strapped to a wooden chair in the center of the house, as though surveying the time-honored proceedings. Animal sacrifices are made and the meat passed to the entire gathering. Bronze gongs (*gangsas*) clang deep into the night, while the people dance in a circle with fluttering, bird-like motions. Rice wine, or *tapuey*, is served from centuries-old jars traded from some Chinese junk, ladled with aged coconut shells. Invocations are said to a pantheon of spirits, including Kabunyian, the creator, and Lumawig, a folklore hero.

Baguio

The road to the highlands from Manila usually runs through **Baguio** ㉙, a six-hour bus drive from Manila (four hours by private car). Nestled aloft a 1,500-meter (4,900-ft) high plateau in the Cordilleras, Baguio's cool climate and pine-clad hills have consistently lured visitors. It shows little evidence today of an earthquake which severely damaged the city in 1990.

TIP

Roads throughout the Cordillera are necessarily rugged, but gratifyingly scenic. Be sure to bring a heavy sweater or coat, as bitter cold might seep through the open-sided jeepney at higher elevations.

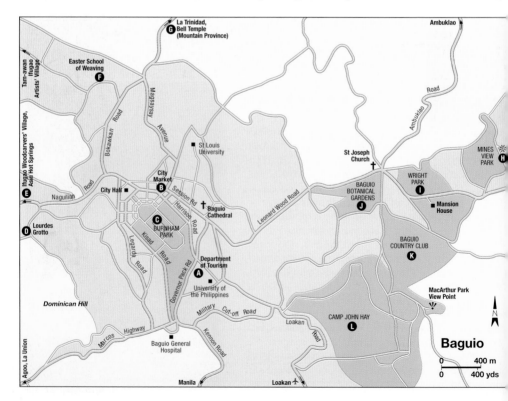

Baguio

0   400 m
0   400 yds

There is not a whole lot to see – Baguio is better known for the leisure and relaxation offered by its pine-covered hills. The city serves as a summer getaway from the crowds and heat of Manila, refreshingly averaging 18°C (64°F) throughout the year. Baguio seduces with clean parks, lovely gardens, quaint churches, and a variety of restaurants and hotels. Accommodation is easily available in Baguio, except during Holy Week. Maps and information on lodgings are available free at the **Department of Tourism Ⓐ** office on Governor Pack Road.

A highlight in Baguio is the month-long **Baguio Flower Festival**, or **Panagbenga**, which means the "season for blossoming" in the Kankanaey dialect, held every February with parades of floral floats, marching bands and dance troupes.

Getting around Baguio is easy. Jeepneys congregate at the northern end of Session Road – at the bottom of the hill – and follow regular routes. However, taxis here are exceedingly reasonable, and sensible for extended trips through this incredibly sprawling city – such as down Naguilian Road for the sunset over the Ilocos coastline, or up to Mt Santo Tomas for a view of the South China Sea.

Head for the market

Long walks seem to be the most popular form of recreation in Baguio, the time-honored route being up and down **Session Road**, with its gamut of bookstores, bakeries, Chinese restaurants, coffee houses, pizza parlors and cinemas. At the northern end of Session Road, opposite the jeepney terminus, is **Baguio City Market Ⓑ**. The well-stocked market offers fresh produce from both highland and lowland farms, from Spanish tomatoes and yams to blueberries, sausages and other assorted delicacies, as well as a rich variety of woven bags, baskets, woodcarvings, jewelry, clothing and kitschy souvenirs.

Maps:
Area 170
City 204

If you don't mind having stuffed animal heads stare at you, try staying at the Safari Lodge in Baguio, tel: 074-442 2419.

BELOW:
Baguio market.

TIP

North of Baguio is the
Mountain Trail, or
"Halsema Highway" –
rough, partially paved
and often washed out
in the rainy season –
running to Bontoc.
Although Bontoc,
Banaue and points
south to Baguio are
accessible by bus,
other towns here have
only a limited service.

Burnham Park C, with a manmade lake, sports ground and orchidarium, stands at the center of Baguio, south of Session Road. Between far-flung Naguilian Road and Mt Santo Tomas sits **Lourdes Grotto D**, where devotees climb 252 steps to the Lady of Lourdes shrine and a good view of the city. From Lourdes, head west 5 km (3 miles) to the **Ifugao Woodcarvers' Village E**, where prices are lower than in town. Another 16 km (10 miles) northwest of Baguio is **Asin Hot Springs**, with lush vegetation and hanging bridges.

North of the city center is the **Easter School of Weaving F**, where export-quality native cloth and curio items sell for bargain prices. Local weavers using backstrap-looms are the main attraction. Go downstairs to watch them make the cloth. Further north, up Magsaysay Avenue and some 10 minutes' drive from downtown, is **Bell Temple G**, a collection of temples bedecked with dragons and Chinese ornamentation, where monks or priests practice a blend of Buddhism, Taoism, Confucianism and Christianity, and can tell your fortune. On the border with La Trinidad is the **Tam-awan Ifugao Artists' Village** (tel: 047-446 2949), styled in the tradition of native Ifugao houses, and opened in 1996 to help foster a deeper understanding of the culture of the Cordilleran people, with some 10 native Cordilleran huts of different tribes.

In the northeastern part of the city, **Mines View Park H** affords a view of Benguet's mineral bowl. Plenty of shopping stalls abound here too. Coming back toward the city, Leonard Wood Road leads to **Wright Park I**, where children can take pony rides. Opposite is the **Mansion House**, summer residence of Philippine presidents. Further down Leonard Wood Road, is the **Baguio Botanical Gardens J**. South of Mansion House are **Baguio Country Club K** and **Camp John Hay L**, once an American military retreat.

BELOW:
Baguio boy offering
pomelo fruits.
RIGHT: Baguio's
Botanical Garden.

Beyond Baguio

Benguet Province, the southernmost mountain province, surrounds Baguio. Its capital, **La Trinidad**, stands just north of Baguio, and is a great place to load up on fresh strawberries. Out from La Trinidad, the partially paved Mountain Trail winds northward to Bontoc. **Kabayan**, a four-hour drive from Baguio, is worth a trip. At the 52-km marker on the Mountain Trail, near the Natubleng Vegetable Terraces in Buguias, follow the right fork south to Kabayan town, the base for trekking **Mt Pulog** ❸, held sacred by the Ibaloi. The second highest peak in the country – and the highest in Luzon – towers 2,928 meters (9,606 ft) above sea level. For climbers, a ranger station is located on the main Kabayan road.

Trekking Mt Pulog is best from February to April; allow at least three days to reach the peak for a stunning view of the **Cagayan Valley** and **Sierra Madre** range, and the Philippine Sea in the distance. Pine stands give way to oak forests, then alpine and bamboo grass-covered slopes, which thin out towards the peak, explaining Pulog's name, meaning "bald." Mt Pulog also has three mountain lakes – Tabeyo, Incolos and Bulalakaw – and several unexplored caves around its base.

Towering **Tinongchol Burial Rock**, once home to the mummified remains of Ibaloi ancestors, awaits near Kabayan. Unfortunately, many of the remains have been stolen. Nearby, on **Mt Timbac**, are more burial caves, with mummies at least 500 years old. Unlike wrapped Egyptian mummies, these are naked and with tattoo marks of geometric patterns still visible. They lay in the fetal position, in wooden coffins carved from tree trunks. Some of these mummies are displayed at the interesting museum by the Kabayan town hall.

Maps:
Area 170
City 204

The forests of Kabayan are mired in a controversy about patents on certain native herbal medicines. A local medicine man supposedly gave information on local herbs to US pharmaceutical companies, who now stand to profit from the development of life-saving drugs.

BELOW:
mummified remains at Mt Timbac.

TIP

To view inscriptions on
Sagada's hanging
coffins, be sure to
bring along a powerful
pair of binoculars.

Mountain Province

The Mountain Trail winds 110 km (68 miles) towards the provincial capital at Bontoc, 6–12 hours from Baguio, depending on road conditions. Mountain Province was created in 1907, during American rule, and included most of the Cordillera highlands. Its inhabitants are mostly Bontoc, Kankanaey and Balangao, along with some Gaddang, Ifugao, Bayyo and Ibaloi, among others.

Although all practice similar planting and harvesting customs, their burial and wedding rituals differ wildly. Towards the 90-km marker, near Sabangan, a road to the left ascends to **Bauko**, an eerily quiet logging center shrouded in mountain mist. Though offering little beyond pleasant hikes through the pine forests, this is the best place to spend the night along the southern Mountain Trail. Try the Mt Data Lodge – it has an excellent restaurant, and a huge fireplace for cold nights.

Rice terraces and burial caves

An hour from Bauko, the road descends to the Chico river, running parallel with it to Bontoc and beyond. **Bontoc** itself offers not much more than gas and provisions. Traveling by bus means staying the night, which can be done comfortably and cheaply at a number of lodges.

Situated in a low valley, Bontoc can be quite warm in the daytime. Hikes away from town provide a good survey of how rice terraces are maintained. These rice terraces are unlike the more famous ones in Banaue. Here, the walls are made from rocks instead of mud. Locals say that their terraces, though smaller than the massive spread of terraces in Banaue, are more difficult to construct, and therefore more picturesque. A visit to the **Bontoc Museum** (open daily 8am– noon and 1–5pm; entrance fee) is a must for insight into Cordilleran culture.

BELOW: hand-woven material hung out to dry.

THE HOMECOMING OF APO ANNO

Apo Anno, famed 12th-century Kankanaey hunter of Benguet, the half-mortal son of a goddess, lived for 250 years and was revered throughout the community. Tattoos covered his body from head to toe, portraying the extraordinary events of his life.

Upon Anno's death, the Kankanaey mummified his body, laying it to rest in a coffin beneath a rocky outcropping in Nabalicong, Benguet. Here, Anno remained peacefully for 600 years, until a European, Hans Meir, came across the mummy in 1885. Tragedy struck in 1918, when unknown grave robbers stole the body. The displeased spirit wreaked havoc, bringing heavy rains and landslides to the region.

Anno's whereabouts remained a mystery, after surfacing briefly at the 1922 Manila Carnival – and bringing uncharacteristic downpours to the capital city – and then vanishing again. Finally, in 1984, a mummy showed up in an antique shop, and was obtained by the National Museum. In a fortunate twist of fate, a Benguet tribal priest (*mambunong*) identified the mummy as local son Apo Anno. In May 1999, Anno made the triumphant journey home amidst much ritual, being re-buried in his home during a grand feast lasting three days. After the culmination of the event, a rainbow appeared in the sky.

Much of the charm and coziness lacking in Bontoc, with its harsh trading-post atmosphere, can be found in **Sagada**, an hour away by bus or Jeep. It has become increasingly popular among travelers, and there are quite a few inns and hotels here. Pleasant hiking is the order of the day in this upland valley town which has lime and shale formations, plus burial caves. Wooden coffins are stacked together at the mouths of several caves a short walk from town. Others, called "hanging coffins," dangle over cliff edges, as Sagadans are traditionally buried with full exposure to sunshine, wind and rain. Many of the trails to the caves are poorly maintained; hire a guide at the town hall to maximize your visit.

A number of attractions are within an hour's hike of town: an underground river; Kitongan bottomless pit that supposedly remains unfathomed; the tiny Bokong Waterfall, with its swimming hole; and Lake Danum – more pond than lake.

Banaue

Banaue ㉛ in **Ifugao Province**, 50 km (31 miles) southeast of Bontoc, marks the usual continuation of any mountain trip. The bus leaves Bontoc in the morning for the two-hour ride over the exhilarating Mt Polis highway. Terraced fields with spiral beds, oak trees gnarled to perfection and mountain orchids are fascinating sidelights for travelers. Banaue and the surrounding *barangay* remain the best sight in the Cordilleras – and one of the best in the Philippines (see *page 212*). The massive expanse of rice terraces covering entire mountainsides is bound to awe even the most jaded traveler. Built 2,000 years ago, the terraces cover more than 260 sq. km (100 sq. miles) of steep mountains.

Banaue sits in the heart of Ifugao country. In a way, it is the soul of these proud people. The word *ifugao* simply means hill – and for the Ifugao people, the "hill"

Bright jewel-like colors is the hallmark of Sagada weaving.

BELOW: Bayyo village on the Bontoc-Banaue Road.

means everything. An extensive social system exists here. Those who own the lower, larger terraces are the wealthy elite. The peasants till the upper, narrower terraces. As one Ifugao put it, "We cannot but do what our ancestors told us to do."

The Banaue Hotel and Youth Hostel frequently offers cultural dance performances in the evenings for a modest fee, as well as accommodations with a spectacular view – but the same can be said of many cheaper lodging places in this dedicated backpacker town. Behind the Banaue Hotel, 240 steep steps lead down to **Tam-an village**, where Ifugao people tend their rice terraces and produce woodcarvings and beadwork to supplement their income. Heading north along the road by jeepney or pedicab, one reaches the Banaue Viewpoint, where handicraft stalls line the path that leads to a breathtaking vista of the rice terraces. Ifugao elders in full tribal dress will pose for pictures – for a small fee.

In Banaue, be sure to check out the small museum (open on request) at the Banaue View Inn, run by the family of H. Ottley Beyer, an American anthropologist who studied the Ifugao, eventually taking a native wife and dying here.

Reached by a series of steps from the road below Banaue center, **Bocos** has some interesting sights. The huts are adorned with the skulls of *carabao* and wild pigs, which indicate the status of the families. Villagers keep their most sacred idol, *bulol*, the rice god, in the granary. It only comes out at harvest time to be bathed in the blood of sacrificed animals.

A footpath leads down from the road to **Poitan**, a village with a collection of houses roofed with both traditional cogon grass and sheets of galvanized iron. Here you can get a good view of the stone post protected and idolized by the Ifugao, and the stone-lined pit where elders gather to discuss problems and affairs.

Some 4 km (2½ miles) from Banaue, about a 45-minute walk, is an ideal spot

TIP

For a more romantic view of the Ifugao Rice Terraces – touted as the eighth man-made wonder of the world – hire a guide to take you further afield. Vertigo sufferers beware! The terrace edges are steep.

BELOW:
Ifugao child at play in the mountains.

for a picnic. A small waterfall tumbles into a natural pool in Guihob. Take a dip in the crystal-clear waters and gaze at the surrounding rice terraces. **Hapao**, 16 km (10 miles) southwest of Banaue, offers one of the most beautiful, stone-lined rice terraces in the mountains, thought to be the oldest in the area. Other terraces in **Banga-an**, 14 km (9 miles) from Banaue, are accessible up steep stone steps.

The spectacular, amphitheater-like terraces of **Batad**, 16 km (10 miles) from Banaue, are reached by a 4-km (2½-mile) footpath from the road. Here tattooed men and women work the fields. For a truly memorable journey, hire a guide to Batad, but first spend the night in Cambulo, where you can cool off by swimming in the rushing river. About an hour beyond Batad, by difficult footpath, cascades Tappiya Falls, with its enormous natural swimming basin.

Mayoyao, 44 km (27 miles) northeast of Banaue, offers a breathtaking view of rice terraces. From Banaue, backtrack to Bontoc and Baguio, or descend to the lowlands and the National Highway through **Lagawe**, Ifugao Province's capital city. In Lagawe, visitors can explore the Bintakan and Nah-toban caves, and a fine museum of Ifugao culture.

Kalinga, Apayao, and Abra Provinces

From Bontoc, the adventurous should proceed directly to **Kalinga Province** – north of Mountain Province – one of the most rugged provinces in the Cordillera region and home of the Kalinga people. The Kalinga-Bontoc Road runs 130 km (80 miles) to Tuao on the Cagayan-Apayao border. From Tuao, a spur road (210 km/130 miles) leads all the way to the South China Sea in Laoag, Ilocos Norte.

In **Tinglayan**, 2 hours north of Bontoc, you can find an impressive self-sustainability project in the tours offered by **Chico River Quest** (www.chico riverquest.com), an ecotourism operator set up by local guides and an American rafting company. They offer some of the best whitewater rafting in the country, and cultural tours and trekking to traditional villages and rice terraces in the area. Several hours to the north from Tinglayan is the **Balbalaasang National Park**, near the Abra border, and it is known for its unspoiled, natural beauty, sweet oranges and cultural heritage.

Apayao Province, to the north of Kalinga, is named after its main river, the Apayao, and noted for its clear waters, wildlife and old growth forest. The river is accessible through Kabugao, 70 km (43 miles) from Tuao, where motorised boats can be hired. The **Agamatan National Park and Wildlife Sanctuary** is located by the Ilocos Norte border, in Calanasan. Waterfalls abound in this province, including some of the tallest in the country. Be prepared for multi-day hikes to some of the most impressive falls.

A very poor road connects to Abra Province to **Balbalan**, but Abra is usually accessed from Ilocos Sur. The provincial capital, **Bangued**, is known for its handicrafts, such as sturdy baskets and fine weaving. The capital serves as a good jump-off point for exploring the seldom-visited hinterlands of Abra, such as the Abra River, once known for the fine horses bred along its valley. Today, however, only the natural landscape remains. ❏

Map on pages 170–71

BELOW: tattoos are believed to offer protection from harm.

THE FABLED RICE TERRACES OF IFUGAO

The hardworking Ifugao people tend to their rice terraces, hewn from the steep hillsides, as their ancestors have done for the past 2,000 years

Spread throughout the entire province of Ifugao but most often seen at Banaue, the Ifugao rice terraces are a testimony to the early technological advancement of the Ifugao people. Constructed 2,000 years ago, employing simple tools and backbreaking labor, the exquisitely sculpted terraces are a distinctive trademark of Ifugao culture. An ingeniously designed irrigation system directs water through carefully placed sluices on the terraces, delivering the right amount to the young rice shoots.

In Ifugao, the most mountainous part of the Philippine Cordillera, rice is king, and the coarse, homegrown variety is preferred to store-bought rice. Sweet potatoes are grown in forest clearings, but only rice appears during celebratory feasts – that is, alongside chickens, pigs, ducks, and the occasional lowland water buffalo, or *carabao*.

CHANGING TIMES

Although the Ifugao covet mountain-grown rice, today, few families can claim self-subsistence from the terraces which once supported their forebears. Over time, the terraces require extensive repairs, and the irrigation system must be dredged periodically to maintain water flow. A growing population dictates that each child inherits an increasingly smaller plot of land. Sadly, most of the younger generation – attracted to the lures of city life – is reluctant to undertake the laborious chore of rice farming.

▷ **THRESHING RICE**
Ifugao women pound rice with a wooden pestle, separating the heavier grains from the chaff.

△ **STAIRWAY TO HEAVEN**
Hiking along the precipitous rice terraces offers panoramic views. Little wonder that UNESCO has recognized the rice terraces as a World Heritage Site.

△ **RIDING HIGH**
Locals cheerfully perch atop a jeepney, the most efficient form of transportation in this hilly province.

▷ **WELL-WATERED**
A carefully designed and well-maintained irrigation system brings the right amount of water to each terrace.

MUCH-REVERED RICE GOD

Holding a special place in the Ifugao pantheon is the *bulul*, or rice god. Standing watch over each family's granary is a pair of *bulul* figures, carved from narra wood. During ceremonial rituals, Ifugao elders will slaughter chickens, recite divine incantations and pour the sacrificial blood of chickens over the head of the *bulul*. In turn, it is believed that the *bulul* will watch over the rice, and also help increase the yield of the coming harvest. Although the tradition of honoring the *bulul* persists, it is increasingly difficult to find a finely carved old rice god in situ, strapped to the wall of an Ifugao house. Antique collectors offer princely sums of cash to families willing to part with such treasures. These include not only the *bulul*, but also the structures integral to an Ifugao house: the pine posts flanking the doorway and the support beams.

△ **RACKED BRAINS**
Animal skulls on the exterior of a Ifugao home indicate the relative wealth of the family. *Carabao* skulls are sparse, as it's difficult to bring the water buffalo up to these heights.

▷ **OMINOUS OFFERINGS**
Despite strong missionary presence over the past century, the Ifugao cling to their animistic roots.

△ **HANDICRAFTS HAVEN**
To supplement incomes, many Ifugao families have turned to handicrafts. Women weave baskets, while men create decorative woodcarvings.

BICOL PENINSULA

Bicol's remarkable natural attractions – active volcanoes, stunning caves, spectacular waterfalls and even the world's biggest and smallest species of fish – make it an absorbing destination

Map on page 216

In a lake near the world's most perfectly shaped volcano swim the world's tiniest freshwater fish. Steam drifts through the palm trees where geothermal power is tapped for electricity. Offshore are islands with some of the whitest sand beaches and clearest coral-reefed waters one is ever likely to see. Amidst the islands are well-kept secrets of undiscovered wilderness.

On stormy nights, the raw force of typhoons whips off the sea, battering the region from the Pacific side. Every decade or so, one of the archipelago's most active volcanoes spews off deadly lava. In small Donsol Bay is the largest-ever recorded gathering of whale sharks, the largest fish in the world. Add to these extreme attractions the horrible, one-eyed, three-throated *ponong*, which the curious traveler might still glimpse on one of those classic, dark and moonless nights… This is the Bicol region, a peninsula of wild diversity, fire and fury, located at the southeastern-most tip of Luzon.

Camarines Norte

Camarines is derived from the Spanish *camarine*, literally meaning granary or storehouse. The name referred to the rice granaries here that had caught the attention of a Spanish mission exploring the region in 1569. In 1929, the province of rich mineral and agricultural resources known simply as Camarines was divided into Camarines Norte and Camarines Sur.

Camarines Norte occupies the northwestern portion of the Bicol region. It faces Basiad Bay on the west, the Pacific on the north, and San Miguel Bay to the east. Inland, Quezon Province bounds it on the southwest and Camarines Sur on the south. **Daet ❶**, the provincial capital, is known as the most accessible surf site along the Philippines' east coast, reached by a 45-minute flight, or eight-hour bus ride, from Manila. Its famous historical landmark is the country's first Rizal monument, built in 1898, in front of the Municipal Hall. Nearby is the 940-meter (3,100-ft) Mt Labo, Bicol's northernmost volcano.

While not quite like the monster waves of Catanduanes or Siargao, the province's beach break surf sites are suitable for novice surfers. For instance, the white-sand **Bagasbas Beach**, 5 km (3 miles) from Daet, has relatively small breaks that are easier to ride. More experienced surfers head straight for the picturesque fishing village of **Mercedes**. It has a 2-km (1½-mile) gray-sand beach, and 1–1.5-meter (3–5 ft) waves on ordinary days, which swell to 2–3 meters (6–10 ft) during typhoons. The adrenaline and brine of the surf can be washed away at the natural hot spring of nearby Lanot Beach, and then Mercedes' underwater **Canton Cave** can be explored at low tide.

LEFT: resort pool with Mayon Volcano in the distance.
BELOW: *banca*, or local pumpboat.

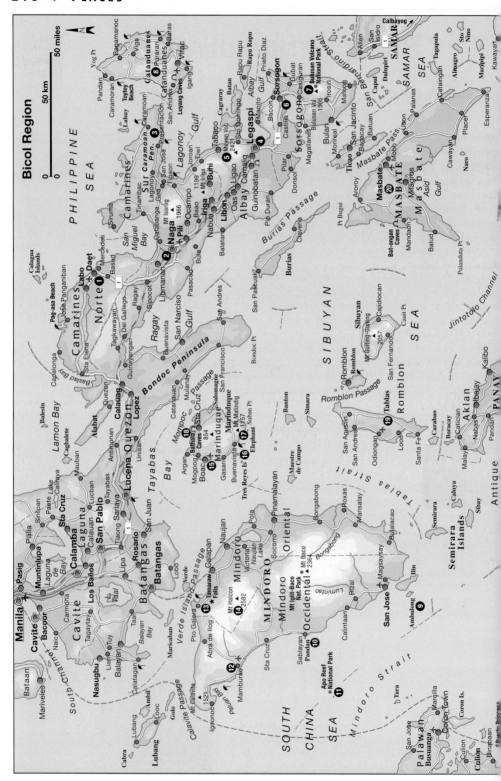

Bicol Region

N

50 miles

50 km

Camarines Sur

Like its northern sister, **Camarines Sur** is an agricultural province. Rice and coconut are the main products, with abaca and banana next. Mining is a growing industry, too, while fishing has, since time immemorial, supplemented all other livelihoods. The locals have also taken on embroidery and bamboo craft.

The high point of the year for the province's largest city of **Naga ❷** is when the great barge, or *casco*, starts its colorful voyage from near the market. This is the water parade in honor of the Virgin of Peñafrancia, housed at the **Peñafrancia Basilica**.

Wander around the city to research the history of the region. Visit the **Naga Metropolitan Cathedral**, built in 1578. Look at the centuries-old San Francisco Church, the province's first, where a Spanish governor surrendered to Filipino revolutionaries toward the end of colonial rule. Don't miss the Quince Martires monument, built in honor of the 15 Filipino martyrs who were executed by the Spaniards. Nearby is the sprawling 1873 Holy Rosary Minor Seminary, one of the oldest seminaries in the country. The well-preserved Colegio de Sta Isabel, founded in 1868, was the first school for girls in the Philippines.

Within the city is the sprawling **Provincial Capitol Complex**, which has a children's park, a modern amphitheater, a jungle garden for relaxing promenades, swimming pools, mini golf and tennis, as well as life-sized statues of legendary Bicolano lovers *Daragang Magayon* and *Handiong*.

Though Camarines Sur is still largely agrarian, there have been developments of interest to tourists, especially in the Bicol area, in recent years. These include the **Camsur Watersports Complex** (open daily 8.30am–9.30pm; entrance fee; tel: 054-477 3159; www.camsurwatersportscomplex.com), which has the largest

Map on page 216

Naga's Metropolitan Cathedral has led a highly eventful life: destroyed by fire in 1768, rebuilt by 1843, damaged by a typhoon in 1856, restored again by 1879, once more damaged by an earthquake in 1887, and rebuilt in 1890.

LEFT: harvested rice stalks.
BELOW: celebrants at the Peñafrancia festival.

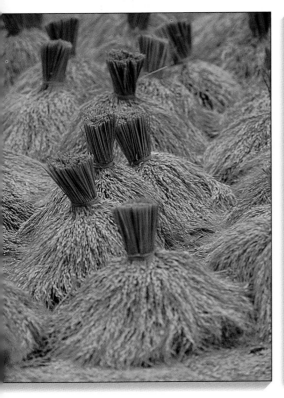

The Leaning Tower of Bombon.

cable-pulled wakeboarding center in Asia as well as organized tours around Bicol, such as to the unexplored Caramoan Peninsula.

Natural Playground

The **Kulapnitan Caves of Libmanan** – named for the thousands of *kulapnit* or cave bats that hang on its gold-crusted ceilings – present a breathtaking spectacle of limestone formations. Along Quirino Highway is the Villa Esperanza Resort in **Sipocot** town, a modern resort in a tropical setting. **Del Gallego** houses the PNR Marker Park, where the late President Manuel L. Quezon drove a golden nail during the inauguration of the north- and south-bound railroad tracks, which finally linked Manila and Legaspi.

From Naga, take a jeepney to *barangay* **Panicuason**, home to the 13-meter (43-ft) Malabsay Falls and Nabontolan Spring, located near the edge of a riveting ravine. Farther on is the 1,966-meter (6,450-ft) **Mt Isarog**, a dormant volcano whose many springs and streams make it an important watershed in the region. Isarog's virgin rainforest, with a wide variety of rare flora and fauna, has easy trekking trails. At its crater is the Magragobdob Falls, small yet alluring.

Halfway along a rough road to **Tigaon** is Consorcep Resthouse, 550 meters (1,800 ft) above sea level. Up north is the **Leaning Tower of Bombon**, the local counterpart of Pisa's famous landmark. In the next town of Calabanga is the brick-made **Ladrillo Church of Quipayo**, built in 1616. Rare artifacts excavated in this church are displayed in a museum behind the altar.

BELOW: wild orchid in the rainforests of Mt Isarog.

Lagonoy town has the twin attractions of Bolan-ogan Falls, located in a lush forest setting, and Adiangao Cave, whose underground marvels have attracted many cavers. Sabang Beach in **San Jose** features crystal-clear waters and powdery sands, as does **Atulayan Island**.

Off the eastern coast of San Jose is the ultimate adventure destination of **Caramoan Peninsula** ❸. With a feast of bays, islands, islets, protruding rocks, brooding limestone cliffs and heavily forested highlands that are home to abundant wildlife, Caramoan has all the attributes of a prime ecotourism destination. For a treat, cycle to breathtaking **Gota Beach**. Nearby are numerous white-sand islets, surrounded by caves accessible by foot. While Caramoan is ideal for island-hopping, sea-kayaking, scuba diving, snorkeling and hiking, infrastructure is fairly minimal, so arrange your plans before heading to the area.

About 15 km (9 miles) southeast of Naga is the city of **Pili**, named after the pili nut, one of Bicol's more popular exports. The capital is known for Boncao Hill, the last Japanese stronghold in Bicol. The next town of **Bula** has the milky-white Nalalata Falls, and boasts of an 18th-century church, while **Nabua** town has Lake Bato, an inland lake habitat of wild ducks.

Sheltering in the shadow of the 1,196-meter (3,924-ft) Mt Iriga, also known as Mt Asog, is **Iriga City**, thought to be the youngest city in Bicol. The volcanic mountain is popular for its relatively easy trails and the spectacular view from its peak.

The neighbouring town of **Buhi** is home to numerous, scenic waterfalls, spring-resorts and little lakes. The Church at Buhi has the tallest belfry and reputedly the most pleasant bell sound in Bicol. **Lake Buhi** is the habitat of *tabios*, the world's smallest freshwater fish, locally known as *sinarapan,* and measuring about 3–4 mm (⅛-inch). Like most endangered species, the *sinarapan* once formed part of a substantial fishing industry. The introduction of predatory species and over-fishing, however, has endangered the tiny creatures. **Roca Encantada**, an enchanting island in the middle of the lake, is popular for picnics and strolls.

Albay

Overland from Iriga City is the province of **Albay**, considered the "land of fire and fury," which does not, however, stop travelers from visiting and returning. There are daily flights to **Legaspi ❹**, capital of Albay, and various bus services on the Legaspi–Manila route.

Volcanoes and rolling hills covered with coconut plantations, rice fields and patches of forests dominate Albay's terrain. Legaspi is a bustling commercial center, sitting in the shadow of Mayon Volcano, reputedly the world's most perfectly cone-shaped volcano. Visit in October and see the week-long Ibalong Festival, which honors the heroes of Ibalon. The festival is a blaze of colorful costumes, ranging from the beautiful to the bizarre, and a riot of music, both traditional and modern. The smell of exotic Bicolano dishes will waft through the air.

Legaspi City Museum (open Mon–Fri 8am–noon and 1–5pm; free) showcases old photographs, documents, religious and cultural objects of local importance.

Mayon Volcano

Beautiful it is called and is truly so – with a threatening, deadly allure. **Mayon Volcano ❺** takes its name from *magayon,* or beautiful in the Bicolano dialect.

Map
on page
216

TIP

To see the wriggly *sinarapan* – the world's smallest freshwater fish – swimming, visit Buhi Freshwater Demonstration Fish Farm, or the Municipal Aquarium at the Buhi Town Hall.

BELOW:
dugout canoes line the shores of Lake Buhi.

Because of its constant activity, trekking Mayon Volcano is considered dangerous. Time and time again, Mayon erupts yet again, forcing thousands of villages in its surroundings to be evacuated. Anyone planning a climb should check first with the Philvolcs office in Legaspi.

BELOW:
Mayon Volcano with the ruins of Cagsawa Church.

It first erupted for European eyes in 1616, when a passing Dutch ship witnessed its explosive abilities. Since then, Mayon has erupted over 50 times – and as recently as August 2006.

In 1814, Mayon erupted with brief but massive violence, sending a bombardment of red-hot boulders to bury the settlements of Cagsawa and Buiao in the town of **Daraga**. Local inhabitants ran for shelter to Cagsawa Church, but a mighty tide of lava flowed right into it, killing at least 1,200 people. Today, **Cagsawa Ruins**, most of it submerged 40 meters (130 ft) below the ground, reminds visitors of this tragic eruption, considered to be Mayon's worst. On a hilltop overlooking the town 5 km (3 miles) away from Mayon stands the overgrown **Daraga Church**, which the locals built right after the 1814 eruption.

Considered to be the most active volcano in the Philippines, erupting almost every 8 to 10 years, the 2,420-meter (7,940 ft) **Mayon Volcano** covers an area of 465 hectares (1,150 acres) and was proclaimed a national park in 1938. Its eco-system is home to endemic and endangered flora and fauna such as bleeding heart pigeons – so-called for the red marking on their breasts. At the foot of Mayon's slopes are farms that take advantage of the rich volcanic soil.

Non-trekkers wanting to see Mayon will find equally interesting sites nearby. Nestling right on the volcano, at an altitude of 760 meters (2,500 ft), is **Mayon Skyline Hotel and Convention Center**, formerly the Mayon Resthouse. An excellent resort with temperatures similar to that in Baguio, it offers an exhilarating view of the Pacific Ocean and Eastern Albay. Within the resort is the **Holy Rosary Mountain**, whose giant rosary beads garland a huge cross on a slope right above the hotel.

Of course, there's more to Albay than Mayon Volcano. The mountains of

Masaraga, Malinao and Catbuwaran are just waiting for trekkers to conquer them, and the islands of San Miguel, Cagrary, Batan, Rapu-Rapu and Buhatan – off the eastern coast of Legaspi – have several dive spots.

Map on page 216

Whistling caves

In the town of **Camalig** are the **Hoyop-Hoyopan Caves** (literally "blow-blow" – derived from the sound of the wind whistling through the main entrance), part of an extensive series of limestone caves. Carrying a smoky flare, the guide leads visitors down a twisting subterranean path that eventually ends on the other side of the mountain. A steep climb up the hill arrives at another entrance and then dives back underground. A fourth access point offers a magnificent vista of green coconut plantations, with Mayon towering above them. Finally, the hike re-emerges at the original entry point.

Calabidong Caves, 2 km (1½ miles) farther away, have a small underground stream and a dense population of bats. Altogether, over a dozen caves have been discovered within an 8-km (5-mile) radius of the main caverns. Pototan and Cagraray Caves, in Liguan Island, have large chambers and stalactites.

North of Legaspi, at the town of **Sto Domingo**, is Mayon Spring Resort, well equipped with facilities and dotted with pine trees, perfect for a picnic. The next town of **Bacagay** has almost unspoiled **Sogod Beach**, known for its clean, black sand. Its coconut palms and lush vegetation provide cool shade.

Limestone formation at Calabidong Caves.

In **Malilipot** town is the magnificent 245-meter (800-ft) Busay Falls, which has seven tiers of white foam cascading down to a major basin that branches out into several smaller ones. The next town of **Tabaco** has Buang Spring Resort, where a natural spring-fed swimming pool and other facilities surrounded by trees provide a romantic and enjoyable forest atmosphere. Nearby San Lorenzo Beach has a breathtaking view of Tabaco Bay. Off the coast of Tabaco is the green, soft-looking and quiet island of **San Miguel**, home to the white-sand and clear-water Punta Beach. Amater Resort in **Malinao** town has a natural spring-fed swimming pool.

BELOW: black-sand Sogod Beach.

In **Tiwi**, the surging ocean comes upon sweeping Putsan Beach. It features magnificent rock formations and the jet-black sands, used to make the region's ancient ceramics. The beach teems with magnificent rock formations and fishing boats. Every third Saturday of August, thousands of devotees flock to small *barangay* **Joroan** in Tiwi to pay homage to the miraculous image of Nuestra Señora de Salvacion, patroness of Albay. The event, popularly known as the Pilgrimage to Joroan, features a procession carrying the saint down to the beach. Large, well-decorated pumpboats then ferry pilgrims and devotees to the shores of the village at Sogod, where a mass is held. Along Tiwi's highway are steep cliffs that roll dangerously down, but don't be intimidated. Those who are not easily cowed are rewarded with views of the vast Pacific Ocean at strategically-placed rest areas along the way.

Sorsogon

A fine drive along a coastal, cliffside road south of Legaspi loops across mountain ridges that plummet

It is generally believed that when the Bicolano is not enjoying mundane life to the hilt, he is contemplating it in the church or in the seminary, for many Filipino priests come from the Bicol region.

straight to the sea. This takes you to **Sorsogon Province**, the southernmost in Bicol. At least 10 buses (involving 13 hours of travel) from Manila reach the capital city, **Sorsogon ❻**. Or one can fly to Legaspi, then take a jeepney.

Sorsogon is pleasant and progressive. At the center is the attractive Provincial Capitol Building, while Sorsogon National High School is considered one of the most impressive and beautiful high school buildings in the country.

Seven km (4 miles) away is a white sand beach in Bacon, with cottages and picnic huts. Twenty kilometers (12 miles) distant is Rizal Beach in **Gubat**, a long, crescent-shaped strip of white sand, ideal for boating, swimming and beachcombing. A little way south is **Barcelona**, noted for its church and fortress ruins, and its good beach.

Farther south is **Lake Bulusan**, dubbed the "Switzerland of the Orient," lying 600 meters (1,970 ft) above sea level and expanding over a circular area of 16.5 hectares (40 acres) inside the 3,670-hectare (9,070-acre) **Bulusan Volcano National Park ❼**.

A 2-km (1½-mile) hiking trail winds around the lake and up to the 1,565-meter (5,130-ft) **Bulusan Volcano**, which leaps like a giant from the middle of a forest, that is home to more than a hundred kinds of plants and flowers. At its foot is San Benon Spring, which has a mixture of sulfuric, steaming, lukewarm and cool waters. Just 7 km (4 miles) away is **Masacrot Spring**, a man-made pool with bubbling, cool and natural soda water.

Namuat Falls in **Casiguran** is surrounded by a variety of flowering plants. Bulus Spring of **Irosin** has clear and cool water springing out from obscure fissures. The nearby scenic Mapaso Spring is believed to have curative effects, its falling water emitting thin smoke. Along Sorsogon Bay is Pepita Park, complete with rest houses, cemented walks, beaches, a children's playground and lush greenery. Overlooking the bay is the Paroja Hill Grotto.

Sorsogon's current crowd-drawer is the town of **Donsol**: off here, the gentle *butanding* or whale sharks, are spotted seasonally. The best time to go is between February and May, when spotters and *butanding* interaction officers from the municipality guide boat-loads of people to swim and interact with the gentle giants.

Catanduanes

A flight northeast from Legaspi takes you up over the black sand beaches along the coast. The various small islands in the Albay Gulf, fringed with fine, white sandy beaches, disappear below, and, for a few minutes, the plane skims over the wave tops. Then, slowly, the hilly island of Catanduanes comes into view.

Way off the beaten track, the 15,110-sq. km (5,830-sq. mile) island province of **Catanduanes ❽** is a huge mountain mass with thick forests of hardwoods, one of the main sources of Philippine mahogany. Called "Land of the Howling Winds," Catanduanes lies east of Luzon and bears the first impact of the typhoons that regularly strike the area, seriously hindering its economy. There is, however, a positive side to typhoons, appreciated by that group of sports enthusiasts called surfers. To them Catanduanes is simply

BELOW: a warm smile beckons.

home to a fickle surf break called Majestics, and, when it's not pumping, to other local breaks in Coconut Point, Twin Rocks, Morning Point, Rocky Point and Bintikayan.

As the island slowly gains interest as a surfing destination and attracts more visitors, its sleeping secrets are slowly being awakened, such as **Toytoy Beach** and **Igang Beach**, previously enjoyed only by locals, are becoming modestly developed to provide rest stops for eager surfers.

Spectacular beaches

Around town are a couple of hotels and restaurants, providing a base, when the weather is good, for exploring more of the island. Puraran Beach is clean, white and invigorating, with a dining hall and surfing area. Mamangal Beach is lined with trees, has pavilions and sheds, and is ideal for weekend picnics and scuba diving, its waters clear, and the reefs swarming with all sorts of colorful fish. Toytoy Beach has a clean, white beach and underwater coral formations, while the white-sanded Igang Beach has nearby caves and more coral. Catanduanes Island Resort has white and brilliantly clean beaches ideal for surfing, skindiving and sports fishing, as well as an 18-hole golf course.

Lush vegetation, forests and wildlife provide an excellent backdrop for hiking and climbing around **Nahulugan Falls**. The scenic **Binanuahan Waterfalls** has picnic grounds and sheds for overnight stays, and is good for swimming, diving and hiking, while **Luyang Caves** feature a grotto-like limestone formation. Indeed, such natural attractions, coupled with the booming surf scene, suggest that the Catanduanes economy may one day equal that of its urban neighbors. ❑

TIP

When surfing the reef breaks at Catanduanes, always use protective gear, such as rash guards and booties and be prepared for cuts and scrapes.

BELOW: Sorsogon fish ponds.

LUZON'S ISLANDS

These offshore havens offer untouched beaches, virgin forests, mysterious caverns, soothing hot springs, and the simple pleasures of camping beneath the stars

Map on page 216

Most of those who have traveled to the islands of Mindoro, Marinduque, Romblon and Masbate would talk of bumpy roads and lack of infrastructure in some areas. But do not be intimidated: try the islands' simple delights and uncomplicated pleasures. If you're bold enough to take on the challenge, excitement is guaranteed as you come face to face with adventure and mystery.

Lying just south of Manila is the large island of **Mindoro**. Its name comes from Spanish, *mina de oro*, meaning gold mine, though no major gold deposits were discovered there at any time. But perhaps the Spaniards weren't actually referring to a precious metal when they named the place, for the island's tourism potential is undoubtedly a gold mine of a different sort. The island is divided by the Mindoro Mountains into Mindoro Oriental, on the eastern side, and Mindoro Occidental, to the west.

Mindoro Occidental

Bounded on the north by Verde Island, on the west and south by the Mindoro Strait, and Mindoro Oriental on the east, **Mindoro Occidental** is endowed with numerous attractions. Mostly natural, these include virgin forests, beautiful white sand beaches, islands and islets rich in marine life, coral gardens, caves and waterfalls. There are abundant but barely tapped natural land and marine resources. The offshore waters are rich in tuna, marlin and swordfish.

There are cheap accommodation throughout the province, some without electricity. But who cares when you're trekking the interior of the mountains, visiting Mangyan settlements, or trying to steal a glimpse of the wild *tamaraw?* Who needs light when the moon and stars are bright?

There are regular flights to Mamburao and San Jose from Manila, and boats and fast ferries depart every hour from Batangas to Calapan. On the island, buses ply the Puerto Galera and Bulalacao route.

On the southwestern coast of Mindoro Occidental is the sprawling city of **San Jose**, off which sits the 3,000-hectare (7,400-acre) **Ambulong Island ❾**. White beaches, cliffs and underwater caves characterize the island. There is a fishing village on the sheltered side, and coral gardens and tropical fish in numerous coves. Dive spots, such as Iling Point, Baniaga Reef, Ambulong Bank, Dungan Reef, Sardines Reef, Manadi Island and Apo Reef are accessible from San Jose.

The budget traveler can visit **North Pandan Island ❿**, off the coast of Sablayan, for leisurely water sports activities. Surrounding the little resort

LEFT: ready to meet the sun. **BELOW:** a *banca* moored off Mindoro.

are snorkeling, fishing, boating and swimming sites, as well as excellent rock formations. When all accommodation in Mindoro is fully booked, especially during Holy Week, North Pandan Island offers a paradisical slice of tropicana to visitors looking to dodge the crowds. Camping here is a nice option for those so inclined; otherwise, Pandan Island Resort offers bungalows.

Apo Reef

North Pandan Island is the major gateway to **Apo Island**. Located on this island is the **Apo Reef National Park ⓫**, acclaimed as one of the best dive sites in the Philippines. Apo itself is less than 1-km (½-mile) long, but the extensive reef holds enough underwater interest to keep divers busy for a week. Some 400–500 coral species are present in the waters around the island, and Shark Ridge presents the best underwater adventure on the reef. The best time to visit Apo is March–early June, between the monsoons and when the seas are calmer. Between dives, one can also birdwatch on the islands of Binangaan and Cajos del Bajo.

When crossing to San Jose from Ambulong, stop off at **Ilin Island** for a glimpse into life in a Philippine fishing village. The White Island at Ilin has a long beach with smooth and powdery white sand, ideal for swimming, scuba diving and fishing. Marine turtles occasionally bury their eggs in the sand here.

In the heart of Mindoro is the 75,450-hectare (186,400-acre) **Mt Iglit-Baco National Park**, home to the last significant population of *tamaraw* (wild upland dwarf buffalo) and the endangered Mindoro imperial pigeon. It is considered one of the least known, least visited national parks in the country, and a sanctuary for the *tamaraw*. To search for these endangered beasts, hire a guide (P150–350 per day) at the Tamaraw Conservation Project.

BELOW: an Apo Island fisherman caught unawares.

Tayamaan Beach in **Mamburao** , the provincial capital, is a 1-hectare (2½-acre) strip of sand lined with coconut trees and native cottages. The secluded 14-hectare (35-acre) Mamburao Beach Resort, has a 4-km (2½-mile) light gray sand beach, ideal for swimming, scuba diving, windsurfing, snorkeling, deep sea fishing and water skiing. Glass bottomed boats, speedboats, and outrigger boats are also available.

Caving challenges

Unexplored caves dot the mountains of Mindoro. Experienced cavers may want to take the challenge of **Luyang Baga** (Lung Cave) in Cabacao, Abra de Ilog. Getting to the cave, however, is tough. After a jeepney ride from Mamburao to Abra de Ilog, you need to hire a Mangyan guide from the settlements near Cabacao to take you to the entrance. Be prepared with everything: supplies in town are sparse.

From Cabacao the trek takes eight hours, and involves 21 river crossings in chest-deep water. During rainy season, the current is very strong and the trail virtually impassable. But the trail has its rewards. Once in the caves, visitors can marvel at the white crystalline floors and walls, spelothems, and deep pools of gin-clear water. Many of the deep pools and connecting chambers have yet to be explored. Consult with your guide to make sure you are adequately equipped to tackle the more difficult passages, some of which are tiring, horizontal and narrow.

Northwest of the province is **Lubang Island**, where Japanese soldier Hiroo Onada was found in 1974, surrendering as a prisoner-of-war after 30 years of hiding in the mountains.

Northward is **Ambil Island**, a favorite fishing ground for sports enthusiasts,

Map on page 216

TIP

Watch the tide when visiting Ilin Island. Some of its beaches are fringed with reefs, making passage difficult during low water.

BELOW: a Mangyan man and child.

THE MANGYANS OF MINDORO

Mangyan is the collective name given to Mindoro's indigenous proto-Malayan people, who settled on the island around 3,000 years ago.

Several tribal groups – the Alangan, Buid, Iraya, Tugayda, Tatagnon and the Hanunoo – make up these people, who traditionally wear native G-strings. Most Mangyans live a nomadic life, hunting wild animals, fishing and gathering native fruits.

Their small villages comprised houses made of palm wood and covered with palm straw. Some of them practice sustainable slash-and-burn farming.

Like other tribal groups in the country, Mangyans have their own cultural systems and beliefs – and, regrettably, their own tales of harassment and social stereotyping, as they continue to struggle to preserve their own identity and hold on to their precious lands. The typical Filipino, for instance, jokingly (some more seriously) refers to the Mangyans as "people with tails."

Illegal loggers, Christian settlers and ranchers have booted the Mangyans out of the lands that they once occupied. Elusive and shy, these people have now retreated deeper into the mountains, many deliberately avoiding contact with outsiders.

BELOW: trekkers near Puerto Galera.

who cross the narrow channel from Manila to Nasugbu. On Ambil is the scenic Besay Falls, consisting of a series of waterfalls each cascading into a crystal clear basin about 5 meters (16 ft) in diameter.

A 30-minute pumpboat ride northwest of Lubang is the sports fishing fan's favorite, **Cabra Island**. Generally flat, Cabra has golden-hued sandy beaches on its southwestern part and magnificent rock formations along its east coast.

Mindoro Oriental

In a sheltered inlet, where the scenic harbor seems perfect for those with a little sea gypsy in their soul, sits **Puerto Galera** (PG) ⓭ , or "Port of Galleons". Today, the place marks its days with the comings and goings of increasing numbers of visitors, as it has become developed – some would say over-developed – into a resort area.

Although **Sabang Beach** was once described as "Little Ermita," the number of bars has decreased in recent years. There are plenty of peaceful, pleasant spots along the coast, ideal for water skiing, kayaking, scuba diving, snorkeling, sunbathing and swimming. **Small La Laguna Beach** has coral reefs, good for snorkeling and scuba diving. **Talipanan Beach** and **Punta Guarda Beach** are not as busy as the other beaches in Puerto Galera, and are perfect for swimming. **White Beach** has nice beaches for swimming, and some entertainment facilities, but gets over-crowded during local holidays, such as Holy Week. **Aninvan Beach** is close enough to White Beach to walk to, but far enough from the noisy nightlife.

A trek up the hills above Puerto Galera makes a nice break from the all-beach scenery; Mangyan tribal settlements dot the interior. If you want a beach all to yourself, hire a boat to take you to **Bikini Beach**.

Inside the Roman Catholic convent is **Puerto Galera Museum** (open Mon–Fri 8am–5pm; free), exhibiting valuable artifacts dating from Spanish and pre-Spanish times. These include large jars, porcelain dishes and the legendary black rice of Puerto Galera, believed to be the sea water-preserved remains of a rice granary that caught fire in the 16th century. There's also the **Marble Cross** at Muelle, a famous landmark in memory of the crew of the Spanish warship *Canonero Mariveles*, which sank during a storm on November 18, 1879 while guarding the waters of Puerto Galera.

Also visit the marble quarry at Mt Talipapan, where 17 different varieties of marble are extracted from the mountainside, and see the polished marble floors of the Marblecraft Guest House.

Ponderosa, an exclusive 9-hole golf club sitting on an 800-meter (2,600-ft) elevation, offers Puerto Galera's shimmering beauty on one side, and mist caressing the deep-green mountains on the other. The 130-meter (430-ft) high **Tamaraw Falls** is located alongside the roadside 15 km (9 miles) southeast of Puerto Galera and has a natural swimming pool at its base. Its cascading waters attract the attention of passers-by. Hire a jeepney to get there.

Further southeast of Puerto Galera, **Calapan**, the provincial capital, lies in the shadow of 2,582-meter (8,471-ft) **Mt Halcon ⓮**, the highest in Mindoro, and the Philippines' fourth highest. Considered one of the country's finest trekking peaks, it has several rivers and rock formations and is a notable haven for wildlife. Its wild terrain, however, must be treated with respect. If considering a climb, get a guide.

Continuing southeast, **Naujan Lake**, the largest freshwater lake in the province, is home to freshwater species that enter the lake to feed before going to the open sea to spawn. Hunting and fishing inside this wildlife sanctuary are regulated by national park personnel.

Adjacent is the volcanic **Pungaw Hot Springs**, located among large boulders. Its surroundings pools – filled with bubbling hot springs water – are believed to be therapeutic. Go to the nearby Dome Hill and see the breathtaking view of the lake, the vast agricultural plains and the Butas and Lumangbayan rivers.

Marinduque

An isolated volcanic mass surrounded by coral reefs, **Marinduque** lies between Mindoro Island and Quezon Province's Bondoc Peninsula. Legend would have the heart-shaped island rising from the seas as a consequence of a tragic love story. A powerful southern Luzon king named Datu Batumbacal prevented his daughter Marin from accepting the love of a fisherman-poet, Garduke. When the pair persisted in meeting secretly, the king ordered the beheading of Garduke, but the lovers sailed out to sea and drowned themselves instead. At that instant, Marinduque Island rose from the sea.

Boac ⓯, the provincial capital and seat of business and commerce, lying on the west coast, is best accessed by sea from Lucena, Quezon. There's also a 40-minute flight from Manila. Although still in the throes of rebuilding its former glory, this naturally, historically and culturally rich province continues to attract tourism.

The **Battle of Pulang Lupa** was the first known major battle won by the Filipinos over the Americans

Map on page 216

In 1981, a sunken galleon was found between the waters of Gaspar and the mainland, yielding millions of pesos worth of artifacts and treasures, mostly porcelain.

BELOW: nearing Marinduque.

In 1996, Boac made international news when mine wastes from the mountaintop operations of Marcopper Mining Corporation – which used to produce 20 percent of the country's copper – smothered the pristine Boac river system that begins in the hills.

on July 31, 1900. Despite having inferior weapontry, the group of Filipino soldiers overcame their American enemies, thereby forever earning their place in Philippine history books. A marker stands at the site, which is now surrounded by dense vegetation.

Mainit Hot Springs, a flowing brook of hot spring water, considered highly therapeutic, is Marinduque's version of a hot spa, while 18th-century **Boac Cathedral** features Filipino-Hispanic Gothic architecture, with much of the original structure faithfully preserved – the facade and main body, the belfry, and the altar. The cathedral also houses the reputedly miraculous Lady of Biglang Awa (Sudden Mercy).

Three Kings

Thirteen kilometers (8 miles) south of here is Gasan, from where one can take a 30-minute ride by motorized outrigger to **Tres Reyes** (Three Kings) **Islands** , the favorite snorkeling and diving site of the province – and where an ancient Chinese junk capsized in the 15th century. Most of its remains have since been removed however. The largest of the three, and closest to Marinduque's southwest coast, is Gaspar Island, with Melchor Island and Baltazar Island beyond.

These islands are ideal for fishing, swimming and snorkeling, with their precipitous shore cliffs and wonderful underwater caves and reefs. Marine species such as grouper, snapper, mackerel and sweetlip are abundant in the area, while coconut crabs called *igod* are frequently found on the beach.

Dominating the south of Marinduque is **Mt Malindig** , an inactive volcano which rises 1,160 meters (3,800 ft) above the sea and is accessible from Santa Cruz. Dense forest covers its upper half, but the rest is nearly deforested due to

BELOW: Boac, provincial capital of Marinduque.

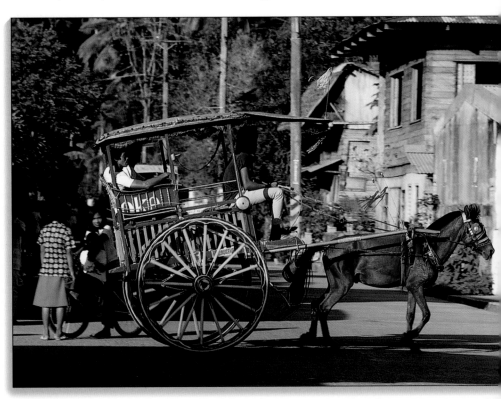

slash-and-burn farming. Fortunately, this does not affect the mountain's reputation as an excellent place for climbing, camping and bird watching. At the volcano's base are the therapeutic waters of **Malbog Sulfur Springs**, where two swimming pools of warm, though slightly sulfuric, waters offer relaxing baths to visitors.

Off the coast of Buenavista town are sheer cliffs, with a lengthy beach of white sand and crushed corals surrounding **Elephant Island**, one of the small islets dotting the seas of Marinduque.

Map on page 216

Around Santa Cruz

In the town of Santa Cruz is the mysterious **Bathala Caves** ⑱ complex. Only four of the seven caves have so far been explored. The first is called the Simbahan (church), owing to its cathedral-like interior where stalagmites form a rough likeness to an altar, a bell and a silhouette of the Virgin Mary carrying the Child. The second cave is darker and deeper, and reputedly guarded by a python. The third has an underground river, and the fourth cave harbors human bones, thought to be the remains of World War II soldiers.

Off the coast of Santa Cruz are the islets of Polo, Mompong and Maniwaya, characterized by white sand beaches and sandy cliffs. The nearby, privately owned **Salomague Island** has a long white beach of sand and crushed corals. There is a good dive spot northeast of the islet.

On the northwestern tip of Marinduque is scuba diving haven **Natangco Islet**, an 8-hectare (20-acre) islet with a short stretch of powdery white sand that gradually slopes into the sea, filled with corals and aquatic life. Coasta Celina, another diving favorite, further south in Torrijos town, is flanked by cliffs on both sides, with an undersea wall that is rich in marine flora and fauna.

LEFT: masked revellers at the Moriones Festival.
BELOW: Bathala Caves.

*Marinduque island is
where the colorful
Moriones Festival is
held each year
during Holy Week
(April or May). The
crucifixion and
resurrection of Christ
comes alive before
your very eyes.*

BELOW:
marble products
on sale at Romblon.

The week-long Moriones Festival, celebrated in the towns of Boac, Mogpog and Gasan every week before Easter, is another Marinduque attraction. It is a religious festival featuring masked men colorfully dressed in the likeness of Roman soldiers. Some of the masks, made of local *dadap* wood, are sold to tourists immediately after the festival, while others are kept for the following year's event.

Romblon

Southeast of Marinduque is the province of **Romblon**, which consists of three major islands and several islets. The biggest island is **Tablas** 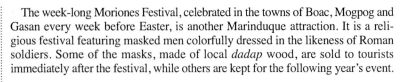, where the provincial airport is located. The province is completely surrounded by deep waters and lies on the Sibuyan Sea, between the islands of Masbate and Mindoro. There are several 45-minute flights a week, and also twice-a-week, 14-hour boat trips, from Manila.

Known as "Marble Country," Romblon features topography that is rich in marble and other rock types, all of which supply materials for sculpture and building. It has extraordinary white sand beaches and clear waters, beautiful during both sunny and stormy weather. Places of interest include Bonbon Beach, Cambon Beach, Bita Falls, Tinagon Dagat (Hidden Lake) and magnificent waterfalls in San Andres and Odiongan towns.

The province also offers **Romblon Cathedral**, which features a Byzantine altar and several icons and paintings, and two old forts, **Fort Santiago** and **Fort Andres**, once used as lookouts for pirates during the Spanish regime.

Masbate

Many places in the Philippines derived their names from the locals' response to a misunderstood question from the Spaniards. **Masbate** was born out of such a miscommunication. A squad of Spanish soldiers saw a couple here preparing beverages out of cocoa. One of them asked the locals the name of the region. Thinking that the soldier had asked what she was doing, the woman answered "Masa bati, masa bati," which literally meant to mix and beat more and more. From then on, the place was called Masbate.

On the northwestern tip, limestone cliffs rise almost perpendicular along the Sibuyan Sea. In the interior, rolling hills cascade with verdant forest. The province is composed of three main islands – Masbate, Ticao and Burias – plus several small islets. It is accessible by plane from Manila or by boat from both Manila and Bicol.

Cattle Country

Known as "Cattle Country of the Philippines" because of its abundant grazing pasture and its status as the country's primary beef source, **Masbate**  also teems with stunning beaches, springs, caves and waterfalls. Dacu Beach in Mobo town is a favorite site for weekend picnics, coconut-lined Aroroy Beach is fast-becoming popular for excursions, and Talisay Beach is a booming resort, famous for its "diving board" rocks. There is also Ubo Falls, Masbate's version of Pagsanjan Falls without the hassle of touts, and the

18-meter (60-ft) Tagoron Falls, which plays host to a variety of colored fish at or close to its base. Lush vegetation and wild animals live around the single-tier Catandayagan Falls.

Just 1.5 km (1 mile) from the national road at **Botongan** is a cave with three openings. One, at the base, is very wide and has a church-like formation, giving an eerie yet religious atmosphere. Another is at the center and the third is found at the top of the cave. Inside is a large tunnel, connecting to another cave in **Zapatos Island** in Balud town. About 120 meters (390 ft) from the cave is the cool and fresh **Botongan Underground River**, ideal for pleasurable dips. Not far away is the **Matang Tubig Spring**, which has three sources. Its surrounding giant trees and rich vegetation makes it popular with budding artists and poets seeking inspiration.

Owing to the region's central location, Masbateños suffer from a sort of identity crisis. The province is part of the Bicol Region, whose people speak Bicolano. Depending on location, however, Masbateños speak only Cebuano, Ilonggo or Masbateño.

Offshore Islands

Ticao Island and **Burias Island** are only day-trips away from Masbate, and they offer something even more remote than their "mainland" island, Masbate, with beaches and fishing villages. For those into island hopping, boats connect Claveria, on Burias, with Donsol, Sorsogon. The latter is also the home of a huge cave which was discovered in 1999, which had a trove of prehistoric gravestones and Ming Dynasty porcelain. Ten km (6 miles) from Ticao Island is Ticao Pass, where giant manta rays have been knwn to gather en masse, giving divers quite a treat.❏

Map on page 216

Though Masbate has only a handful of cattle ranchers, there are a lot of local cowboys who compete in the annual Rodeo Masbateño, usually held in May, June or July.

BELOW: eye-catching jeepney on Masbate Island.

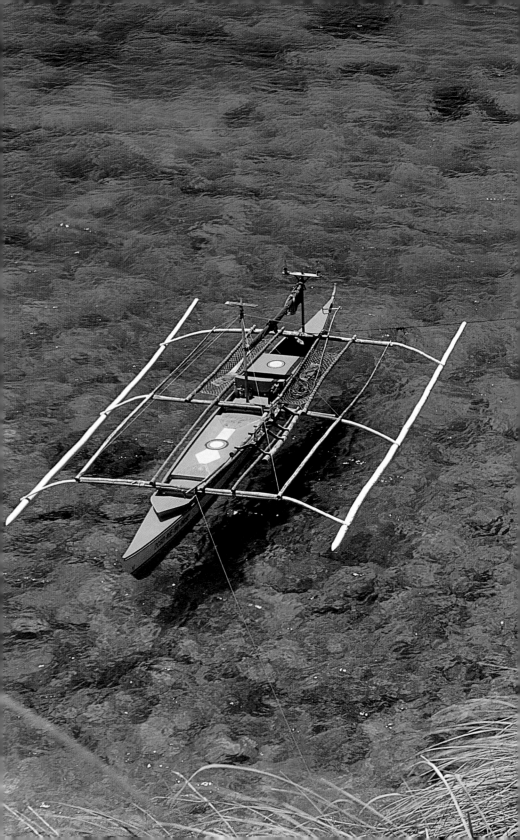

VISAYAS

These laid-back islands offer more than dramatic natural beauty: they have a historical significance, too

They were described by one poetically inclined visitor as "islands of now in a sea of yesteryear." Strung like a necklace of uneven beads, held together by sundry seas, straits and gulfs, the Visayas lend themselves readily to such wistful descriptions. The six major land masses and fringe groups of isles – sandwiched between Luzon and Mindanao – parade a series of idyllic images – calm waters, shimmering coves and palm-fringed beaches. Seafood is always enviably fresh, and the sun ever a handmaiden. The slower pace gives a seductive lilt to the Visayans' speech.

Bisaya, or Visayan, is the term generally accorded to the people of the Visayan Islands, although there are actually three distinct cultural and linguistic groups: the Waray of Samar and Leyte, which comprise Eastern Visayas; the Cebuanos, of their island province in Central Visayas; and the Ilonggos of western Negros and southern Panay in Western Visayas.

On March 16, 1521, the Portuguese sailor Ferdinand Magellan anchored off the tiny island of Homonhon in Leyte Gulf. While he stands credited with the discovery, it was a Malay slave who uttered the first greeting between Spaniard and Filipino. Enrique de Molucca, Magellan's Moluccan slave, hailed a small boat of eight natives from the rail of the *Trinidad*. The natives understood him perfectly; the world had been circled linguistically, and Enrique de Molucca became the first known person to circumnavigate the globe.

Six weeks later, Magellan was dead. Sailing north to the island of Cebu, he "Christianized" the rajah and 500 of his followers. Lapu-Lapu, a minor rajah of Mactan – a muddy coral island where Cebu's international airport now stands – was not as accommodating. He defended his island with some 2,000 warriors against 48 armor-clad Spaniards, the battle claiming Magellan's life. Today, a tall white obelisk on Mactan Island marks the spot where Magellan fell. The dedication on one side of the base records the event as a tragedy for Magellan; on the opposite side, it records a triumph for Lapu Lapu.

The best way to visit the Visayas is by boat. Only then may one experience the islanders' disdain for the dubious benefits of speed. Jets whisk travelers from Manila to Cebu and most other Visayan capitals in under an hour. However, speed does not leave time to savor the subtleties of transition. It takes 20 hours to sail from Manila to the Visayas, and the passage compensates for the chaotic pier bustle and the likely delays before departure. As the Manila skyline recedes, one feels one has given metropolitan clutches the slip. ❑

PRECEDING PAGES: Apo Island in Negros Oriental has all the requisites of a perfect beach: crystal clear waters, powder white sands and a spectacular reef.
LEFT: hauling a bag of sugar to one of the remote islands in the Visayan group.

EASTERN VISAYAS

*Colorful festivals, wonderful seafood, superior trekking,
endless water fun and sobering reminders of recent conflict:
these are the varied attractions of Samar and Leyte*

Map on pages 240–41

Manila

The provinces of Northern, Eastern, and Western Samar; Leyte, Southern Leyte; and Biliran are collectively known as Eastern Visayas or Region 8. Its combination of rich history, sprawling jungles, and mystery spells adventure – for the thrill-seeking traveler at least. Even with the three cities of Ormoc, Tacloban, and Catbalogan in the region and with local tourism slowly picking up, there's still no mistaking the rural charm of this region. Despite much wartime strife, Eastern Visayas, which cradles some of the country's lushest forests and pristine shores, is still very much land, sea, sky, and history.

Adventure tourists and budget travelers do not find the region's "ruralness" a problem. Samar and Leyte offer ample opportunities for action sports, historical tours, and scenic leisure strolls. And the islands' isolation means you'll have everything all to yourself, almost.

Natural wealth

Owing to its rich ecosystems, most of the region's people are engaged in farming and fishing. Region 8 has rich natural resources. Its plains and valleys are fertile, producing hemp, copra, corn, rice, tobacco, bananas, papayas and pineapple. The swamps teem with nipa and mangrove, and the mountains are abundant with rattan and timber. There are thousands of hectares of virgin forests.

LEFT: rice planting on Leyte Island.
BELOW: pineapple plantation cowboy.

Eastern Visayas has no distinct dry or wet season. Its driest months are April–August, with November–January the rainiest. Typhoons from the Pacific usually hit Eastern Samar, sparing most of the region from the calamity. Most people speak the Leyte–Samar dialect, Waray, although some are also conversant in Cebuano, Filipino, and English.

Eastern Visayas abounds in ritual. During the cropping season, farmers perform ceremonies invoking nature and ancestral spirits for a good harvest. This is complemented by Christian customs like the recitation of a *novena*, a nine-day prayer of devotion among Catholics. Fisherfolks, likewise, ask permission from the water spirits for safety at sea and a good catch. Fiestas are celebrated with prayer, food and drink, dance and music. The locals say the only way to walk is to dance, and the only way to talk is to sing.

June is party time. The Pintados Festival revives the tradition of painting the body and dancing to the rhythm of bamboo sticks. Fishermen in the coastal villages of the region celebrate the Subiran Regatta, an annual race for native sailboats.

Regarding food, seafood lovers can feast on Eastern Visayas' fare of fresh fish, shrimps, scallops, *lapu-lapu*, blue marlin and crabs, cooked in a variety of styles.

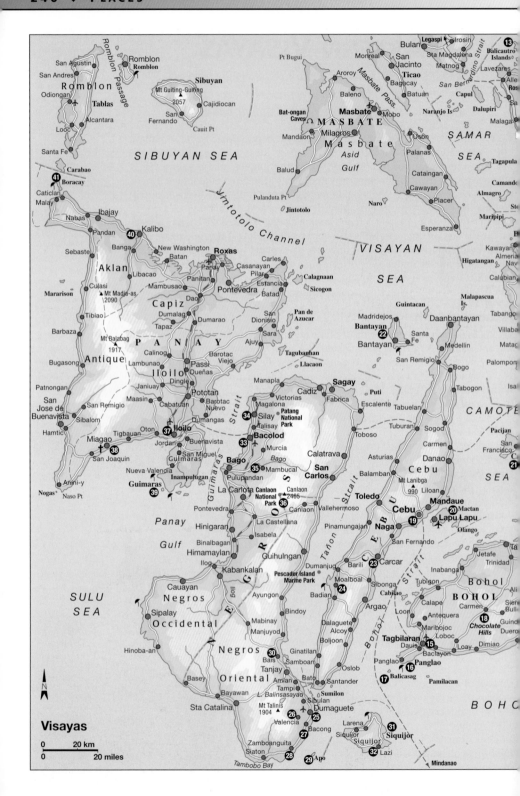

San Agustin
San Andres
Odiongan
Romblon Passage
Romblon
Romblon
San Agustin
Tablas
Alcantara
Looc
Santa Fe

Sibuyan
Mt Guiting-Guiting
2057
San Fernando
Cajidiocan
Cauit Pt

Pt Bugui
Monreal
Aroroy
Bagacay
Baleno
Bat-ongan Caves
Mandaon
Milagros
Masbate
MASBATE
Masbate
Asid Gulf
Balud
Pulanduta Pt

Bulan
Legaspi
Irosin
San Jacinto
Ticao
Batuan
Mobo
Uson
Palanas
Cataingan
Cawayan
Naro
Placer
Jintotolo

Monreal
Sta Magdalena
Matnog
San Bernardino Strait
Capul
Naranjo Is
13
Balicautro Islands
Lavezares
Allen
Ros
Sa
Dalupiri
Malaga
SAMAR SEA
Tagapula
Camando
Almagro
Ste
Maripipi

SIBUYAN SEA

Carabao
41
Boracay
Caticlan
Malay
Ibajay
Nabas
Pandan
40
Kalibo
Banga
Batan
New Washington
Roxas
Aklan
Libacao
Sebaste
Culasi
Mt Madja-as 2090
Mararison
Tibiao
Barbaza
Mt Balabag 1917
Bugasong
Antique
Patnongan
San Jose de Buenavista
Hamtic
Miagao
38
San Joaquin
Anini-y
Nogas
Naso Pt

Jintotolo Channel

Jintotolo

VISAYAN SEA

Esperanza
Kawayan
Higatangan
Almeria
Nav
Calubian
Malapascua Is.
Tabango
Villaba
Matac

Paray
Panay
Panitan
Mambusao
Dumalag
Tapaz
Dumarao
Dao
Calinog
Lambunao
Maasin
San Remigio
Sibalom
Tigbauan
Oton
Jordan
San Miguel
Buenavista
Guimaras
Nueva Valencia
Guimaras
39
Inampulugan
Capiz
Pontevedra
PANAY
Iloilo
Janiuay
Dingle
Cabatuan
Barotac Nuevo
Dumangas
Pototan
Passi
Dueñas
Barotac Viejo
34
Silay
33
Bacolod
Murcia
35
Bago
Mambucal
Pulupandan
La Carlota
Pontevedra
Guimaras Strait
Carles
Casanayan
Pilar
Estancia
Batad
San Dionisio
Sara
Ajuy
Manapla
Victorias
Magalona
Talisay
Bago
San Carlos
Calatrava
Canlaon 2465
36
Canlaon
Vallehermoso
Calagnaan
Sicogon
Pan de Azucar
Tagubanhan
Llacaon
Sagay
Cadiz
Fabrica
Escalente
Tabuelan
Toboso
Asturias
Balamban
Mt Lanibga 990
Liloan
Cebu
Puti
Guintacan
Madridejos
Bantayan
22
Santa Fe
San Remigio
Bogo
Tabogon
Medellin
Daanbantayan
Sogod
Carmen
Danao
CAMOTES
Pacijan
San Francisco
C.
21

Patang National Park
Tuburan

SIBUYAN SEA

Panay Gulf
Hinigaran
Binalbagan
Himamaylan
Ilog
Kabankalan
Cauayan
Negros
Sipalay
Occidental
Hinoba-an
SULU SEA

La Castellana
Isabela
Guihulngan
NEGROS
Boll
Ayungon
Mabinay
Manjuyod
Bindoy
Pescador Island Marine Park
Dumanjug
Moalboal
Badian
Pinamungajan
San Fernando
Naga
Barili
Carcar
Sibonga
Cabijao
Argao
Dalaguete
Alcoy
Boljoon
Oslob
Santander
Sumilon
Dauis
Baclayon
Panglao
Balicasag
Cebu
19
Mandaue
20 Mactan
Lapu Lapu
Olango
Jetafe
Trinidad
Inabanga
Tubigon
Loon
Calape
Antequera
Maribojoc
Loboc
Tagbilaran
15
Dimiao
Loay
18
Chocolate Hills
Guind
Duero
BOHOL
Ali
Sierra Bull
Bohol
Carmen
Tanjay
30
Amlan
Tampi
L. Balinsasayao
Mt Talinis 1904
Bais
Samboan
Ginatilan
Bato
23
24
Toledo
Cebu
Tañon Strait
Cebu Strait
Bohol Strait
Bacong
27
Valencia
26
25
Dumaguete
Larena
Siquijor
Siquijor
31
32 Lazi
Ago
29
28
Siaton
Zamboanguita
Tambobo Bay
Sta Catalina
Bayawan
Sibulan
Basey
Negros
Oriental

CAMOTE SEA

VISAYAN SEA

SEA

N
Visayas

0   20 km
0   20 miles

Mindanao

BOHOL

Pamilacan
Panglao
16
17 Balicasag

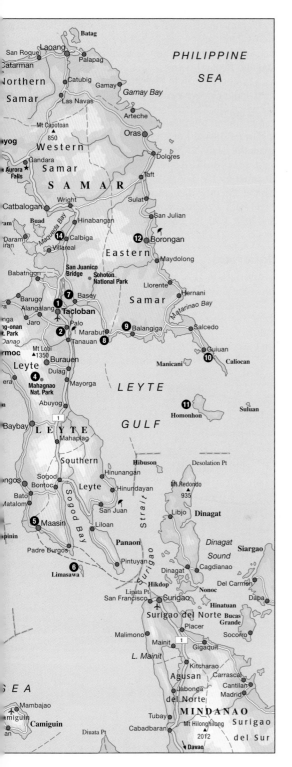

The region has an array of lodging facilities, ranging from luxurious to smaller hotels, inns and pension houses. Cozy, native huts and cottages for back-to-nature tourists are also available. Those wanting to learn more of the local culture can avail of homestay programs through the local tourist office. Note, though, that power supply is erratic in some towns, and rainwater is the most common drinking water among rural households. In contrast, you can easily find facilities for ballroom and disco dancing. The more adventurous visitors can engage in surfing, trekking, mountain and rock climbing, caving as well as watersports.

The central location of Samar and Leyte makes the place readily accessible by land, sea and air. The most favored destination in the region is Tacloban, served daily by one-hour flights from Manila and a half-hour flight from Cebu. Several bus companies ply the Manila–Quezon–Bicol–Samar–Leyte route via the Maharlika Highway; the estimated travel time is 24 hours. A good road network connects the region's municipalities and *barangays*, which are accessible by buses, jeepneys and other private vehicles.

Shipping lines offer regular trips to the region's major ports of call. The Manila–Tacloban route has three round-trips a week, and travel from Cebu is by high speed Supercat and Waterjet. Ferries cross the Surigao Strait from Maasin southeasterly to Lipata Point, in Surigao del Norte, from where the highway proceeds across Mindanao. Outlying islands, on the other hand, can be reached by pumpboat.

Leyte

The capital of Leyte Province – and regional capital of Eastern Visayas – is **Tacloban City ❶**. At the end of the 16th century, Tacloban was still under the municipality of Basey, Samar, but because of its strategic location, it became a vital trading point in the region. On June 12, 1952, it was proclaimed a chartered city.

The statue of an Asian Madonna at the Maria Kannon Garden in Tacloban City is a peace gift from the Japanese.

Visitors should start by picking up information at the regional Department of Tourism office in Children's Park.

At the corner of Magsaysay Boulevard and Sen. Eñage Street are the Tacloban City Park and Playground and Plaza Libertad, where a Filipino version of the Statue of Liberty stands. In front is the **Leyte Provincial Capitol**, once the seat of the Philippine Commonwealth Government under President Sergio Osmeña Sr. While there, visit the Leyte SME Assistance and Trade Center for a glimpse of local culture/art and investment opportunities. Just off Magsaysay Boulevard is the **Leyte Park Resort**, nestled on the sea shore of San Pedro Bay, overlooking Mt Danglay on the island of Samar.

Farther along to the right is the **Maria Kannon Garden**, with a lovely statue of an Asian madonna donated by the Japanese people as a symbol of peace between the Philippines and Japan. Adjacent is the Philippine-Japan Peace Commemoration Statue and Park. Perched on a hilltop in the next compound is the Tacloban City Hall and Park, with the **Balyuan Tower/Mini Amphitheater** below, offering a panoramic view of scenic Kankabatok Bay.

MacArthur's Headquarters

At the end of the road, turn right to J. Romualdez Street. On the left side is Rizal Park. Further along is the **CAP Building** (formerly Price Mansion: open Mon–Fri 8am–noon and 1–5pm; free), the official headquarters of General Douglas MacArthur during the liberation of Leyte in 1944. The MacArthur Room is preserved for public viewing.

BELOW: returning fishermen, Tacloban market pier.

One block southeast, on the corner of T. Claudio and Sen. Eñage streets, is the **Redoña House**, residence of President Osmeña during the liberation of Leyte.

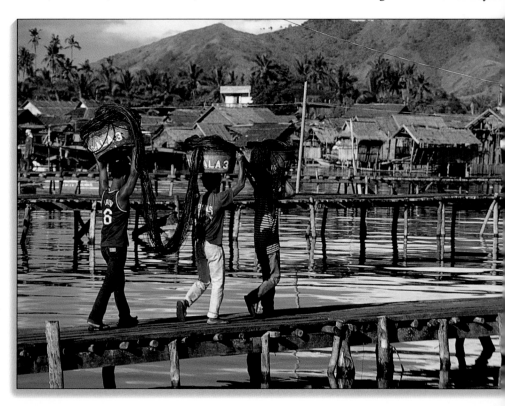

Along Avenida Veteranos Extension, towards Serin district, are the **Stations of the Cross**: 2-meter (7-ft) concrete statues of Jesus and other biblical characters. On top of the hill is the 5.5-meter (18-ft) Sacred Heart monument.

Close by is the **San Juanico Bridge**, which, at 2.2 km (1¼ miles), is Southeast Asia's longest bridge, and crosses over San Juanico Strait to Samar.

Wartime reminders

Back in Tacloban City, at the rotunda in front of Coca-Cola Bottling Company is the **Boy Scout Monument**, erected in 1941. Going straight south to San Jose, on the right side is the **Dio Resort** (also known as Baluarte San Jose), where the Japanese pillboxes are still preserved. Farther along is the Daniel Z. Romualdez Airport, a battle area during World War II. Not too far away is the 9-hole golf course and driving range at the foot of the city's most prominent peak, **San Gerardo Heights**, locally considered Tacloban's version of Makati's ritzy Forbes Park.

At the rotunda by the Coca-Cola plant, turn left to the national highway. At Pawing, before entering the Leyte Government Center, is the **Monument of the Filipino Soldier**, a tribute to the Filipino World War II veterans. Turning left leads to Leyte Government Center, a 130-hectare (320-acre) area for all national government agencies.

Further on, at Red Beach, Candahug, in **Palo ❷**, the **Leyte Landing Memorial** shows where MacArthur landed in 1944 with his Allied Liberation Forces to fulfill his famous "I shall return" promise to the Filipinos, booting out the Japanese invaders. Bronze statues, at 1.5 times bigger than life size, mark the site of the landing and give visitors a great photo opportunity. Close by is the

Map on pages 240–41

San Juanico Strait is considered to be the narrowest navigable strait in the world. It cradles beautiful islets, infinite whirlpools and rushing waters.

BELOW: the CAP building in Tacloban was used by General MacArthur as his headquarters.

50th Leyte Landing Commemorative Rock Garden, and adjacent is the imposing MacArthur Beach Resort, where one can view the enlarged authentic photographs of MacArthur during the liberation days, as well as the panoramic Leyte Gulf.

Palo Metropolitan Cathedral, built in 1596 by Augustinian friars, was converted into an evacuation hospital for the Americans, and served as a refuge for Filipino civilians during the war. Nearby are La Purisima Shrine, an old image of Mary dating back to Spanish times, and **Hill 522**, a battle area during World War II.

Back in Tacloban City, along Real Street is **Sto Niño Shrine and Heritage Museum** (open daily 8–11am and 1–4pm; entrance fee), housing Imelda Marcos' collection of statues of the infant Jesus, and other art objects, as well as tastefully decorated guestrooms with varied Filipino motifs, and a spacious ballroom. Since its sequestration during the Aquino presidency, however, the museum has been left in a state of disrepair.

Adjacent is the **People's Center and Library** (open daily 8–11am and 1–4pm; entrance fee), equipped with a social hall, gymnasium and a reading room which contains 82 ethnic tribe dioramas, historical documents and books on humanities. Turn left to Avenida Veteranos, then right, passing Rizal Avenue, to shop for souvenirs and local delicacies.

Hunter's paradise

West of Palo is **Jaro's Mt Kankahanay**, a hunter's paradise of scenic grandeur, virgin forests and very cool climate, rising 1,230 meters (4,000 ft) above sea level. To the north is the town of **Barugo**, site of the battle between Filipino

BELOW: the Leyte Landing Memorial at Red Beach where General MacArthur landed in 1944.

guerrillas and Japanese Imperial Forces in August 1944, significant for the lack of Filipino casualties, while all the Japanese except one were killed. A monument made up of three stairs marks the site, which is fenced by big silver-colored chains and three flagpoles that resemble bayonets.

The next town, **Carigara**, is popular for Sunduan Ha Carigara, an annual Easter Sunday celebration of cultural, social and religious activities, with a float parade contest, cockfighting, songs and dances. The **Break Neck Ridge**, in neighboring Capoocan, was the site of one of the bloodiest scenes in the battle to free the Philippines from Japanese occupation.

Leyte Mountain Trail

On Leyte's western coast, thousands of Japanese and American soldiers died in Buga-Buga Hills in **Villaba**, during the latter's assault to capture this area during World War II. Inland, the **Leyte Mountain Trail**, outstanding for trekking, runs 40 km (25 miles), from Tong-onan to Lake Danao, continuing southeast to Mahagnao National Park. The trail passes through exhilarating rainforest, beautiful lakes, the spectacular Guinaniban Falls and the Amandiwing mountain range.

North of **Ormoc City** is the **Tong-onan Hot Springs National Park**. The springs are known for their curative powers, and have also become a vital geothermal power source in the lush forest. Just southeast sits the violin-shaped **Lake Danao**, 640 meters (2,100 ft) above sea level and hemmed by cloud-capped mountain ranges and forests.

From Lake Danao continues the Leyte Mountain Trail, wending its way to temperate **Mahagnao National Park ❹**, home to inspiring craters, hot springs, lakes of multi-colored mud and rocks, and virgin forest with giant ferns and orchids – not unlike a scene from *Jurassic Park*. Nearby, one can ride the exciting **Daguitan Rapids** in makeshift rafts of banana trunks, or steadier rubber tired fashioned into rafts for a unique way to see the countryside. From Lake Mahagnao, hike north to the town of **Burauen**, where horses can be rented to explore the surrounding area.

South again from Ormoc is the town of **Baybay**, home to Visayas State College of Agriculture, situated on the foothills of the Baybay mountains. Further south is **Hilongos**, where Hilongos Bell Tower, the highest existing bell built during the Spanish era, is located. **Kaupnit Balinsasayaw Park**, located along the Baybay-Mahaplag road, is a favorite stopover and campsite for travelers.

Beyond Baybay, the road follows the western coastline to **Maasin ❺**, provincial capital of Southern Leyte. Maasin is home to such attractions as the Esfa Beach Resort and the Busay Falls. **Maasin Cathedral** holds images and saints dating back to the Spanish era.

Off the southern tip of Leyte is historic **Limasawa Island ❻**, where the country's first Catholic mass was arguably celebrated. Northeast is **Panaon Island**, where the popular Bitu-on and Maamo beaches can be found.

Map on pages 240–41

The Japanese invasion in 1942 marked the onset of the darkest period in the history of Tacloban. The Battle of Leyte Gulf is one of the biggest naval battles in modern Philippine history.

BELOW: Japanese monument to the dead at Break Neck Ridge.

BELOW: a Basey fiesta clown.

Biliran

Across Carigara Bay and connected to Leyte's northern coast by a bridge lies the picturesque **Biliran Island ❸**, a 55,540-hectare (137,200-acre) island province. Its busy main port, which is crowded with rows of buses and jeepneys, belies the highly rural nature of the province. Head out from Naval on the island's circumferential highway, and the hustle and bustle is literally left behind. Noticeably green, Biliran is abundant with waterfalls, countless streams, hot springs, and fine sand beaches, the most notable of which are Agta Beach in Almeria and Banderrahan Beach in Naval. Biliran's resident highest peaks, **Tres Marias** (literally, Three Marias) is a trio of seemingly equidistant mountain tops, a favorite of local climbers and home of the Philippine spitting cobra.

Located on the island's eastern coast is the town of **Caibiran**, which has the spring-fed San Bernardo Swimming Pool and Tomalistis Falls, both of which were once claimed as having the sweetest water in the world. Off Caibiran are the hot sulfur springs of Mainit and Libtong.

Around Biliran are smaller islands, the most popular of which are the pristine **Maripipi Island**, **Higatangan Island**, and **Sambauan Island**. For the more physically inclined, mountain biking on the National Cross Country Highway is an interesting change – from the beach and sand setting, one is surrounded by cool forest cover and dense vegetation.

The comparative lack of level ground on Biliran compels farmers to build hillside mud terraces, which are nourished by the province's numerous streams, and turned into beauty spots. The **Iyusan Rice Terraces** in Almeria are just one example.

FIESTA IN BASEY

Melanie is a 45-year-old school teacher from Pasig, Metro Manila. As early as July, she advises her school principal about her annual leave, which she conveniently schedules to coincide with the September 29 fiesta of her hometown, Basey, Samar.

This signals the start of her preparation for the event, for which the Basaynons (people of Basey), regardless of where they might be, excitedly return home.

Her earnings as a teacher barely enable her to make ends meet, but she allows herself one whole week of "pampering" and wining and dining with the "big people" of Basey. Though she doesn't have an ancestral home to use as a base, she knows her relatives and friends will eagerly accommodate her, and her friends from Manila, in their homes. The mayor, the town's fiesta host, is her distant relative and he will be offended if she doesn't stay a night or two in his newly renovated house, much more so if she doesn't show up to eat there. He has friends who come all the way from the US for the occasion.

Such is Basey's fiesta. Unreasonably extravagant, yet giving the migrant Basaynons a sense of belonging, without which they can all just grow old in North America, or Manila, and forget about their birthplace.

Samar

At the south end of San Juanico Bridge, joining Leyte to the neighbouring island of Samar, sits **Basey** ❼, site of **Sohoton National Park** with its limestone walls, arches and caves, all swathed in verdant vegetation. Tourists can visit this majestic attraction on board a native outrigger, just a 1¾-hour ride through small, picturesque villages along the **Basey Golden River**. Rawis, a barrio near the river, houses the still unexplored **Rawis Cave**, which, the locals who have been there swear, is better than Sohoton itself.

Basey's church – the **Church of Basey** – was built in 1864, and it features a watchtower built a decade earlier. Every year, on Sept 29, this sleepy town suddenly comes to life as it celebrates the feast of St. Michael, the town's patron saint. The outlandish partying lasts an entire week. The most-awaited festival, however, is the **Banigan-Kawayan Festival**, a cultural street-dancing showcase of props and traditional attire made of bamboo and mats.

To the southeast is the town of **Marabut** ❽, home to the Marabut Marine Park, which features 15 towering rock islands with secluded beach coves and coral gardens, perfect for sea kayaking. **Malatindok**, a magnificent 21-meter (70-ft) X-shaped rock formation located off Calabuso Beach, has challenged countless rock climbers, few of whom have been successful in conquering its peak.

Farther on is Eastern Samar, considered the "eastern gateway to the Philippines." Its extreme topography makes it a must-see destination for the adventurous traveler. **Balangiga** ❾ was the site of a controversial historic incident between the Philippines and the United States. After locals launched a surprise attack on American soldiers on September 28, 1901, the American military retaliated by killing thousands of Filipinos and removing the town's church

Map
on pages
240–41

TIP

Mobility at the Sohoton National Park is partly limited by water tide, so bring a packed lunch and start the tour early in the morning.

BELOW: massive caves at Sohoton National Park.

bells, which were used as a signal during the raid. The incident was dubbed the "Balangiga Massacre" by the American press, and to this day, ownership of the bells – they are on display on an airbase in Wyoming, USA – remains a dispute between the two countries.

Guiuan

South leads to **Guiuan ⑩**, near Suluan Island, home of the first Filipinos to make contact with Magellan's Spanish colonizers. The town's **Church of the Immaculate Conception** is a beautifully preserved 16th-century structure with hand-carved altars and doors, considered the most beautiful antique church in Region 8.

The Guiuan World War II Operating Base has a 3-km (1½-mile) runway, constructed by American Seabees, for the B-29s that dropped the atomic bombs on Japan. Sulang Beach is an ideal site for deep-sea fishing and scuba diving; multi-colored schools of fish are a common sight.

Off the southernmost tip of Guiuan town is **Homonhon Island ⑪**. This is where Magellan's fleet first landed in 1521. **Navy 3149 Base** was one of the biggest American PT (patrol torpedo) boat bases of World War II, with over 300 boats and 150,000 American soldiers then. The base commands a fantastic view of the Pacific Ocean.

Northwards along the eastern coast of Samar lies the town of **Maydolong**, which houses Menasnge Park and its awesome natural rock formations. Next is **Borongan ⑫**, the provincial capital of Eastern Samar; this town is noted for cattle and swine breeding. Other attractions in Borongan are the stone-walled Hamorawon Spring, Guintagican Beach, San Julian Beach and the Santa Monica Caves.

BELOW:
this little pig lives in Borongan, noted for its swine-breeding.

Canhugas Beach in **Hernani** town is said to be legendary, having a 200-meter (650-ft) footbridge from the reef to the sea built by a "giant." There is also a rock formation that looks like man-made steps, the waters slamming against it flowing down through the steps like a waterfall.

Map on pages 240–41

Last true province

Following the eastern coast leads to **Northern Samar**, considered to be one of the last remaining true Filipino provinces where seeing foreigners is still strange for locals. Inland, Las Navas and Catubig house the star-like **Pinipisikan Falls**. Off the western tip of the province is **Biri Island** ⓭, which features magnificent corals, shells and rare tropical fish, beautiful, exotic scenery and natural wonders like the Magasang boulders. Its colorful Pintados, Sarakiki and Buyogan festivals are considered three of the best in the country.

Other attractions in Northern Samar are Rosario Hotsprings, Victoria Falls, San Isidro Viriato Falls, and Flying Dog Beach on Dalupiri Island. Ojay Beach is Scimitar-like, with cool blue waters for swimming and surfing. The beach is lined with swaying coconut trees and offers picturesque scenery.

Farther south is Calbayog, then **Catbalogan**, the provincial capital. In between is Gandara, with its Blanca Aurora Falls. The road continues southward, circling the rich fishing grounds of Maqueda Bay, to **Calbiga** ⓮, where spelunkers can enjoy the **Gobingob-Lanugan Cave**, said to be the second-largest karst cave in the world.

Mussels by the basketful in Northern Samar

A smooth and pleasant drive along scenic coastal mountains then takes you back to the San Juanico Bridge, which crosses over the strait – the narrowest navigable strait in the world – back to the island of Leyte. ❑

BELOW: pristine Biri Island.

CENTRAL VISAYAS

Picturesque coves, white sand beaches, colorful flora, ancient landmarks, fantastic diving and the cosmopolitan city of Cebu make Central Visayas a good vacation choice

Map on pages 240–41

The usual entry point to Central Visayas, which comprises the islands of Cebu and Bohol, is Cebu City, from where one may take plane hops to certain capital cities of the neighboring islands, a fast ferry service to some destinations, or travel by slow boat to major cities, including those in Mindanao. The island of Bohol is most easily reached via Tagbilaran by air, or by ferry from Cebu or elsewhere.

Bohol

For its relatively small size, **Bohol Island** has much to offer in terms of history and natural attractions. Miguel Lopez de Legazpi, the Spanish colonizer who became the first governor-general of the Philippines, anchored briefly at the island in 1563, sealing a blood pact with a chieftain, Sikatuna.

Boholanos are known to be an extremely clannish and industrious lot, and possibly for this reason are often pointed out as bogeymen in a region generally more familiar with lassitude. The province is one of the largest coconut-growing areas in the country, and cottage industries continue their impressive production of delicacies and various handicrafts, which find their way to most markets, from the Visayas all the way to Luzon.

Notable among the Boholano weaver's products are mats and sacks made of *saguran* fibers, Antequera baskets combining bamboo and nito, and items woven out of local grasses and reeds. Antique wooden furniture and *santos* (saints) – now fashionable decorative items in Manila – are often sourced from Bohol's far-flung towns. Here, families may be willing to part with period tables and chairs, or the handcarved, quaintly painted wooden altars which proliferated in the homes of religious folk during colonial times.

A good road system circles the 160-km (100-mile) circumference of Bohol. The coastline is marked by picturesque coves and clean, white-sand beaches, most of them a short ride from **Tagbilaran ⑮**, the provincial capital and main port of entry. Ferries also cross over from Cebu to Tubigon town on the northwestern coast, as well as from Leyte to Cogtong in the east.

The marked religiosity of Boholanos is deduced quickly enough from a stroll through the small city's relatively clean and orderly streets. One notes, perhaps while walking past the Divine Word Academy – the capital's premier educational institution – the distinctive, heavily built tricycles. In Bohol, not only do their metal bodies look sturdier, but they also serve as a convenient medium for honoring the Lord by way of quotations from the Bible.

The Mangga public market in the northern outskirts is where you can find the freshest seafood in Central

LEFT: Bohol's Chocolate Hills are best seen in summer. **BELOW:** dawn breaks over Bohol.

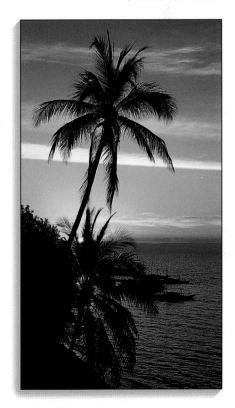

Visayas, with the day's catch usually sold late in the afternoon. For a small charge, you may take your selection to the back of the market, have it cooked Boholano style, then gorge on your choices right on the spot, where there are tables and benches. A good selection of handicrafts and delicacies is available at the centrally located Torralba market. Try the purple yam called *kinampay*.

Most visitors prefer to stay outside Tagbilaran at beach-side areas such as Panglao, but there is also a good range of accommodations in the capital, from budget inns to high-end hotels. Tagbilaran has two major bus terminals, with information on fares and schedules announced on prominent whiteboards. The buses – regular and mini – link the capital to all the main towns. Jeepneys ply the same routes but on shorter hops, as well as more rugged roads leading to the forested interior. Metered taxicabs are also available, largely for ferrying tourists to and from beach resorts and scenic attractions. Then there is the "motorela" – a cross between a motorized tricycle and a jeepney.

Colonial gems

Some of the best-preserved Spanish churches, watchtowers and fortifications in the country are found in Bohol. For an excellent tour, compare the lavishly painted church ceilings and ornate decor of the impressive colonial architecture found in the towns of Baclayon, Dauis, Panglao, Loay, Loboc, Dimiao, Jagna, Cortes, Balilihan, Maribojoc, Loon and Calape.

Some 7 km (4 miles) east of the city proper is **Baclayon Church**, one of the country's oldest, built by the Jesuits in 1727. The Recollects built an L-shaped convent in 1872, connecting the already fortified church with a bastion that has been overgrown with shrubbery and now lies hidden behind a grotto of the

BELOW: seafood from the waters around Bohol.

Virgin of Lourdes. The church has an interesting museum housing a rich collection of religious relics, ecclesiastical vestments, and old librettos of church music in Latin inscribed on animal skins. Both the church and museum are open daily during daylight hours.

Close by is the **Blood Compact Marker**, commemorating the historic agreement between Rajah Sikatuna – also reputed to have been the King of Bohol in some accounts – and the Spanish expeditionary leader Legazpi.

Panglao Island

About 10 km (6 miles) south of the capital is the town of **Dauis** on tiny **Panglao Island** ⓰, linked to Bohol Island by two short causeways. Here a concentration of dive camps and budget cottages has turned **Alona Beach** into Bohol's primary tourist accommodation area. The beach is said to have remained nameless until Alona Alegre, a buxom movie star from Manila, on a location shoot in the 1970s, regaled locals and backpackers alike by showing off the first bikini ever worn in Bohol.

Long **Dolho Beach**, close to the town of Panglao, offers a sand flat at low tide where locals comb the tidal pools for edible crustaceans. Particularly succulent is sea urchin roe, locally called *swaki*, which is collected by old women in small bottles, dipped in vinegar and *calamansi* juice, and peddled as an aphrodisiac. **Momo Beach**, on the west side of Panglao, is a quiet cove, with accommodations provided by rustic cottages at the jungle's edge. Popular among locals for weekend picnics is **Dumaluan Beach** in Bolod. Nearby, on another fine stretch of white sand, is the Bohol Beach Club, a luxury resort with a pool, sauna, jacuzzi, tennis courts, the works. If you tire of these amenities, there

Map on pages 240–41

In the 16th century, Rajah Sikatuna and Spanish explorer Legazpi are said to have slashed their arms and allowed their blood to mix in a historical act of bonding.

BELOW: a swinging beach boy.

THE PAINTED ONES

The Spanish called Visayans *Pintados* (Painted Ones) because of their extensive, intricately designed tattoos. Jesuit chronicler Francisco Colin describes the practice in a book printed in Madrid in 1663: "It was a custom… a mark of nobility and bravery, to tattoo the whole body from top to toe when they were of an age and strength sufficient to endure the tortures of the tattooing which was done… with instruments like brushes, or small twigs, with very fine points of bamboo."

Earlier documentation is provided by an illuminated manuscript dated 1590, reputedly commissioned as a gift for the King of Spain and purchased in 1947 by historian C. R. Boxer. Illustrations of the Pintados are complemented by effusive text: "The Bisayans are accustomed to paint their bodies with some very elegant paintings. They do them with iron or brass points heated with a fire, and they have artisans who are adept at it. They do them with such order, symmetry, and coordination that they elicit admiration from those who see them. They are done in the manner of illuminations, painting all parts of the body… The women paint only the hands very elegantly. To the men these paintings serve as if they were dressed, and thus they seem although they usually go naked…"

TIP

Whale- and dolphin-watching cruises are conducted almost year-round by resorts, with arrangements often including packed lunches, experienced guides and wildlife spotters. Contact dive shops for more details.

are always the blue starfish which gather by the hundreds close to the shore.

Other attractions on Panglao Island include **Dauis Church**, built by the Recollects in 1784, beside which is a hexagonal watchtower erected a decade earlier that features delicate carvings on its limestone blocks; the four-story, octagonal **Panglao Watchtower**, the country's tallest coastal tower, which stands behind the seaside ruins of a baroque church; and **Hinagdanan Cave** with its underground bathing pool half-lit by a pair of natural skylights.

Diver's haven

Panglao also serves as the access point for reef-fringed **Balicasag Island ⑰**, a diver's haven with well-appointed cottages, and for pumpboat cruises for whale and dolphin watching off **Pamilacan Island**. Balicasag's marine sanctuary, protected by its own community, is well known as one of the country's top diving sites. Among its highlights is the Black Forest, a gradual slope of black coral on the island's northeastern side. For those who don't scuba dive, the snorkelling can also be absolutely fascinating. The Philippine Tourism Authority (PTA) maintains the Balicasag Island Dive Resort, with comfortable accommodations. A service boat ferries guests to and from Tagbilaran.

On Pamilacan, nearly an hour's ride by pumpboat from Baclayon or Tagbilaran, stands a partially ruined, 19th-century triangular fort. Pamilacan has a long history of whaling, but locals, who now guide ecotourists seeking dolphins and whales, can give visitors a unique insight into their former prey. Simple cottages are available for overnight stays.

Northeast from Tagbilaran and through the hinterland of Bohol is **Corella**, home of the **Philippine Tarsier Sanctuary** (www.philippinetarsier.org) where

BELOW: budding musicians from Balicasag Island.

one can trek through a 6-hectare (15-acre) mahogany forest and have a look at the Philippine tarsier, popularly, but erroneously, dubbed the smallest monkey in the world. Among other forest wildlife are the flying lemur, grass owl, Tarictic hornbill, emerald dove and the Philippine sailfin lizard. Forest guards maintain this sanctuary, keeping a pen of captive tarsiers in their native habitat for viewing.

A further 19 km (12 miles) from Tagbilaran is the town of **Loboc**, where one may visit the **Museo de Loboc** (Loboc Museum; open Mon–Fri 9am–5pm; free) and an old stone church. Alternatively, embark on a scenic river cruise that wends past lush greenery alternating with women washing clothes along the riverbanks. After 7 km (4 miles), the meandering route ends at a modest waterfall, where one may bathe with the playful locals, mostly young boys, before the trip back. The regular cruises are conducted on motorized *banca* or large bamboo rafts outfitted with palm-weave roofs and tables for a pleasant picnic lunch.

A short distance north of Tagbilaran is **Maribojoc**, with the much-visited **Punta Cruz Watchtower**, a two-story, triangular fortification built by the Recollects in 1796, and which they called Castillo del San Vicente Ferrer. The landmark stands within a park, overlooking the Cebu Strait. Northwest of Maribojoc is the mountain town of **Antequera**, where a legion of visitors converge daily, but especially on Sundays, for the woven baskets and other bargain handicrafts. The coastal road from Maribojoc leads to **Calape**. Here, **Calape Church** attracts visitors for its famous and reputedly miraculous Virgin Mary image.

Chocolate Hills

But what remains Bohol's most famous attraction, and with which the island has become synonymous, is a unique panorama in the vicinity of **Carmen** ⑱, a town 55 km (34 miles) northeast of Tagbilaran. Here, 1,268 hills – formed by limestone, shale, and sandstone, in an area once covered by ocean – rise 30 meters (100 ft) above the flat terrain. They are called the **Chocolate Hills**, for the confectionery-like spectacle they present in summer, when their sparse grass cover turns dry and brown. Two of the highest hills have been developed, offering a hostel, restaurant, swimming pool and observation deck. Legend has it that teardrops from a lovelorn giant helped form the hills.

It is possible to go around the entire island by following the coastal road, which makes for a very scenic trip indeed, although one must be prepared to lodge in modest surroundings, or rely on the kindness of strangers. A counter-clockwise course is recommended, passing through the towns on the southern and eastern coast. Among these is **Anda**, a two-hour drive from Tagbilaran with its low-key beachside accommodation.

The next stop from Jagna is the sleepy town of **Duero**, from where a 26-km (16-mile) drive inland leads to a pleasant valley where the Eskaya tribe has drawn anthropological attention for adhering strictly to traditions. These include forbidding both marriage to anyone not of the village, and the wearing of trousers by females. Most curious is the continued use of an ancient script and dialect distinct from any spoken on the rest of the island. The Eskaya have been Christianized to some extent, but believe that Christ

The tarsier, a primate but not a monkey, is found not only in Bohol: besides also being found on Samar and Mindanao, similar species inhabit other parts of the Indo-Pacific region. The nocturnal creature has bulging round eyes and a tail longer than its 10–12 cm (4–5 inch) body. The tarsier is a protected species in the Philippines.

BELOW: tiny tarsier at Corella.

was originally a Boholano born in Dauis on Panglao Island. Also in Duero is a seaside compound owned by a National Artist for Sculpture, Napoleon "Billy" Abueva, worth a visit for its sculptural attractions.

Hundreds of fringe islands and islets surround Bohol. Most have fishing communities, while a few have modest resorts for visitors. Even those that are uninhabited are easily accessible. **Cabilao Island**, off the western coast and reachable from Loon or Calape, has a lighthouse, a mangrove lagoon, excellent reefs for the intrepid diver, and an inexpensive resort. Nearby is **Sandingan Island**, which is linked to the mainland by a bridge, while northeast lie the islands of **Pangangan** and **Mantatao**. Off the northern coast is a group of several large islands populated by hardy fisherfolk, while off the northwestern town of Tubigon is **Inanoran Island**, with dense mangrove. Here, an Australian has established a small resort. The tiny, attractive islet of **Pungtud**, off Panglao town, lies right in the middle of a great lagoon. Day trips are recommended to this idyllic tropical isle, only 250 meters (800 ft) in length at high tide. It may be reached in 20 minutes by pumpboat from the tip of Panglao Island. A fun alternative is the overnight sea-kayak camping trip on this island, offered by **Bohol Xtreme** (tel: 0919-479 2809; e-mail: gil45.geo@yahoo.com).

Cebu Island

The island province of **Cebu** is bounded by the Visayan Sea in the north, the Bohol Strait – which separates it from the islands of Leyte and Bohol – in the east, the Bohol Sea in the south, and Tañon Strait, which divides it from the island of Negros in the west. From Manila, the WG&A Super Ferry sails daily and reaches Cebu City in 21 hours, with accommodations ranging from luxury

"Bai" (pronounced "buy") is the familiar term of endearment used by Cebuanos to address all males, just like "man" or "guy." "Day" (pronounced "dye") is used to address females.

BELOW: the Cebu Strait divides Cebu from Bohol Island.

Maps:
Area 240
City 257

cabins to economy class. Other inter-island shipping lines, some of them with rather decrepit vessels, ply the same route, and onwards to Mindanao.

Cebu has in recent years become a model for independent industrial development. With its splendid deep-water port, international airport and attractive beaches and resorts, the city and province of the same name are magnets for investment, both Filipino and foreign. The city of **Cebu** ⑲ is the oldest in the Philippines, the commercial and education center of the Visayas, and the hub of air and sea travel throughout the south. A 30-minute drive takes visitors from **Mactan International Airport** into the city, passing through **Lapu Lapu City** on **Mactan Island** ⑳ and **Mandaue City** on the mainland. Jeepneys ply regular routes connecting the three cities.

Cosmopolitan heritage

Cebu is a busy capital, second only to Manila in commercial activity and cosmopolitanism. The original settlement of Sugbu was an important trading community even before the arrival of the Spanish; ships from the East Indies, Siam and China paid tribute to the local chief for the right to berth here and barter. Legazpi successfully began colonization in 1565, making Cebu the capital until the takeover of Manila six years later.

A large wooden crucifix that was left by Magellan in 1521 commemorates the archipelago's first encounter with the West. **Magellan's Cross** Ⓐ, at upper Magallanes Street, is Cebu's most important historical landmark. Its supposed remnants are encased in a black cross of *tindalo* wood and housed in a kiosk, which also serves as a shrine commemorating the initial conversion of the islanders to Christianity. Historical accounts contend, however, that Chief Hum-

For a fantastic view of Cebu city, head up to Tops, one of the best parks in the Visayas. Drive west from Lahug for about half an hour along Busay Road (Osmena Highway) and take a left immediately after La Tegola Restaurant. A commanding view of Cebu city spreads below.

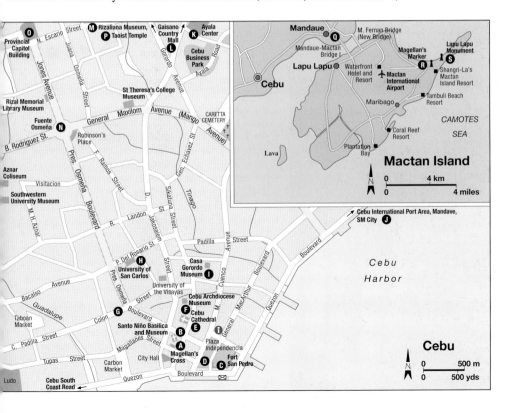

abon and his men destroyed Magellan's cross soon after the Spanish force was routed in Mactan by Lapu Lapu. Perhaps they did leave a stump. What is known is that Legazpi replaced that original cross of evangelization four decades later. A semanticist may then insist that it be called "Legazpi's Cross," but Cebuanos believe in leaving things well alone, since the name "Magellan's Cross" honors the fellow who first planted, if not a cross that survived, at least the seeds of a new religion that thrives to this day. Cebuano devotees may be seen visiting the shrine, pausing for prayer, lighting candles or dropping coins into the alms box.

Nearby, off Osmeña Avenue, is the **Santo Niño Basilica and Museum** B (open on request; free), formerly known as San Agustin Church, which was built in 1565 to house the country's oldest religious relic, the Image of the Holy Child Jesus. This was presented by Magellan to Queen Juana of Cebu on her conversion to Christianity. One of Legazpi's men found the image intact 44 years later, when Spain resumed its colonization of the Philippines. It has since survived fires and earthquakes. To this day, many Cebuanos believe that their old city withstood successive attempts at plunder by Muslim, Dutch and Portuguese pirates owing to the protective power of the Holy Infant. The church's conversion into a basilica was ordered by the Vatican in 1965 in recognition of its importance as the cradle of Christianity in Asia.

In January, also known as the "Santo Niño month," the area around the church swarms with pilgrims from all over the country. Religious fervor reaches a peak with the staging of the Sinulog Festival in the third week of January, with thousands of revelers parading and dancing with organized, wildly costumed groups up and down the steeets of downtown Cebu, to the frenzied beat of drums, the toot of whistles, and shouts of *"Pit Senyor!"* in honor of the Christ Child.

As the oldest Spanish settlement in the country, Cebu has numerous sites that depict its rich colonial heritage. The foremost is the Fuerza de San Pedro or **Fort San Pedro** C (open daily, 7am–10pm; admission fee), a Spanish fort built in the 17th century and reinforced in 1738 to repel attacks by Muslim or European raiders. It is a triangular fort with bastions at each point, and an earth embankment. The walls are 6 meters (20 ft) high and 18 meters (59 ft) thick, with the bastions rising some 9 meters (30 ft). Two of its sides face the sea, with a 15th-century gun emplacement still in place. Other, smaller Spanish cannons are similarly preserved. It has a total floor area of 2,025 sq. meters (21,800 sq. ft). The largest building, called "Cuerpo de Guardia," used to house the fort's defenders, while an adjacent structure called "Viviendo del Teniente" served as living quarters for the highest official. The fort has since been used as a prison for Cebuano rebels during the Spanish era, a military outpost by the Americans, and a prisoner of war camp during the Japanese occupation. Eventually, it was transformed into a park with a zoo run by a religious sect, and an office for tourism officials. Its main building now houses a museum.

Across Fort San Pedro is **Plaza Independencia** D, formerly Plaza Libertad, a tree-shaded promenade square where stands an obelisk honoring Legazpi. Nearby is the Department of Tourism office.

BELOW: Magellan's Cross, Cebu's most important historical marker.

Colon Street

A few blocks away are the **Cebu Cathedral ⓔ** and **Cebu Archdiocese Museum ⓕ** (open Mon–Fri, 9am–5pm; free). Farther up is **Colon Street ⓖ**, named after Christopher Columbus. It is the oldest street in the country, situated within the Parian district, Cebu's original Chinatown. The Chinese community is much in evidence in Cebu, and is said to be largely responsible for its continued growth as an industrial and commercial center.

Colon used to be Cebu City's main street, where all the moviehouses and ritzy shops were found, and all jeepney routes began and ended. Young people who wanted to hang out would simply agree to meet in Colon and decide what to do once they got there. A business address in Colon meant that one's restaurant, shop or office was in the very heart of the capital. Today, Colon is usually so crowded it has become off limits to most jeepneys. Shoe and watch repair stalls stand alongside an eclectic mix of hardware, machine, electrical and noodle shops. It has lost its attraction as a central meeting place, as continuing urban growth has given the city several social, commercial and financial centers.

A block north of Colon is the **University of San Carlos ⓗ**, on the site of the oldest college in the country, first built in 1595. It has a fine biological museum and the Cebuano Studies Center. Several streets eastward is **Casa Gorordo Museum ⓘ** (usually open daily 9am–5pm; free), a century-old residence turned into a private museum displaying artifacts and memorabilia related to Cebu's traditional lifestyle. The museum actually had been the residence of the first Filipino bishop of Cebu, who was descended from the wealthy Gorordo family. Historical works from the 18th century are among the extensive exhibits.

Map on page 257

TIP

Visit the Museum of Traditional Tattoo Arts, a tattoo parlour-cum-museum on Colon St to get a glimpse into the traditional culture of the *pintados*, or the "painted ones," as the Visayans used to be known, due to their intricate tattoos. (www.geocities.com/tattoomuseumphil)

BELOW: the 17th-century Fort San Pedro.

Shopping pleasures

Further eastward, several long blocks from Casa Gorordo, is the **Cebu International Port Area**, directly north of which are two of the capital's enormous malls, **SM City ❶** and **Ayala Center ❻**, the latter within the Cebu Business Park, which has taken over what used to be the Club Filipino Golf Course in the Lahug district. **Gaisano Country Mall ❶** is further north in the Banilad district, which also has Banilad Town Center and Crossroads. These major shopping malls compete as consumerist delights, landmarks of cosmopolitanism, local hangouts, and leisure and activity centers. All are quite distant from downtown Cebu, on the way to Mandaue City and the two bridges connecting Cebu to Mactan Island.

Rizaliana Museum

Close to Gaisano Country Mall in the northeastern part of Metro Cebu is the **Cebu Country Club and Golf Course**. Right before it may be found the **Sian Tian Temple** on Archbishop Reyes Avenue, further evidence of Chinese presence and influence in the capital. Off Salinas Drive nearby is the **University of Southern Philippines' Rizaliana Museum ⓜ** (open Mon–Fri 9am–5pm; free), which exhibits a substantial collection of memorabilia of national hero Dr Jose Rizal. Here are some of his first literary writings, a *cerrada* coat and other articles of clothing, etchings and personal letters to his family, poems written for his wife, Josephine Bracken, and the oil lamp used inside his cell at Fort Santiago when he wrote his valedictory poem, *Mi Ultimo Adios*. Southward on Gorordo Avenue is the campus of the **University of the Philippines Cebu**.

Getting closer back to the city center, there are three more small museums maintained by educational institutions: **St Theresa's College Museum** on E.

Pond Extension, the **Rizal Memorial Library Museum** on G. Garcia Street, and the **Southwestern University Museum** (all open Mon–Fri 9am–5pm; free) in the Sambag II district, close to **Aznar Coliseum**, the venue for sporting events and big music concerts by visiting artists.

Sooner or later one winds up at **Fuente Osmeña** (Osmeña Circle) , a roundabout that is virtually at the center of the city. Here are smaller shopping arcades, midtown hotels, nightspots, restaurants, beer houses and barbecue stalls that seem to thrive only when dusk descends. A fountain is situated in this circular park that connects the **Avenue of Nations**, flanked by narra trees that blossom into a shower of gold in summer, and **President Osmeña Boulevard**, which leads directly to the Capitol Building. The park and the boulevard are named after Cebu's "Grand Old Man of politics," Sergio Osmeña Sr, who served as the country's third president during turbulent times, 1944–46. Osmeña remains a "magical name" in Cebu. The late president's descendants are still prominent nationally, as well as locally.

Of pre-war vintage, the **Provincial Capitol Building** – seat of the provincial government – is unrivalled in grandeur throughout the country, with a backdrop of undulating hills highlighting its majestic dome, visible all the way from the Avenue of Nations and Fuente Osmeña.

Taoist Temple

Northward is the posh residential enclave of **Beverly Hills**, atop which is the much visited **Taoist Temple**. Devotees engage in traditional rites on Wednesday and Sunday, but there is a daily crowd of tourists for picture-taking, as well for the commanding view of the city sprawl and Mactan Island across the narrow channel. Nearby is **Nivel Hill**, location of the now-closed Cebu Plaza

Map on page 257

TIP

Jones Ave is also often marked as President Osmeña Boulevard, which leads to some confusion for those poring over a city map.

BELOW: there is a commanding view of Cebu city from the Taoist Temple.

TIP

The Lapu-Lapu
Monument at Punta
Engaño overlooks a
seafood market
surrounded by
restaurants on stilts.
This popular dining
center is called STK,
standing for "Shoot-
to-Kill" on the street,
but really "Sinugba-
Tinola-Kinilaw" –
grilled, stewed or
vinegared – the
preparation methods
for the day's catch.

BELOW: the most
outstanding of
Cebu's three Lapu
Lapu monuments.

Hotel; from here, you will have a gorgeous view of the city, especially at night.

First-class to mid-priced hotels in the city center can be found mostly around Fuente Osmeña. Any number of pensions and budget inns dot downtown Cebu, most in the bustling streets off Fuente Osmeña, and along President Osmeña Boulevard all the way to the port area. Another concentration of economy lodging places is near Ayala Center at the Business Park, where on the high-end side, there is Marriott Hotel. On the heels of the Waterfront Hotel and Casino, located right outside the Mactan International Airport, is the Waterfront Hotel in the Lahug district, which is designed to evoke the splendor of famous Southeast Asian temples but looks straight out of an ersatz Las Vegas instead. The Waterfront Beach Hotel, thankfully more laid back in architectural style, has also been established in Mactan. Of the three, the last alone lives up to its name, since the other two are very much inland.

Contiguous to the capital, **Mandaue City** ⓠ is a bustling industrial site with an otherwise singular attraction, the centuries-old **St Joseph Church**. This is also commonly called the Church of the Last Supper for its life-sized statues of Jesus and the apostles, handcarved during Spanish times. A popular Lenten ritual held in this parish is the *Pasyon sa Mandaue*, a dramatic presentation lasting 24 hours that re-enacts the Passion and Death of Jesus Christ.

A historical relic that has unfortunately been overwhelmed by urban blight is the **Mandaue Watchtower**, a cylindrical rubble tower built in the 19th century, when raiders shifted their seasonal attacks from Cebu's well-defended southern parts to the northern towns of the island. It may still be glimpsed from the Mandaue-Mactan Bridge I, jutting out among a sorry landscape of shanties and gasoline depots.

Mactan Island

For many visitors, Cebu means handcrafted guitars and ukuleles made of soft jackfruit wood. The guitar-making industry is centered in Maribago and Abuno on Mactan. Visitors can watch the local craftsmen at work, or be entertained by a quality-control expert trying out a freshly completed guitar. Soon enough all the locals in the vicinity may be expected to join in for an impromptu sing-along session.

Magellan's Marker ⓡ, which was erected in 1886, marks the spot where he was slain on Mactan's shore, while the **Lapu Lapu Monument** ⓢ stands just a lance's throw away. The latter portrays the Mactan chieftain with his *kampilan* (a machete-like weapon) raised above his head, ready to strike, although his back is diplomatically turned to the old foe's marker. Another statue of Lapu Lapu is erected at the plaza fronting the Lapu Lapu City Hall. This time the weapon is held downward, and the local hero is without a shield. Yet another Lapu Lapu monument stands at Punta Engaño, near the **Mactan Tourist Souvenir Shop**. Its statue is undoubtedly the most handsome, with the *kampilan* held at mid-thigh level and the shield strapped to the hero's left arm. All three statues are bronze-hued, if not actually made of bronze and all of them glint golden in the harsh sun. On 27 April every year, history comes to life at the **Kadaugan sa Mactan Festival** with the re-enactment

of Magellan's fatal encounter with Lapu Lapu, on the waters off Mactan Island.

Cebu is well-known for its sun-drenched, white sand beaches and year-round tropical climate. The coastal waters off the entire elongated island offer superlative scuba diving. In terms of accommodation, unrivaled beach resorts from mid-priced to posh is concentrated on Mactan Island, making it an inviting destination for visitors who plane in directly for weekends without having to pass through Manila.

Visitors to Mactan Island sometimes decide that they don't even have to cross the strait to mainland Cebu to have a pleasant vacation. After all, if it's leisure and relaxation they came for, then the assorted beach resorts in Mactan fit the bill, while a Gaisano Mall and other shopping centers in Lapu Lapu City and Maribago can satisfy consumerist or souvenir needs. Crossing either of the two bridges to Mandaue and Cebu City means re-introducing oneself to the urban menace of dust and heavy traffic: "Why, it's almost like Manila" is a complaint often heard. A one-day tour of the capital's historical and cultural attractions is often enough for the short-term visitor, especially if one comes from a foreign city, likely another Asian capital, where the hustle and bustle were what one escaped from in the first place. Unless one has business meetings in Cebu City, or decides to try out a fine dining restaurant absent in Mactan, this little island has much of the best Cebu has to offer – beach strips, watersport activities, casino entertainment, at least one grand massage parlor and great seafood. Most of all, Mactan maintains the still unspoiled charm of the relatively uncongested countryside.

To experience other points of interest on the rest of Cebu Island or the Visayas, of course, one has to brave it through the capital. But it's easy enough to find direct transport to the egress points for fast-ferry service to neighboring islands, or bus depots for traveling north or south of Cebu City.

Map on page 257

A Cebuano is often said to be like a fish out of water when not caressing a guitar. Cebu is well known as the guitar-producing capital of the Philippines.

BELOW: low tide at Mactan maroons this *banca.*

Camotes Islands and Northern Cebu

Past the town of **Sogod**, some 60 km (40 miles) north, lies Allegre Beach Resort, which has its own private stretch of white sand, luxury cottage accommodations, and restaurant facilities. Off Sogod are the **Camotes Islands ㉑**, in the middle of the Camotes Sea below Leyte.

The slow ferry ride to these unfrequented but charming islands can take as much as four hours, from Cebu City to the town of Poro in Poro Island. The other large town is San Francisco, in the adjoining Pacijan Island. The three large islands, each about the size of Mactan, have great potential with their splendid white sand beaches and wildly colorful flora.

A 33-km (20-mile) drive north of Cebu City is **Danao City**, newly industrialized but offering delicious native cheese and, curiously enough, an assortment of snakeskin bags and shoes. An hour northeast by pumpboat is **Gato Island**, where Japanese fishermen discovered a bounty of sea snakes back in the 1930s. This led to a sea snake industry in Barrio Tapilon of Danao, where the sea snakes are sold not only for their hide but also for esoteric cuisine, with the meat believed to be yet another aphrodisiac.

Off the northwestern tip of Cebu Island is **Bantayan Island ㉒**, now becoming popular among venturesome beach fanciers with a taste for excellent softshell crabs. Ferryboats provide a daily shuttle, since the fishing grounds off Bantayan are a major source of Cebu City's seafood. In the towns of **Santa Fe** and **Madridejos** are the remains of small stone forts built circa 1790.

Malapascua, a small island off the northern tip of Cebu, has earned itself an enviable reputation of late as one of the most rewarding places to dive in the country, thanks to a healthy population of thresher sharks, dolphins, manta rays,

BELOW: Cebuano children and their winsome smiles.

Map on pages 240–41

the occasional whale shark, and other marine life. Thresher sharks are not usually found at such shallow depths in other parts of the world. The island is accessible via a half-hour boat trip from the town of Maya. Tourists and the infrastructure that come quick on their tails have sprung up in the last few years here, and the fear of over-expansion is a real concern for the future.

Southern Cebu

An hour's drive south of Cebu City is the idyllic and upscale Pulchra Resort in **San Fernando**. The next big town is **Carcar ㉓**, the "orchard town," which is worth a visit for its array of well-preserved Antillan houses, a few of which are open for an intimate look at well-maintained period appointments. Farther on is **Argao**, with another old stone church and the Casay Beach Resort.

The road leading south from Cebu City is an extremely scenic drive, especially along the eastern coast, with Mediterranean-like views when it ascends cliffside turns with emerald waters shimmering in small coves a sheer drop below. As in Bohol, the southern part of Cebu Island is studded with towns that formed part of the Spanish defense perimeter against marauding pirates. The stone fortifications and watchtowers remain particularly impressive in the towns of Argao, Dalaguete, Obong, Coro, Alcoy, Boljoon, Caceres, Oslob and Looc. The southernmost town is **Santander**, where old flame trees line the coastal road, presenting a magnificent sight when abloom in summer. A short trek leads to **Pontong Lake**, the reputed habitat of a rare species of bird that is said to have the ability to go under water for much of the day.

Moalboal and the South

Moalboal, 3 hours south of Cebu City, is another one of the area's renowned dive spots. Blessed with three marine reserves – Tonggo Island, Ronda Island and Pescador Island – the area teems with corals, fish, and, frequently, dolphins and whale sharks.

The hub of activity is **Panagsama Beach**, which is a dense collection of restaurants, dive shops and lodgings. A huge typhoon washed the beach away several years ago, however. By contrast, the adjacent **White Beach** is a good alternative with its quiet, expansive beach, inviting sunbathers and beach walkers to give it a visit. Everything shuts down here earlier, however, so check with your resort beforehand if you need anything after 7pm.

Four towns north of Moalboal, and closer to Cebu City, is **Barili** with the Barili Hot Springs, the first choice among city folk who want to camp out for the weekend. South of Moalboal, about 17 km (11 miles) away, or a 30-minute ride on a bumpy road, is **Badian**, known for **Kawasan Falls**, which, with three natural pools, are arguably the best in the island.

Nearby is the upscale Badian Island Resort on **Badian Island**, a 10-minute pumpboat ride from the mainland town. Certified honeymooners are treated to a special tree-planting ceremony in the resort's back garden. As the couple plant their so-called love tree, they are serenaded by staff with a love song of their choice. So utterly Visayan. ❏

BELOW:
beach service at
Panagsama Beach.

WESTERN VISAYAS

Stunning natural beauty and powerful cultural and spiritual traditions merge on these islands, attracting beach addicts, history enthusiasts and lovers of carnival

Map on pages 240–41

I sland-hopping from Cebu to Negros Island may be done by fast ferry, a two- to three-hour trip by air-conditioned hovercraft to Dumaguete City, by ship (about six hours), or by bus down Cebu Island to Bato and then by slow ferry across Tañon Strait to Tampi, south of Amlan – an hour's ride by jeepney to Dumaguete. All in all, this overland and ferry crossing takes at least six hours.

Negros Oriental

The capital of Negros Oriental (Eastern Negros) Province, **Dumaguete ㉕** is a small university town built around the Protestant-run **Silliman University**. Locals have dubbed their hometown "The City of Gentle People." Visitors can't help but agree, as there's a quaint charm to Dumaguete not found in most cities, even in the generally laid back south.

Silliman University sprawls over a good portion of the city, its central quadrangle bordered by old acacia trees presenting a "groves of academe" postcard view. On one end is a Protestant chapel; on the other the **Silliman University Anthropological Museum** (open Mon–Fri 9am–noon and 1–5pm; free), housed in a period wooden structure with notable filigreed eaves. Among the items on display are instruments of sorcery from neighboring Siquijor Island, including ritual candles and voodoo dolls.

Beyond the museum may be glimpsed an occasional ship gliding on Tañon Strait. This seafront end of the campus calls for a lingering visit. **Rizal Boulevard**, an esplanade that stretches along the seawall from the wharf, is an ideal promenade area at all hours, especially at sunset, as shell and seaweed gatherers roaming the tidal flats call it a day. Makeshift beer-and-barbecue stalls sprout for an al fresco treat, rivaling the seafront row of cafés and restaurants.

Two good hotels are well situated on the breezy boulevard, including the five-story Bethel House, the tallest and most modern building in the city, which has rather stringent rules governing occupancy. Guests are not allowed to bring drinks or smoke inside the building. The proprietor is known to be a devout Catholic, so that visitors are often wakened early by the staff's morning prayers and religious songs.

Downtown, the omnipresent tricycle creates a perennial buzz. Jeepneys and minibuses are taken only for longer out-of-town routes. Any trip within the city is taken on a tricycle. The main street is chock-a-block with banks, student canteens, cinemas and a department store with the only escalator in town – always a hit with the local children. The **Ninoy Aquino Freedom Park** faces the centuries-old **Dumaguete Cathedral**, its vine-grown belfry once used as a lookout for marauders, whose seasonal attempts at pillage

LEFT: why settle for a picture when you can have the real thing at Boracay.
BELOW: giant squid.

gave Dumaguete its name – from *dumaguit,* which means "to swoop down."

Southwest is the pretty garden town of **Valencia** , where *suman budbod kabog* (a steamed delicacy wrapped in banana leaves) and thick native chocolate make inexpensive treats at the market. A tricycle ride can take you up to **Camp Look-out** in the foothills of Mt Talinis, also known as Cuernos de Negros (Horns of Negros) for its twin peaks. This sylvan setting offers a commanding view of Negros' southern portion, the islands of Siquijor, Cebu and Bohol across the strait, and, on a clear day, the northern coast of Mindanao.

Also accessible from Valencia is the towering **Casiroro Falls**, which may be reached by riding up a dirt road, trekking down a gully, and following a boulder-strewn stream. Closer to town is the **Banica River Resort** with fresh-water pools, bathing streams and picnic settings.

A long stick does the trick when paddles won't work.

Bacong

On the highway leading south, the first town is **Bacong** ㉗, a 20-minute drive. It has an interesting old church fronting the sea, a habitable treehouse by the beach, and, close by, a weaving room and stonecraft shop for good souvenir buys. Bacong's park has modest monuments to Dr Jose Rizal and local hero Pantaleon Villegas, a revolutionary general also known as Leon Kilat ("Lightning").

Kilat's reputed amulets and acrobatic prowess helped him rise quickly up the Katipunan ranks in the south. He led Cebuano forces in laying seige to the Spanish defenders of Fort San Pedro, before bombardment from a gunship forced a retreat to Carcar where Kilat was eventually assassinated. The close relations between Cebu and Negros Oriental, both of which speak the Cebuano language, are reflected in this historic episode, in much the same way that rev-

BELOW: an Apo Island fisherman mends his nets.

olutionary leaders from both Negros Occidental and Iloilo, which both speak Ilonggo once closed ranks against their Spanish colonizers.

A good stop on the road south is **Zamboanguita** ㉘, for its quaint Zoo Paradise World and World Peace Museum, maintained by a religious sect called the Lamplighters, who still walk barefoot and sport very long hair. Off Zamboanguita is the coastal village of **Malatapay**, which comes alive every Wednesday with a colorful open-air market, offering anything from livestock to seafood and handicrafts. Pumpboats may be hired for the 45-minute crossing to **Apo Island** ㉙, a marine sanctuary with a dive camp and a couple of budget resorts run by Europeans.

Farther south is **Siaton**, off which is **Tambobo Cove**, which has been transformed into a marina by retired expatriates who recognized the boat-building skills of the locals. The approach to the cove is gloriously scenic in summer, when rows of old flame trees put on a roadside show of fiery resplendence.

North of Dumaguete are several interesting towns, beginning with **Amlan**, from where you can hike up to the twin crater lakes of **Balinsasayao** and **Danao**. Before Amlan is a beach hotel called Wuthering Heights, appropriating the name of the former picnic area lorded over by a grassy promontory. The three-story hotel at sea's edge leaves little room for a pocket beach below, but its rooftop restaurant and open terrace offer a panoramic view of the strait, coconut plantations, and the misty peaks of Mt Talinis.

North of Amlan is **Tanjay**, which has a colonial-era church beside a plaza that lights up on weekends with open-air ballroom dancing. With its well-trained choirs and generations of musicians, the town prides itself on being the "Music Capital of Negros."

Map on pages 240–41

Dumaguete's easy pace is confirmed by the rare sight of a tartanilla – a horse-drawn carriage. The pedicab and motorized tricycle have nearly rendered the tartanilla a vanished breed, but a few holdovers are subsidized by the regional tourism office.

BELOW: spearing fish in Apo Island.

SORCERY AND SPECIAL POWERS

The story is still told of how an old lady named Mameng – the most powerful white sorcerer in the 1970s and 1980s – was once summoned to call on Imelda Marcos, who was said to have been stricken by a strange skin disease that dermatological experts couldn't treat.

The tale goes on to recount how Mameng diagnosed the affliction to be the result of a curse placed on the First Lady by mermen who had been injured during the construction of San Juanico Bridge linking Samar and Leyte islands. Mameng was supposed to have counseled Imelda to make a conciliatory offering, which she did by the base of the "love bridge" that had been built in honor of the First Lady by Ferdinand Marcos. Her skin disease disappeared, and Mameng was amply rewarded.

Siquijor's star attraction in recent years has not exactly been a sorcerer, but a man with unusual kinetic powers. Just ask to be taken to Jess, who will accommodate anyone with a demonstration of his special skills.

He cuts out a pair of figures from cigarette cartons, goes into trance, and starts making the male-female pair dance. He has been well documented on video and film by visiting academicians, documentarists, and incredulous foreigners seriously into psychic research.

On the approach to Bais, check out the antiquated steam locomotive on the roadside as you come within sight of the sugar mill, which has towering, cylindrical chimneys.

BELOW:
a mat weaver.

Bais City

An hour's ride north on the coastal highway from Dumaguete is **Bais City** ➌, where tourists flock, especially during the hot months, for whale-and-dolphin-spotting cruises on Tañon Strait. Bahia de Bais, a hilltop hostel run by the Philippine Tourism Authority (PTA), offers modest rooms at reasonable prices, a small restaurant, and a splendid terrace with a majestic view of Bais Bay and the surrounding lowlands. The PTA regulates the popular cruises in coordination with the Coast Guard. The full-day tour first takes a party to a mangrove swamp where an extended boardwalk has been laid out. Other stops include a sandbar for swimming, and an islet for a picnic lunch in between the morning and afternoon sessions of cetacean spotting.

Bais is identified with an influential *mestizo* community descended from early Spanish settlers. On a stretch of highway leading to the city, century-old trees form a thick canopy, alongside which stand vintage wooden residences where local sugar mill officials were once housed. Throughout the small city may still be found the occasional Antillan house made of stone. By a military camp stands another statue of General Leon Kilat, looking rather lumpy in white paint, and apparently uncomfortable astride a horse.

Another three hours of traveling northwestwards, through Negros Island's mid-section, will take you to Bacolod City. En route, you will cross the area of the **Canlaon National Park**, where Negros' last forest stands atop a dormant volcano, off upland **Canlaon City**, Negros Oriental's "summer capital."

Siquijor Island

Siquijor Island ➌ is accessible by an hour's fast ferry from Dumaguete. Long

recognized as the center of sorcery in the south, it was called Isla del Fuego, or Island of Fire, by the Spanish, a name which seems to tally with the Siquijodnons' story of their island having risen from the sea amid the crash and flare of thunder and lightning. Some 50 or so of the 100,000 islanders are *mananambals*, or folk healer-sorcerers. These people are classified as "white" or "black" sorcerers, depending on the nature of their abilities, and some of them actually have better talents as healers rather than as agents of harm.

The ferry berths at the capital town of **Siquijor**, near where the barrio of Siquijor San Antonio serves as the center for shamanistic activities. Here, *mananambals* from all over the Visayas and Mindanao gather during Holy Week for a ritual called *tang-alap*. Medicinal plants and various elements from surrounding forests, caves, and cemeteries are gathered, after which the adepts, laughing and joking, form a circle and chip off a piece of each ingredient to make several piles. The final ritual, at dawn, sees the sorcerers distribute samples from the consecrated piles among themselves.

You can motor easily around the island to visit the towns of **Larena** and **Lazi** ➌. The former is the island's main port, and the latter is particularly interesting for its centuries-old church with a pink-colored façade, and across the street, an impressively large but now-deserted two-storey convent. It has been proposed for rehabilitation and conservation as a World Heritage Site because of its hard-wood plank flooring, capacious interiors with period furniture, and lovely colored glass windows. Along the route one will find splendid white sand beaches, some of which are attended by modest resorts such as Sandugan and Paliton.

Map on pages 240–41

Negros Occidental

Ilonggos are considered the most laidback, if not decadent, of the southerners. In a sense, they bring the Visayas' essence to a lofty distillation, marked by genteel pursuits and a disdainful regard for the harsher facets of living. This is mainly due to the profitable production of sugar, which used to be the key word to the Ilonggo's lifestyle.

Haciendaros – landowners, most of whom can trace their lineage to early Spanish settlers – were often regarded as an idle and profligate group with strong political clout. From the time commercial sugar production on Negros Island had its beginnings in the late 19th century, they lorded it over migrant workers called *sacadas,* who streamed seasonally into Negros from the rest of the Visayas. The fall in sugar prices in the 1980s delivered a relative comeup-pance, forcing the gentry to shift to other, less profitable crops, or try their hand at new industries. But the attempts to diversify the economy into prawn breed-ing, corn, rice and native crafts have since regressed, owing to a recent, if tem-porary, resurgence in the sugar industry.

The capital of Negros Occidental (Western Negros) Province, **Bacolod** ㉝, is a relatively new city that has flourished somewhat haphazardly from the rise and fall of sugar profitability. It has experienced several decades of lean years after fat ones, when, for a time, it ranked second only to Manila in the number of reg-

BELOW: Visayan sugar plantation workers.

TIP

While in Bacolod, treat yourself to *chicken inasal* (barbecued chicken with lemongrass) found on sidewalk stalls, or at Manukan Country, a concentration of barbecue stalls by the reclamation area, popular among budget diners.

istered motor vehicles. This may have been typical of the old profligacy, but the Ilonggos of Bacolod have shown resilience. Urban development continues unabated in terms of commercial centers, and it remains the most financially advanced and modernized city on Negros Island.

Central Bacolod

Sprawling over 2 hectares (5 acres) of manicured lawns is the **Provincial Capitol Park**, bounded by Gatuslao Street, North Capitol Road and South Capitol Road. It is the most elegant park in Western Visayas, with a large lagoon and central fountains fronting the imposing capitol building. More popular for promenaders is the **Bacolod City Plaza**, similarly endowed with trees, park benches, concrete gazebos and water fountains that are colorfully lit in the evenings. Cultural programs are staged regularly on weekends, with orchestral bands and smaller musical groups alternating in providing free entertainment to park visitors. The **Bacolod Cathedral** stands across one side of the plaza, which is also flanked by the Central Public Market, Seabreeze Hotel and the City Hall.

Not far from the city plaza is the **Negros Occidental Provincial Museum** (open Mon–Fri 9am–noon and 1–5pm; free), also known as the "Sugar Museum" for its display of facets of sugar technology, while on Lacson Street, nearby, is the **Negros Showroom**, featuring regular handicraft exhibits. Bacolod has its fair share of restaurants, cinemas and shopping malls, as well as an upscale concentration of nightspots and girlie bars called Golden Fields, where the Casino Filipino is also located.

A few minutes' drive north is **Silay** ❹, small and sleepy, but with several interesting old houses recalling the Castilian past, when Silay was the cultural

BELOW: the fiery depiction of Christ at St Joseph the Worker Chapel.

center of the region, known as the "Paris of Negros." At 21 de Noviembre Street is the **Hofileña Art Collection**, which includes a Picasso and a Goya among paintings by Philippine masters such as Juan Luna. An artwork by Dr Jose Rizal is also on exhibit. Another usual stop is Ideal Bakery, a byword for its Castilian delicacies such as *hojas, pan de ara,* and *pio nono* (a sugared roll commemorating Pope Pius IX).

A bit further north is **Victorias Milling Company**, reputedly the largest sugar cane mill and refinery in the world. Within the "Vicmico" compound is **St Joseph the Worker Chapel**, with an awesome mural in full technicolor depicting a furious Jesus and his disciples. Other attractions, such as saints depicted with Filipino features and garb, and a psychedelic mosaic made of broken pop bottles, make this a must-visit. It is sometimes referred to as the Chapel of the Angry Christ. Locals still proudly recall how it gained global recognition decades ago when it was featured in *Life* magazine.

Around Bacolod

Off **Cadiz City** at the province's northern tip, 64 km (40 miles) north of Bacolod, is **Llacaon Island**, 9 hectares (22 acres) of gleaming white sand beaches fringed by coral reefs. On the northeastern tip, 94 km (60 miles) from Bacolod, **Escalante** has several resorts that face the mouth of Tañon Strait. A 10-minute pumpboat ride will take you to **Isla Puti** (White Island). Escalante is also known for its processed crab meat and freshly salted *danggit*, the crispy dried fish that is such a favorite that it regularly makes its way to Manila groceries.

Some 45 minutes' drive southeast of Bacolod, through **Murcia** town, is **Mambucal Summer Resort** ㉟, with a tourist lodge, several cottages, camp-

Map on pages 240–41

TIP

For a good look at the culture and a peak into lives during Silay's glorious days, visit Balay Negrense in Silay. Owned by the Jalandoni family, the residence has been turned into a private museum.

BELOW: old-world architecture at Iloilo City.

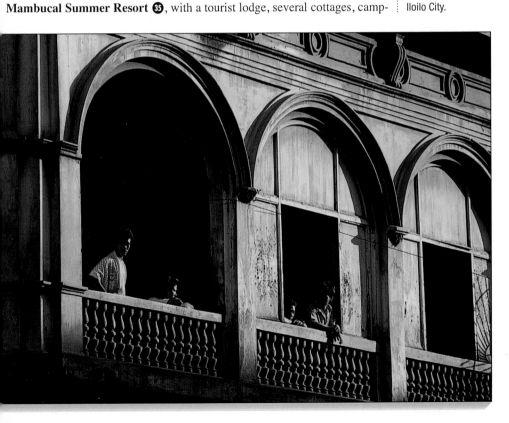

ing grounds, swimming pools, and seven waterfalls, three of which are easily accessible along concrete pathways. The best feature at the resort is a bathhouse, where, for a minimal fee, one can soak in hot sulfuric water.

Mountain climbers might try **Canlaon Volcano** , which rises 2,465 meters (8,087 ft) to a summit of twin craters, one extinct and the other active. The usual starting point for the climb is Kanlaon, 100 km (60 miles) from Bacolod and 170 km (100 miles) from Dumaguete. Some of the Negros Occidental towns at the volcano's foothills also serve as jump-off bases. One trail starts near Ara-al, a *barangay* of **La Carlota** where hot springs abound, while another one that is better marked and easier to follow ascends the southwest side, starting near Biak-na-Bato. **Hacienda Montealegre** has become the starting point for an organized trek led by the local guides.

A night is usually spent halfway up at a surprising 2-hectare (5-acre) stretch of white sand called **Margaha Valley**. A second night may be spent by leisurely climbers at the volcano's shoulder, some 600 meters (1,970 ft) below the craters. From the summit, one can peer into the 100-meter-wide (330-ft) active crater, which descends to a depth of 250 meters (820 ft).

Sipalay, 160 km (100 miles) south, has a major lure in Tinagong Dagat (Hidden Sea), accessible through a narrow channel between Dinosaur Island and the mainland. Corals and tropical fish teem in this seaside lake. Nearby, Maricalum Bay has similarly abundant marine life, and attracts deep-sea anglers with varieties of mackerel, barracuda, grouper and tuna.

Panay

From Bacolod, it is just a leisurely two-hour ride across Guimaras Strait to **Iloilo City** . Negros Navigation provides daily ferry services, which can be most pleasant at sundown. Past Guimaras Strait, the ferry turns into Iloilo Strait, which separates Panay and Guimaras Island, then wends its way up the Iloilo river into the city's excellent protected harbor, whose jutting form gives the city its name – *ilong-ilong* or "like a nose."

The capital of Iloilo Province on the southeast coast of **Panay Island**, Iloilo City is considered a culturally older Ilonggo center that has retained much of the distinctive charm of its Castilian heritage, while remaining the most important port in the region since it was opened to international shipping in 1855. Hearing of Iloilo's excellent harbor, Legazpi came over from Cebu in 1569, and subsequently made Iloilo his base for explorations northwards to Manila.

By the river's mouth is **Fort San Pedro**. Originally constructed in 1616 with earthworks and wooden palisades, it was transformed in 1738 into a stone fort, quadrilateral in shape with a bastion at each corner, and defended by 50 guns. In 1937, Fort San Pedro became the quarters for the Philippine Army. The barracks was eventually removed and the fort turned into a promenade area, popular in the early evening hours.

J. M. Basa Street is the main thoroughfare, and together with Guanco, Iznart and Ledesma streets, makes up Iloilo's commercial center. It would be a mistake to expect a flurry of activity here. There is no rushing the Ilonggo resident; even commercial activities submit to languor. Some good Chinese restaurants may be found on J.M. Basa, as well as department stores, and movie houses that have taken over the old shells of art deco buildings.

The **Museo ng Iloilo** (Iloilo Museum; open Mon–Fri 9am–noon and 1–5pm; entrance fee) on Bonifacio Drive showcases prehistoric artifacts from the many burial sites dug up on Panay Island, including gold-leaf masks for the dead, seashell jewelry, and other ornaments worn by pre-Spanish islanders. Also of note is an exhibit of the cargo recovered from a British ship that sank off Guimaras Island in the 19th century: Victorian chinaware, port wine and Glasgow beer are among the shipwreck's treasures.

Molo district

Molo district has a Gothic-Renaissance church completed in the 1800s, and the Asilo de Molo, an orphanage where little girls hand-embroider church vestments. Molo has become famous outside Panay for a noodle dish known as *pancit Molo*, just as La Paz, another Iloilo district, is the home of the original (although restaurants from Manila to Bacolod will claim this popular adjective) La Paz *batchoy*. Both are variations of the Chinese *mee* (noodles) and are regulars in most restaurants in Western Visayas. Panaderia de Molo (Molo Bakery), the oldest bakery in the South, is a favorite. Biscuits, breads and assorted delicacies are packed in round tins for convenient *pasalubong* (take-home gifts).

Jaro district also has a Gothic cathedral, with a ruined belfry, found at the edge of the town plaza. Jaro has been the traditional center for loom-weaving and hand embroidery of *piña* and *jusi*, delicate fabrics used for the Filipino *barong tagalog* (traditional shirt). **Arevalo** district is called the "Flower Village"

Map on pages 240–41

Weaving abaca, a fiber made from hemp, and used in a variety of goods like mats, bags and place mats.

LEFT: Molo Church.
BELOW: baked goodies at Molo Bakery.

for its traditional production of leis, bouquets and wreaths. In the 16th century, Arevalo was a shipbuilding center and served as a supply base for Spanish expeditions to Muslim Mindanao and the Moluccas.

Out from Iloilo

The presence of many old churches underscores the high regard the Spanish colonizers had for Iloilo Province as a religious and commercial center for the region. Some 13 km (8 miles) north is the Renaissance-inspired **Pavia Church**, with red brick walls and window frames of coral rock. Construction began in 1886, but somehow the church was never finished. Farther up is the neoclassical **Santa Barbara Church**, where Ilonggos first gathered to declare the revolution against the Spanish rulers.

At kilometer 25 on the same northward road is **Cabatuan Church**, also of neoclassic style and built in the early 1880s. Nearby is Cabatuan Cemetery, walled in with coral rock and sandstone.

More untapped islands lie off the northeastern coast of Panay, amid the rich fishing grounds of the Visayan Sea. From **Ajuy**, one can proceed northward to **Estancia**, a fishing town dubbed by local geography books as the "Alaska of the Philippines." A 20-minute pumpboat ride from Estancia leads to **Sicogon Island**, former site of one of the poshest resorts in the Visayas.

Westward from Iloilo, along the southern coast, runs a more frequented road past beach resorts and Iloilo's more distinctive old churches. At kilometer 22 is the coastal town of **Tigbauan**, worth a stop for its baroque church, sadly ruined by an 1948 earthquake, like so many of the country's churches.

At kilometer 40 is the **Miagao Fortress Church** ❸, built in 1786 as a place of worship, as well as an impregnable fortress. The most impressive among Iloilo's formidable array of centuries-old churches, its unique facade features a stunning bas-relief of intricate botanical motifs fairly reminiscent of Aztec art. Largely because it best exemplifies what is called the tropical baroque style of architecture, the church has been declared a world heritage and conservation site by UNESCO.

Guimaras Island

Fifteen minutes by pumpboat from Iloilo is the island province of **Guimaras** ❸, the site of the much-admired **Roca Encantada** (Enchanted Rock), summer house of the distinguished Lopez family. Perched on a promontory overlooking Guimaras Strait, it is visible on the ferry ride to or from Bacolod. Across the promontory is **Siete Pecados** (Isles of Seven Sins), a curious counterpoint to the attractions of spiritual value found in Guimaras.

The capital town of Guimaras is **Jordan**. Just to its west is **Bala-an Bukid**, a favorite Catholic pilgrimage site atop Bundulan Point. To the south, at San Miguel, is a Trappist monastery, the only one in the country. Off the town of San Isidro is **Inampulugan Island**, which is entirely taken over by a first-class resort named Costa Aguada. In **Santa Ana Bay**, accessible from Lawi, or 45 minutes by pumpboat from Fort San Pedro pier in Iloilo, is Isla

BELOW:
sunset fishing at
Guimaras Island.

Naburot Resort. Lovingly created by the Saldaña family, this delightful place to stay has unusual features, such as antique wooden doors that double as windows.

In the southern coastal town of **Nueva Valencia** is **Catilaran Cave**, where Ming jars have been unearthed. On Good Friday, the *pangalap* ritual, similar to that of Siquijor island, is held here. Hundreds of devotees recite Latin prayers while crawling through the 500-meter cave, believing they will acquire supernatural powers, useful against countering evil spirits. Nearby, **Tatlong Pulo** (Three Islets) offers smaller caves, plus excellent swimming, snorkelling and island-hopping.

Antique Province

Past kilometer 53 is **San Joaquin**, the southernmost town of Iloilo Province. San Joaquin Church, dating back to 1869, is of gleaming white coral, and has another unusual facade, depicting the historic Battle of Tetuan, where Spanish forces routed the Moors in Morocco in 1859. From here, the road continues northward through rolling terrain to **Antique Province**, which hugs the western coast of Panay. A high and rugged range of mountains runs parallel to this coast, lending the province an isolated character, which is underscored by roads that have been paved in recent years.

San Jose de Buenavista, the capital, is 100 km (60 miles) from Iloilo. Several beach resorts are found in the *barangay* of San Jose. Close by is Hamtik, the site of the landing of the 10 Bornean Datuks, or princes, in 1212, which is the beginning of the timeline for Malay people in the Philippines. An hour's drive south leads to Anini-y. Off Anini-y is **Nogas Island**, which has a white sand beach and is ideal for scuba diving and snorkeling. Located in *barangay*

Map on pages 240–41

Salt pan workers near Iloilo City.

BELOW: Miagao Fortress Church.

Dapog of Anini-y is **Sira-an Hot Springs**, which is close to a fairly good swimming beach.

North of San Jose de Buenavista is the town of **Tibiao**. Whitewater kayaking is organised by the Kayak Inn, as are enjoyable hikes up the seven-tiered Bugtong Bato Waterfalls. The next town up the coast is **Culasi**, off which is coral-ringed **Mararison Island**. Rising 2,300 meters (7,500 ft) is the legendary **Mt Madja-as**. An extinct volcano, it is believed to have been the home of Bulalakaw (Comet), whom early pagan settlers worshiped as the supreme deity. The mountain was then called Orang Madja-as. It has several upland lakes and a proliferation of waterfalls. Deer and wild boar still roam the area, and local hunters still make it a practice to bag a trophy or two as prized game meat during fiestas. The big festival in Antique is the Binirayan Festival, which takes place for three days at year end. Tumultuous street dancing goes on all over the capital in remembrance of the Hamtik landing.

North of Culasi, you cross over into **Aklan Province**, located near Panay's northwestern tip. The port town of **New Washington** handles inter-island shipping connections. Those who have failed to make early plane or ship reservations can fly or take the ship to Roxas instead, then travel by bus to **Kalibo ⓵**, the oldest town in Aklan and home of the famous Ati-Atihan festival. Its enormous success has led to replication of the street dancing in various other cities in the Visayas and northern Mindanao, where local versions are staged in honor of historic episodes or favorite religious icons. The infectious Ati-Atihan beat, as well the ethnic costumes and body paint, has become a highlight also of Independence Day celebrations held by Filipino communities in various US cities.

BELOW: painted Ati-Atihan dancer.

THE PHILIPPINES' MARDI GRAS

In the year 1212, as popular folklore would have it, 10 Bornean *datu* (chiefs), fleeing the collapse of the once-mighty Srivijayan empire, sailed northwards with their followers and landed on the island of Panay. There they bought the coastal lands from the native Negrito inhabitants with gold, pearls and other ornaments.

This legendary barter between Malays and native inhabitants is commemorated yearly in what is the most popular and colorful festival in the whole country. On the third weekend of January, the small coastal town of Kalibo, in Aklan Province, plays host to thousands of Filipinos and foreign visitors who join the three-day revelry and fiesta known as Ati-Atihan.

The festival is planned by local people long in advance. Their costumes are wildly original and no one in town, local or visitor, dares traipse around without a painted face, a camera, and a beer bottle or jug of coco wine in hand. Hotel prices rise considerably during this fiesta period, and rooms can be very difficult to find.

Ati-Atihan celebrations have been copied elsewhere in the Philippines and also in other countries. The Ati-Atihan dancing contingent, for instance, is a much-awaited Independence Day photo opportunity in Manhattan, US.

Boracay Island

Off the northeastern tip of Panay Island is world-famous **Boracay Island** . Shaped like a slender butterfly drawn in powder-fine white sand, Boracay has become a fabled paradise for both budget and posh resort travelers. It was first "discovered" back in the 1960s, when beachcombers went looking for its rare *puka* shells. By the 1970s, Boracay was on the hit list of every intrepid adventurer in Asia. They came in small numbers at first, staying in the nipa huts along White Beach, for a couple of dollars a night. But, as with every other magical spot with a pristine environment and an increasing cachet amongst backpack travelers, the word spread. By the 1980s, the adventurers had become the hoards, and boutique resorts sprang up all along White Beach. It was still a journey to reach, as it remains today, but that was part of the draw. Nowadays, the easiest way is to fly from Manila to Caticlan via turbo-prop flights and take the 15-minute pumpboat crossing to the island. One can also take the more regular jet flight to Kalibo, and ride a jeepney or van (two to three hours) to Caticlan for the crossing. Banca boats, which take visitors from the port in Caticlan to the boat jetty in Boracay, stop service at sunset.

Upscale resort

Today, Boracay has moved way upmarket. Since the mid-1980s, it has attracted the well-heeled of Europe, America and Asia, as well as Filipinos, who have begun to outnumber foreign visitors lately. The sight greeting arrivals is nothing but spectacular: a gentle aquamarine sea, the whitest of white beaches, tall palms swaying in the breeze. It is hard to take a less than stunning photo here. For an arresting view of Boracay and its surrounds, head up to the **Mt Luho View Deck**.

Maps:
Area 240
Isle 279

TIP

Don't worry about dressing for dinner on Boracay. The island's undressed code (bare feet and bikini) is acceptable even in the smarter joints. Sandals are recommended, though, in case of occasional objects in the sand.

BELOW: learn how to dive at Boracay.

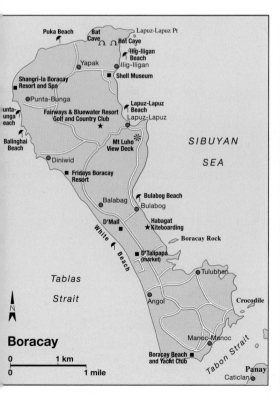

Boracay map

Colorful lanterns at one of numerous handicraft and souvenir shops that line Boracay's White Beach.

BELOW: Boracay's White Beach is well... white.

New arrivals stake out a stretch of sand and lie in Boracay's special sun. Visitors can hire sailboats, kiteboards and windsurfers at any of the score of rental shops. Bicycles are available for exploring the tiny island, which is only 7 km long by 3 km wide (6 miles by 2 miles). Yapak village, located on the northern end of the island, is where everyone heads to find *puka* shells, although you are more likely to find them at a tourist shop than on the beach, thanks to one too many collector. There are also endless choices of watersports, such as jet skiing, parasailing and scuba diving.

Boracay dining, which was once simple and based on good island fare, now ranges from haute Filipino to haute French, with Indonesian, Thai, Italian, Chinese, Swiss, and English available. Some restaurants offer dancing on the beach beneath the stars.

There are still some basic nipa huts, but mostly resorts are found on the beach now. An uproar was caused in the late 1990s with the establishment of the posh Fairways & Bluwater Resort Golf and Country Club, which takes up all of 118 hectares (292 acres) in Yapak, off Lapuz-Lapuz Beach, on the northeastern side. But the proprietors of the world-class leisure hub have since successfully addressed concerns about overtaxing the island's water supply and other natural needs.

As for the expected upturn of jetsetters descending on Boracay's beaches, the locals can't complain, since employment and business opportunities – and livelihood – are only further enhanced with more arrivals. Residents also believe the backpackers will still be there, as will the increasing crowds of Manileños and venturesome fellow-Visayans, so what's one more species to add to the social whirl under the tropical sun, as long as the golf balls avoid hitting a windsurfer offshore?

Growing pains

Boracay has now become a firm player in Asian tourism, despite a rough beginning during which hasty and uncontrolled growth led to severe environmental issues. A coliform scare in 1997 passed in a few months, but not before concerned tourism officials had sat down the island's proprietors for lessons in environmental management. Thereafter, sewage and water pipes were laid to the mainland, and a new jetty was also built to make the Caticlan embarkation process a smoother affair. In rough conditions, both the Caticlan and Boracay landing areas may be moved to more leeward areas. These days, change is still in high gear, and visitors will easily notice one or two resorts that look more like roadside motels than tropical beach getaways.

Boracay's sand, marvelously cool to the sole even at high noon, comes from finely crushed calcareous materials, in other words corals and seashells that have expired in the course of time. Marine biologists warn that if the reefs fringing the island are left unprotected, the sand would not be replenished, and it could go the way of the daily tide. Eventual erosion would see the white beaches diminishing in size. Granted that this will take a long time, environmentalists, together with tourism, health and science officials, still look at endless meetings ahead of them – with the residents and resort proprietors in alert attendance – to figure out a long-term program for conserving the island's natural assets. In the meantime, Boracay beckons irresistibly at the universal beach fancier, its continuing allure a veritable beacon this lucrative side of paradise.

Capiz Province

Roxas City is the capital of Capiz, Panay's northeast province. Anglers will find the Capiz coastline a rich fishing ground. **Napti Island**, off nearby **Panay** town, offers great varieties of seafood and pretty beaches. Capiz's thriving fishing industry is known to supply many of Metro Manila's fine dining restaurants with quality seafood: from oysters and bamboo clams to the largest, freshest groupers, marlin, jacks, squid, octopus and prawns.

Panay Church has a marble floor and 3-meter-thick (10-ft) walls of white coral. The interior is decorated with *retablos* (altar pieces) of silver and hardwood. The Panay Cemetery also has walls and a chapel made of coral.

Capiz's coastline has a number of good beaches. **Baybay Beach** for instance offers modest tourist accommodation, while nearby is **Olutayan Island**, whose surrounding waters are another anglers' paradise. The **Ivisan Coves** in the barrios of Basiao and Bataring are popular natural bathing pools.

Over an hour's drive south from the capital will take you to **Dumalag Church**, built in the 1800s. Nearby is another attraction, Suhot Cave. East of Roxas, some 45km (30 miles) is Casanayan Beach.

Capiz's version of street revelry is the Halaran Festival held June 22–25 throughout the province. On the Feast Day of Our Lady of the Immaculate Conception, on December 8, Roxas City also celebrates, a little more solemnly, a religious festival in honor of its patroness. ❑

Maps:
Area 240
Isle 279

TIP

Tribal Adventure Tours (www.tribaladventures.com), based in Sand Castles Resort in Boracay, offers adventurous mountain biking and kayaking tours in the rugged terrain of northwestern Panay. Tours start from Caticlan.

BELOW: the Visayan Sea's bounty is well known.

LIVING SEAS: SOURCE OF LIFE AND PLEASURE

Whether for recreation or sustenance, the abundant marine resources of the Philippines continue to serve both tourists and locals

The figures are stunning. With more coastline than the continental USA fringing the 7,107 islands and islets of the Philippines, and 1.7 million sq km (656, 375 sq miles) of territorial waters, the country was once considered as repository of one of the world's richest fishery resources. Since time immemorial simple fisher-folk have been living off this life-giving abundance.

One-tenth of the world's 20,000 fish species are found in these waters, and in 1987, the value of the local fishing industry was pegged at US$2 billion, with nearly 2 million people involved in fishing and its related service industries.

Visitors wax lyrical over the country's world-class white sand beaches, lonely islets and surf-sculptured rock formations. Watersports enthusiasts have turned to its pounding waves, pristine reefs and waters clear as gin.

Recent events, however, are reversing trends. Studies show the country's marine environment has deteriorated to crisis levels. Illegal fishing through the use of dynamide and cyanide, and other destructive activities are destroying the seas. Unless these are stopped, it may only be a matter of time before tourists shun its beaches, and Filipinos bid goodbye to one of nature's greatest bounty.

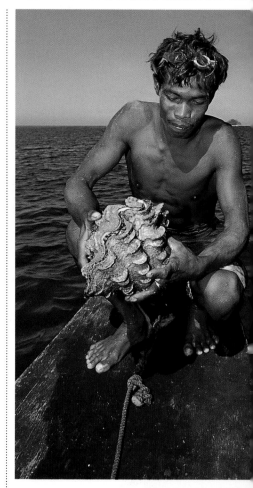

△ **GIANT CLAM**
Diving is not just recreational. For many Filipinos – who dive without the aid of expensive scuba gear – it's a livelihood. The clam is a much-sought after delicacy.

▽ **BALANCING ACT**
The Samal people of southern Mindanao are the poorest and least independent of the Muslim groups. They live over the sea, in villages perched on stilts above coastal waters.

◁ **SAY HELLO**
A close encounter with a colorful ribbon eel. Divers from the world over are drawn by clear waters and the fascinating underwater world.

SCUBA DIVING AND WRECK HUNTING

△ SKI SET
At tourist beaches, jet skiing is a popular option for those who like to stay above water. It is an expensive sport though, averaging US$50 an hour.

▽ BOAT BOY
For the sea-loving Badjao people of the Sulu Seas, the water is home as well. Literally born and bred on water, they often set foot on land only to die.

◁ SUN DRIED AND SALTED
Preserved salted fish is big business among fishing communities. For the poor, it is a cheap food staple that needs no refrigeration.

▷ WEED FROM SEA
Seaweed is such a popular export commodity that Filipinos have taken to even cultivating certain species.

There's a very good reason why people get easily hooked on diving in the Philippines. Its warm tropical waters teem with an astounding variety of marine life – including the largest ever recorded gathering of whale sharks in the world – and extensive reefs. For divers, this is a watery nirvana as they plunge into its clear waters to suss out its more than 488 of the worlds 500 species of coral and over 1,000 fish species.

Although numerous dive sites abound all over the archipelago, dive fiends will undoubtedly wax lyrical about the Tubbataha Reef in the Sulu Sea, accessible only by live-aboard dive operators. So superlative is the marine environment here that UNESCO has deemed it a World Heritage Site. Wreck divers should head for sunken ships in Subic Bay and Batangas, Coron Bay in Palawan, and the Leyte Gulf. For more information on Philippine diving, check out www.diver.com. ph.

△ THE DAY'S CATCH
A common early-morning scene at coastal villages. Casting nets from the shoreline is one of the cheapest and quickest ways to catch fish.

PALAWAN

The natural attractions of this long, isolated finger of an island are only enhanced by the roughness of its road system

On the southwest corner of the Philippine archipelago lies the elongated island province of **Palawan**, pointing like a *keris* (a Malay wavy short sword) towards northern Borneo. A quarter of the country's islands are found in the Palawan group, but their geography has meant virtual isolation until recently.

Petroleum companies are now drilling in Palawan's offshore areas. The Malampaya platform, off Palawan, already supplies 40 percent of Luzon's electricity and natural gas. "Black gold" was not in Pigafetta's mind when, in the 16th century, he cited Palawan as the "land of promise," but Magellan's chronicler must have deduced from the islands' natural potential and sparse population that one day this lucrative afterthought to the rest of the archipelago could be exploited.

When the Spanish arrived, the sultans of Jolo and Borneo controlled Palawan. It wasn't until the 19th century that Spain managed to gain a foothold in the town that was later to be called Puerto Princesa and is now the provincial capital.

Ten centuries earlier, this same settlement on the eastern coast had moved the Chinese to call the island Palao-Yu, or "land of beautiful safe harbor." It was then inhabited by settlers of proto-Malay stock, whose descendants still exist today as the Batak, Palawanon and Tagbanua. Their migration from the Indonesian islands is popularly believed to have been by way of the land bridges that once attached the Philippine archipelago to the Asian subcontinent. The theory is supported by the distinctive fauna and flora of Palawan, which, like those of Mindanao, are uncommon to the rest of the country.

In the 13th century, more settlers filtered in from the Majapahit empire of Java. Today, despite continuing migration, Palawan remains sparsely populated, since it is still considered too remote. Improvement of the infrastructure will certainly change this, but until then, roads remain atrocious and travel even around the main island is done mostly by boat. But for the intrepid – whether explorer, naturalist or beach mandarin – seeking fringe locations, Palawan's rough going yields rewards of considerable merit.

Visitors might watch the birds' nest gatherers at work, scaling cliffs for the prized nest of swiftlets that will make its way to some Chinese restaurant. It's possible to motor up a subterranean river to marvel at limestone cathedrals, visit a cave complex containing important archeological finds or take the pick of handicrafts from a unique farm prison. Alternatively, savor the fabulous sunsets off the western coast, or watch more than a 100,000 birds darken the skies as they come home to roost in their island sanctuary. ❏

PRECEDING PAGES: netting a hefty red grouper near the white-sand Pamalican Island puts a smile on the face of this fisherman.
LEFT: rose-tinted sunset at Dinakya Island in Palawan.

NORTHERN PALAWAN

This collection of remote, unspoiled islands has become a resort paradise where wildlife abounds, towns are sleepy and the diving simply fascinating

Map on page 296

Manila

Northern Palawan refers to the outlying islands north of the Palawan mainland, as well as the area within its northern tip. The fringes include the Calamian island group, with the three major islands of Busuanga, Culion and Linapacan; the Quiniluban island group, with the main island of Agutaya; and Cuyo Island. These last two are quite distant from the mainland, in the middle of the Sulu Sea that separates the Palawan archipelago from the Visayas.

Palawan is not only unspoiled, but incredibly rich in terms of tropical flora and fauna, much of it uncommon. The waters off the entire east coast abound with game fish, and exotic wildlife roams the interior. This includes the Palawan peacock pheasant, the smallest of its kind in the bird world; the 30-cm high (1-ft) mousedeer or chevrotain, the smallest of Asiatic hoofed animals; the monkey-eating eagle; and the *tabon* bird, whose large eggs are collected from beach burrows to make a prized omelet, as well as the Palawan mongoose, hornbill, bearcat, civet, stink badger, scaly anteater, porcupine, flying squirrel and the giant sea turtle, which lays eggs on certain beaches at the end of the year.

Calamian Islands

A slow boat makes the weekly trip from Manila to Puerto Princesa city in Central Palawan, stopping halfway at **Coron ❶**, on **Busuanga Island ❷** in the Calamian group. While in Coron, find out how long the ship will stay docked for cargo. Chances are you'll have enough time to wander about the old town for some good handicraft buys, an extremely cheap gallon of pure wild honey, and dried sea cucumbers sunning on some pavement fronting a Chinese store. WG&A Superferry now plies this route weekly, leaving Pier 15 at Manila's South Harbor Friday evening, reaching Coron early Saturday, and returning by early Monday. This convenient schedule allows weekenders a good opportunity to savor Coron.

This area used to be difficult to get to, as with most other parts of the Palawan mainland. However, daily flights from Manila now land in the new Coron airport in Busuanga Island, which, together with **Coron Island ❸** (not to be confused with Coron town), have, by word of mouth, built a reputation as an adventurer's delight. The town itself is sleepy, often used only as a point of passage, but numerous destinations are within reach by pumpboat or rickety bus.

Maquinit Hot Springs may be the best in the entire country, if only for its unusual site that is accessible by road or a 20-minute pumpboat ride from Coron. Here one can bathe in hot sulfuric water in twin waist-deep pools set by a mangrove stand, and flanked by a Virgin Mary grotto. It is highly recommended, especially

LEFT: aerial shot of the Palawan coast.
BELOW: the bearcat is one of numerous unique fauna found in Palawan.

TIP

Diving in Lake
Cayangan (better
known as Barracuda
Lake), whose depth is
unknown, is quite an
experience. Local dive
operators ride a *banca*
to a crack in the
limestone wall, where
divers must scale 25
meters (80 ft) of razor
sharp coral, in full dive
gear. A descent into
the warm lake leads to
the sooty zone, where
visibility drops to zero.

Below: Lake
Cayangan in Coron
Island is believed to
be sacred by locals.

for those who develop kinks from third-class boat travel or light plane hops. When the therapeutic water becomes unbearably hot, bathers can always jump out and run across the gray-sand beach to the sea.

Coron Island is a jewel for a trekker with a taste for upland lakes. Cross over from Coron town and scale trails past limestone cliffs for an hour or so, until you behold **Lake Cayangan**, a basin of emerald water trapped in a virtual circle of tropical verdure and karst formations. Tagbanua natives regard Lake Cayangan as sacred. It is also the home of a giant barracuda, which frequently shows up during lake dives – hence its more common name, Barracuda Lake. Due to reputed volcanic activity underneath, there are alternating layers of hot and cold water. Calm and quiet, the lagoon is perfect for kayaking. Another upland lake, Cabugao, is much larger but farther off and requires longer than a day trip out of Coron Island. This area is the first land in the country to be returned to a tribal people's (the Tagbanua) control, and laws and practices are still being developed. As Coron Island is almost entirely under Tagbanua jurisdiction, check accessibility, fees, and other rules such as camping and kayaking parameters, before visiting the beaches, lakes and other attractions.

Fascinating dives

All around **Coron Bay**, south of Busuanga Island, are terrific dive sites (plenty of dive operators provide equipment and services), with the world-renowned feature of numerous wrecks, mostly of Japanese ships and planes that went down during World War II. In September 1944, US reconnaissance planes spotted 24 tiny islands in the waters off Coron which kept moving. The islands – Japanese ships camouflaged in green leaves and shrubbery – were sunk by a convoy of US Navy SB2C Helldivers shortly after. The wrecks have become historical underwater landmarks. An abandoned Japanese submarine is also said to be lurking in difficult waters. Dive Link Resort on **Uson Island**, barely 10 minutes by pumpboat from Coron, is a good jumping off point for underwater adventure, with a dozen Japanese wrecks lying at depths of 20–40 meters (65–130 ft). It also provides amenities and leisure for non-divers. Brightly painted cottages at the seaside are set against a backdrop of hillocks lush with hardwood trees.

A rough road leads westward from Coron, passing the relatively big towns of Concepcion, Salvacion and Old Busuanga, off which is another airstrip. In the hot season, the Palawan cherry tree turns this road into a scenic route strewn with pink-and-white blossoms. Offshore are hundreds of islets, most uninhabited, yours for the taking on any given day, and easily accessible on a calm sea.

Off the northern tip of Busuanga Island sits the remarkable **Calauit National Wildlife Sanctuary** on **Calauit Island ❹**. Giraffes, elands, zebras, bushbacks, impalas, gazelles and waterbucks were shipped here in 1977 by arrangement between President Marcos and an African potentate. For a while the game preserve was rumored to be a private shooting range for presidential son "Bongbong" Marcos. The Conservation and Resource Management Foundation

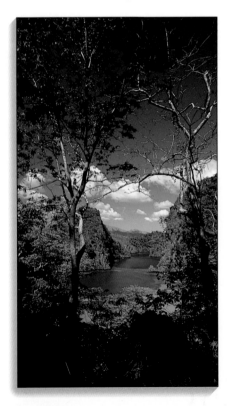

Map on page 296

(CRMF), tasked to oversee the sanctuary, has done such a good job, despite occasional poaching by disgruntled former islanders, that the African animals have prospered to help make the island a singular destination for photo opportunities.

To get to Calauit, take the pumpboat from Buluang, the end town of the provincial road, or make arrangements with any of the few resorts in the area. Two of these, Las Perlas and Las Hamacas Beach Resort, are found close to **Old Busuanga** town, while the upscale Club Paradise (www.clubparadisepalawan. com) occupies **Dinakya Island** off San Jose, the last town on the even rougher road to the northern coast. Another resort close by is Maricaban Bay Resort. Resort-bound tourists usually fly directly from Manila to the Yulo King Ranch (YKR) airstrip off San Jose, or take a pumpboat ride around the coast from Coron.

South of Busuanga is **Culion Island ❺**, anathema to most Filipinos during less enlightened days, when it was home to a leper colony. Culion's old church still has a towering belfry for a panoramic view of the surrounding islands. There is also a small museum displaying records of the town's painful past, but heartwarming tales of courage and sacrifice are also highlighted. A stone fort beside the church, dating back to 1683 and renovated in 1740, was partially demolished in the 1930s, but a round bastion and part of the wall remain.

The Quiniluban and Cuyo Islands, southeast of Culion, may be reached in good weather in about half a day by motorized outrigger. There are well-preserved Spanish forts on both **Agutaya Island** in the Quiniluban island group and **Cuyo Island**. Great beaches include Caymanis Beach on the southern part of Cuyo, and Matarawis Beach in Agutaya. At the northern end of the Quiniluban islands is the **Halob Island Bird Sanctuary**, while the exclusive Amanpulo Resort occupies all of **Pamalican Island**.

African wildlife on the tropical isle of Calauit is a strange sight – shipped here from Kenya in 1977.

BELOW: the high life at Amanpulo Resort, Pamalican Island.

Taytay

Close to the northern tip of Palawan is the old town of **Taytay**  ⑥ , one of the first Spanish fortifications to be built on Palawan. Founded in 1622, Taytay was once the Spanish capital of the province that the early Spanish colonizers renamed Paragua. Close by is the island of **Paly**, with waterfalls and white sand beaches, where giant sea turtles lay eggs in November and December. Off Taytay is **Malampaya Sound**, an angler's paradise that has been dubbed, rather tediously, the "fish bowl" of the Philippine archipelago.

Soups and resorts

Northwest of Taytay, 50 km (30 miles) away, is **El Nido** ⑦ , where towering black marble cliffs provide swiftlets with enough nooks and crannies in which to build their nests, so popular in soups throughout the Chinese world. Gatherers clamber up rickety bamboo scaffolding to collect the nests from crags and deep caves in the cliffs. About 1 kg (2 lbs) of these prized nests may net a professional cliff-scaler tens of thousands of pesos, a minimal sum compared to what they will fetch in Manila or elsewhere in Asia, where a traditional Chinese meal often starts with delicately flavored birds' nest soup.

El Nido town can be reached from Puerto Princesa, by plane or by a rough road that takes about nine hours or less depending on the weather. Alternatively, from Sabang – home of an underground river – hire a pumpboat for the seven-hour trip.

El Nido is the base for excursions to the surrounding limestone islands of the **Bacuit Archipelago**. A bonus of visiting these islands is a stay at one of the superior and far-flung resorts, like Club Noah Isabelle on **Apulit Island** in Taytay Bay or El Nido Resort on **Lagen Island** and **Miniloc Island**. These are

Some cheap cottages are available in El Nido, a sleepy town of some 27,000 residents, where the houses bear a personal touch: instead of numbers, signs announce the names of the owners.

BELOW: upscale Club Noah Isabelle on Apulit Island.

havens for divers and lovers of aquatic sports – and of El Nido's fabled shrimp and lobster dinners.

Map on page 296

El Nido Resort opened with its Miniloc operations in 1982 with just one diveboat and 15 cottages. Soon it drew attention as an environment-friendly resort. Some of its native cottages stand on stilts right over the edge of a cove. Other outstanding features include a daily fish-feeding program by the wooden pier, where the fish gobble offerings right from a visitor's hand; great coral formations to be enjoyed by simple snorkeling; and a small lagoon, land-locked but for a narrow passage at low tide, where the swimming and snorkeling can be memorable amidst the unspoiled jungle setting.

As El Nido grew in popularity, another resort set up a similar operation on Apulit Island, named Club Noah (later appending the Isabelle), and manned by well-trained Filipino staff. Club Noah Isabelle and El Nido Lagen have more lavish facilities, while El Nido miniloc retains its peaceful and homey atmosphere.

The Department of Environment and Natural Resources allows a maximum of only three resorts on El Nido's 45 islands. The third is a health spa, the Malapacap Island Retreat, on **Malapacao Island**.

Green sea turtle near Pangulasian Island.

Crusoe's islands

Pangulasian is 40 minutes by pumpboat from El Nido village. The Robinson Crusoe-type island, with its long stretch of paradisical beach and trails snaking off into the hibiscus jungle, can be visited on day trips from other resorts. Other islands in the Bacuit Archipelago worth visiting include Snake Island, with its white sands and turquoise waters, and Pinasil, with its jaw-dropping Cathedral Cave, which is big enough to drive a motorboat into.   ❑

BELOW: night diving off Pangulasian Island.

PUERTO PRINCESA

The environmentally progressive, sprawling capital of Palawan is an excellent base for exploring the beaches, bays, caves and jungles at the center of the island

Map on page 296

Situated near the middle of the eastern coast of Palawan Island, **Puerto Princesa** ❽, the capital of Palawan Province, serves as the hub of travel here. Various airlines fly daily from Manila, touching down in about an hour, and at least three major shipping lines convey passengers and cargo to the well-sheltered port in Puerto Princesa Bay. The trip by sea takes about 24 hours. Some boats, such as the WG & A Super Ferry, stop in Coron en route.

The early Spanish colonizers regarded the bay as "a princess of ports," thus giving the name to what was just a small coastal settlement surrounded by wild frontier land. Puerto Princesa was slowly developed into a base for naval operations, until it became a town with a dozen roads and a hospital by 1883. The colonial government appeared to have been extraordinarily prescient when it cited Puerto Princesa, well before the turn of the century, as one of the most beautiful towns it had helped develop. A government report dated 1884 said: "It had orderly streets, buildings and houses, and the community kept it clean."

Eco-city

In recent years, Puerto Princesa, which occupies 253,980 hectares (627,000 acres) and sprawls over 106 km (66 miles) from north to south, has gained the distinction of being a model city and an ecotourism haven. It has perennially set the standard for environmental awareness, and has the country's most acclaimed local government unit (LGU).

Its consistent achievements have been due largely to the no-nonsense leadership of three-time Mayor Edward Hagedorn, a reformed "bad boy" who has inspired his constituency to acquire a paragon image for the capital. Hagedorn's former exploits as a toughie and his dramatic conversion into a dynamic local executive have resulted in two feature-length movies based on his life, with no less than the "King of Action Movies," the late Fernando Poe Jr, portraying him in one of the "biopics." Biographies have also been written about the mayor, now the media's darling, whose political stock has risen so fast that various political parties have been trying to entice him to run for higher national office.

His success may largely be traced to his enlightened partnership with cause-oriented non-governmental organizations (NGOs), whose numbers and active efforts have helped establish a strong civil society in the Philippines, so that the country has often been hailed as the "NGO capital of the world."

Puerto Princesa has thus turned around from its former image of a distant, sleepy capital to a precedent-setting model for other provincial cities. It has already earned awards for environmental conservation and

LEFT: Puerto Princesa is one of the most attractive cities in the Philippines. **BELOW:** cooling down.

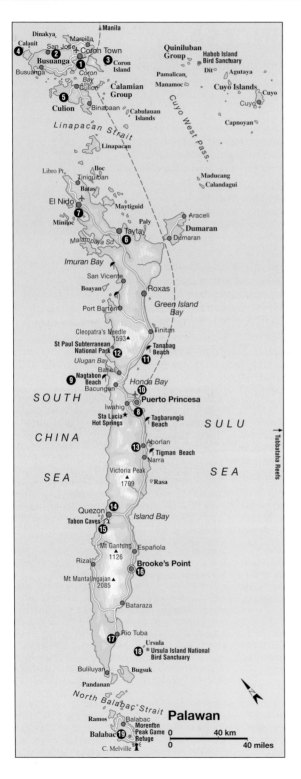

Palawan

protection, and for its program for peace and order, and public education for all age groups.

Only recently, Puerto Princesa was judged the best LGU in the much-coveted National Literacy Awards contest, in recognition of its integrated and comprehensive city education enhancement program. This was launched by Hagedorn in an effort to put its quality of education on a par with that of Metro Manila. The Puerto Princesa Functional Literacy program has been established to introduce the three Rs and other basic skills to tribal and indigenous groups like the Bataks and Tagbanuas, in an effort to help them cope with the changing times, and make it easier for them to interact with the so-called lowlanders. Ten "satellite libraries" have been built, one for each *barangay* with a high school, while three others have been set up in strategic locations. These are equipped with encyclopedias, dictionaries and a variety of "how-to" reference materials, covering pertinent topics like health, farming and family planning.

Clean and orderly

A stroll through the city streets quickly impresses the visitor with its unusual level of cleanliness and apparent sense of order, which stand in stark contrast to most other cities in the country. Wide, tree-lined avenues are an occasional feature, but, for the most part, the city sprawls over a large land area, with no discernible center except for where the **Provincial Capitol** building introduces a relatively busy section of several blocks that ends at **Rizal Park**. This is alongside the main thoroughfare of J. Rizal Avenue – leading eastward from the airport – just as it crosses the national highway, which runs north.

Along this avenue are several pensions and mid-priced inns, the most popular of which are Badjao Inn and Casa Linda Inn. Both have a small stage by the bar and dining area where folk singers are nightly attractions for the NGO crowd and a good number of expatriates, most serving as foreign consultants. Many more budget inns are found toward the parallel main of Manalo Extension and Abad Santos Extension south of J. Rizal Avenue. The **Children's Park** and **Immaculate Conception Cathedral** are found close to Rizal Park, right before the seaport. Midway are **Mendoza Park** and the **Palawan Museum**, open during regular office hours.

A couple of large, three-star hotels are located north of the airport and along the dense mangrove stands of Puerto Princesa Bay are numerous resorts and restaurants. A popular hangout for the culturally inclined is Karimikutan Café and Art Gallery, which is intricately designed with bamboo and other indigenous materials. It regularly exhibits artworks by a strong core of local artists and features poetry reading sessions as well as ethnic-rock bands. The hottest nightspot is the newly established Club (pronounced *Clue-B*) Uno.

Roads, not all of them decent enough to be called such, branch out from Puerto Princesa only to stop at certain points, from where further travel is undertaken by coast-hugging boats.

Around and about

Close to the city is the **Palawan Wildlife Rescue and Conservation Center** (formerly known as the Crocodile Farming Institute), where tourists often stop for an educational tour and souvenir buys of sundry items made of crocodile skin, such as bags and shoes. There is also a mini-zoo featuring a few of Palawan's uncommon fauna. Farther southeast, 16 km (10 miles) from the city, is the unique "prison without walls." At the **Iwahig Prison and Penal Farm** (formerly called Iwahig Penal Colony), most prisoners roam freely within the reservation's 37,000 hectares (90,000 acres) of beautiful undulating rice fields and orchards. Handcarved items

BELOW: serving out sentences at Iwahig Prison and Penal Farm.

BELOW: coastal view of Puerto Princesa city.

of *kamagong* (ebony) and mother-of-pearl inlay work are among the best of the handicrafts turned out by the inmates to supplement their income from agriculture. Two river resorts within the colony are favorite excursion retreats for Puerto Princesa residents: the **Balsahan River Swimming Resort** and **Panagurian Falls**.

South and north

A little farther south on the provincial road is **Sta Lucia Hot Spring**. This road continues southward until it reaches the eastern coast near Turtle Bay, from where it hugs the coastline all the way to the municipality of Aborlan. Along the way is **Tagbarungis Beach**, serviced by Blue Sky Sport & Beach Resort. Off the beach is **Pontog Island** with superlative white sand beaches.

The provincial road leading south from Puerto Princesa also branches westward past Iwahig, until it reaches the coast on the other side of the narrow island, facing the South China Sea. **Napsan Beach** is a favored destination, while nearby, reached after a bit of a trek, is **Salakot Waterfalls**, which has several deep pools that invite a cold plunge.

The road gets rougher as it hugs the majestic coastline leading north, veering inland after some 20 km (13 miles) to reach the town of **Bacungan**, from where the national highway leads back south to Puerto Princesa. En route is **Santa Lourdes Hot Spring**. From the Bacungan junction, a secondary road leads back west to **Nagtabon Cove**. Here the kilometer-long (½-mile) **Nagtabon Beach 9**, some 45 km (30 miles) or over an hour's drive from Puerto Princesa, offers a fine stretch of beige-colored sand, lapped by clear turquoise waters. Offshore are Dry Island and the improbably named Hen and Chicken Island. Sunsets over the South China Sea are particularly splendid here.

Relatively undiscovered by travelers, despite its proximity to the capital, Nagtabon Beach has two small resorts – Pablico's and Georg's Place – situated at either end of the placid strip flanked by undulating hills and green cliffs. A retired German pilot, Georg Bauer, became enamored of the idyllic cove during a visit two decades ago. It wasn't only the cove that had beguiled him, however. He courted and married, and together with his Filipino wife, decided to start out with a single duplex cottage. They have since added half a dozen other simple yet attractive bamboo cottages. Don't expect luxury features such as air-conditioning, however. Solar-powered lighting is provided, along with spartan amenities that include one or two beds per cottage, clean showers and toilets, screened windows with curtains, and interestingly, mosquito nets imported from Germany.

The islands in **Honda Bay 10** northeast of Puerto Princesa have become very popular frolicking grounds for beach fanciers and watersports enthusiasts. Here one can select any of the good number of islets for a day trip, or overnight accommodation at a simple resort. Island hopping is also recommended, as snorkeling or scuba diving ensures a varied selection of coral wonders. The more popular, bigger islands offering facilities for watersports, restaurants and accommodation include Starfish, Meara, Fondeado, Cowrie, Snake, Buguias and Arrecife. The northeast coast some 50 km (30 miles) from the capital has excellent beaches, with the most attractive **Tanabag Beach** ⑪, serviced by San Rafael Beach Resort and Green Beach Resort.

From Tanabag, serious trekkers usually set out for a cross-country jungle expedition that may take them all the way to **Cleopatra's Needle**, a rugged mountain with a sharp peak that rises to 1,593 meters (5,226 ft). On the north-western coast, **Ulugan Bay** is popular for its excellent dive spot off lovely **Rita Island** and a cluster of islets known as Tres Marias.

Map on page 296

Underground river

Most visitors to Puerto Princesa opt to visit the famous **Underground River** in **St Paul Subterranean National Park** ⑫ in Sabang. This is reached by travel-ing overland north of Puerto Princesa to **Baheli**, close to the western coast, 60 km (40 miles) away, and proceeding on motorized outriggers or pumpboats for another two hours. *Banca* trips may be arranged for delving into St Paul cavern – a fas-cinating passage through a subterranean world of exquisite cathedrals with mas-sive stalactites; icy lagoons where the eerie quiet is occasionally pierced by shrill cries of swooshing bats; and cavewall formations that resemble a George Lucas film set. High-powered lamps handled by the expert guides illuminate these attrac-tions. It is an exhilarating experience that can range from an hour-long incursion into the half-submerged bowels of the earth to an extended exploration of two to four hours. Day trips can be arranged from Puerto Princesa, but visitors wishing to tarry longer in the area may register with the park wardens for overnight camp-ing at any of the white sand beaches surrounding the entrance to the subterranean river, or check in at one of modest resorts in the vicinity. ❑

Ask a tricycle driver to take you to Puerto Princesa's Vietnamese Village where there are restaurants serving Vietnamese cuisine.

BELOW: St Paul Subterrannean National Park.

SOUTHERN PALAWAN

Broken roads rambling aimlessly south lead the adventurous to a land of historic caves, glorious wildlife, gentle indigenous people and merchants still plying historic Muslim trading routes

Map on page 296

Manila

O n the road south from Puerto Princesa, at kilometer 69, or about two hours' drive along the eastern coast, is the municipality of **Aborlan** ⓭. This is an agricultural town where a reservation has been set aside for ethnic and minority groups. Princesa Holiday Beach resort and Camille del Sol are the prime attractions, along with **Tigman Beach**. Some 30 km (18 miles) farther south is the town of **Narra**, off which is an interesting inlet called **Tinagong Dagat**, or Hidden Sea. **Rasa Island**, offshore from Narra, is a bird sanctuary and a unique ecotourism destination. Inland from Narra is a rugged mountain called **Victoria Peak**, with **Estrella Waterfalls** on its northern slopes. Another 30 km (18 miles) south of Narra is King's Paradise Island Bay resort, past which the road branches westward to cross to the South China Sea coast.

Tabon Caves

About 155 km (100 miles) southwest of Puerto Princesa – four hours by bus or jeepney – is the town of **Quezon** ⓮ on the west coast, from where one may take a half-hour boat ride to **Tabon Caves** ⓯. Another prime destination on the Palawan mainland, Tabon features a huge and fascinating complex of some 200 caves, of which only 30 or so have been explored. Here, human remains were found and carbon-dated to 22,000–24,000 years ago, the oldest traces of *Homo sapiens* in the Philippine archipelago.

With the Tabon relics were found Stone Age implements and artifacts of later eras, including burial jars and kitchen utensils. Overlooking a bay studded with small islands, the entrance to Tabon Caves is situated about 30 meters (100 ft) above sea level, on a promontory facing the South China Sea. The large mouth leads to an equally imposing dome-shaped chamber, beyond which are numerous sections where archaeological work is still patiently, and literally, being carved out. From anywhere within Quezon town, ask a tricycle driver to take you to the **Tabon Museum**, which exhibits artifacts and reading material on the archeological story behind Tabon Caves.

Close to Quezon, along Kanalong Bay in **Tarampitao**, runs a 10-km (6-mile) stretch of white sand beach where the swimming is good and the viewing fine for majestic sunsets. Also close by is the **Quezon Mini Underground River**, not quite as extensive as St Paul's but also worth a few hours' exploration.

The road proceeds southward toward the small town of Rizal, from where it extends further south, until re-crossing the island to meet the provincial highway skirting the eastern coast. This highway is in very poor condition, mercifully ending before it reaches the southernmost tip of the mainland. The preferred route to this unfrequented area is the highway along the eastern

LEFT: Palawan's waters are famous for harboring pearl-wielding clams.
BELOW: Underground River exploration.

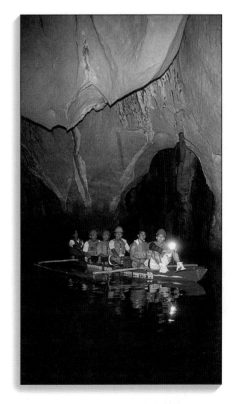

coast, so that one should backtrack from Quezon and turn south toward the town of **Española**. The only tourist stop of note here is the pretty **El Salvador Park**.

Muslim traders

Further south, 150 km (90 miles) from Puerto Princesa, and reached only over very rough roads that make the drive painfully slow, is **Brooke's Point** , another progressive municipality. Here one may note the sudden preponderance of Muslim traders, who are not seen much in Central and Northern Palawan. The old trading and migratory routes that had established a bond between the southernmost part of mainland Palawan and the islands south of Mindanao, way off to the southeast, as well as the northernmost islets of Malaysia directly south, are still evidently serviceable for maritime people whose mental and cultural maps transcend notions of political boundaries.

Check out **Port Miller & Lighthouse Tower**, from where you may imagine the romance of slow centuries when this lookout point served as a beacon for seafarers and shoreline communities. From Brooke's Point, accessible by way of determined trekking, are **Mainit Falls**, off the *barangay* of Mainit, and **Sabsaban Waterfalls**, further northeast, on the foothills of Mt Gantung.

Still further south, more easily reached by sea, are the predominantly Muslim communities of **Bataraza** and **Rio Tuba**. The rugged road ends at Rio Tuba, which has been thriving of late, thanks largely to a large copper mining company that provides employment, but whose presence unfortunately renders much of the town perennially choking in the red dust stirred up at the mine pits.

A tribe distinct from the Batak and Tagbanua of the north used to enjoy preeminence in this area, calling themselves, simply, Pala'wan. But the inroads

The world's largest pearl, the "Pearl of Lao-tze," was found in the shell of a giant clam off Palawan in 1934. It weighed in at 6.6 kg (15 lbs) and measured 24.2 cm (9½ inches) long and 14 cm (5½ inches) in diameter. Valued at more than US$40 million, it's kept in a San Francisco bank.

BELOW: Palawan rural scene.

Map on page 296

made by mining firms and both Christian and Muslim settlers may be tragically encroaching on these gentle folk, who have long been noted for their age-old mystic practices in communion with revered spirits. In unusual communal sessions, they chant and play traditional string and wind instruments, until some go into a trance and start dancing in the middle of the enchanted circle.

Recently, video filmmakers from Manila, one of whom traces his roots to the tribe, helped them stage a waterborne protest against the activities of a pearl farm operator who had cordoned off a sandbar where they used to gather clams and other marine delicacies. The documentation was shown on Manila television, but up to now a contingent of Marines has stood guard to keep them away from what had been their treasured sandbar.

Nearby islands

Some 5 km (3 miles) off Rio Tuba sits the **Ursula Island National Bird Sanctuary ⑱**. This bird sanctuary was severely hit by a rat plague several years ago, and most of the birds moved to far-off **Tubbataha Reefs** in the middle of the Sulu Sea. Now, with the establishment of the sanctuary, some of the birds are starting to return. Some migratory birds from China and Siberia also roost here from November to February. The sanctuary can be reached most easily by a five-hour pumpboat ride from Brooke's Point.

Off the southern tip of Palawan Island are **Bugsuk Island** and, close to the endpoint of Palawan province, **Balabac Island ⑲**, famous for its rare seashells. Other interesting features are **Basay Waterfalls** close to Balabac town, the **Morenton Peak Game Refuge**, and **Melville Lighthouse**, overlooking the Balabac Strait that separates the Philippine archipelago from Malaysia. ❑

The brown booby bird nests in the atolls that dot remote Tubbataha Reefs.

BELOW: butterfly fish in the pristine waters of Tubbataha Reefs.

SULU'S SEA LIFE

Lying remote in the Sulu Sea, Tubbataha Reefs make up a 33,200-hectare (56,000-acre) expanse of diverse corals, serving as a rich habitat for pelagic fish, marine mammals, birds and invertebrates. According to the World Wildlife Fund (WWF), 300 coral species, 46 coral genera, 379 fish species, seven sea grass species and 71 species of algae make up the rich diversity of the reefs. In 1993, UNESCO declared Tubbataha a World Heritage Site.

According to WWF, Tubbataha's marine diversity is virtually unparalleled by any other area in the world today. Large marine life is often present, including manta rays, tuna and jackfish. Four species of dolphins and two species of marine turtles also inhabit the surrounding waters. The small sand cays in the area offer breeding grounds for several species of seabirds, including boobies.

Unfortunately, Tubbataha Reefs – despite their remote location – have fallen prey to the destructive practices of humans, including extensive dynamite and cyanide fishing. Since there are neither sizable islands nor fresh water to support human habitation of any sort, the Philippine navy can only send intermittent patrols to protect Tubbataha – and then only during the dry season, when the open seas are calm enough for the exercise.

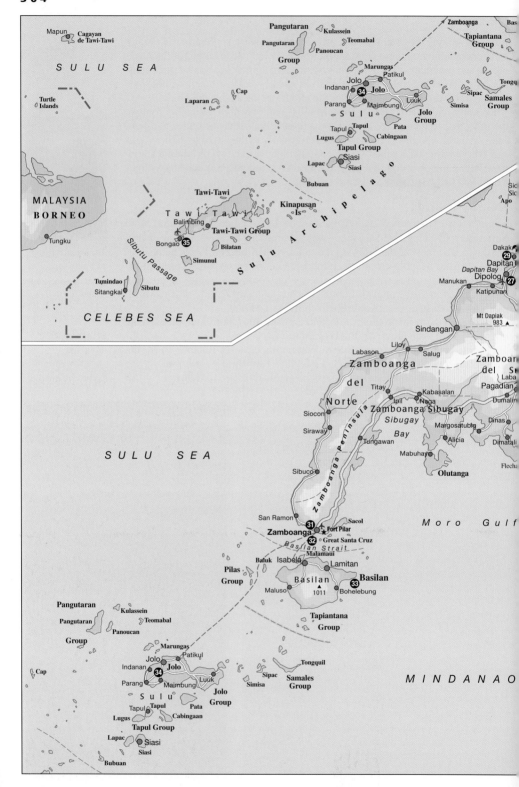

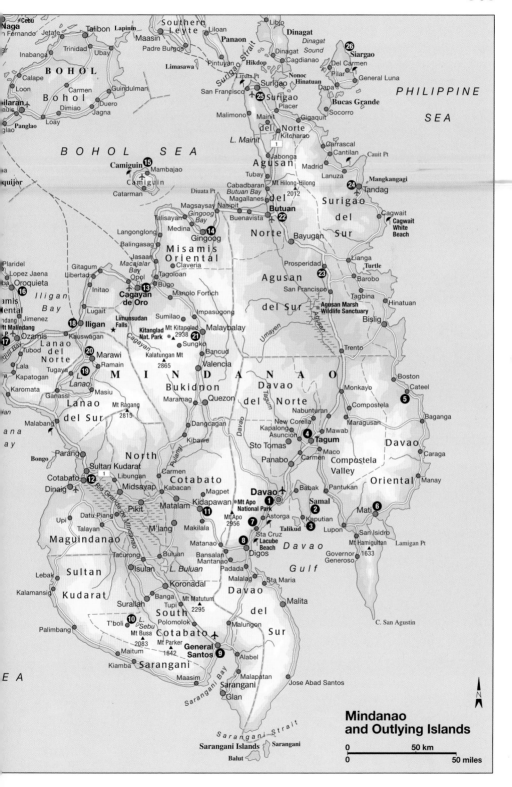

Mindanao
and Outlying Islands

MINDANAO

A land of extremes, marvelous Mindanao is a vacation paradise, providing the traveler is well prepared

Covering 94,630 sq. km (36,530 sq. miles), Mindanao, second in area in the Philippines only to Luzon, is a land of superlatives. The region has the world's largest eagle; the world's most expensive shells; the world's richest nickel deposits; the world's largest city by area; and some of the world's deepest waters. Within the Philippines, Mindanao cradles such extremes as the highest peak, Mt Apo; Ali-wagwag Falls, the highest waterfall; and Agusan Marsh Wildlife Sanctuary, the largest freshwater wetland and the largest mangrove swamp.

Mindanao promises to be a holiday hideaway of endless white sand beaches, islands, lagoons, mangrove swamps, mountains, valleys, ocean, rivers, lakes, waterfalls, rock formations, forests, springs and marshland. For the sports enthusiast, the island teems with excellent places for hiking and trekking, scuba diving, white-water action, surfing, climbing and caving. To the culture buff, the island offers a rich and diverse cultural mosaic of fiestas and festivals, traditional arts and crafts, and tribal rituals.

Some 22 million people of various ethnic and cultural origins inhabit the island. It holds about 80 percent of the country's iron reserves, all its nickel deposits and an abundant supply of other minerals. It is the country's leading producer and exporter of banana, pineapple, corn and coffee as well as a major producer of livestock and crabs.

Though most of Mindanao's rich natural resources remain untapped, those already exploited – by illegal logging and rampant gold mining, for instance – have experienced serious environmental degradation. Until recently, the province's economy suffered from both government neglect, and law and order problems. A lack of basic infrastructure still hurts tourism and business establishments, while some places continue to be hotspots for crime.

Tourists traveling to western Mindanao should check local conditions with embassies and local officials before departure, as some parts remain volatile due to Muslim insurgency. A major offensive by Philippine government troops during the Estrada administration, followed by the involvement of American forces during the current Macapagal-Arroyo presidency have heightened tensions in the area *(see page 335)*. The US, Japanese and other governments have issued stern travel advisories about parts of Mindanao. Sadly, some areas of this wild, spectacular section of the Philippines simply should not be visited, even by the most intrepid traveler. These trouble spots include Basilan Island and the Sulu Islands. There are hopes that a military crackdown on the terrorist kidnap gang Abu Sayyaf and increased investment in the area will put these fascinating places back on the traveler's map in future. ❏

PRECEDING PAGES: T'boli tykes from the village of Sebu in southern Mindanao.
LEFT: haughty beauty all decked out in the tribal finery of the Yakan tribe from Basilan Island, south of Zamboanga.

SOUTHERN AND CENTRAL MINDANAO

From primitive handicrafts to Internet cafés, endangered species to modern resorts, fundamentalist revolutionaries to international industries: this region is an absorbing mix of yesterday and today

Manila

Change has certainly found its way to **Davao City ❶**, the world's largest city by area and the starting point of most Mindanao adventures. Going downtown in a cab from the airport, you'd never think it had been a "laboratory" of urban death squads, led by communist guerrillas operating with impunity in the early 1980s. Back then, radio announcers read death tolls in a blasé tone, as if reading a weather report.

Nowadays, Davao – in the northernmost part of **Davao del Sur** – is a booming city with a rich cultural and ethnic mix – but without the characteristic violence of yore. Only adventure, romance, history and culture remain, highlighted by Davao's popular Kadayawan Festival, celebrated every August. More flights now arrive from destinations all over the country, Singapore, and the dive meccas Manado (Indonesia) and Palau.

Head of the Gulf

The city sits at the head of Davao Gulf in the island's southeastern quadrant. Heading south to the town center from **Davao International Airport**, midway to the city along J. P Laurel Avenue is **Insular Village ❹**, home of the Waterfront Insular Century Hotel, sprawling on immaculately kept grounds. On its grounds is the **T'boli Weaving Center ❺**, also known as Dabaw Etnika, where tribal women in native attire weave *dagmay*, a fabric made from *abaca* fibers. Bags, wallets and other accessories with intricate designs are made from *dagmay* cloth. Close by is the **Davao Museum ❻** (open Mon–Fri 9am–noon and 1–5pm; tel 082-300 8046; admission fee), featuring ethnological maps, dioramas, photographs and displays of tribal artifacts. Call before visiting, as plans are afoot to relocate the museum.

After Insular Village, the road veers west, passing Lanang Golf and Country Club, until it crosses **Cabaguio Avenue**. Here stands **Lon Wa Buddhist Temple ❼**, the biggest Buddhist temple in Mindanao, in a setting of candle trees and bamboo. The temple features Italian marble slabs, a magnificent Buddha, carved wood ornamentation depicting the life of Buddha, carp-filled lily ponds, and high-ceilinged halls.

Further on, after crossing **Bolcan Street**, is **Puentespina Orchids and Tropical Plants ❽**, a garden featuring several varieties of native orchids, including the rare and beautiful *waling-waling*. Nearby is **Agdao District**, which in the 1980s was renamed "Nicaragdao," in reference to Nicaragua in Latin America, where a brutal civil war raged at around the same time.

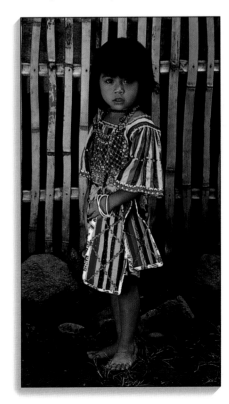

LEFT: the Philippine eagle – most commonly found in Mindanao.
BELOW: a T'boli girl.

Many women in rural communities have turned to weaving as a means of supplementing the family income.

The road continues on to **Leon Garcia Street**, where lies **Magsaysay Park ❻**, named to honor the third president of the Philippines. In Magsaysay Park is the only statue of a durian in the country and the regional Department of Tourism with its staff eager to show guests the jewels of Davao. Not far away is the Sta Ana Wharf, the most common take-off point for diving around the islands and reefs in the Davao Gulf.

Central Davao

In the town center stand many governmental and private establishments. Near the post office on **Ramon Magsaysay Avenue** is the University Mall, filled with Internet cafés. Across is the Marco Polo, Davao's tallest luxury hotel. On **C. M. Recto Street** is Ateneo de Davao University and Aldevinco Shopping Center, which has a compact nest of unique shops with good selections of Muslim brass and tribal artifacts from around Mindanao, plus Chinese wares. To the south, on **San Pedro Street**, is **St Peter's Cathedral ❼**, the oldest church in a city comprising a blend of Muslim and Christian architecture. Westwards passing the city hall, the road crosses **Legaspi Street**, where Apo View Hotel is located.

North of the town center, on J. P. Laurel Avenue, is **Gaisano Mall ❽**, and the sprawling 9-hectare (22-acre) **Victoria Plaza ❾**, which offers fine foreign and local cuisine, shopping and bowling. Further on, a diversion road leads to **Ladislawa Subdivision**, the city's most prestigious residential center, populated mostly by expats, *balikbayans* (returned Filipinos, who have lived overseas) and foreigners retiring in Davao. Nearby is **University of the Philippines, Mindanao ❿**, home to an art gallery (open Mon–Fri 9am–5pm; free) showcasing contemporary Mindanao works, plus national and international artists.

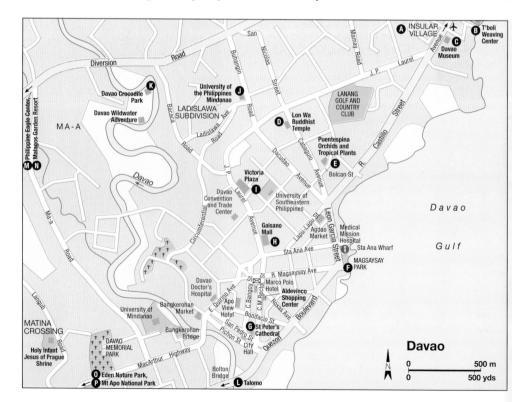

West of the city, on a hill behind the Davao Memorial Park, in suburban **Matina**, is the **Holy Infant Jesus of Prague Shrine**, which is a replica of an original statue in Prague. The shrine offers an excellent view of the city and gulf.

Further along the main road is the Apo Golf and Country Club, then a road on the right leads to **Caroland Resort**, a beautiful and unspoiled savanna with fruit trees and wild ducks. Horseback riding, and fishing in a lagoon can be enjoyed.

In **Ma-a**, about 15 minutes from the town centre, visit the **Davao Crocodile Park** Ⓚ at the rapidly expanding Riverfront Corporate City subdivision. The Park was opened in 1996, but has only been in this location since 2006. Several sizable enclosures show the reptile in different stages of growth, but it is Pangil, the 6-meter (19-ft) long crocodile that is the star. The park also hosts a retinue of tropical birds, monkeys and deer – some endemic to Philippine forests – and Buloy, a 3.3-meter (11-ft) long albino Indian python that you can put on your shoulders for photographs. Located in the back of the Davao Crocodile Park is **Davao Wildwater Adventure** (tel: 082-301 2020; www.davaowildwater.com). It has white-water rafting from easy to the medium grade to cater to rafters of various levels.

At Matina Crossing, the road veers northwest, passing by the black sand beaches of Talomo, Talisay, Salokot and Guino-o, to name a few, interesting for their proximity to fishing villages. **Talomo** Ⓛ was the scene of the Japanese landing in 1942, and the American landing in 1945. Farther south on Doña Candelaria Drive is the Growth with Equity in Mindanao (GEM) office.

Eagle center

Northwest of Talomo is the **Philippine Eagle Center** Ⓜ in **Malagos**, Calinan, a camp established as a sanctuary for the monkey-eating Philippine Eagle, or

With 18 colleges and four universities, Davao has the most universities outside Metro Manila.

BELOW:
wild mousedeer
at the Philippine
Eagle Center.

Locals wax lyrical about the durian – while Westerners invariably turn up their noses. Someone once likened the fruit to "onion custard forced down a drain pipe."

haribon. It is also home to other bird species, wild deer, tarsier and a python. En route to the sanctuary, stop briefly at Sul Orchids, a 2-hectare (5-acre) orchid farm where a variety of crossbreeds are grown to perfection.

The **Malagos Garden Resort N** in Calinan hosts the best works of National Artist awardee Napoleon Abueva. In this garden setting, Abueva's bronze *Miss Li* lifts her hands like a free spirit, golden brown hair blown by imaginary orchid-scented winds, while the *Bridge of Love* forms an erotic arch of two naked lovers locked in a passionate kiss. *Kaganapan*, a marbled pregnant woman, is one of the sculptor's masterpieces, while the stainless steel *Ring of Gods* once so caught Imelda Marcos's attention that she kept it for her collection. Its name changed accordingly to "Imelda's Doughnut."

About an hour and a half to the south, in **Toril District**, a road leads to **Eden Nature Park O**, a hilltop garden resort which offers a magnificent view of the whole city. At night, one can hear the sounds of crickets and other creatures in almost the same rhythm as the flickering of lights in downtown Davao. Westwards is **Mt Apo National Park P**, home of the country's highest peak *(see page 321)*.

Agro-industrial tours

BELOW: three chefs and their fish.

While in Davao, try the agro-industrial tours at farms scattered in suburban areas. Nenita Stock Farm, a ramie/sorghum plantation, also breeds cattle and pigs. Gap Farming Resort is a 10-hectare (25-acre) pomelo, rambutan and sweet tamarind plantation. Lapanday Development Corporation is a vast banana plantation, while Lola Abon's Durian Factory and Mindanao Industrial Confectionery processes *durian* into jams and candies. Finally, at Bago Oshiro Experimental Station, one can examine projects on crossbreeding native fruit trees and orchids.

While on the agro-industrial spree, drive north of the city, along the seemingly endless expanse of banana plantations in **Panabo**, **Carmen** and **Sto Tomas**, Davao del Norte. In between the giant plots are unpaved private roads, very dusty in the dry, hot season. Inside the plantations are packing plants, guesthouses and employee housing. The nearby **Davao Penal Colony** is popular for woodcraft items, plus citrus fruit, banana, ramie and rubber plantations, as well as a forest where one can hunt small game animals, a botanical garden, a zoo and Lake Imelda.

Samal Island

The nearby stretches of white sand, clear blue waters, mangroves, coral reefs, rolling hills and caves in **Samal Island** ❷ await the visitor who wants to relax, or pursue adventure. Located 700 meters off the southern coast of Davao City, Samal is a 28,000-hectare (69,000-acre) archipelago of nine islands, accessible via a 5-minute *banca* ride from Buhangin town in Davao. The world-class 11-hectare (27-acre) **Pearl Farm Resort**, in a secluded cove in the town of **Kaputian** ❸, is Samal's most popular attraction. It was once a pearl farm, where Sulu Sea oysters were cultivated for their pink, white and gold pearls. It features Samal Houses, patterned after the stilt houses of the Badjaos of Sulu. You can enjoy the sight of tiny fish frolicking between the sturdy poles of the houses during the day, and the sound of waves crashing against them at night.

Watersports are the main reasons to visit Samal: almost all resorts have facilities and there is much to explore. Kaputian, for instance, has two sunken World War II Japanese vessels. The land-based adventurer will also find Samal good for trekking, mountain biking and caving. **Mt Puting Bato**, the main hiking destination, offers a superb view of Davao City, Davao Gulf, and the surrounding islands at sunrise and sunset, from its peak. Rappel down the cascades to the cool, clear water pools of Hagimit and Tagbaobo waterfalls. Caliclic Cave in **Babak** features four rooms with skeletal remains, believed to be those of the Kalagan tribes, while Talikud Caves allegedly contain giant pythons and an underground passage crossing Davao Gulf to Malalag, Davao del Sur.

Davao del Norte

After Kapalong, in the western part of Davao del Norte, is the town of **Talaingod**, a 65,000-hectare (161,000-acre) settlement of a tribal group called Talaingod. The town has rich natural resources, including a 6,000-hectare (14,830-acre) virgin forest, Nabantalan Cave, Mt Masimalon (150 meters/500 ft), the 60-meter (200-ft) Kalapatan Falls, and the 7-hectare (17-acre) Kilomayon Lake. The town hall, built on a mountain top, 275 meters (900 ft) above sea level, overlooks the village of a people plagued by tribal frictions and poor infrastructure, though in recent years the area has become more attractive to visitors.

Tagum ❹, the provincial capital of Davao del Norte, features **Mainit Springs**, composed of a cold and hot spring which meet in a river. Go to the white-sanded **Tagnanan Beach**, 45 km (28 miles) southeast of Tagum, to swim, hunt shells, fish and scuba dive. Explore the cave of **Mawab**, 865 meters (2,835 ft)

TIP

Just outside Davao are numerous fruit and flower plantations. Although most welcome visitors, it's best to check with the local tourist office at the city hall (tel: 082-222 1956) for opening hours before proceeding.

BELOW:
Pearl Farm Resort.

A jar of water (banga) and a coconut shell dipper are placed near the entrance to each house for the guests to wash away the sand after a day of bare-footing it on the beach. In local custom, this gesture symbolizes the cleansing of the spirit.

long, with curtain-shaped stalactites and huge calcite pillars. A small subterranean waterfall tumbles into a lake. The 345-meter (1,130-ft) long **Tuburan Cave** in Monkayo, however, requires technical skill and climbing equipment because of the 15-meter (50-ft) pit inside. The rappel down is worth it: a potable spring and crystal-clear underground river await the diver and the fish and crab catcher. Contact the Tagum City Hall for details on guided tours.

Compostella Valley

Legislated as a new province in 1998, **Compostella Valley**, or Comval, is famous for two things: gold and wilderness. With one of the largest deposits of gold in the country, the town of Mankayo is synonymous with the wild-west style of anarchy it once represented, at the heyday of the gold rush. Things have calmed down a bit, and adventuresome travelers are starting to explore its other gifts from Mother Nature; endless beach resorts, expansive caves, and hundreds of waterfalls bisecting verdantly forested mountain ranges.

Of particular note to nature lovers is a trek up **Mt Candalaga**, which can be arranged with the town of Maragusan, or through the Regional DOT in Davao City. During the course of this 3-day hike, hikers will see over 30 waterfalls and 100 cold springs, thick primary rainforest and wildlife of startling variety. Other eco-tours are being offered to the Nabunturan caves and the Malumagpak waterfall, and educational tours to the gold fields are in the works.

Davao Oriental

East of Monkayo is **Davao Oriental**'s town of **Cateel ❺**, home of the Aliwagwag Falls picnic area, consisting of a forest, a river and the towering

BELOW: one of the hundreds of breath taking falls to be found in Southern Mindanao.

AGELESS PEOPLE OF TALAINGOD

The day was hot and humid, Layna Anlungay recalled, when she started feeling pains in her belly. Then a thought suddenly struck her: she was going to give birth.

Layna nervously went to the village *hilot* (traditional midwife), who attended to her. An eternity of pain later, Layne gave birth to a baby girl. The village welcomed her first-born with merrymaking – and everybody had a story to tell about the baby's birth.

Ando, Layna's husband, who was burning dried grass at their farm, almost put the entire village aflame when, in his haste to go home, he forgot to put out the fire. Onik, her elder sister, braved the waist-deep, leech-infested river, so she could cut the traveling time to her sister's in half, swearing she'd never do it again.

Several years later, such stories are still vivid in the minds of their tellers. All details are recalled – except for the birth date of the child.

"It's not important. The real Talaingods don't know their age," declared Ando, seemingly unmindful of the curiosity, and perhaps even envy, their agelessness has aroused in people too willing to lie, at every opportunity, about their real age.

Who says simplicity doesn't have its rewards?

Aliwagwag Falls. At 340 meters (1,110 ft) high and 20 meters (65 ft) wide, it is considered to be the highest falls in the country and one of the most beautiful in Mindanao, although it is actually a series of 84 falls appearing like a stairway, with each step ranging from 2–34 meters (6–110 ft).

Mati ⑥, the provincial capital, teems with fine beach resorts and is home to the 250-hectare (620-acre) Menzi Citrus Plantation where guests can stay in a refurbished Castillian-style house, with rooms and a pool. Scuba dive on **Pujada Island**, 155-hectare (385-acre) white-sand island, 1 hour by pumpboat from Mati. Pujada is host to the Pujada Bay Marine Conservation Area, and plans are afoot for an ecotourism program for dolphin and whale watching.

For the really adventurous traveler, San Isidro town an hour southwest of Mati, is home to **Mt Hamiguitan**, whose narrow, leech-infested and slippery trails run across steep, unforgiving slopes. The worst ascent is a 60-degree climb of about 350 meters (1,150 ft). But consider these as life's little inconveniences on the journey to a puzzling natural phenomenon: the uninhabited **Tinagong Dagat** (Hidden Sea), situated 300 meters (975 ft) above sea level, in the midst of a virgin forest.

Further south, towards **Governor Generoso**, is the Cape of San Agustin, where St Francis Xavier was supposed to have said mass. Off Governor Generoso, accessible by a 30-minute *banca* ride, is **Sigaboy Island**, an exact replica of a giant whale floating over the calm sea. On the islet are such attractions as caves, a green canopy of palm trees and a white sand beach.

Davao del Sur

Southwards from Davao City, passing through Tagabuli Industrial Estate and the San Miguel Brewery Complex, is the town of **Sta Cruz ⑦**, home to **Sibulan River Rapids**, site of an adrenaline-pumping craze known to adventure buffs as white-water tubing. Similar to the better-known sport of white-water rafting, tubing involves riding atop an inflated rubber tube – usually the interior of a truck's tire – and being carried downstream by the current.

Watch the locals make salt, or go swimming, boating, spear fishing, and shell hunting on the fine beaches of **Astorga**, 10 km (6 miles) north of town. Or rappel down the 90-meter (300-ft) Tudaya Falls, just below the foot of **Mt Apo** (see *page 321*).

At 4pm, pack your camping stuff and head west across Mt Apo to **Kapatagan** for a rewarding drive in the hills. The sunset reflects an awesome pinkish gold hue in the sky. A number of vacation houses, mostly owned by expats, dot the hilly *barangay*. When the night gets colder, spread those portable beds, lie down under thick clothing, and start gazing up at the stars.

Visit Mt Carmel in Kinuskusan, **Bansalan** and see how a foreign-initiated experimental farming project, called SALT, or Sloping Agricultural Land Technology, has improved the lives of its beneficiaries. Also in town is the provincial nursery called Pagkain ng Bayan, growing all varieties of Philippine fruits and fresh goat's milk.

Digos ⑧, the provincial capital of Davao del Sur, is built on seven hills surrounded by rice fields. **Sinawilan Hot Spring**, 4 km (2½ miles) away, is nestled within a forest. One can go bat-spotting along a grey-sand beach

Jeepneys are often packed like a can of sardines in an effort to accommodate all and sundry.

BELOW: Mt Apo, the highest peak in Philippines.

Map on pages 304–5

in **Talucanga**, 6 km (4 miles) from town, or stay at the Holiday Beach Resort in *barangay* Dawis, which has beautiful cottages and watersports facilities. Lumayon Spring in **Balabag** is ideal for bathing, surrounded by hills and forest.

Trudge an hour on rough but picturesque roads to experience the colorful culture of the B'laan tribe at the **Bolon Sabak Bilaan Village** in Matanao, or enjoy its waterfalls, cattle ranches, and hot and cold springs. Ethnic arts and culture are also preserved in the Binaton Bagobo Village. Piapi Beach in **Malalag** is dotted with picnic huts and offers panoramic views of Malalag and the nearby wharf. In **Padada**, south of Digos, Japanese forces once used the Tulugan Caves as a hide-out during World War II. In the next town of **Malita** is Aqua-Culture Investor Corporation, a modern prawn farm. Go shipwreck diving or deer watching in its forest, or simply wander around the caves, springs, and beach with crystal clear water. Off the southern tip of San Jose town are the **Sarangani Islands**. On Ballestic Island are the fortress remnants of the late Roy Lopez Villalobos, a Spanish explorer, while Balut Island features white sand beaches, and hot and cold springs.

South Cotabato

Perched on **Sarangani Bay**, on the southern tip of Mindanao, is **General Santos City ⑨**, or "Gensan," transformed from a backwater into a boomtown by US$270 million in foreign aid and private investment. There are an increasing number of flights between General Santos and Manila, Cebu and other cities.

Makar Wharf, Gensan's international seaport, is one of the most modern installations in the country. There's also an international airport, which, along with the wharf, has made Gensan the center of SOCSKSARGEN, a business district made up of South Cotabato, Sultan Kudarat, Sarangani and Gensan.

Map
on pages
304–5

Gensan's rich marine resources include such rarities as the big eye and yellow-fin tuna, and skipjacks. In its fertile valleys grow pineapples, bananas, coffee, rice, corn and asparagus, while cattle and pigs are farmed. Beaches, natural spring resorts, caves and a rich culture are its major tourist attractions.

In **Polomolok**, 20 km (12 miles) northwest of Gensan, cavers can explore the stalactites and stalagmites of **Salkak Cave**, which has a series of multiple chambers leading to an underground river. Trekkers can climb the 2,290-meter (7,515-ft) **Mt Matutum** through dense forests and the Blaan tribal highlands, and gape at monkeys, exotic birds, wild pigs and deer. **Dole Philippines**, a 10,000-hectare (24,700-acre) pineapple plantation and cannery, lies near the mountain. Its clubhouse is the usual base for climbing; overnight stays can be arranged through the company's personnel department. Across is Mt Parker, whose lower slopes have been denuded by illegal logging. **Lake Maughan**, its crater, is the source of five big rivers, and part of a 50,000-hectare (125,000-acre) proposed provincial park and wildlife sanctuary – the lake abounds with wild fauna and flora endemic to South Cotabato.

The ultimate caving challenge is at the nearby **T'boli Cave**, in T'boli town, where only the first 250 meters (810 ft) of calcite pillars and crystalline formations have so far been explored. Be technically prepared, though.

Around the spectacular 365-hectare (900-acre) **Lake Sebu ⑩**, surrounded by rolling hills and mountains, live some ethnic minorities. Among them are the cave-dwelling Tasaday and the T'boli, believed to be the most visually and culturally fascinating tribe in the country.

T'boli women often wear an *abaca* turban, a colorfully ornate, broad and round hat. *T'nalak* cloth, made from pounded bark, is T'boli's famous weave. The T'boli also have intricate beadwork, beautifully woven baskets and traditional brass ornaments. The Sta Cruz Mission runs 27 schools, including a college, in T'boli territory, and sells traditional artwork. The annual September T'boli Festival, a tribal thanksgiving, is celebrated with horse fights, traditional dances and games.

North of Polomolok, past Tampakan, site of the Western Mindanao Mining Corporation, and Koronadal, South Cotabato's capital, is **North Cotabato** province. **Kidapawan ⑪**, the provincial capital, is the most popular route to Mt Apo, accessible by a two-hour bus ride from Davao City. New Israel is famous for its numerous monkeys, while **Flortam Hot Spring**, known as the "Fountain of Youth," is where visitors go to cure their arthritis and rheumatism. The **Pisan Cave** in Kabacan nearby is full of bats and snakes.

Revolutionary territory

From Kabacan, the national highway heads west to Midsayap, Libungan and finally **Sultan Kudarat**, the provincial capital of **Maguindanao** province. North of this point is the former territory of the Muslim revolutionary group known as the MILF or Moro Islamic Liberation Front *(see page 335)*. Much of the area, including the MILF's headquarters, **Camp Abubakar**, was retaken by the Philippine military during a broad offensive under the Estrada administration. The area remains contentious and is unsafe for tourists.

A woman decked out in her T'boli traditional finery.

BELOW: T'boli woman playing a bamboo instrument.

Map on pages 304–5

TIP

Even the most dangerous parts of Mindanao are deceptively peaceful. But there are active kidnap gangs targeting foreigners operating in many remote areas. Travel with supreme caution in rural Mindanao. When in doubt about a place or a route, don't take chances.

BELOW: pineapple plantation.

Cotabato City ⑫, reachable by land from Kidapawan and by air from Manila, houses the **Autonomous Region in Muslim Mindanao (ARMM) Compound**, which showcases an unusual blend of modern and Muslim architecture. Inside are the Shariff Kabungsuan Cultural Center, Regional Museum (open Mon–Fri 8–11.30am and 1.30–5pm; free) and Regional Library. The museum houses artifacts of the Maguindanao, Maranao and Tiruray tribes of Muslim Mindanao.

P. C. Hill, a towering 28-meter (90-ft) stone fort, which now houses the City Internal Defense Command, is Cotabato City's most famous landmark. This hill served as a watchtower for the natives in their drive to detect and repel enemy assaults during World War II. From here, there is a panorama of the city and the Rio Grande de Mindanao or Pulangi, the second largest river in the Philippines and the longest in Mindanao, some 180 km (115 miles) long and 96 meters (310 ft) wide. Watersports and boat racing are the river's popular attractions.

Fertile soil

South of Maguindanao is the province of **Sultan Kudarat**, whose soil is one of the richest and most fertile in the Philippines. Buluan Lake and the *waling-waling* orchid are its main tourist attractions, though it is a little unsafe to visit. Alternatively, head further south to **Sarangani** and its beautiful beaches, most of which are undeveloped. The surrounding waters, particularly Sarangani Bay, are rich fishing grounds, hosting as many as 2,400 species.

Sarangani has had much of its marine resources lost to destructive fishing practices, but the tide seems to have turned with fish and corals rebounding at an incredible rate. Divers are now returning to enjoy the waters of Maasim and Takot Malbang islands, among other dive spots. ❑

Mount Apo

From the depths of Mindanao island soars Mount Apo, the "grandfather" of Philippine mountains, for whose tribal mystery and legend, not to mention rich natural wonders, outdoor enthusiasts conquer a towering 2,950-meter (9,700-ft) peak.

The name Apo, which means "Lord," came from the Bagobo tribespeople living on its slopes, who believe that the "Garden of Eden" had its beginning in the tropical rainforest around Lake Venado, one of Apo's mountain lakes. Now a national park, Mt Apo straddles a long mountain range traversing the boundaries of Davao del Sur, North Cotabato and Davao City. Its volcanic peak commands a 72,800-hectare (180,000-acre) base of lush tropical rainforest, boiling mineral springs, sulfur vents, lakes and waterfalls. Such rich environs host an equally diverse fauna, including monkeys, wild pigs and the endangered Philippine eagle. So far, the only recorded eruption was in 1640. All physical indications, however, point to continuing volcanic activity deep below.

Climbing Mt Apo usually takes three or four days, depending on one's physical fitness, and the route taken. Most hikers, however, prefer to take their time and enjoy the scenery on the way. There are now three official trails, each offering unusual features. These are the Magpet, Kidapawan, and Sibulan trails. Security, however, is still erratic, so, most of the time, only two of the trails are open. Check with the regional DOT in Davao City.

Vandalism has become rampant, as some visitors have etched or spray-painted their names on trees or rocks along the trails, creating a need for tighter security as tourism officers and mountaineering clubs try to prevent further deterioration. Apo's treasured geothermal energy deposits have sparked similar environmental controversy, as local resistance to the construction of Mt Apo Geothermal Plant II continues to grow.

Still, the conquest of Mt Apo remains a goal for mountaineers. The Davao Tourism Office (DTO) holds the prestigious "Conquer Mt Apo" climb every Easter weekend and an "Octotrek" climb every October. The Mt Apo Climbers Association, reachable through the DTO, also organizes regular trekking events. Paid guides are required, although they can also be porters and perform other services like cooking, pitching tents and providing drinking water for trekkers at the same time.

DTO trek schedules for Mt Apo offer two route options: Kidapawan and Magpet. The choice of trail determines what can and cannot be seen. The most popular, Kidapawan Trail, jumps off at the continuously boiling Lake Agco, passing through a part of the Marbel river, the Mainit Hotspring and the Malou Shi Waterfalls. The Magpet Trail, on the other hand, starts at Magcaalam, passing through Manobo Tico and Mab'bu Falls. Just before reaching the peak, both trails pass by famous Lake Venado, where trekkers from one trail can camp and wander around the crystal clear waters to meet trekkers from the other. Three hours' hike away is the Philippines' highest peak. Atop awaits an unobstructed panoramic view of the whole of Mindanao. ❑

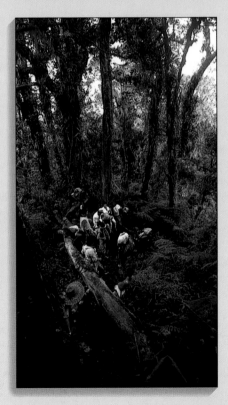

RIGHT: climbing Mt Apo takes three to four days, depending on fitness levels and route taken.

NORTHERN MINDANAO AND CARAGA

Map on pages 304–5

This region of mixed cultures offers a hoard of natural treasures, plus the contrasting pleasures of simple, remote communities and busy, industrialized cities

Manila

After visiting Davao, just when you start thinking that you've seen the best parts of Mindanao, stop. You're about to experience the equally historical, cultural, highly urbanized, even magical, destination of Northern Mindanao and Caraga – a land of raging rivers and wild waves, of languid lakes and spectacular sunsets, of dreams, daydreaming and delirium.

Misamis Oriental

The easternmost province, **Misamis Oriental**, is the export manufacturing and processing center of Northern Mindanao, with a land area of 3,570 sq. km (1,380 sq. miles) and a long, sheltered coastline with deep, natural harbors. Rivers traverse its rugged mountain ranges and lush valleys, flowing past 173,945 hectares (429,820 acres) of fertile cropland and 168,850 hectares (417,220 acres) of forest. **Cagayan de Oro City** (CDO) **⓭**, is the regional capital and main entry point, served by flights from Manila and Cebu, as well as boats from Manila, Cebu and other ports. From the city, one can go to any point of Mindanao by land, taking advantage of a well-paved road network.

CDO is highly urbanized, with a wide range of lodgings, restaurants, markets and shopping centers. Jeepneys and *motorela*, six-person motor scooters in front of a chassis, ply the streets. The Cagayan river bisects this large and sprawling city. On its eastern side, near the bridge, is Gaston Park, surrounding **San Agustin Cathedral**, with an unusual water tower. On Corrales Avenue is Xavier University, housing the **Museo de Oro** (open Mon–Fri 8am–noon and 1–5pm; free) featuring archeological finds, Hispanic antiquities and tribal artifacts, complemented by the Santillano Shell Museum, exhibiting over 1,000 priceless shells from around the world.

CDO's best beach is 9 km (6 miles) west of the city in **Opol**. West of the national highway, in **Laguindingan**, is Cueva Con Agua, where water drips from a cave roof. Past Gitagum and Libertad is **Initao** and Initao Cave, home to unusual bats with cauliflower-like noses. Some 14 km (9 miles) southeast of CDO is **Macahambus Cave**, where, in 1899, Filipino revolutionaries scored a major upset over American forces. Walk through the cave to emerge among gigantic rocks and savage trees overlooking Cagayan river.

From Opol, a road inland at **Cugman** leads to the small but attractive Catanico Falls, with a swimming hole and picnic area. Seven km (4 miles) onwards is *barangay* **Bugo**, site of the Del Monte Philippines cannery plant (tours by appointment, 8am–2pm).

LEFT: rocky coastline of Camiguin Island. **BELOW:** boat boy.

A handful of fish.

From Bugo, a steep twisting road strikes inland, offering superb views of **Maca-jalar Bay**, with a 175-km long (110-mile) shoreline, ideal for windsurfing and jet-skiing. In 1944, the Americans considered landing here, below the typhoon belt. However, Leyte was chosen instead. On a hill overlooking the bay is the 200-hectare (495-acre) eco-village of **Malasag**, which affords a beautiful view of the entire city. Within the eco-village are the "tribal houses," where various Mindanao tribes are authentically represented. To visit, contact the local Department of Tourism (DOT) for lodging and tour arrangements.

Northeast of the city is **Villanueva**, where Phivedic Industrial Estate, the country's largest, can be found. Eastward, at the town of **Claveria**, is the Noslek Canopy Walk, with hanging bridges and viewing decks as high as 18 meters (60 ft) up the trees, giving splendid views of lush virgin forests.

Coastal towns

Along the coastal highway north, after several other towns, is **Lagonglong**, where the limpid, cool Sapong Spring is located. Farther on, at **Talisayan**, is government-run Calamcan Beach. The next town, **Medina**, has a few white sand beaches, with the cool Alibwag Spring nearby. **Duca** has a good dive site, with underwater gardens, and 30 minutes away by pumpboat are **Pampangon**'s sunken pontoons, overgrown with marine life.

The next stopover, **Gingoog City** ⓮, has several great waterfalls, including Libon-Lawit, Tiklas and Odiongan. The Badiangon Beach and Spring also has two known caves, Agay-ayan Sunog and Tinuluyan. The Don Paquito Lopez Pass, or **Kisoong Ridge**, stands 1,280 meters (4,200 ft) above sea level. An underwater hill, sitting atop a plateau dotted with caverns and abundant marine

BELOW: White Island, a sand bar connected to Camiguin. In the background is Hibok-Hibok Volcano.

growth, sits unperturbed in **Gingoog Bay**. **Magsaysay**, the province's last town on the eastern side, houses Punta Diuata, a series of 13 connecting caves.

Map on pages 304–5

Camiguin

Off the coast of CDO is the island province of **Camiguin** ⑮, a peaceful pear-shaped island with steep volcanoes, lush jungles, wonderful waterfalls, white sand beaches, and hot and cold springs. Do not be dissuaded by its remoteness. To the adventurer and the urbanite alike, Camiguin is like a paradise.

Start out in the province's capital, where sleepy old houses still bear the intricate work of 19th-century artisans who specialized in cut-out ceilings and other wooden panels that resemble lacework. The area springs to life in the third week of October for the Lanzones Festival, which takes its name from a fruit with pale brown skin and sweet translucent flesh.

In the heart of the island is the **Ardent Hot Springs** mineral pool, which is fed by the active **Hibok-Hibok Volcano** (1,330 m/4,370 ft). Picnic here, beneath the sheltering trees, or cool off in springs of varying degrees of heat. Alternatively, swim at the isolated snowy sand bar called **White Island**, which can be accessed from Paras Beach Resort in **Barangay Yumbing**.

Head further south along the highway as it winds up a mountainside. Off the coast, what looks like a lighthouse from afar is actually a huge cross. It marks the spot where a village and its cemetery wound up below sea level after a Spanish-era eruption of Old Vulcan, one of Camiguin's seven volcanoes. Nearby are the ruins of **Gui-ob Church**. Loll about on the grassy area where the church pews would have been: thick stone walls are now the church's only remnants from the same eruption.

Towards the eastern side of Camiguin is pretty **Mantigue Island**, which hosts a small fishing community. For a small fee, partake of the daily catch while learning about the locals' simple, island life. It also possible to head out to **Kabila Beach**, where rare *taklobo* (giant clams) are being propagated.

To cool off, rappel down the stunning 76-meter (250-ft) **Katibawasan Falls** to a pool surrounded by orchids and ferns, or trek along a rocky riverbank to reach the magnificent **Tuasan Falls**.

Misamis Occidental

Surrounded on three sides by water, and on the south-western side by Zamboanga, the province of **Misamis Occidental** features fishing grounds teeming with marine life. Except along the coastal area, hilly and rolling lands characterize its terrain, which becomes particularly rugged towards the western border. Industry revolves around coconut processing and fishing.

Visitors do not go to Misamis Occidental for comfort or luxury. Tourism in the province is associated more with abundant seafood, a little history, mountaineering and beach life. Inexpensive hotels and pensions or family-run rooms supply accommodation, with travel provided by either tricycle or jeepney.

Oroquieta City ⑯, the provincial capital, sits in the northeastern part, accessible via a seven-hour Cagayan de Oro–Pagadian–Dipolog bus ride. At its

TIP

Rent a motorcycle or scooter for an intimate look at Camiguin. The 64-km (40-mile) circumvential road and all of the roads that lead off it offer unlimited potential for exploring an area with the highest number of volcanoes per square kilometer of any island on the planet.

BELOW: Mt Malindang forest.

heart is the **Provincial Capitol**, one of the most beautiful in the country, with flower gardens, fountains and a children's park. **Camp Ceniza**, 2 km (1 mile) away, has scenic views, trees and a floating pavilion. El Truinfo Beach is lined with shades and cottages for picnickers, while **Oroquieta Agro-Industrial School Mini-Park** is noted for its natural ecology and wildlife.

North of the city, at the town of **Lopez Jaena**, are two *barangay*, Biasong and Peneil, whose fine beaches are potential tourist spots. Farther on is **Plaridel**, where Nazareno Dam, an old irrigation canal considered to be one of the best of its kind in the country, was built years ago by townsfolk, without the aid of sophisticated machinery. From Plaridel, the road veers west to the town of Calamba and the Bulawis Spring, with several mini-falls and springs developed into a swimming pool.

Wildlife watershed

South of Oroquieta is **Mt Malindang**, a 53,000-hectare (130,960-acre) national park and wildlife sanctuary, halfway to Ozamis. The Malindang Range is a watershed of over 20 rivers, and home to a variety of wildlife such as the Philippine eagle, deer, giant bat, python and a unique rodent species called the Malindang rat. Spanning 4 hectares (10 acres), **Lake Duminagat** is the most prominent of its waterways. The protected park has received P800 million from an ecological work fund, most of which comes from foreign donors. However, there has been controversy over the construction of a new road, which the Subanen tribe claims crosses its place of worship.

BELOW: multi-hued parrot at Malindang national park.

The town of **Panaon** has several beaches and the 2-meter (6-ft) high Imeldanita Fall, framed amidst green trees and boulders. Farther south is **Ozamis**

City **⑰**, which holds the province's cultural treasures. Near the wharf is Fort Santiago, also called Kota, an old Spanish fortress built in 1707 to protect this region from pirates. At the Immaculate Concepcion Cathedral is a pipe organ from Germany, the biggest in Mindanao. The City Hall Complex and Doña Prospera Park is billed as the largest, most impressive city hall in the region.

Regina Swimming Pool, a natural pool fed by cold springs, is 3 km (2 miles) from Ozamis. **Tangub City** or the "City of Fish Traps" along **Panguil Bay** is famous for the tiger shrimp in its bay, which is exported to countries like Japan.

Lanao del Norte

Southeast of Misamis Occidental is **Lanao del Norte** province, best reached from Cagayan de Oro City via a two-hour bus trip to **Iligan City ⑱**, known as the city of steel and waterfalls. It is highly industrialized, and environmental activists describe it as a city waiting to explode, because of poor city planning. Shopping malls, restaurants and lodging houses abound.

Fast boats and ferries ply the waters to Iligan from Cebu and Manila. Its deep harbor is home to giant companies, including National Power Corporation (NPC). The 98-meter (320-ft) **Maria Cristina Falls**, fed by the Agus river, has supplied most of Mindanao's electricity since being harnessed for hydroelectric power in 1952. The Mabuhay Vinyl Corporation Park and Lagoon, on top of a hill within the plant, has a small park rimming the lagoon. Iligan City Hall stands atop **Buhang-inan Hill**, 45 meters (150 ft) above sea level, providing a magnificent sunset view.

A *Sinulog* Festival is held every September 29, when Iligan celebrates the feast of its patron saint, San Miguel the Archangel. **Iligan Museum** (open Mon–Fri 8–11am and 1–5pm; free) is located in an old residential house along

The National Power Corporation (NAPCOR) complex at Iligan has an underground plant which can be viewed by prior arrangement. Visitors can arrange to have the water to the majestic Maria Cristina Falls switched on.

BELOW: Maria Cristina Falls.

Badelles Street. The Togolan tribe, descendants of the earliest inhabitants of Iligan, lives in the mountain hamlets.

Spectacular falls

Just 54 km (34 miles) from the city is the two-tiered **Limunsudan Falls** in *barangay* Rogongon, said to be the country's highest waterfall at 265 meters (870 ft), while, in the deep forest, is Sadyaan Cave, a three-chambered cavern with stalactites and stalagmites looking ominous to strangers and sacred to the natives. The 27-meter (90-ft) high Mimbalut Falls in *barangay* Buru-un is the most accessible of Iligan's 20-plus waterfalls, just 11 km (7 miles) from downtown. Nearby is Tinago Falls, hidden in a deep ravine and cascading into a calm, deep pool, a thrill to swim in.

Dodiongan Falls in *barangay* Bonbonon is a 20-meter (65-ft) high cascade gushing down a boulder, surrounded by lush vegetation. Cathedral Falls, with a natural swimming pool at the base, can be found in *barangay* Kapatagan at **Tubod**, the provincial capital. Timoga Cold Spring and Kalubihon Spring are among Iligan's finest, and there are some popular beaches.

Lanao del Sur

Southeast of Lanao del Norte is **Lanao del Sur** province, home of the Maranao, people of the lake. The first town, **Balo-i**, signals that the traveler has crossed over from the land of the cross to that of the crescent. On the left of the road is the first of innumerable mosques, brilliantly painted in reds, yellows and greens. Truck bumpers are blazoned with *Trust in Allah* rather than *Trust in Jesus*, and girls are dressed in the tubular step-in *malong* rather than skirts.

As the road continues on through several municipalities, first-time travelers to these parts might feel a euphoric mix of excitement and, possible dread at heading into an area renowned for religious unrest. Your attention may be diverted by colorful streamers and billboards, hung along the highway, congratulating a family member for passing a board exam or winning an honor.

The countryside is lush and green with corn; horses are nearly as common as jeepneys. Just 40 km (25 miles) after leaving Iligan, **Lake Lanao** , the second largest and deepest lake in the Philippines, and Mindanao's largest freshwater lake, comes into view. The road descends a little later to the Islamic City of **Marawi** , so called for its 65 mosques, the largest number in any city in the entire country. This is an easy 30-minute ride from Iligan, along a well-paved and checkpoint-studded national highway. West of Quezon Boulevard, across the bridge over the Agus river, is the 40-meter (130-ft) **Signal Hill**, from where battle signals were sent to Camp Vicar and Camp Overton during World War II. Turning right on the next diversion road leads to Camp Keithley, the former residence of American soldiers in Mindanao. **Dayawan** is popular for hand weaving and ornate Maranao designs, and **Tugaya** is the local brassware capital.

Two km (1¼ miles) beyond is the main campus of **Mindanao State University**, the country's second-

The Maranao people – or People of the Lake – of Lanao del Sur are known for their brassware.

BELOW: King Faisal Mosque, Marawi.

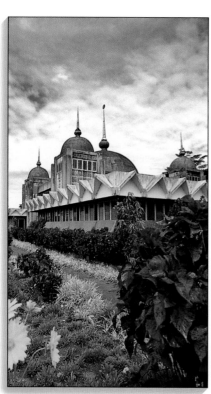

largest state university. It serves not only as an educational institution but also as a center of social and cultural integration. Students of different ethnic origins are housed in the same dormitories to further cultural understanding.

The **King Faisal Mosque** and **Institute of Islamic and Arabic Studies** stand just within the university gates. The road then climbs through the sprawling 1,000-hectare (2,500-acre) campus, considered the most beautiful in the country.

On the left, just before the ascent, is the Marawi Resort Hotel, the only hotel in Lanao del Sur, sitting in a near-paradise location, and composed of bamboo cottages. The **Aga Khan Museum** (open Mon–Fri 8–11.30am and 1–5pm; free), at the crown of the campus, features Maranao and Moro artifacts.

Bukidnon

East of Lanao del Sur is **Bukidnon**, the only land-locked province in Mindanao. Literally translated as "people of the mountains," Bukidnon is a land of pineapple plantations and coffee fields, extensive forests, lofty mountains and deep canyons. Buses ply the Cagayan de Oro–Bukidnon–Davao route, and public utility jeeps service commuters to and from the different municipalities of the province. There are no commercial flights to Bukidnon, although it has several airstrips used by private firms. **Malaybalay ㉑**, the capital town, is only a two-hour ride from CDO.

The **Pines View Park**, also called "Little Baguio" for its abundant pine trees, stands at the back of the Provincial Capitol. This popular camping destination also hosts festivals, foremost being the Kaamulan, where ethnic tribes decked in colorful costumes gather to sing and dance, compete in indigenous games and perform rituals. Farther on, towards **Bancud**, is Matin-Ao Spring and Nasuli Spring, which is covered with trees and plants and ideal for diving enthusiasts.

Map on pages 304–5

The some 50,000-strong Bukidnon people of east Lanao are a tribe of fiercely independent highland dwellers.

BELOW:
Muslim students outside the Aga Khan Museum.

Tribal center

About 1½ hours' drive along an unpaved road from Malaybalay is the village of **Sungko**, inhabited by the Talaandig tribe. The **Talaandig Center for Living Traditions** here is a two-story nipa and bamboo house where children learn long lost traditions. Not far away, national artist Leandro Locsin designed the **Monastery of the Transfiguration**.

Kitanglad National Park (31,300 hectares/77,350 acres) in North Central Bukidnon, consists of more than a dozen peaks and hosts many rare bird species. Vanilla, which is actually a type of orchid, grows here in the wild environs, and holds the promise of being locally cultivated. Towering Mt Kitanglad (2,938 meter/5,639 ft), held sacred by many tribes since pre-hispanic times, constantly challenges climbers, who have to scale through forest for five hours to reach the summit.

Northwards, in San Roque in Sumilao, is the 2,745-meter (9,000-ft) **Palaopao Hill**. Its sides contain caves, rock shelters and wooden artifacts with designs dating back to the metal age. At the southeastern part of the hill is the Paiyak Cave.

At 14,000 hectares (34,600 acres), Del Monte Philippines, straddling the towns of Manolo Fortich, Libona, Sumilao and Impasugong, and employing around 5,000 people, is thought to be the biggest pineapple plantation in Asia.

The next town of Manolo Fortich features the zigzag road of **Mangima Canyon**, home of the Mangima Challenge, an annual contest for monster-truck and four-wheel-drive enthusiasts. The elliptical **Stone Marker of Yoshitois Grave** bears two sets of inscription for high-ranking Japanese officials killed during World War II. South of Malaybalay is **Valencia**, home to the 25-hectare (60-acre) Apo Lake, ideal for boating and fishing.

BELOW:
Lake Lanao doubles
as a laundromat.

Caraga

Caraga, the country's newest geopolitical region, is a one-stop shop for history, anthropology, business, daydreaming and adventure. **Butuan City ㉒**, provincial capital of **Agusan del Norte** and the region's major jump-off point, is served by daily flights from Manila. The Golden Tara of Agusan, a faded, gold-painted statue of an ancient goddess, stands outside the airport, waiting to greet each visitor.

Butuan, a city of antiques and archeological finds, has three museums: **Balanghai Shrine Museum** showcases skulls and burial coffins from the pre-historic age; **Butuan Regional Museum** has a huge repository of artifacts that support the city's thriving pre-hispanic existence; and the **Diocesan Ecclesiastical Museum** houses a prized collection of religious artifacts (all open Mon–Fri 8am–noon and 1–5pm; free).

Endangered species

The long and winding Agusan river passes through Butuan City – the "Timber City of the South" – and the two provinces of Agusan. Located smack in the center of the river basin is the 68,000-hectare (168,000-acre) **Agusan Marsh Wildlife Sanctuary**, both the largest freshwater and the largest mangrove, swamp in the Philippines, and home to rare and endangered flora and fauna as well as tribal communities. Between the river and the coast runs the rugged, twisting valley of the **Sierra Madre of Mindanao**.

West of Butuan are the three coastal towns, Buenavista, Nasipit and Carmen, which feature fine beaches. A domestic port in Nasipit opens the province to Manila, Cebu, Bohol and other major Philippine cities.

A historic marker commemorating the first mass in Mindanao stands in

Map on pages 304–5

Highly stylized floral motifs called okir are used by the Maranao people to decorate their homes, boats and domestic utensils.

BELOW: Mindanao's Sierra Madre.

Magallanes, a town north of Butuan. Also in Magallanes is a century-old *bitaug* tree lit by thousands of fireflies at night; Phimco, the only match factory in Mindanao; and Sta Ines Plywood Corporation, a wood processing complex.

The undiscovered jungle passages of 2,012-meter (6,601-ft) **Mt Hilong-hilong**, in the town of Remedios T. Romualdez, the highest in Agusan del Norte, challenge climbers wanting to douse in its waterfalls and reputedly enchanted lake. Farther on, the road leads to Cabadbaran, starting point for **Mas-ai Peak**, considered one of Mindanao's best, and least known, destinations for trekking.

Highly recommended, the **Tubay Mountain Beach Resort** is located between Tubay forest and Butuan Bay. From the national highway, one can bike a 5-km (3-mile) road through panoramic forest to the pick-up point, from where a covered motorized *banca* takes visitors to the resort.

Overland south of Butuan is **Agusan del Sur**, the country's most thinly populated province. **Prosperidad ㉓**, the capital, houses Binataba Falls, believed to be linked to an underground stream. The town of **San Francisco** has an abundance of giant Toog trees. But the main attractions of the province are its people and their culture.

The Manobo, who have settlements in **Bayugan**, are known for their planting and harvesting rituals, and traditional wedding ceremonies. The Higaonon live in high, swaying treehouses which consist of small family rooms linked by gangplanks to a central communal area. Other groups include the Bunawan, Matigsalug and the fierce Magahat and Talaandig.

BELOW: a Mandaya weaver from Surigao del Sur.

Surigao del Sur

Northeast of Agusan del Sur is Surigao del Sur, home of the Surigaonon and the tribes of Manobo, Ubo, B'laan and Mandaya. **Tandag ㉔**, the provincial capital,

is a backwoods surfing paradise with a lovely coast and wild swells, an undisclosed twin sister of Siargao Island. It is ideal for excursion, picnicking, and fishing, and features three guano-filled caves and white-sand beaches. Among the most popular breaks are Big Star, Moshi-Moshi and Glenda. Three km (2 miles) off Tandag is **Mangkangagi Island**, whose three guano-filled caves and white sand beaches make it ideal for excursions, picnicking and fishing.

Northwards is the town of **Lanuza**, one of the most charming towns on Mindanao's east coast, with a laid-back ambience, the best longboard surf waves, and one of the best boardwalks in the country. Further up the highway is **Cantilan**, where Maletangtang Cave, known for its beautiful boat shape and cool springs, and the white sand Malinawa Beach are located. **Carrascal** houses the huge Iron Mountain, so called for its immense iron reserves.

South of Tandag is the famous white sand beach in **Cagwait**. **Turtle Island** in Barobo has an 8-hectare (20-acre) white sand beach whose multi-colored coral reef adds to its attraction.

Inside **Picop Plantation**, one of the biggest pulp and paper companies in the Far East, are the beautiful Nyholm and Borboanon Falls. From Mangagoy wharf in **Bislig**, pumpboats go to black sand Barcelona Beach and Hagonoy Island, a scuba diving site.

Surigao del Norte

Finally, on the northernmost part of Mindanao, is **Surigao del Norte**, home to mineral deposits and native baskets, hats and embroidery. This is a great place to take a break, and to go kayaking, caving, snorkeling, diving, or swimming.

Surigao City , the provincial capital, is accessible via fast Supercat ferry from Cebu. Known as the gateway to northern Mindanao, this is where Manila-Davao buses depart and arrive via ferry to Maasin.

Casa Real in the city is the residence of a former Spanish governor. Around the city are Sabang Beach, with a long black sand shore, Ipil Beach with white pebbles, and Mabua Beach with rock formations that serve as natural diving boards.

Day-asan Floating Village, also known as the "Venice of Surigao City," features houses built over shallow water and canals for boats.

Weird rocks

In the gulf between Surigao City and Siargao Island are a collection of interesting islands and rocks. **Raza Island** has low tide on one side and high tide on the other. **Sibaldo Island** is home to the 10-meter (33-ft) high Zaragaza Rock Formation and the solitary rock islet known as Tamulayag, where trees grow without soil, giving it the look of a huge floating flower vase.

Hikdop Island has a white beach rich in rare seashells, and on its northeastern portion is Punta Kalabera, a naturally sculptured stone formation that looks like a human skull from a distance. **Bayagnan Island** has fascinating offshore whirlpools that appear and disappear with tides, an effect of converging currents in the area. Also worth visiting is the **Cantiasay Foot Bridge**. It joins the two islands of San Jose and

Surigao del Norte in northern Mindanao is famous for its delicate hand embroidery.

BELOW: fiesta time in Surigao City.

Map on pages 304–5

In the old days, bodies of cholera and smallpox victims from the adjoining barangay are said to have been dumped on Sibaldo Island and left to rot.

Cantiasay, and is reputedly the longest wooden foot bridge in the country.

Other interesting places around the city are Manjagao Island, ideal for boating; Nabago Pearl Farm, Sagisi and the Sumilom Islands, excellent for their bizarre rock formations. **Nonoc's** nickel quarries can be reached after a 30-minute boat ride from the city. **Placer** is famous for its ancient gold mines and "gold rush" panning, but, unfortunately, has fallen prey to mining waste spillage.

Northwards, on **Dinagat Island**, is a good snorkeling site. **Lake Bababu** is a mountain lake with steep vertical inclines and lush vegetation, while the rock formations on the neighboring islets of San Roque and Hagakgak resemble a duck, turtle, ship, eagle and candle. **Desolation Point**, on the northern tip, was where American troops first landed on October 17, 1944 to liberate the Philippines from the Japanese. Farther on is the 10-hectare (25-acre), 20-meter (65-ft) deep **Tambongan Lagoon** in the town of Tubajon.

Siargao Island

One hour's fast ferry from Surigao City is **Siargao Island ㉖**, famous for **Cloud 9**, a world-class reef break off **General Luna** town, or "GL." Westwards, **Del Carmen** has huge tracts of mangroves, rugged, forested foothills, and startling rock formations. **Bucas Grande Island**, part of Socorro town, is where the famous **Sohoton Lagoon** is situated. Explorers can experience the eerie yet magnificent passage through the cave at low tide, into a lagoon of countless islets, or scuba-dive in the waters around Socorro. The "natural swimming pool" at **Magpupungko**, off the town of **Pilar**, is an amazing sight in low water, when it is cut off from the ocean. Dako and **Guyam Islands** make for a fun day boat trip, the latter being a tiny speck of trees and sand that has graced many a book cover and postcard. ❏

Below:
professional Aussie surfer Andy King riding a wave at Cloud 9.

A Regional Conflict

The conflict in Mindanao has never been a simple one. The minority Muslim population live in some of the most resource rich areas in all of the Philippines, but they traditionally are among the last to receive the economic benefits. The country's highest poverty rates can be found in Muslim Mindanao.

The area's problems are profound and the situation is not helped by the fact that the people are ruled by a Christian government in Manila. Groups such as the Moro Islamic Liberation Front (MILF) have responded to this situation by taking up arms against the government. Though the MILF has been involved in ongoing negotiations with the government and claims no link to terrorists or kidnap gangs in Mindanao, the presence of these armed factions and their splinter groups and imitators make the area a dangerous and difficult travel destination.

The most menacing of these smaller groups is the Abu Sayyaf, a band of terrorists operating around Basilan and the Sulu islands with suspected links to Indonesia's Jemaah Islamiya and the Al Qaeda terrorist network – who were responsible for the attacks on New York's World Trade Center in September 2001. Though they claim to fight for the same ideals, their tactics – kidnapping, ransoming, raping and beheading foreign and Filipino civilians alike – make questionable any claim by them to legitimacy.

After a major offensive against the MILF by Joseph Estrada's administration, the group called a ceasefire in March 2001 and asked to hold talks with the government. The renegade Abu Sayyaf group, however, showed no interest in such fence mending and continued a series of raids on tourist resorts in Mindanao, Palawan and in Sabah (Malaysia) to grab and ransom off foreign hostages.

Foreign governments have paid millions of dollars in ransom to the Abu Sayyaf, which the group quickly invested in faster speed boats, higher powered weapons and satellite phones to assist in their kidnapping operations. In anger, the Philippine government called off its talks with the group and sent thousands of troops to Basilan to rescue the two Americans and one Filipino held hostage since May 2001.

After months without success, the US government – invited by President Gloria Arroyo-Macapagal – sent its troops to the area to assist. On June 7, 2002, in a firefight between the Philippine military and the kidnappers, American hostage Martin Burnham and Filipino nurse Deborah Yap were killed. Burnham's wife Gracia was wounded but escaped alive. Since then tensions in the area have remained high, and in 2002, parts of Mindanao became much more dangerous than in years past.

The US, Australian and Japanese governments, amongst many, have recommended against travel in Western and Central Mindanao and the entire Sulu archipelago from Zamboanga to Tawi-Tawi.

The conflict in Mindanao has reportedly cost more than 130,000 lives. Many of the children of those killed by government soldiers grow up harboring the same deep feelings of injustice that drove their fathers to arms. It is difficult to see how this situation will resolve itself in the forseeable future. ❏

RIGHT: assault rifle with the MILF logo.

ZAMBOANGA AND THE SULU ISLANDS

*Mindanao's southwestern tip is a rich cultural mosaic:
a variety of indigenous peoples share its wealth of fertile
agricultural land and the bounty of its seas*

Mindanao's westernmost provinces of Zamboanga del Norte and Sur, Basilan, Sulu and Tawi-Tawi share a long history of unyielding resistance to foreign control. Previously called the Zamboanga Peninsula, it was part of the Sultanate of Sulu, the oldest seat of government, at a time when "Manila was a swamp and Cebu was a beach," at least according to historian Oswalda Cadel.

Spain finally captured Sulu in the 1870s, transferring the seat of power to Zamboanga. American forces established the Department of Mindanao and Sulu in 1914, making Zamboanga a province. In 1952, Zamboanga was split into two provinces, Norte and Sur, and lumped into Western Mindanao. In 2001, Zamboanga Sibugay Province was carved out of Zamboanga Sur.

In 1989, Tawi-Tawi and Sulu were placed under the political jurisdiction of the Autonomous Region of Muslim Mindanao (ARMM). But the provinces' rich marine resources still link them to close neighbors through the Zamboanga-Basilan-ARMM (ZBA) economic area.

There are flights from Manila and Cebu to the cities of Dipolog, Pagadian and Zamboanga, and various boat services to Zamboanga City and Dipolog City. Overland, ZBA is accessible via the national highway through Ozamis, connecting Dipolog to any point in Mindanao. Jeepneys and pedicabs ply the roads of mainland Zamboanga, while *kumpit* (long, deep, enclosed motorboats) serve the outlying islands.

LEFT: a Badjao stilted village in Tawi Tawi.
BELOW: Yakan dolls from Basilan Island.

Zamboanga del Norte

The 6,600-sq. km (2,550-sq. mile) province of **Zamboanga del Norte** (pop. 750,000) is bounded on the north and west by the Sulu Sea, on the east by Misamis Occidental, and on the south by Zamboanga del Sur and Zamboanga Sibugay. Hilly and mountainous, its average elevation is 244 meters (800 ft). Mt Dabiak (2,600 meters/8,530 ft), south of Katipunan town, is the province's highest peak. The main inhabitants of its northern part are Christian migrants from the Visayas, while in the south are the Muslim groups of Tausug, Samal, Yakan and Kalibugan. Cebuano is the main dialect.

Provincial capital **Dipolog City** ㉗ is considered the gateway to Western Mindanao. Christmas and New Year are the best times to visit, when Dipolog comes alive with fireworks. There is also the *Sinulog* festival in January, and special Holy Week celebrations in April. The city offers a range of hotels and discos, and at its heart stands Holy Rosary Cathedral, a century-old church designed by the Philippine national hero Jose Rizal. Though renovated, the basic

design has been preserved. About 15 blocks across is Punta Corro, a cross to symbolize the religious character of the inhabitants.

Visitors can climb 1,001 Concrete Steps to **Linabo Peak**, the city's highest point at 460 meters (1,500 ft), offering a panoramic view of the twin cities of Dipolog and Dapitan. In *barangay* **Dicayas** is the **Pamansalan Forest Park**, a 10-hectare (24-acre) restoration site, now a bird sanctuary, and the **Japanese Memorial Park**. Farther on are the Sicayab Beach and Miputak Beach Resort.

Dapitan City

Only 14 km (9 miles) northeast of Dipolog is historical **Dapitan City** **28**, site of the **Rizal Shrine** (open daily 8am–5pm; entrance fee) inside a 16-hectare (40-acre) estate where Rizal spent his exile from 1892 to 1896. Featured are his residence, clinic, school and a water system, all built using indigenous materials. The adjacent Rizaliana, a modern, concrete building constructed in 1972, houses Rizal-related books, periodicals and other historical exhibits.

Beyond the Rizal Shrine is **Dakak Beach Resort** **29**, a 750-meter private beach blanketed with powdery white sand. Natural spring water and tumbling waterfalls feed the resort's two pools, whilst a private, open-air jacuzzi affords the ultimate in blissful refinement. The resort's Aqua Sports Center features most watersports.

Dapitan Bay, whose sunsets are said to be more beautiful than those of Manila Bay, stretches along the northern coast of the city and is a popular swimming and diving site. Overlooking the bay is **Ilihan Hill**, home to **Fort de Dapitan**, a Spanish military fortress built in 1762. The island *barangay* of **Aliguay** and **Silinog**, located 10 km and 14 km (6 and 9 miles) respectively from Tagolo Point, have white sand beaches and rich aquatic resources.

BELOW: Dakak Beach Resort is fronted by a spectacular white sand beach.

Zamboanga del Sur

South of Dipolog is **Zamboanga del Sur**. It has an irregular coastline scattered with bays, and a flat, coastal plain that gives way to interior mountains. Southwards and a small peninsula extending into the Moro Gulf. The dry season lasts from January to March; the rest of the year is rainy.

Provincial capital **Pagadian City ㉚** is the only Christian-dominated place in the province. Tausug, Yakan, Badjao, Samal and Subanon populate the rest of the province. It was the Subanon who set up a fishing and trading village near the coast and called it Pagadian, a corruption of the Maguindanao word *padian*, meaning marketplace. Often referred to as the Philippines' "little Hong Kong," Pagadian features idyllic islets and tribal boathouse villages.

A 10-minute pumpboat ride across the city wharf is Dao-Dao Island, or **Pajares Island**, ideal for swimming and sunbathing. Southeast of the seaport is **White Beach**, with clear, deep water. **Pulacan Falls** is a beautiful picnic and camping site in the town of **Labangan**, 12 km (8 miles) from Pagadian City.

Along the Pagadian–Zamboanga City national highway towers Mt Palpalan (210 meters/690 ft). The mountain gives a good view of the urban center and the clear waters of **Pagadian Bay**. The 18-meter (60-ft) Lison Valley Falls, in *barangay* Lison Valley, 40 km (25 miles) from Pagadian, has a catchment pool area of 1,500 sq. meters (1,800 sq. yards).

Further along the highway is **Zamboanga City ㉛**, known as the city of flowers. The capital of this southern island throughout the Spanish regime, Zamboanga sits at the southern tip of Mindanao's westernmost arm. Chavacano, a dialect of pidgin Spanish and Cebuano, is the lingua franca. The inhabitants are Christians, Tausug, Yakan, Badjao, Samal and Subanon.

**Map
on pages
304–5**

TIP

Though Zamboanga City is a great destination, its past peace and order problems with Muslim insurgents have made it unpopular with tourists. Before visiting, check the latest situation with the local tourism department.

BELOW:
mooring a boat on Dapitan Bay.

Behind the wharf lies **Plaza Pershing**, named after Governor John Pershing, the first American governor of Moro country. The quasi-baroque city hall, completed in 1907, stands at the southeast corner of the plaza and houses the post office. From here, along Valderros Street, is the Lantaka Hotel, where the Department of Tourism (DOT) offices are located. Adjacent to the hotel is Pettit Barracks, occupied by the US Forces after their capture of the city on November 16, 1899. A 15-minute walk away is **Fort Pilar**, built in 1635 by a Jesuit priest to ward off attacks from Moros and foreign invaders. A shrine to the Lady of Del Pilar, the patron saint of Zamboanga is found in the eastern wall. A short distance to the east is **Rio Hondo,** a 23-hectare (57-acre) coastal colony of Tausug, Samal and Badjao who live in houses-on-stilts called *sahaya*.

Around Zamboanga

Make arrangements at Lantaka landing (behind Lantaka Hotel) to rent a pump-boat for the 25-minute voyage to **Great Santa Cruz Island** ㉜, known for its pinkish sand beach, lagoon, fishing village and old Samal graveyard. The area surrounding the island hosts an extensive variety of coral formations, which in turn support a medley of tropical fish.

Some 20 km (12 miles) east of the city is **Taluksangay**, a quieter village on stilts. Its mosque, with silvery dome and turrets, is most photogenic. Westward from Zamboanga, the road immediately enters the 2-km (1½-mile) long **Cawa Cawa Boulevard**. This pocket-sized version of Manila's Roxas Boulevard, lined by old acacia trees, is the favorite gathering place of the locals. At the far end of the boulevard are several beer parlors. Farther is a small colony of Yakan families, who will demonstrate their weaving and sell the cloth for visitors.

Beyond is **Yellow Beach**, where American forces landed in March 1945 to liberate Zamboanga.

At 22 km (14 miles) east is the **San Ramon Prison and Penal Farm**. Souvenirs, mainly in the form of woodcarvings, can be purchased at this 19th-century Spanish-built prison farm. The salesman will probably be an old man who had been incarcerated for some crime, which he will tell you he did not commit.

Seven km (4 miles) north of Zamboanga City is **Pasonanca Park**, 150 meters (500 ft) above sea level. Most travelers will find it more interesting for its view than its scout camp and swimming pools. Also on a hill, in a 1.5-hectare (2½-acre) lot at the Regional Government Center in Cabatangan, 5 km (3 miles) from Zamboanga City, is **Astanah Kasannangan** (Palace of Peace), a mosque-like edifice of the executive office of Region 10. About 7 km (4 miles) along the western coast is **Yakan Weaving Village**, which produces some of the finest weaving in the country.

A two-hour voyage south from Zamboanga City, across the 25-km (16-mile) Strait of Basilan to the island, brings travelers to **Basilan Island** ㉝. The island has been the site of fierce fighting between the Philippine government and the terrorist group Abu Sayyaf. Maximum caution should be exercised if visiting, but a better option still might be to skip Basilan completely. En route, the boat skirts Great Santa Cruz Island. The last part of the voyage, before reaching **Isabela**, the capital and port, is through a 1-km (½-mile) wide mangrove channel banked by palm trees and adorned with nipa huts on stilts. Across is **Malamaui**, a new island resort, expensive for a far-flung province. The only other lodging place, Basilan Hotel, is conveniently located downtown but, for security reasons, is not recommended. Make arrangements for lodgings with the mayor's office instead.

Map on pages 304–5

Muslim insurgency

Yakan, Tausug, Samal and Zamboangueños have migrated to Basilan, bringing with them their distinct cultures, which now make up the province's rich mosaic. The sunset over the rubber plantation in Menzi, with swaying rubber trees reflected in a nearby lagoon, paints a picture of near-paradise in this would-be tourist destination. Unfortunately, Basilan is a haven for Muslim rebels. Fielding's *World's Most Dangerous Places* guidebook describes it as the lair of the dreaded Abu Sayyaf *(see page 335)*, an extremist Muslim rebel group. The government is working on stamping out the Abu Sayyaf and making Basilan safe for tourists. Recent cooperative exercises with American military forces have had some effect on scattering the Abus, but your Basilan beach vacation may still be a few years off.

Handwoven textiles from Basilan Island.

A rough road southward from Isabela through rubber, palm-oil and coconut plantations, and past stands of coffee and pepper, leads, after 32 km (20 miles) to **Maluso** fishing village, which the DOT advises visitors to avoid. A similar road to the northeast passes citrus groves and rubber plants. After 30 km (20 miles), it arrives at Basilan's most "peaceful" town of **Lamitan**, where **Datu Kalu's Park and Shrine** is located. The Yakan, the town's inhabitants, hold the **Lami-Lamihan Festival** every June to revive their cultural heritage.

BELOW: Muslim students.

The Sulu Archipelago

Jolo ㉞ (pronounced "Ho-Lo"), capital of **Sulu Province**, is accessible from Zamboanga City by a nine-hour ferry ride or three-hour fast boat. It has never been a particularly safe place to visit, with even reports of kidnapping in millennia-old Chinese trade records. It's the only Muslim-dominated place that Spanish colonizers were able to conquer, but not until the last 23 years of their rule. In 1974, Jolo was burned to the ground when fighting broke out between rebelling Muslims and government troops.

Sulu consists of over 400 scattered and almost isolated islands, stretching from the tip of Zamboanga southwestward towards Borneo. As in Basilan and Tawi-Tawi, Muslims dominate Sulu. The main dialect is Tausug; although Samal, Cebuano, Chavacano, Tagalog and English are also spoken. Lying outside the typhoon belt, Sulu is blessed with a year-round bounty of harvests from land and sea. Its soil and climate allow it to grow a greater variety of agricultural products than elsewhere in the country, and the area abounds in timber resources. The main industries are fishing, boat building, coffee processing and fruit preservation. Although some locals fashion souvenirs out of turtle shells, avoid these at all costs. The export of such products made from protected species is prohibited worldwide.

The brick **Walled City of Jolo** – the world's smallest – is historic for having deterred enemies for many centuries. At its entrance are four gates – once used as watchtowers – and several mounds used as burial grounds for Spanish and American soldiers who died at the hands of Muslim warriors. The Provincial Capitol, built by Governor Murphy Sangkula, has a Moorish-inspired architectural design. The **American Calvary Monument** (open Mon–Fri 8–11am and 2–5pm; free), Sulu's only existing museum, is just outside Jolo.

BELOW: a Badjao sea gypsy boy.

THE BADJAO SEA GYPSIES

It could have been one of those typical scenes in the coastal Philippines, with the women waiting on the seashore to buy fish from the fishermen. Except that Badjao fisherman Lagani, 25, didn't want to sell his catch to a particularly well-dressed female customer – simply because she wasn't going to pay him in coins.

Such is one of the idiosyncrasies of the Badjao, or sea gypsies, the smallest ethnic minority in the Sulu Archipelago. They live a nomadic sea existence as fishermen along the coasts of Jolo, Siasi, Tapul Island, Sitangkai, Subutu and Tawi-Tawi Islands.

Apart from being migrants who kept to their boats and maintained a nomadic way of life, no one knows for certain the origins of the Badjao. Nevertheless these are a hard-working, peace-loving and thrifty people.

The Badjao's typical boat is known as a *lipa*. Long and thin, the wooden vessel has a small stove at the stern in which the catch can be cooked. However, most now live in houses made of *nipa* and bamboo which are built along the seashores and coral reefs. Because of their aquatic lifestyles, the Badjao are renowned for their swimming and diving ability. Their simple way of life is reflected in the fact that many Badjao children go to school almost bare-ass naked.

Within kilometers of Jolo town are the white sand beaches of Maubo, Tandu and Tadjung, while off the mainland is the Pearl Farm at **Marungas Island**, a 30-minute pumpboat ride away. However, despite all its coastal allure, Sulu is one of the poorest provinces in the country. True, the signing of a peace agreement between the Moro Islamic Liberation Front and the Philippine government has improved, if only a little, its law and order, but some family feuds have expanded into political wars, and guns are still widely used. Connecting the province to the rest of Mindanao and other neighbors through the development of BIMP-EAGA (Brunei-Indonesia-Malaysia-Philippines East Asean Growth Area) might finally help the island recover from its war-torn past.

Map on pages 304–5

Tawi-Tawi

The Sulu Sea to the north and Celebes Sea to the south surround the 300-plus islands of Tawi-Tawi, the Philippines' southernmost province. **Bongao ⬤**, the provincial capital, is accessible by fast ferries and slower boats that regularly ply the Zamboanga–Bongao–Sandakan route. There are several flights weekly from Zamboanga to Bongao – the only place in Tawi-Tawi with even the simplest amenities. Bongao Peak, considered sacred by locals, hosts a monkey sanctuary.

Badjao fisherman building a lipa – a traditional fishing vessel.

The Samal people dominate the population, which also includes smaller numbers of Badjao, Jama Mapun and Tausug people. Locals usually wear colorful wrap-around sarongs, called *malong*. Samal is the most common dialect, but Tausug, Filipino and English are also spoken.

Badjao Village, a series of simple houses tucked into a labyrinth of docks doubling as pathways, offers visitors direct access to handicrafts. The docks also provide a personal glimpse of the sea gypsies at home.

BELOW: traditional mat weaving in Tawi Tawi.

Tubig Indangan, on the island of **Simunul**, was the first mosque built by Arabian missionary Sheik Makdum in 1380. There is a rock formation just offshore from Simunul called *Manuk-Mangkaw*, meaning "floats like an umbrella." Allied submarines sought refuge beneath this rock structure during World War II.

The Gusong Reef in **Cagayan de Tawi-Tawi** is home to seagulls, locally called *tallah-tallah*, that settle by the thousands into a protected area once a year to nest. Tawi-Tawi's **Turtle Islands** offer a rare opportunity to observe marine turtles up close, and is being considered for future ecotourism development. But, as has happened to many sites of natural bounty in Asia, man's destructive practices threaten the Turtle Islands. Some Sulu natives have been known to sell turtle eggs by the thousands, endangering the entire turtle population. According to WWF, local extinction is imminent if the situation is not remedied quickly. Turtle Island itself is actually jointly administered with Malaysia.

Further out into the Celebes Sea is **Sibutu**, of wild boar fame. Locals rumor that wild boars swim over from Malaysia and are occasionally hunted by shooting parties from Manila. Finally, almost at the border with Malaysia is the Venice of the East, **Sitangkai**, a town built on stilts over crystal-clear waters and a beautiful coral reef. Be sure to try native *kalawa* and *baulo* cakes while sitting out over the water, watching the sun set at the western end of the Philippine world. ❏

INSIGHT GUIDES
TRAVEL TIPS

CONTENTS

Getting Acquainted

Place

Location The Philippines' 7,107 islands, spanning 1,840 km (1,140 miles) from north to south, are bordered by the Philippine Sea in the east, the South China Sea and Luzon Sea in the west, and the Sulu Sea and Celebes Sea in the south.
Area Total land area is 300,000 sq. km (116,000 sq. miles) but 95 percent of this is formed by the 11 larger islands, on which 95 percent of the people live. Only 2,000 islands are inhabited while 2,500 are still unnamed.
Terrain Mostly tropical and mountainous, except along the indented coastlines and fertile central plain of main island Luzon. The highest peak is Mt Apo (2,950 meters/9,690 ft) in Davao province in Mindanao. There are 22 active volcanoes, including Mt Mayon, which last erupted in February 2000. Four of the six most active volcanoes are located in Luzon.
Geography There are four distinct regions: 1) Luzon, the largest and northernmost island, where the capital Manila is located; 2) the tightly-packed Visayas islands in the center; 3) Palawan on the west, with 1,800 islands; and 4) Mindanao, the second largest island.

Deepest Point

On the Pacific side of the Philippines runs the **Philippine Trench**, or Philippine Deep. Cutting an underwater swath 10,060 meters (33,000 ft) below sea level, its depth exceeds the altitude of Mt Everest, and is the second deepest place in the world.

Land use is varied. There is arable land (19 percent), permanent crops (12 percent), pastures (4 percent), and forest and woodland (46 percent). About 18 percent of the land is irrigated.

Climate

A tropical country, much of the Philippines has a hot and dry climate from March to May. Generally, the southwest monsoon – and the typhoons it brings – predominates from June to October. The dry, cooler season during the northeast monsoon period lasts from November to February. Year-round temperatures range from 78°F (25°C) to 90°F (32°C); mean annual humidity is at 83 percent.

Rainfall varies with the region:
Type 1 has two seasons, dry November–May and wet June–October. Type 1 areas are found mainly in the western half of Luzon (including Manila), Palawan, Coron, Cuyo and the lower part of Antique, Iloilo and Negros.
Type 2 lacks a distinct dry season but has a pronounced maximum rain period December–February. Areas include eastern Bicol, eastern Mindanao, northern and eastern Samar and southern Leyte.
Type 3 areas, which do not have a pronounced maximum rain period but a short dry season of 1–3 (November–January) months, include central Luzon, Visayas and western Mindanao.
Type 4 sees even rainfall throughout the year and is found in the eastern coast of Luzon, Leyte and Bohol, and in central Mindanao.

Sitting in the typhoon belt, the Philippines has about 15 typhoons each year. High season is June–October, with the peak in July–September, coinciding with the height of the southwest monsoon.

People

About 12 million out of a population of nearly 90 million Filipinos live in the greater Metro Manila area. The people are basically of Malay descent, with evidence of Chinese,

Spanish, Arab and American stock. The population increases by 1.6 million every year, or over 2 percent, the highest growth rate in Asia. Attempts to implement family planning programs have met with strong opposition from the Catholic Church. Meanwhile, three babies are born every minute in the Philippines.

The primary religion is Christianity; 80 percent are Roman Catholic, 11 percent Protestant or other Christian; 7 percent Muslim; and 2 percent Buddhist or other religions.

Life expectancy averages 67 years and the functional literacy rate is 84 percent. Pilipino and English are the official languages. At least 110 other dialects or languages are spoken.

Government

The official name of the country is the Republic of the Philippines. In 1972, then-president Ferdinand Marcos suspended a 1935 constitution, declaring martial law and throwing the nation into chaos. Though a new constitution was ratified the following year, Marcos meddled with this till he achieved complete power and authority. After the peaceful February 1986 "People Power" uprising along EDSA that ousted Marcos, the country reverted to a democratic form of government.

In a February 1987 plebiscite, a new constitution was ratified, providing for a democratic republican state and a president. This paved the way for the re-establishment of an elected bicameral legislative body. After a painful 2 decades of Marcos rule, the country limited the presidential term to a single 6-year term.

Gloria Arroyo-Macapagal became President of the Philippines in January 2001 after the brief but disastrous administration of former movie actor Joseph Estrada. Estrada was forced out of office by mass protests – called People Power II by some and mob rule by others. President Arroyo narrowly won elections held in May 2004, which will, if everything goes right, give her a 10-year term, making her the third longest-serving President in the Philippines.

For administrative purposes, the republic is divided into 17 regions, 79 provinces, 117 chartered cities, 1,506 municipalities and 41,993 *barangays*. Provinces consist of several municipalities centered on a provincial capital. Municipalities are sub-divided into the *barangay*, the smallest socio-political unit, headed by a *barangay* captain.

The legal system is based on Spanish and Anglo-American law.

The Economy

In 1997, the Philippine peso lost nearly half its value, falling from an exchange rate of P25 to P45 per US$1. While the tourist paying in dollars would consider this a stroke of good fortune – paying half price for meals or handicrafts – the devaluation was a disaster for the country. The unexpected economic downturn halted a period of incredible growth enjoyed by the Philippines and its Asian neighbors in the early 1990s. The Philippine GDP, which during 1994–97 saw an average annual growth rate of nearly 6 percent, dropped to negative 0.5 percent in 1998. The formerly booming stock market and property sector also suffered massive declines.

While the rest of the region slowly started to climb back from the Asian economic crisis, the Philippine economy was once again dragged down by domestic politics. The mismanagement of the country's economy by former President Joseph Estrada and the months during 2000 spent trying to remove him from office devastated the country's economy. During the height of the crisis, the Philippine peso plunged to nearly P55 to the US dollar.

The installation of Gloria Arroyo-Macapagal (GMA) in 2001, a trained economist, brought widespread optimism from observers certain that the country's economic

situation could be turned around. While aggressively targeting such troublesome areas in the infrastructure as corruption and domestic security, progress has been an uphill struggle, and the peso hit an all-time low in mid-2004. Her courting of foreign investment by promoting privatization and deregulation programs in the country's major industries has earned her kudos in economist circles, and the country's Gross Domestic Product (GDP) hovered around 5 percent towards the end of 2006.

Public Holidays

January 1 New Year's Day. Fireworks and celebratory gunfire ring in the new year.

April/May Maundy Thursday, Good Friday. Flagellants in the streets, processions and *Cenaculos* (passion plays). In Pampanga and elsewhere, devout Catholics are voluntarily crucified.

April/May Easter Sunday Morning processions; family celebration.

April 9 Araw ng Kagitingan (Day of Valor/Bataan and Corregidor Day). Celebrations at Fort Santiago in Intramuros commemorate the bravery of Filipino soldiers during World War II.

May 1 Labor Day. A tribute to the Philippine worker.

June 12 Independence Day – from Spain in 1898. Parades at Rizal Park in Manila.

October/November Eid al Fitr – a recently declared public holiday passed to respect the country's other dominant religion, Islam. Marks the ending of Ramadan.

November 1 All Saints' Day. Most Filipinos travel home to visit ancestral tombs and spend the day with their family.

November 30 Bonifacio Day celebrates the birth of nationalist leader Andres Bonifacio.

December 25 Christmas Day.

December 30 Rizal Day. Wreath laying ceremony at National Hero's Monument in Rizal Park (Manila), in honor of the revered Jose Rizal.

December 31 New Year's Eve.

Note: In the Muslim provinces of western Mindanao, four other Islamic holidays are also recognized.

Business Hours

Shops are open Monday–Saturday, 10am to 7 or 8pm. Outside Manila, the Philippine attitude of *bahala na* (whatever happens) prevails; shops and museums are lackadaisical about schedules. If a museum or attraction is closed, ask around; it might very easily be opened if you ask the right person.

Government and business hours are Monday–Friday 8am–5pm and workers break for lunch noon–1pm. Some businesses are open on Saturday 8am–noon. Banks are open Monday–Friday 9am–3pm.

The National Flag

The Philippine flag shows a white triangle with yellow sunburst, and three stars over horizontal fields of blue and red. In times of peace, the blue is over the red field, while in war the red field is over the blue.

The eight rays of the Philippine sun, in the triangle, represent the first eight provinces to revolt against Spanish domination. The three stars at the triangle's corners indicate the three major island groups: Luzon, the Visayas and Mindanao.

Planning the Trip

Everyone entering the Philippines from abroad must hold a valid passport. Visitors from nations with diplomatic ties are granted a 21-day visa upon arrival. All visitors must hold onward or return tickets.

Visitors who wish to extend their stay from 21 to 59 days should contact the Bureau of Immigration, Magallanes Drive, Intramuros, by Jones Bridge (open Mon–Fri 8am–5pm). Avoid the cumbersome process by hiring a travel agent, or obtaining a 59-day visa before arrival.

Customs

Each arriving passenger is allowed 400 cigarettes (20 packs) or two tins of tobacco, and two 1-liter bottles of alcohol.

Filipinos living overseas bring home huge amounts of goods – many of them dutiable – to their families back in the Philippines. As a result, you will see passengers walking stacks of boxes through the "Nothing to Declare" Customs line at the Manila airport. In general, customs regulations are not strictly enforced but officials will sometimes use the rule of law on a selective basis, particularly when it comes to bringing electronics into the country.

Porter Services

About P20–30 per bag is an appropriate charge, more for heavy packages.

Health & Insurance

Yellow fever vaccination is necessary for those arriving from an infected area. Do note that outside some parts of Palawan and Mindanao, malaria is fairly rare in the Philippines. However, there is a risk of malaria year-round below 600 meters (2,000 ft) in elevation, except in urban areas; the malignant *falciparum* strain is present, highly resistant to chloroquine. Anti-malarial drugs are suggested for travel in remote areas. Mosquito-borne dengue fever has seen a resurgence in recent years; wear insect repellant and cover exposed skin to prevent insect bites.

Rabies is present. If bitten by any mammal, seek medical treatment immediately. Since bilharzia (schistosomiasis) may be present in fresh water, do weigh the risks of swimming in lakes or rivers.

Although pharmacies such as Mercury Drug are found everywhere, visitors may be unable to find the selection of medications available at home. Carry a first aid kit with necessary prescription drugs, plus aspirin, anti-inflammatory tablets, Imodium (anti-diarrhea pills) and antibiotics.

It is best to avoid drinking tap water; stick to bottled water.

Money Matters

The peso (P) is the monetary unit and there are 100 centavos to one peso. The Bangkong Sentral

Holiday-time Travel

Travel during the holiday season – especially Easter and Christmas – can be difficult and chaotic. Make reservations far in advance, or avoid travel during these periods. One interesting exception to this rule is Easter in Manila. This is the biggest travel time of the year in the Philippines and the capital city empties. Though many stores and museums are closed, the usually congested city is nearly vacant. It is a very relaxing time to see the city and many smaller Manila hotels offer discounts because there are so few customers at this time.

Medical Travel Insurance

International insurance is recommended; hospitals may require advance payment before treatment. In emergencies, ask your hotel for help.

(Central Bank) issues the following bank notes: P20, P50, P100, P200, P500 and P1,000. There are 5c, 10c, 25c, P1, P5 and P10 coins. The US dollar, pound sterling, Swiss franc, Canadian dollar, Australian dollar and Japanese yen are easily convertible – though the US dollar is widely accepted.

At time of press the exchange rate was US$1 to P50.

Especially outside Metro Manila and Cebu, the Philippines is a cash economy. Even travelers' checks can present something of a challenge in Manila; bring your purchase receipt and passport to a bank and be prepared for a queue.

ATMs are open 24 hours and easily found in major cities, although international banks may not be accessible. Maximum daily withdrawal is about P20,000. During holidays, withdraw cash early, before ATMs run out of cash.

Credit cards are widely accepted throughout Manila, although service charges prevail. In more rural areas, only major establishments accept plastic. Be prepared with cash. Many a traveler has cut short a trip in the provinces for lack of money. Licensed moneychangers on Mabini Street in Ermita and P. Burgos Street in Makati offer reasonable rates.

Taxes

When shopping, taxes are included in the listed price. Major restaurants and hotels add a 10 percent service charge; hotels tack on an additional 12 percent VAT.

Tipping

Larger establishments will add a service charge. Smaller establishments leave tipping to discretion but it is best to leave something. The local habit is to leave a token fee rather than a percentage of the total bill, usually less than P100. The relatively low cost of travel here makes it easier for foreign visitors to be generous.

Time Zone

The Philippines is 8 hours ahead of Greenwich Mean Time (GMT). Sunrise and sunset occur around 6am and 6pm, respectively.

Electricity

The standard voltage in the Philippines is 220 volts AC, 60 cycles. Many areas also have 110 volts capability. Major hotels will provide adapters. Plugs are of the North American configuration, without the grounding slot.

Weights/Measures

Though the metric system predominates, the imperial system is well understood. Temperatures are listed in Centigrade, with weight expressed in grams and kilograms. Distances are listed in meters and kilometers.

What to Wear

Dress in loose, lightweight clothing to beat the heat. Few locals wear shorts or sleeveless shirts in the city, but tourists can bend the rules somewhat. To blend in better, dress like the locals – in jeans and T-shirts. If visiting a church, make an effort to dress conservatively.

Umbrellas are useful against sun and rain. If heading to the mountains, pack a fleece jacket, as chilly conditions surprise many travelers.

Tourist Offices

EUROPE

France: Service de Tourisme, Ambassade des Philippines, 4 Hameau de Boulainvilliers 75016, Paris, tel: 331-4265 0234; e-mail: dotpar@wanadoo.fr.
Germany: Tourism Attachè, Kaiserhofstrasse 7 D-60313 Frankfurt Am Main 1, Frankfurt, tel: 4969-20893/94; e-mail: phildot-fra@t-online.de.
United Kingdom: Philippine Department of Tourism, 146 Cromwell Road, London SW7 4EF, tel: 4420-7835 1100; e-mail: infotourism@wowphilippines.co.uk.

NORTH AMERICA

Canada: Philippine Department of Tourism, 151 Bloor Street, West Suite 1120, Toronto, Ontario, M5S1S4, tel: 416-924 3569; e-mail: info@wowphilippines.ca.
Chicago: Philippine Consulate General, 30 N Michigan Avenue, Suite 913, tel: 1312-782 2475; e-mail: pdotchi@aol.com.
Los Angeles: Philippine Consulate General, 3660 Wilshire Boulevard 900, Suite 216, tel: 1213-487 4525; e-mail: pdotla@aol.com.
New York: Philippine Center, 556 Fifth Avenue, tel: 1212-575 7915; e-mail: pdotny@aol.com.
San Francisco: Philippine Consulate General, 447 Sutter Street, Suite 507, tel: 1415-956 4060; e-mail: pdotsf@aol.com.

ASIA-PACIFIC

Australia: Philippine Department of Tourism, Level 1, Philippine Centre, 27-33 Wentworth Avenue, Sydney, tel: 612-9283 0711; e-mail: cgjones@pdot.com.au.
Hong Kong: Philippine Consulate General, 6/F, Room 602, United Centre, 95 Queensway, Hong Kong, tel: 852-2866 7643; e-mail: pdothk@netvigator.com.
Japan: Tokyo Embassy of the Philippines Tourism Attache 5-15-5 Roponggi, Minato-ku, tel: 813-5562 1583; e-mail: dotjapan@gol.com; Osaka Philippine Tourism Center 2F, Dainan Building, 2-19-23 Shiommachi, Nishi-ku, tel: 8166-535 5071; e-mail: dotosaka@crux.ocnne.jp.
Korea: 403 Renaissance Building.

1598-3, Socho-dong, Socho-ku, Seoul, tel: 822-598 2290; www.wowphilippines.or.kr.
Singapore: Philippine Tourism Office, #06-11 Orchard Towers, 400 Orchard Road, tel: 65-6738 7165; e-mail: philtours_sin@pacific.net.sg.
Taiwan: Manila Economic & Cultural Office, Tourism Center, 4/F Metrobank Plaza, 107 Chung Hsiao East Road, Section 4, Taipei, tel: 8862-2773 5724; e-mail: philtour@ms57.hinet.net.

Tourism Websites

Note More information on tourism in the Philippines can be found at the Philippine Department of Tourism's catchy websites www.wowphilippines.com.ph, www.visitmyphilippines.com and www.wowpinoy.net.

Getting There

BY AIR

More than 500 international flights arrive in Manila weekly. There are two operational international terminals and one domestic terminal.

The **Ninoy Aquino International Airport** (NAIA), also known as Terminal 1, serve all international flights except Philippine Airlines' (PAL). It is located 7 km (4 miles) from the city center. The **Centennial Terminal**, also known as Terminal 2 and located about 1 km (½ mile) from NAIA, is the base of all PAL and Air Philippines domestic and international flights. All other domestic flights originate from the **Domestic Terminal**, which is 3 km (2 miles) from NAIA (about a 10–15 minute taxi ride away). The new NAIA Terminal 3 is completed but not yet operational amid much controversy.

With the Manila terminals reaching capacity, more passengers are bypassing Manila altogether and using the **Mactan Cebu International Airport** (MCIA) as a hub. MCIA has increased its international connections in recent years. Other cities with international airports are **Laoag**, **Davao**, **Subic** and **Clark**.

Airline Offices

Philippine Airlines, the national carrier, flies to Hong Kong, Taipei, Beijing, Shanghai, Seoul, Pusan, Tokyo, Osaka, Fukuoka, Las Vegas, Vancouver, Okinawa, San Francisco, Honolulu, Guam, Los Angeles, Melbourne, Sydney, Riyadh, Bangkok, Kuala Lumpur, Singapore, Jakarta, and Ho Chi Minh City. The office is at PAL Center, Legaspi Street, Legaspi Village, Makati City, tel: 02-855 8888; www.philippineair.com.

Cebu Pacific, a good-quality discount carrier in the Philippines, has expanded its international routes to Hong Kong, Jakarta, Bangkok and Kuala Lumpur. Level 1, Robinsons Galleria Mall, EDSA corner Ortigas Avenue, tel: 02-636 4938, www.cebupacificair.com.

Air Philippines has chartered flights to Southeast Asian cities and Korea. Call for current offerings, tel: 02-855 9000; www.airphils.com.

Air France–KLM connects to Paris via Hong Kong. 39/F, Yuchengco Tower, RCBC Plaza, Ayala Avenue corner Buendia Avenue, Makati City, tel: 02-887 1202; www.airfrance.com.

American Airlines has flights to cities in the US, most via Tokyo. G/F, Olympia Condos, Makati Avenue corner Santo Tomas Street, Makati City, tel: 02-817 8645; www.aa.com.

British Airways flies to London via Hong Kong several times a week. Filipino Merchants Building, Legaspi corner De la Rosa Street, Legaspi Village, Makati, tel: 02-817 0361; www.british-airways.com.

Cathay Pacific flies to Hong Kong from Cebu and Manila several times a day. Manila: 22/F, LKG Tower, 6801 Ayala Avenue, Makati City, tel: 02-757 0888. Cebu: 12/F, Ayala Life FGU Center, Mindanao Avenue, Cebu Business Park, tel: 032-231 3747. Davao: M Floor, Royal Mandaya Hotel, J. Palma Gil Street, tel: 082-222 8901; www.cathaypacific.com.

Emirates Airlines flies directly to Dubai 10 times weekly. 18/F Pacific Star Building, Makati Avenue corner Gil Puyat (Buendia), tel: 02-811 5278; www.emirates.com.

Japan Airlines connects to Narita twice a day. 2/F, Sky Plaza, 6788 Ayala Avenue, Makati City, tel: 02-886 6868; www.jal.co.jp.

Korean Air connects Manila to Seoul twice a day. G/F, LPL Plaza Building, 124 L.P. Leviste Street, Salcedo Village, Makati City, tel: 02-893 4909; www.koreanair.com.

Lufthansa flies daily to Frankfurt, continuing onward to other European destinations. 39 Plaza Drive, Rockwell, Makati City, tel: 02-580 6400; www.lufthansa.com.

Northwest Airlines links to the US through Osaka, Tokyo and Nagoya. E-ticketing services available. 9/F, Athenaeum Building, 160 Leviste Street, Salcedo Village, Makati City, tel: 02-841 8800. Also G/F, La Paz Center, Salcedo and Herrera Street, Legaspi Village, Makati City, tel: 02-810 4716; www.nwa.com.

Qantas Airways flies to Brisbane and Sydney several times a week, with connecting flights from these cities to other parts of Australasia. Manila: c/o HT&T Travel Philippines, 10/F Salustiana D Ty Towers, 104 Paseo de Roxas, Makati City, tel: 02-812 0607. Cebu: tel: 032-254 9604; www.qantas.com.

Singapore Airlines provides direct service from Manila to Singapore. 33/F, LKG Tower, 6801 Ayala Avenue, Makati City, tel: 02-753 5151/2, www.singaporeair.com.

Thai International Airways flies daily to Bangkok and Osaka. G/F, Country Space 1 Building, H.V. de la Costa Street, Salcedo Village, Makati City, tel: 02-812 4744, www.thaiair.com.

BY SEA

Freighters and cruise ships stop in Manila Bay, though most travelers arrive by air.

There are two sea routes from Mindanao to Southeast Asia frequented by backpackers, but the government discourages these excursions because of Moro rebels and piracy in the area.

The Philippines' Sampaguita Shipping Corporation operates a passenger ferry from Pagadian to Zamboanga (both in Mindanao), a quicker and safer alternative to overland travel. The ferry continues to Sandakan, Sabah, a few times weekly. Passengers are mostly Muslim Filipinos from Mindanao.

Aleson Lines also runs a Zamboanga-to-Sandakan ferry, Monday and Wednesday.

At the Airport: Arrival and Departure

Arrival: Manila's Ninoy Aquino International Airport (NAIA) Terminal 1 services most international airlines, while flag carrier Philippine Airlines uses Terminal 2 (Centennial Terminal) for international and domestic flights.

After clearing customs and claiming baggage, rent a car or take a taxi. Rental cars in Manila come with a driver; traffic in this city should not be underestimated. If opting for a "coupon" taxi, pay a fixed rate to your destination at one of the counters inside, then head outside to wait for the next taxi. Cheaper street taxis can be found on the departure level. Most taxi-related crimes happen when travelers are coming from the airport with all their valuables, passport and luggage in tow. Saving the few dollars difference between a street taxi and coupon taxi is not advised, but for those on a tight budget, regular taxis can be found by heading upstairs to the departure area, where taxis drop off passengers. Most Manila hotels offer free or inexpensive shuttles. Look for the people holding up small signs with the names of hotels.

Departure: It is easiest to reach the airport by private car or taxi. Give yourself plenty of time, especially during rush hour, typhoons and holidays.

Most airline counters open 3 hours prior to departure. Independent travelers should reconfirm their tickets 48–72 hours before departure; Philippines Airlines insists on reconfirmation.

The Manila airport departure tax is P550 or US$11.

Practical Tips

Media

NEWSPAPERS AND MAGAZINES

The myriad daily newspapers in English include the *Manila Bulletin, Philippine Daily Inquirer, Manila Standard* and *Philippine Star*, most of which are available online. The *Fookien Times* is published in English and Chinese. Local free weekly newspapers published in English include *What's On & Expat* (www.whatson-expat.com.ph), and *Foreign Post* (www.theforeignpost. com). *Citiguide* is a bi-monthly, smaller-format newspaper listing events, dining, nightlife and shopping opportunities, available at newsstands and restaurants.

A large selection of foreign publications is available: *Newsweek, Time, Far Eastern Economic Review, Asian Business, The Economist, Reader's Digest, Vogue, Yazhou Zhoukan, Asian Wall Street Journal* and *International Herald Tribune*. These are sold in major hotels, bookstores, supermarkets and at newsstands.

Useful Links

An excellent website with links to all things Filipino is www.filipinolinks.com. For great information on restaurants, hotels and nightclubs, try www.clickthecity.com.

TELEVISION

Government-owned People's Television (Channel 4) broadcasts a variety of programs, including the latest national and foreign news, sports events, live coverage of government-sponsored events, variety shows, and soap operas.

Other independent stations include: Radio Philippine Network (RPN) channel 9; Greater Manila Area TV (GMA) channel 7; Intercontinental Broadcasting Network (IBC) channel 13; Alto Broadcasting System-Chronicle Broadcasting Network (ABS-CBN) channel 2, ABC channel 5, Studio 23, and channel 23. Most hotels have cable or satellite television, offering a cosmopolitan range of international news and programming. A tourism channel called Living Asia TV promotes domestic rediscovery of the Philippine islands, broadcasting airline arrivals and departures between programs.

RADIO

Most radio stations are privately owned, broadcasting a range of music, news, commercials and entertainment talk. Station 100.3 FM plays soft rock and love songs. 89.1 Wave FM plays R and B, lounge and house. 105.1 FM features easy listening hits while 107.5 FM plays alternative music to cater to young listeners.

Postal Services

Post offices are open Monday–Friday, 8am–5pm, Saturday 8am–noon. The Philippine Postal Corporation is at Lawton Plaza (Liwasang Bonifacio), Intramuros, Manila. Hotel desks provide the most convenient services for purchasing stamps and posting letters. At Ninoy Aquino International Airport, the post office is in the arrival area.

The Philippine mail system is slow and unreliable. It is fine for postcards but not much use for anything else. Private courier services like DHL (tel: 1800-1888 0345), Fedex (1800-10 855 8484), UPS (tel: 1800-10 742 5877), and TNT (tel: 02-551 5632) offer inexpensive and reliable mail service within the Philippines, as well as speedy overseas deliveries.

Post Offices in Manila
Manila Post Office Liwasang Bonifacio, Manila
Makati Post Office corner Gil Puyat Avenue (Buendia) and Ayala Avenue
Pasay Post Office F.B. Harrison, Pasay
San Juan Central Post Office Pinaglabanan, San Juan

Telecommunications

Most of the larger Philippine hotels have IDD, telex, fax and Internet facilities, available to guests at a small charge.

Public payphones require P2–3 or prepaid telephone cards. Some small shops also provide informal phone services.

CELLULAR PHONES

The Philippines, which has always had notoriously bad telephone

Telephone Codes

International access code: 00
International operator: 108
Domestic operator: 109
Directory assistance: 114 or 187
Philippines country code: 63
City codes:

Manila	02
Angeles	045, 0455
Bacolod	034
Baguio	074
Batangas	043
Boracay	036
Cagayan de Oro	088, 08822
Cebu	032
Clark	045
Davao	082
General Santos City	083
Iloilo	033
Subic	047

The prefix 0 must be dialed for all calls made within the Philippines. When calling the Philippines from overseas, dial the international access code, followed by 63 and the phone number (without the preceding 0).

service, has embraced cellular phones wholeheartedly and they are now as reliable as, or in fact more reliable than, many land lines. Their reach is impressive – from the remote regions of Mindanao to the northern islands of Batanes.

The competition for cell phone users is intense, with Smart and Globe commanding the lion's share of the market, and Sun Cellular is a recent entry into the market. Cellular phone prefixes are 4 digits, and start with 09, the 0 to be dropped when dialing from overseas.

Cellular phones in the Philippines use the GSM network. If your cell phone has a roaming facility, it will automatically hook up to one of the country's networks. However, cellular phones from Korea, Japan, and the US sometimes have compatibility problems.

A simple and convenient telecommunications solution is to buy a cheap (US$40 new, US$20 used) cellular phone upon arrival and use it with prepaid calling cards, available everywhere. It can be resold upon departure at small cellular shops for about half of its original purchase price if it is still in good condition. Cell phone dealers are found throughout the city.

If compatibility is not an issue, you can also make calls on your cell phone with a prepaid local SIM card (around US$8), with which you get a local number.

Regional Tourist Offices

Metro Manila
• Department of Tourism (DOT), DOT Building, Room 207, T.M. Kalaw Street, Ermita, tel: 02-524 2345.
• DOT, Ninoy Aquino International Airport branch, tel: 02-832 2964.

Southern Luzon
• DOT, DOT Building, Room 208, T.M. Kalaw Street, Ermita, Manila, tel: 02-524 1969.

Central Luzon
• DOT, Paskuhan Village, San Fernando, Pampanga, tel: 045-961 2665.

Ilocos
• DOT, Oasis Country Resort National Highway, Bgy, Sevilla San Fernando, La Union, tel: 072-888 2411.
• DOT, Ilocano Heroes Memorial Hall, Laoag City, tel: 077-771 1473.

Cotabato
• DOT, 2/F, Comse Building, Quezon Avenue, Cotabato City, tel: 064-421 1110; e-mail: dot12@mozcom.com.

Northeastern Luzon
• DOT, 2/F, Tuguegarao Supermarket, Tuguegarao, Cagayan, tel: 078-844 1621.

Cordillera Administrative Region
• DOT, DOT Complex, Gov. Pack Road, Baguio City, tel: 074-442 6708; e-mail: dotcar@mozcom.com.

Bicol
• DOT, Regional Center Site, Rawis, Legazpi, tel: 052-482 0712; e-mail: dotr5@globalink.net.ph.

Eastern Visayas
• DOT, G/F, Foundation Plaza Building, Leyte Park Resorts Compound, Magsaysay Boulevard, tel: 053-321 4333; e-mail: dotev@skyinet.net.

Central Visayas
• DOT, G/F, LDM Building, Lapu-Lapu Street, Cebu, tel: 032-254 2811. Airport office, tel: 032-340 8229; e-mail: dotr7@cvis.net.ph.

Western Visayas
• DOT, Western Visayas Tourism Center, Capitol Ground, Bonifacio Drive, Iloilo, tel: 033-337 5411, e-mail: deptour6@iloilo.net.
• Boracay Field Office, Balabag (by Boat Station 2), tel: 036-506 0094.

Southern Mindanao
• DOT, Door No. 7, Magsaysay Park Complex, Sta. Ana District, Davao, tel: 082-221 6955; e-mail: dotr11@philwebinc.com.

Northern Mindanao
• DOT, A. Velez Street, Cagayan de

Oro, tel: 08822-726 394; e-mail: dot10@cdo.weblinq.com.

Caraga
• DOT, D & V Plaza II Building, Butuan, tel: 085-225 5712.

Zamboanga
• DOT, Lantaka Hotel By the Sea, Valderosa Street, Zamboanga City, tel: 062-991 0218; e-mail: dotr9@jetlink.com.ph.

Consulates/Embassies

Australia: 23/F, Tower 2, RCBC Plaza, 6819 Ayala Avenue, Salcedo Village, Makati City, tel: 02-757 8100.
Canada: 6/F, Tower 2, RCBC Plaza, 6819 Ayala Avenue, Salcedo Village, Makati City, tel: 02-857 9000.
China: 2/F, World Center Building, Gil Puyat Avenue, Makati City, tel: 02-844 3148.
European Union Commission: 30/F, RCBC Plaza, Tower 2, Makati City, tel: 02-859 5100, www.delphi.cec.eu.int.
France: 16/F, Pacific Star Building, Sen. Gil Puyat (Buendia) corner Makati Avenue, Makati City, tel: 02-857 6900.
Germany: 25/F, Tower 2, RCBC Plaza, Makati City, tel: 02-702 3000.
Italy: 6/F, Zeta Building, 191 Salcedo Street, Legaspi Village, Makati City, tel: 02-892 4531.
Japan: 2627 Roxas Boulevard, Pasay City, tel: 02-551 5710.
Korea: 10/F, Pacific Star Building, Gil Puyat corner Makati Avenue, Makati City, tel: 02-811 6139.
Malaysia: 107 Tordesillas Street, Salcedo Village, Makati City, tel: 02-817 4581–5.
New Zealand: 23/F, BP1 Buendia Center, Sen. Gil Puyat Avenue (Buendia), Makati City, tel: 02-891 5355.
Singapore: 35/F, Tower One, Enterprise Center, Ayala Avenue, Makati City, tel: 02-751 2345.
Taiwan: 41/F, Tower 1, RCBC Plaza, 6819 Ayala, Makati City, tel: 02-887 6688.
Thailand: 107 Rada Street, Legaspi Village, Makati City, tel: 02-815 4219.
United Kingdom: 17/F, L.V. Locsin

Building, 6752 Ayala Avenue corner Makati Avenue, Makati City, tel: 02-816 7116.
United States: 1201 Roxas Boulevard, Ermita, tel: 02-528 6300.

Women Travelers

Foreign women with any modicum of common sense should experience little trouble traveling independently here. Most Filipinos will be surprised at lone female travelers – theirs is a culture that travels in groups. However, your independence will only increase their admiration. Filipinos are generally friendly and helpful.

Local men enjoy whistling and giving out catcalls. No disrespect is meant. Any response on the woman's part may be seen as an invitation or, more likely, would embarrass the perpetrator.

Life is different here: even seven-year-old girls describe themselves as "sexy" before family and friends – a term synonymous with "beautiful" and just as harmless.

At times, a woman may be inclined to invent a boyfriend she is on her way to meet. Filipina women are wary of traveling alone and may invite themselves to sit next to you on the bus or in the lobby to ward off unwelcome male attention.

Tampons are not easily available outside Manila, so bring your own. The same goes for birth control pills.

Traveling with Kids

Filipinos love children and will be more than happy to accommodate yours. Talking about your family is a good icebreaker in conversation.

A family with young ones can make a day trip to the top of Taal Volcano by either riding or hiking. For indoor entertainment, Megamall Powerplant and Mall of Asia have bowling alleys, ice-skating rinks and video arcades. Here are some other suggestions for Manila and beyond.
Avilon Zoo: Rodriguez (Montalban), Rizal, tel: 02-941 8393; avilonzoo.com.ph. Open daily 8am–5pm with guided tours every hour until 3pm. With over 500

species on display. Entrance fee.
Enchanted Kingdom: San Lorenzo South, Sta Rosa, Laguna, tel: 02-843 6073–8. Open Friday–Sunday, 10am–10pm. An amusement park 30 km south of Makati, off the South Superhighway. Entrance fee.
Manila Zoological and Botanical Gardens: Adriatico corner Quirino Avenue, Malate, tel: 02-523 3014. Open daily 7am–6pm. Visit at 9am or 3pm to watch zookeepers feed the animals. Entrance fee.
Museo Pambata (Children's Museum): Roxas Boulevard corner South Drive, Manila (beside US Embassy), tel: 02-523 1797/98, 400 7558, www.museopambata. org. Open Tuesday–Saturday 8am–12.30pm and 1.30–5pm, Sunday 1–5pm. Hands-on displays. Entrance fee.
National Museum of the Filipino People: Finance Building, Burgos Street, Rizal Park, tel: 02-527 1233. Open Wednesday–Sunday 10am–4.30pm. Hands-on displays – guests can virtually "play" a variety of musical instruments in the ethnographic section. Entrance fee (free on Sunday).
Ocean Adventure: Camayan Wharf, Subic Bay Freeport Zone, Zambales, tel: 047-252 9000; Manila: 02-633 4185 or 638 2282, www.oceanadventure.com.ph. Open daily 9am–6pm. Shows featuring performing dolphins, sea lions and whales (including US$50 photo opportunities with the whales). Entrance fee.
SeaFood Wharf Restaurant: Army-Navy Club Compound, South Drive, Luneta Park, tel: 02-536 3522. With an outdoor swimming pool adjacent to dining area; watch your kids swim while you eat.
Splash Island: Southwoods Ecocentrum, Biñan, Laguna, tel: 02-633 5265 or 414 0171. Open Friday–Sunday 9am–6pm. The country's best-maintained water park. Entrance fee.
Star City: Pasay, next to CCP complex, tel: 02-832 0305, 832 0307. The country's largest amusement park with rides and theaters. Entrance fee.

Disabled Travelers

Despite its every effort, the Philippines remains a Third World country struggling to feed its own people. As a result, wheelchair ramps, despite being an increasingly common sight, are rare. Sidewalks are often crumbling and streets usually pockmarked with potholes.

However, owing to Filipino hospitality and a genuine willingness to help, disabled travelers with a noble amount of patience (and keen sense of adventure) can navigate the city with little difficulty.

For those wanting to see how far vacation options for the handicapped have come in the Philippines, check out www.handidivers.com.

Religious Services

Historically, the Filipinos have embraced two of the world's great religions: Islam and Christianity. The former is mostly confined to the south while the latter has followers all over the country.

Two Filipino independent churches are prominent: Aglipay (Philippine Independent Church) and Iglesia Ni Cristo (Church of Christ), founded in 1902 and 1914 respectively. Iglesia Ni Cristo has a considerable membership of about 5 million worldwide, and its spired chapel buildings are a distinct feature in important towns, provincial capitals and major cities.

It is, however, eclipsed by El Shaddai, a Catholic offshoot led by charismatic developer-turned-preacher, Mariano Velarde, better known as Brother Mike. El Shaddai, claiming a following approximately 10 percent of Filipinos, mixes music and celebrity appearances in its modern Christian celebrations. Brother Mike's services at various open-air grounds in Manila, such as PICC and Quirino Grandstand, on Saturday evenings, attract hundreds of thousands of devoted fans. The event is broadcast on radio and television nationwide.

Most Christian church services are held on Sunday morning and evening, while Friday is the Muslim day of worship. Details of services are available at hotel desks and tourist information centers.

Medical Services

It is advisable to have medical insurance, as payment must usually be guaranteed before treatment. Major Manila hospitals include:
Asian Hospital: Filinvest Corporate Center, Alabang, tel: 02-771 9000.
Cardinal Santos Medical Center: Wilson Street, Greenhills, San Juan, tel: 02-727 0001–46.
Makati Medical Center: 2 Amorsolo corner de la Rosa Street, Makati City, tel: 02-888 8999, 892 5544.
Manila Doctor's Hospital: 667 United Nations Avenue, Ermita, tel: 02-524 3011–77.
Medical Center Manila: 1122 General Luna Street, Ermita, tel: 02-523 8131/65.
Philippine General Hospital: Taft Avenue, Manila, tel: 02-521 8450.
St Luke's Medical Center: 279 Rodriguez Boulevard, Quezon City, tel: 02-723 0301, 723 0101.
In Davao: **Davao Doctors**

Diving Emergencies

It bears repeating that when you dive, dive safely. Go with a buddy and/or guide and stay within the charted area. In a diving emergency, you can contact:
Manila Armed Forces of the Philippines (AFP) Medical Center, V. Luna Rd, Quezon City, Metro Manila. Attention: Sgt. Ricardo Mengua, Senior Recompression Technician. Tel. 02-426 2701 x 6745, cell tel: 0919-572 2676.
Cebu VISCOM Station Hospital, Camp Lapu-Lapu, Lahug, Cebu City. Tel: 032-232 2464, 253 2325.
Coast Guard Action Center. Tel: 02-527 8481 x 6136.
Batangas Dr Mike Perez. Cell tel: 0917-536 2757.
Cavite Philippine Coast Guard Medical Center. Tel: 02-527 8481 x 6321–3.

Hospital, General Malvar Street, tel: 082-222 0850, local tel: 106.
In Cebu: **Chong Hua Hospital**, Fuente Osmeña, tel: 032-253 9409; **Cebu Doctors Hospital**: President Osmeña Boulevard, tel: 032-255 5555.
Mercury Drug is one of the most widely-found pharmacies in Manila; some branches are open 24 hours.
Recently, foreigners have been traveling to Manila to undergo laser eye surgery, which is cheaper here than elsewhere. Standards for eye care clinics here can be remarkably high, but choose carefully.
As far as possible, avoid medical treatment outside of Manila, as many travelers and expatriates have reported unpleasant experiences.

Security & Crime

The Philippines is generally safe for travelers. In many cases, traveling in the provinces is safer than Manila, where petty theft, not violent crime, is the main concern. Keep valuables safe. Always lock car and taxi doors once inside. Wear a money belt under clothing; use safety deposit boxes.
There have been occurrences of kidnapping both in Manila and Mindanao. Taxi drivers can be scam artists; if a driver refuses to start his meter, find another cab. Pretend to know the city better than you do and be wary of anyone who seems overly friendly – lest they catch you offguard and slip a sedative into your drink in order to rob you, a common scam in Manila.
Travelers should be aware of sporadic problems with communist guerillas (NPA – New People's Army) and Muslim separatists like the MILF (Moro Islamic Liberation Front) and the Abu Sayyaf. Ask locals for accurate updates on security issues; people not in the area might over-dramaticize.
Parts of Mindanao remain dubious for foreign travelers, including the remote islands of Sulu and Basilan, where foreigners have been kidnapped. Before traveling to the countryside, check the situation at the embassy.

Getting Around

By Air

Transportation around the archipelago normally originates in the country's hub, Manila. Cebu City is coming into its own as a regional hub for flights going around the Visayas and into Mindanao. Flying is quick and cheap, with domestic airlines spanning much of the archipelago. Domestic flight schedules are in constant flux; contact the airlines directly for the latest update. Don't forget that most airports charge a nominal departure tax of around P50–200.
Philippine Airlines flies from the Centennial Terminal in Manila to Bacolod, Butuan, Cagayan de Oro, Cebu, Cotabato, Davao, Dipolog, General Santos, Iloilo, Kalibo, Laoag, Legaspi, Naga, Puerto Princesa, Roxas, Tacloban, Tagbilaran, Zamboanga. PAL Center, Legaspi Street, Legaspi Village, Makati City. Tel: 02-855 8888; www.philippineair.com.
Air Philippines flies from Manila to Bacolod, Cagayan de Oro, Cebu, Davao, Dumaguete, General Santos, Iloilo, Naga, Puerto Princesa, Tuguegarao and Zamboanga. From its Cebu hub, Air Philippines flies to Bacolod, Davao, General Santos City, Iloilo and Puerto Princesa, and a few flights criss-cross the Visayas and Mindanao between Bacolod, Davao, Iloilo, Puerto Princesa, General Santos City. Padre Fauna Center, Padre Fauna, corner Del Pilar, Manila. Tel: 02-855 9000; www.airphils.com.
Asian Spirit has special flights out of Manila and Cebu, connecting to Baguio, Basco (Batanes), Busuanga, Calbayog, Catarman, Caticlan (gateway to Boracay), Cagayan de Oro, Clark, Cebu, Davao, Masbate,

Pagadian, San Fernando (La Union), San Jose (Mindoro), Siargao, Surigao, Tagbilaran, Tandag, Virac (Marinduque). G4 BSA Towers, 108 Legaspi Street, Legaspi Village, Makati City. Tel: 02-888 2002; www.asianspirit.com.

Cebu Pacific flies frequently to Cebu, Bacolod, Cagayan de Oro, Clark, Cotabato, Davao, Dipolog, Dumaguete, General Santos, Iloilo, Kalibo, Laoag, Legaspi, Puerto Princesa, Roxas, Tacloban, Tagbilaran, Zamboanga. Robinson's Galleria, Level 1, Ortigas Avenue, Pasig City. Tel: 02-702 0888; www.cebupacificair.com.

South East Asian Airlines (SEAIR) flies to Baler, Basco, Busuanga, Butuan, Camiguin, Cebu, Angeles, Caticlan, Cotabato, Cuyo, El Nido, Jolo, Puerto Princesa, Sandoval (Palawan), Tawi, Zamboanga. 2/F, Doña Concepcion Building, Arnaiz Avenue, Makati City. Tel: 02-884 1521; www.flyseair.com.

Water Transport

Inter-island boat travel was once uncomfortable and not very safe.

Thankfully transport companies have effectively addressed these issues in recent years. They now offer comfortable cabins and a range of travel options suited to all budgets. Travel may take a little longer, but this mode of transport is rewarding: some of the ports have hardly changed in decades. Tickets on major sectors (e.g. Manila–Cebu) can be booked through travel agencies. Check websites for special discounts, package tours and e-ticket bookings.

Negros Navigation's ports of call include Bacolod, Cagayan de Oro, Coron, Dipolog, Dumaguete, Dumaguit (Kalibo), Estancia, General Santos, Iligan, Iloilo, Manila, Ozamiz, Puerto Princesa, Roxas, and Tagbilaran. Pier 2, North Harbor, Manila, tel: 02-245 5588; www.negrosnavigation.ph.

Sulpicio Lines sails to Baybay (Leyte), Cebu, Cotabato, Davao, Dumaguete, Iligan, Iloilo, Maasin, Masbate, Ormoc, Ozamis, Surigao, Tacloban, Zamboanga, General Santos City. 415 San Fernando, Binondo, tel: 02-241 9701. Pier 12, Manila, tel: 02-245 0616.

WG&A SuperFerry sails to Bacolod, Cagayan de Oro, Cebu, Coron, Cotabato, Davao, Dipolog, Dumaguete, Dumaguit, General Santos City, Iligan, Ozamis, Puerto Princesa, Surigao, Tagbilaran, Zamboanga. 12/F, Times Plaza, U.N. Avenue, Manila, tel: 02-528 7000; www.superferry.com.ph.

In the Visayas, several companies ply routes between the islands, in all manner of craft from *bancas* to fast cats. In Cebu, get hold of *The Freeman* newspaper (tel: 032-255 4263) for listings and schedules of routes around Panay, Negros, Cebu, Bohol, Leyte and Mindanao.

By Bus

The areas surrounding Manila and provincial capitals are relatively well serviced by a reasonably good network of roads. Potholes are a feature and traffic moves at a snail's pace – especially through cities. Dozens of bus companies operate services to the main tourist centers and fares are low: the 6.5-hour journey from Manila to Baguio costs around P350 on air-conditioned

Traveling Distances and Time from Manila

Although the distances listed here seem short, roads are often rough, and traffic severe.

Here are some approximations of distance and time to the following places from Manila, unless otherwise stated:

Alaminos, Laguna 78 km (2 hr)
Alaminos, Pangasinan
254 km (4–5 hr)
Angeles City Pampanga 83 km (2–3 hr)
Antipolo, Rizal
29 km (1 hr from Ortigas; 1.5 hr from Makati)
Baguio City, Benguet
246 km (6.5 hr by bus; 5 hr by car)
Baler, Aurora 231 km
Banaue, Ifugao 348 km
(12 hr by bus; 9 hr by car)
Batangas City, Batangas 111 km
Bontoc, Mountain Province 394 km

Cabanatuan City, Nueva Ecija
115 km
Capas, Tarlac 106 km
Cavite City, Cavite 34 km (1–2 hr)
Clark Field, Pampanga
88 km (2–3 hr)
Currimao, Ilocos Norte 464 km
Dagupan City, Pangasinan 216 km
Gen. Luna, Quezon 239 km
Iba, Zambales 210 km (5–6 hr)
Iriga City, Camarines Sur 487 km
Kawit, Cavite 23 km (1–1.5 hr)
Laoag City, Ilocos Norte
487 km (12 hr)
Legaspi City, Albay
550 km (10–12 hr)
Lipa City, Batangas 84 km (2–3 hr)
Los Baños, Laguna 62 km (1–2 hr)
Lucena City, Quezon
136 km (3 hr)
Naga City, Camarines Sur
449 km
Olongapo City, Zambales
126 km (4–5 hr)

Pagsanjan, Laguna
101 km (2–2.5 hr)
Pagudpud, Ilocos Norte 561 km
Pulilan, Bulacan 45 km (2–3 hr)
Rizal, Laguna 97 km
San Fernando La Union
269 km (6 hr by bus; 5 hr by car)
San Fernando Pampanga
66 km (2–3 hr)
San Jose City Nueva Ecija 161 km
San Juan, La Union
278 km (5.5–6 hr)
San Pablo City, Laguna 87 km
Sariaya, Quezon 124 km
Sorsogon, Sorsogon 604 km
Subic, Zambales 138 km (4–5 hr)
Taal, Batangas 130 km (3 hr)
Tagaytay City, Cavite
56 km (1.5–2 hr)
Tarlac, Tarlac 125 km
Trece Martires, Cavite 46 km
Tuguegarao, Cagayan 483 km
Vigan, Ilocos Sur 407 km (12 hr)

Hotlines

Police/Fire/Medical Emergency: 117
Police Headquarters (24 hours): 723 0401. Camp Crame, EDSA, Metro Manila
Manila Police: 523 3378
Makati Police: 899 9014
Pasay City Police: 831 1544
Quezon City Police: 921 5267
Tourist police assistance (24 hours): 524 1660, 524 1728
Tourist information: 524 2384, 525 2000

buses. (The temperature in these buses tend to be very low; it is best to take a light jacket along.) Long-distance buses make frequent stops at rest stops along the way, which offer snacks and "comfort rooms" (toilets), usually requesting a donation of P2 for their upkeep.
Autobus goes to Banaue, Cagayan Valley and Ilocos, tel: 02-735 8098.
Baliwag Transit goes to Bulacan, Nueva Ecija, Isabella, Cagayan Valley and Pampanga, tel: 02-912 3343.
Batangas Laguna Tayabas Bus Co (BLTB) goes to Batangas, Calamba, Iriga, Legaspi, Lipa, Los Banos, Lucena, Naga, Nasugbu, Ormoc, Tacloban, Calatagan, Tagaytay and Sta.Cruz, tel: 02-913 1525.
Dangwa Trans Co. goes to Baguio and Tabuk (Kalinga), tel: 02-731 2879.
Farinas Transit goes to Angeles, Vigan and Laoag, tel: 02-743 8582.
Maria de Leon Transit goes to Angeles, San Fernando La Union, Vigan and Laoag, tel: 02-731 4907.
Dominion Bus Lines goes to San Fernando La Union, Vigan and Abra, tel: 02-741 4146.
Victory Liner (www.victoryliner.com)

goes to Baguio, Bolinao, Cagayan Valley, Dagupan, Dau (Angeles) and Olongapo from its Cubao Terminal, tel: 02-727 4688. From its Pasay Terminal, tel: 02-833 5019–20, it offers routes to Olongopo, Tuguegarao and Baguio.

By Train

Train travel is only for the very brave with lots of time to spare. Manila's sole line runs from Tutuban Station in Tondo south to Legaspi City. The train is slow and costs the same as a bus. It is not recommended.

Public Transport

In Manila

Grouses of travel by public transportation are slow city traffic, and hot and crowded conditions in the vehicles. In Metro Manila, non-air-conditioned bus and jeepney rates start at P7. For air-conditioned buses, the rate starts at P9. The best strategy for figuring out the cost to your destination is to just ask the conductor or your fellow passengers.

The jeepney is the Philippines' most colorful mode of transport, originally constructed from American jeeps left behind after World War II. Routes are fixed.

Air-conditioned buses ply major thoroughfares such as EDSA, Ayala Avenue, Sen. Gil Puyat Avenue, Taft Avenue and the South and North expressways. Air-conditioned bus terminals are located in Escolta, in Binondo, Manila, Ayala Center (Makati) and in Cubao, Quezon City.

Motorcycles with side cars, called tricycles, may be available for short trips on the smaller streets. In many destinations, such as Boracay or Coron Town, they are the only form

of transportation. Ask the locals for a guide to how much to pay.

Manila's elevated rail system consists of two Light Rail Transit lines: LRT1 (yellow line) and LRT2 (purple line), and the Metro Rail Transit line: MRT3 (blue line). The oldest and most crowded of the light rail systems is the LRT1, which runs along Taft and Rizal avenues between Baclaran (near the airport) and Monumento, providing access to many of Manila's historical attractions. The newest of Manila's light rail systems, the LRT2, has 11 stops running east-west along Aurora Avenue from Recto to M.A. Roxas in Marakina, meeting the LRT1 by Doroteo Jose Station, and the MRT3 at Cubao (Aurora) Station. Finally, the MRT3 runs from Taft Avenue along EDSA till North Avenue in Quezon City. The final gap from North Avenue to link with the LRT1 station in Monumento is being constructed.

Private Car

Getting out of Manila by car can be a problem. Traffic is usually a tremendous snarl – this cannot be emphasized enough. In particular, avoid leaving Manila via the North and South expressways on Fridays, when everyone escapes the city. Conversely, avoid returning to Manila on Sunday evenings. It is often easier to fly out or to take a ferry.

Cars may be rented without a driver, but opting for a driver is highly recommended in the Philippines. Even if you know your way around town and can run red lights with the best of the jeepney drivers, parking is a nightmare. If you must drive, make sure you have a valid foreign and/or international driver's license.

Filipino Drivers Play the Numbers Game

Driving in Manila comes with its set of changing rules and responsibilities. As a result, most visitors avail of the services of a driver. Owing to government efforts to reduce traffic congestion, a system inaccurately, but popularly

known as "color coding" is in place. Rental cars, however, are exempt from this sceme.

The last digit on the car's license plate number determines your day off the road. The number system is in effect from 7am to 7pm, and is

strictly enforced. In every city in Manila except Makati, a "window" on your prohibited day from 10am to 3pm exists where your car can be driven. Ask someone who drives locally what new scheme is in place at the time of your visit.

Driving in the Philippines is very different from the rest of the world. Here, stopping at red lights is optional, though a traffic policeman directing traffic has to be obeyed. Most common offenses warranting pulling over are driving on a day your car is banned *(see page 356)*, and an unbuckled seat belt for the driver and/or passenger. This applies to both private vehicles and taxis. However, a few policemen, known as *buwayas* ("crocodiles"), might pull a driver over on a spurious charge and then demand a bribe. It is better to firmly yet respectfully bargain down and pay the bribe than it is to threaten to report him, which could escalate the situation.

CAR RENTAL

Budget has offices in NAIA, the Peninsula Manila, and Subic Bay. In Manila, tel: 02-776 8118–20; www.budget.com.
Dollar Rent-A-Car has rental stations at NAIA and New World Hotel in Manila, tel: 02-528 5892; www.dollar.com.
Safari Rent-a-Car, 1839 Eureka Street, La Paz Village, Makati City, offers vehicles with or without drivers at competitive prices, tel: 02-890 3606; www.safarirentacarinc.com.
Hertz Rent-A-Car, NAIA Arrival Main Lobby, tel: 02-896 1505. Makati City: G/F, El Rico Suites, 1048 Metropolitan Avenue, tel: 02-896 1505; www.hertz.com.
National Car Rental has offices in Manila (NAIA Arrival Lobby, tel: 02-833 0648; 38 Timog Avenue, Quezon City, tel: 02-374 3151; and 5032 P. Burgos Street, Makati City, tel: 02-818 8667) and Baguio City (Room 213, Laperal Building, Session Road, tel: 074-442 6381); www.nationalcar.com.

Tour Operators

For official tour operators and guides registered with the Department of Tourism (DOT), call 02-524 1703. Over 60 tour operators are listed in the Directory of Philippine Tour Operators, all of whom are members of the Philippine Tour Operators Association.
Banca Safaris operates boat tours to some of the farthest corners of the country such as Batanes, Palawan and Mindanao. Tours are organized by a team of top local authors and photographers. Cell tel: 0920-387 5837; www.bancasafaris.com.
Chico River Quest, Inc. specializes in rafting trips in Kalinga and around the country that emphasize on self-sustainability for the Kalinga people. Cell tel: 0917-966 8081; www.chicoriverquest.com.
Freeport Service Corporation runs tours to Subic Bay – the former military base itself – incorporating jungle treks and the survival skills of native Aeta people. 2/F, Building H8211 Burgos Street, Causeway Rd, Subic Bay Freeport Zone, tel: 047-252 2313–5; e-mail: fsc@svisp.com.
Tribal Adventure Tours leads trips true to its name, from rafting on the Chico River in the Cordillera to climbing new routes up Mt Pinatubo. Tel: 02-821 6706; www.tribaladventures.com.
Bataan Tours runs tours throughout Bataan and to Corregidor island. De Guzman Bldg, Saint Joseph Street, Poblacion (near Max's), Balanga City, Bataan. Cell tel: 0917-697 7671, 047-237 1877; e-mail: bataantravel@hotmail.com.
Eagle Ferry Cruises, Bldg. 8429 San Bernadino Road, Subic Bay Metropolitan Authority. Tel: 047-252 8505 ext. 7038. Reservations cell tel: 0919-864 7675 or 0919-425 481. Trips to Corregidor, Manila and Grande Island from Subic Bay, as well as day trips and fishing charters.

Where to Stay

Hotels

The Philippines offers a wide range of accommodation for every budget, from beach resorts and pensions to luxury hotels.
The capital city offers numerous deluxe hotels. "Tourist belt" hotels along Roxas Boulevard and in Malate–Ermita are convenient for conventions, while business travelers wind up in Makati City or Ortigas. Most Manila hotels offer full business facilities.

Price Guide

The following price categories indicate the cost of a standard double room per night:
$$$$$: US$200 and up
$$$$: US$100–200
$$$: US$50–100
$$: US$20–50
$: US$5–20

Rates quoted below are "rack rates." Hotels offer a multitude of different rates, from Internet rates, to walk-in and local resident rates. Promotions are also frequently offered, so always request the cheapest rates.

METRO MANILA

$$$$$
Ascott Makati
6F Glorietta 4, Ayala Center, Makati City
Tel: 02-729 8888
www.the-ascott.com
Set in the heart of the Makati CBD, the Ascott Makati offers some of the best amenities and services in the serviced apartment category.

The rooms are huge and equipped with washing machines and dryers, furnished kitchens and entertainment centers. Other amenities include a spa, salon, pool and tennis courts. Guests are provided butler service.

EDSA Shangri-La Hotel
1 Garden Way, Ortigas Center, Pasig City
Tel: 02-633 8888
www.shangri-la.com
True Shangri-La style; close to ADB, Megamall. Tennis, fitness center, pool. Italian and Chinese dining, popular for business lunches.

Hyatt Hotel and Casino Manila
Pedro Gil corner M.H. Del Pilar, Malate
Tel: 02-245 1234
manila.casino.hyatt.com
The most Zen of Manila's luxury hotels, the Hyatt caters to everyone, from those who seek superb business facilities to casino affionados to other Hyatt loyalists. Impressive array of lounges, restaurants and amenities done in impeccable décor.

Makati Shangri-La Hotel
Ayala Avenue corner Makati Avenue, Makati City
Tel: 02-813 8888
www.shangri-la.com
Among Manila's finest hotels. Outstanding service. Fine Japanese, Filipino, Chinese, French dining. Live jazz music. Tennis, gym, swimming pool.

Mandarin Oriental Manila
Makati Avenue corner Paseo de Roxas, Makati City
Tel: 02-750 8888
www.mandarinoriental.com/manila
The Philippine's Best Business Hotel for five years running. High-class but warm service. Wi-Fi, gym, beautiful pool and a luxurious spa. Excellent restaurants and a brand-new Martini Bar expansion.

The Manila Hotel
One Rizal Park, Roxas Boulevard, Manila
Tel: 02-527 0011
www.manila-hotel.com.ph
This legendary hotel will appeal to history buffs. One of the oldest buildings standing, it has even hosted General Douglas MacArthur.

(If money is no issue, book the MacArthur suite.) The amenities and restaurants are top notch and charming, and a stay here helps one understand the history of Manila, a city that lost much in the fires of World War II.

$$$$

Discovery Suites Ortigas
25 ADB Avenue, Ortigas Center, Pasig City
Tel: 02-683 8222
www.discoverysuites.com
This offers the optimal location for Ortigas-based business travelers, with the CBD spread out right below. Some of the best malls in the city are also in the vicinity. The amenities and services are deluxe, from the business services to the luxurious breakfast buffet on the 22nd floor overlooking the city, to the lounge and conference rooms.

Dusit Hotel
Nikko, Ayala Center, Makati City
Tel: 02-867 3333
www.dusit.com
A stately hotel in the heart of Makati with large rooms. Full business services and landscaped gardens on the premises for peaceful wandering in the midst of the city, near the Glorietta mall complex.

The Heritage Hotel Manila
Roxas Boulevard corner EDSAN Pasay City
Tel: 02-854 8888
www.heritagemanila.com
Conveniently located, mainly Japanese clientele. Gym, pool, casino, Cantonese restaurant, sushi bar.

Hyatt Regency Manila
2702 Roxas Boulevard, Pasay City
Tel: 02-833 1234
www.hyatt.com
Excellent value for money. Surprisingly stylish tourist hotel, has most spacious rooms in the area. Fitness center, pool. Japanese, Italian restaurants.

Manila Diamond Hotel
Roxas Boulevard corner Dr J. Quintos Street, Manila
Tel: 02-526 2211
www.diamondhotel.com
Japanese-owned business hotel. Neutral earth tones, dark woods, bay

view. Japanese, continental dining. Lobby lounge with fountains, lush garden. Fitness center, pool, tennis.

New World Renaissance Hotel
Esperanza Street corner Makati Avenue, Makati City
Tel: 02-811 6888
www.renaissancehotels.com
Good value – four-star hotel with five-star perks. Large rooms in neutral tones. Fitness center. Continental, Chinese cuisines.

The Pan Pacific Manila
Adriatico corner General Malvar Street, Malate
Tel: 02-536 0788
www.panpacific.com
Located close to the World Trade Center, this offers sleek, contemporary-style rooms, with butler service for all guests. All rooms come with bay views while the top-floor Pacific Lounge provide the best city vistas. There is a fitness center, swimming pool as well as several restaurants in Adriatico Square.

Sofitel Philippine Plaza
CCP Complex, Roxas Boulevard, Pasay City
Tel: 02-551 5555
www.sofitel-asia.com
With cozy rooms that overlook Manila Bay and Intramuros. Outdoor pool in tropical setting. Excellent gym, tennis, driving range. Several restaurants in garden setting.

$$$

Atrium Manila Hotel
Taft Avenue corner Gil Puyat, Pasay City
Tel: 02-552 0351
www.atriumhotel-manila.com
Newish boutique hotel. Music lounge, café, business center. Right next to a LRT station.

Bayview Park Hotel
1118 Roxas Boulevard corner UN Avenue, Malate
Tel: 02-526 1555
www.bayviewparkhotel-manila.com
Good-value business hotel dating from 1960s, located opposite the US Embassy. Higher rooms have great bay views. Gym, pool, café, bars.

Hotel Intramuros de Manila
Plaza San Luis, General Luna Street, Intramuros
Tel: 02-524 6730

Small, cozy rooms in courtyard style.

Hotel Rembrandt
26 Tomas Morato Extension,
Quezon City
Tel: 02-373 3333 x 105
www.hotelrembrandt.com.ph
Caters to Japanese businessmen.
Gym, spa, piano bar, café,
penthouse suites, restaurant.

Manila Pavilion Hotel
United Nations Avenue corner
Orosa Street, Ermita
Tel: 02-526 1212
www.manilapavilion.com.ph
Rooms overlook Rizal Park or Club
Intramuros; earthy tones, attentive
service, many repeat customers.
Gym, pool, casino, spa, Chinese
restaurant.

Makati Prime Tower
Kalayaan Avenue corner Mercade
Street, Makati
Tel: 02-750 3010
makatiprimetower.com.ph
Pleasant business hotel near red-
light Burgos Street district. Fully
furnished condotel with a salon,
spa, indoor pool, wine shop and
Internet café.

Millennium Plaza Hotel Makati
Makati Avenue corner Eduque
Street, Makati
Tel: 02-899 4718
www.millenniumplaza.com.ph
Business hotel. Rooms with
kitchenettes available. Pool,
restaurant.

New Horizon Hotel Mandaluyong
778 Boni Avenue, Mandaluyong
Tel: 02-532 3021
www.newhorizonhotel-manila.com
This Mediterranean-inspired hotel is
conveniently located on EDSA.
Offers complimentary Wi-Fi, a gym
and a European-cuisine restaurant.

The Richmonde Hotel
21 San Miguel Avenue, Ortigas
Tel: 02-638 7777
www.richmondehotel.com
Boutique hotel, close to ADB and
Megamall. Fitness center, pool.

Tower Inn
1002 Arnaiz Avenue, Makati
Tel: 02-888 5170, 843 3325
www.towerinn.com.ph
Centrally located in the Makati CBD,
this four-story hotel caters mainly to
businessmen, with function rooms
and meeting areas.

$$

Aloha Hotel
2150 Roxas Boulevard, Malate
Tel: 02-526 8088
Budget rooms. Bayside rooms,
along Roxas Boulevard, can get a
little noisy. Chinese, Japanese,
Korean restaurants.

Malate Pensionne
1771 Adriatico Street, Malate
Tel: 02-523 8304
www.malatepensionne.com
Pleasant pension with antique
furniture, restaurant. A classic
backpackers' haunt with a fresh
facelift. Great location for fun.

Paco Park Oasis Hotel
1032–34 Belen Street, Paco, Manila
Tel: 02-521 2371–4
www.parkhotel.com.ph
Dedicated tourist hotel, motel-style
rooms open to central patio and
pool. No elevator. Popular for its
convenient location.

Pension Natividad
1690 M.H. del Pilar Street, Malate
Tel: 02-521 0524
Clean, well-kept and tucked away
from Malate's bustle. Antique
furniture, restaurant. Simple but
charming.

Ralph Anthony Suites
Maria Orosa corner Engracia Reyes
Street, Manila
Tel: 02-521 1107
www.ralphanthonysuites.com
Small friendly hotel a short walk
from the Robinson's Place shopping
mall in Ermita.

MANILA'S ENVIRONS

Cavite
Island Cove Resort & Leisure Park
Binakayan, Kawit
Tel: 046-434 0210
Manila tel: 02-810 3740, 810 3728
www.islandcovephil.com
Weekend getaway, swimming pools,
boating, fishing, mini-golf, basketball,
volleyball, tennis. $$$–$$$$

Corregidor Hotel
Corregidor Island
Tel: 02-831 8140
e-mail: suncruises@magsaysay.com.ph
Incomparable surroundings. There
are cozy rooms, dark wood décor, a
swimming pool, and a restaurant.

Package includes ferry to Corregidor
Island. $$$

Days Hotel Tagaytay
Aguinaldo Highway, Silang Crossing,
Tagaytay City
Tel: 046-413 2400
e-mail: daystag@arcon.com.ph
Part of the popular American hotel
chain with surprising luxurious
rooms for a moderately priced
hotel. Outdoor pool. $$$

Taal Vista Hotel
Km 60 Aguinaldo Highway,
Tagaytay City
Tel: 046-413 1000
Manila tel: 02-886 4325
www.taalvistahotel.com
Clean rooms overlooking Lake Taal.
Casino, dance performance, nightly
entertainment, Filipino restaurant,
pool. Volcano treks. $$$

Dive Resorts in Anilao, Batangas
Anilao is not known for its beaches,
but rather for offering some of the
Philippines' best diving,
conveniently located a few hours'
drive south of Manila. Try some of
the following resorts:

Bonito Island
c/o Ms Bessie Vasquez
Tel: 02-812 2292
Beautiful private island resort in
Mabini and Batangas. Excellent
diving and snorkeling, amazing
corals. $$–$$$

Vistamar Beach Resort Hotel
Anilao, Mabini
Tel: 02-821 8332
www.vistamaronline.com
Clean, simple rooms. A wide range
of activities including diving,
windsurfing and volleyball. $$

Batangas
Matabungkay Beach Resort
Matabungkay Beach, Lian Town
Tel: 02-819 3080
www.matabungkay.net
Simple, clean rooms. Excellent
European, Japanese cuisines.
Beautiful pool and view, small
beach, limited diving scheduled.
Hash runs from time to time. $$$

Coral Beach Club
Matabungkay Beach, Lian Town
Cell tel: 0917-901 4635
www.coralbeach.ph
Simple beach resort with air-

conditioned rooms with cable TV.
Offers PADI scuba diving lessons. **$$**
Sanctuary Spa at Maya-Maya
Nasugbu, Batangas
Cell tel: 0918-909 7170/909 7167
www.mayamaya.com
With 14 charming Filipino-style
cottages and the Sanctuary Spa
with its comprehensive menu of
scrubs, massages and treatments.
Other amenities include an alfresco
restaurant and bar, the Maya Maya
Yacht Club and Marina, a pool,
recreation areas, Wi-Fi Internet
access, as well as PADI scuba
lessons. **$$**

Laguna
Hidden Valley Springs
Alamiños, Laguna
Tel: 02-840 4112–4
One of the more intriguing resorts
in the country, nestled at the foot of
Mt Makiling, a dormant volcano that
still heats the hot springs in the
area. These are complemented by
cold springs and giant fruit trees
and a primitive forest. The resort is
a bit expensive, but the secluded
setting is worth the price. **$$$$**
Pagsanjan Rapids Hotel
Gen. Taiño Street, Pagsanjan
Tel: 049-808 4258
Simple, clean, carpeted rooms
overlooking Bumbugan River.
Massage, pool. **$$**
La Vista Pansol Resort Complex
Brgy Pansol, Calamba
Tel: 049-545 1850, 244 3645
Simple buildings; water slide, natural
warm springs, tennis, mini-golf, view
of Laguna de Bay, pool closed
Monday. Crowded on weekends. **$**

Quezon
Cote D'Azur Beach Resort
Barangay Abiawin, Infanta
Tel: 042-535 3047
Manila tel: 02-948 7701
www.cotedazurbeachresort.com
Set in a wonderfully rugged part of
the Philippines, 4 km (2½ mile)
from the town center, this resort
has air-conditioned rooms and
bungalows, and a luxurious free-
form swimming pool. **$$**
**Villa Escudero Plantations and
Resort**
San Pablo City

Manila Tel: 02-523 0392
www.villaescudero.com
Good day trip. Slide pools, bamboo
rafts, *carabao* carts, museum. Enjoy
lunch at waterfalls. Native cottages,
some on lakefront. **$$$–$$$$**

Rizal
Seven Suites Hotel – Observatory
Sumulong Highway, Antipolo
Tel: 02-682 0330
www.cravingsgroup.com/seven
Near Valley Golf along Sumulong
Highway. Seven cozy, romantic rooms
overlooking Manila city lights. Pool,
roof-deck lounge, Italian and Asian
cuisines, bar. Request a discount
when booking in advance. **$$$**

CENTRAL PLAINS

Pampanga
Holiday Inn Clark
Mimosa Leisure Estate, Clark Field
Manila tel: 02-845 1888
www.ichotelsgroup.com
Plush accommodation on sprawling
grounds of Mimosa. Golf course,
driving range, casino nearby.
Selection of restaurants. Beautiful
pool. **$$$$**
Oasis Hotel
Clarkville Compound, Balibago,
Angeles City
Tel: 045-625 8301–4
www.oasishotel.com.ph
Bright rooms with wicker
furnishings. Pool, restaurant,
convenient location. **$$–$$$**
The Swagman Narra Hotel
S.L. Orosa Street, Diamond
Subdivision Balibago, Angeles City
Tel: 045-322 5133
www.angelescity.info
Established over 40 years ago, the
Swagman is a very tourist-friendly
establishment with a number of
services for guests, such as a hotel
tricycle for bar hopping and daily
van shuttles to Manila. There's a
great pool, spa, business facilities
and restaurants. **$$**

Tarlac
La Maja Rica Hotel
MacArthur Highway corner Ligtasan
Street, Tarlac City
Tel: 045-611 2053–7

www.lamajaricahotel.net
A convenient stop to break up long
drives up north. With 40
guestrooms, 20 drive-in units, a
pool, several dining facilities, and
amenities for functions and
business travelers. **$$**

Bataan
Montemar Beach Club
Bagac, Bataan
Tel: 02-892 6497, 811 5496
www.montemarbeach.com
Mediterranean-inspired rooms amid
an area where mountains meet
sand and sea. Kayaking, pool,
restaurants. **$$$**

Zambales
Legenda Hotel
Waterfront Road, Subic Bay,
Olongapo City
Tel: 047-252 1888
Manila tel: 02-732 9888
www.subiclegend.com
Best value for location. Plush
business-style hotel with a casino.
Spacious rooms with handmade
Filipino furniture. Pool, health club,
restaurants, disco, karaoke. **$$$$**
White Rock Beach Resort Hotel
Matain, Subic Bay
Tel: 047-222 2378, 232 2857
Manila tel: 02-421 2781
www.whiterock.com.ph
Great place to park the family, with
enough leisure and active options
for everyone, from golf to bowling to
water sports. All set on the idyllic
Subic Bay. **$$$$**
Crown Peak Gardens
Upper Cubi, Subic Bay, Olongapo City
Tel: 047-252 3144
Sprawling hotel complex, swimming
pool, former marine barracks.
Restaurants. **$$$**
By The Sea Resort Olongapo
99 National Highway, Barretto,
Subic Bay, Olongapo City
Tel: 047-222 2888, 224 2494
www.bythesea.com.ph
Ample amenities for families,
business travelers or groups,
including conference rooms,
restaurants and water sports.
Expansive seaside lawns, plus
private beach and picnic huts, and
a comfortable bar offers live music
on some evenings. **$$**

Mango's Bayview Apartelles
116 Beach Boulevard, Barretto,
Olongapo City
Tel: 047-223 4139
www.mangossubic.com
Tastefully decorated apartments
overlooking Subic Bay with big
remote-controlled televisions and
air conditioning. Available daily,
weekly or monthly. **$$**

Zoobic Lodge
Tiara (Crown Peak), Subic Bay
Freeport Zone
Tel: 047-252 2272
www.zoobic.com.ph
A collaborative project of the
Residence Inn and the Subic Bay
Metropolitan Authority (SBMA). A
stay at the Zoobic Lodge can be
incorporated into a visit to the wildly
popular Zoobic Safari, which is the
only tiger safari in the country. The
lodge is affordably priced and, not
surprisingly, safari-inspired. **$$**

ILOCOS

Hundred Islands, Pangasinan
Puerto Del Sol Beach Resort
Barangay Ilog Malino, Bolinao
Manila tel: 02-637 8963,
www.puertodelsol.com.ph
A boutique resort with clusters of
tastefully designed massage
gazebos by a stunning pool. It has a
creative activity menu, including a
Hundred Island tour with options for
island hopping and snorkeling. **$$$$**

SCL Garden Paradise Resort
Barangay Ilog Malino, Bolinao
Manila tel: 02-536 1744
Cell tel: 0921-411 7938
www.sclgardenresort.com
Among the best of a string of new
resorts along the coast in Cape
Bolinao. Ask for the table in the
treehouse for an interesting dining
experience. **$$**

100 Islands Pensionne House
Lucap, Alaminos
Tel: 075-551 2505
Simple backpacker-style lodgings in
front of where the boats to Hundred
Islands depart in the morning. **$–$$**

Maxine by the Sea
Lucap, Alaminos
Tel: 075-551 2537
Simple, clean air-conditioned and

fan-cooled rooms, but with no hot
water. Seafood restaurant. **$**

La Union
Bali Hai Beach Resort
Paringao, Bauang
Tel: 072-242 5679
www.balihai.com.ph
Private aircon cabins in tropical
garden setting. Pool, 24-hr bar,
German, Indonesian cuisines. **$$**

San Juan Surf Resort
238 Brgy Urbiztondo, San Juan
Tel: 072-720 0340
www.sanjuansurfresort.com
Stylish native cottages with
mosquito nets. Restaurant, surfing,
board rentals, hiking, Internet.
Reservations recommended. Waves
best July–February. Hash runs on
Saturday. **$$**

Cabaña Beach Resort
Paringao, Bauang
Tel: 072-242 5585
www.sflu.com/cabana
Private *nipa* huts along beachfront.
Pool, bar. Filipino, Chinese,
American cuisines. **$**

Ilocos Sur
Cordillera Inn
M. Crisologo Street corner Gen.
Luna, Vigan
Tel: 077-722 2727/39
Clean, simple rooms in traditional
house. All rooms are air-conditioned
and come with cable TV. **$$**

R.F. Aniceto Mansion
1 Mena Crisologo Street, Vigan
Tel: 077-722 2383
Fax: 077-722 2384
Traditional Spanish-style house
turned hotel. Much character.
Aircon rooms, no TV. **$$**

The Golden Pine
Corner Carino and Legarda streets,
Baguio City
Tel: 074-444 9965
e-mail: goldenpinehotel@skyinet.net
Well-situated full-service hotel. With a
restaurant and business center. **$$**

Grandpa's Inn
1 Bonifacio Street corner Quirino
Boulevard, Vigan
Tel: 077-722 2118
Fax: 077-722 1446
A well-loved ancestral home.
Gorgeous carvings. Good
restaurant. **$**

Ilocos Norte
Fort Ilocandia Resort & Casino
Barrio Caylayab, Laoag City
Tel: 077-772 1166–70
www.fortilocandia.com.ph
Close to Laoag Airport. Spanish-
inspired architecture coupled with
elegant rooms and service. Golf
course, massive pool, beach,
tennis. **$$$$**

Saud Beach Resort
Saud, Pagudpud
Tel: 077-764 1005
Manila tel: 02-921 2856
www.saudbeachresort.com
Relaxing beach resort. Swimming
beach, karaoke, restaurant. **$$$**

Palazzo de Laoag Hotel
27 Paterno Street, Laoag City
Tel: 077-773 1842
www.palazzodelaoaghotel.com
A comfortable hotel situated in the
heart of town. Swimming pool. **$$**

Hotel Tiffany
Gen. Segundo Ave corner M.H. del
Pilar, Laoag
Tel: 077-770 3550
Fax: 077-771 4360
Near sinking bell tower. Whimsically
decorated in pastels. **$**

BATANES

Pensionne Ivatan
Cell tel: 0921-442 8841
Has a view deck on a hill facing the
South China Sea and the town of
Basco. This is the closest lodging to
the airport, with a variety of rooms.
$–$$

Shanedel's Inn and Cafe
Cell tel: 0920-447 0737
Nestled in the center of Basco,
which is quite an endearing town to
spend the night in. Family owned

Batanes Islands

Life in the Batanes Islands
moves slowly. Travel is dependent
on the weather; cancellations and
changes of plans are inevitable,
although the weather is actually
quite lovely most of the time.
Outside Basco, it's best to stay
with the town mayor or school
principal. www.batanesonline.com

and operated. Good views of the ocean and hearty meals. **$–$$**

Batanes Resort
Cell tel: 0918-273 6964
A nice 2-km (1-mile) walk from Basco town proper, this resort offers eight maroon-roofed cottages, beautiful views of the hills, sea and sunrises over Mt Iraya. **$**

Batanes Seaside Lodge and Restaurant
Cell tel: 0981-993 613
At the end of Basco right off the national road, this is one of the newest resorts in the province with 13 charming rooms tucked into a nice pocket cove poised to catch the sun, waves and wind. Restaurant and vehicle rental. **$**

CAGAYAN

Cagayan
Hotel Lorita
67 Rizal Street, Tuguegarao City
Tel: 078-844 1390
Fax: 078-846 2179
Simple, comfortable rooms with cable TV and hot water. Beside the Capitol and the Tuguegarao Church. **$$**

Hotel Roma
Luna corner Bonifacio Street, Tuguegarao City
Tel: 078-844 1057
Fax: 078-844 7678
Hotel with spacious rooms and one of the best coffee shops in town. **$$**

Callao Cave Resort
Peñablanca
Tel: 078-844 1057
Fax: 078-844 7658
A stone's throw from the cave, with basic facilities. The resort can arrange for caving guides. **$**

Ivory Hotel and Convention Center
Buntun Highway, Tuguegarao
Tel: 078-844 1275
Fax: 078-846 2179
Modest rooms, hot shower, pool, restaurant and phone. Lobby garden sets the homey tone. **$**

Isabela
Carig Plaza Hotel
Mabini, Santiago City
Tel: 078-682 7143
Santiago's biggest hotel. Lush

garden, aircon, cable TV, hot showers, phone, restaurant, mini golf. **$**

King George Hotel
Bonifacio Avenue, Victory Norte, Santiago
Tel: 078-682 8434, 682 8743
Monolithic building. Aircon, hot showers, cable TV. Ballroom, restaurant. Fast service. **$**

Quirino
Aglipay Caves and Campsite
Villa Ventura, Aglipay
Tel: 078-692 5088
Overnight cottages, budget dormitories. Pool, children's park, picnic sheds. Accessible to Aglipay's 37 caves. **$**

Nueva Vizcaya
Saber Inn & Restaurant
National Highway, Bayombong
Tel: 078-321 2222
Air-conditioned rooms, pool and restaurant. **$–$$**

Governor's Garden Hotel
Manzano Street, Solano
Tel: 078-326 5166, 326 5200
Gardens and big pool compensate for hotel's peeling paint. Nueva Vizcaya's largest, voted annually "cleanest and greenest hotel." **$**

Villa Margarita Mountain Resort
Busilac, Bayombong
Tel: 078-326 5083
Comfortable with cool mountain air. Trekking. Excellent sunrise and sunset views from rooms. **$**

Aurora
Bahia De Baler
Sabang, Baler
Cell tel: 0920-904 0177
Great rooms and beachside location. **$**

Bays Inn
Sabang, Baler
Cell tel: 0918-926 6697
A mainstay for surfers – eat your breakfast while checking out the day's waves. **$**

CENTRAL CORDILLERA

Benguet
Concorde Hotel
Europa Center, Legarda Road, Baguio

Tel: 074-443 2048
e-mail: concorde@mozcom.com
Wood and brick interior, lodge-like ambience, good views. Among Baguio's best. Chinese, Japanese restaurants, piano bar, karaoke. Credit cards accepted. **$$$**

Safari Lodge
Leonard Wood Road, Baguio City
Tel: 074-442 2419
Home of a former trophy hunter, stuffed and mounted wildlife trophies fill the room. Restaurant. **$$$**

Forest Inn
Legarda Road, Baguio City
Tel: 074-442 2552
Fax: 074-443 8437
Pleasant, cozy rooms with white wicker furniture, hot showers. **$$**

Tam-awan Ifugao Village
Tacay Road, Baguio City
Tel: 074-446 2949
www.tamawanvillage.com
Artists' village; tourists can stay in traditional Ifugao homes. **$$**

Benguet Pine Tourist Inn
82 Chanum corner Otek Street, Baguio City
Tel: 074-442 7325
Clean, quiet, backpacker lodging near Burnham Park. Restaurant. **$**

Mountain Province
Mt Data Lodge
Km 100, Halsema Highway, Bauko
Manila tel: 02-524 2495
www.philtourism.gov.ph
Simple, quiet lodge, cultural performances. Contact Philippine Tourism Authority (PTA) for booking information. **$$**

Mapia-aw Pension
Cell tel: 0921-390 0560
About 1 km (½ mile) out of town, but a lovely walk. Tucked into the rocks and forest, a family-tended house with a lot of different room offerings. **$**

St Joseph's Guesthouse
Sagada
Cell tel: 0918-559 5934
Simple, Episcopalian-run rooms. Shared bath, restaurant. **$**

Ifugao
Banaue Hotel and Youth Hostel
Banaue, Ifugao
Manila tel: 02-524 2495
www.philtourism.gov.ph

Banaue's priciest, far from town center. Restaurant, pool, cultural performances, near Tam-an Village. Credit cards accepted. Contact Philippine Tourism Authority (PTA) for booking information.**$$**

Banaue View Inn
Banaue, Ifugao
Tel: 074-386 4078
A favorite. Open air views over terraces, plus museum of Ifugao artifacts collected by American anthropologist Otley Beyer (his descendants run the inn). Some meals, parking. **$**

Halfway Lodge and Restaurant
Banaue, Ifugao
Tel: 074-386 4082
Like other lodges here, extremely simple yet clean, with great terrace views. Restaurant with slow service. **$**

BICOL

Camarines Norte

Apuao Grande Island Resort
Mercedes, Daet
Manila tel: 02-523 8541–5
www.swaggy.com
A small, well-run resort on a private island with a good bar and a library. **$$**

Canimog Hotel
San Vicente Road , Lag-on
Tel: 054-721 1624
Fax: 054-721 2602
Beautiful garden lends ambience to otherwise nondescript hotel. **$$**

Wiltan Hotel
Vinzon's Avenue, Daet
Tel: 054-721 2525
Standard amenities, pleasant garden. Slow service. **$$**

Camarines Sur

Camarines Sur Government Lodgings
The Camarines Sur government runs three lodgings on the spacious Provincial Capitol Complex in Naga City. Inquire at the Camsur Watersports Complex (tel: 054-475 0854; www.camsurwatersports complex.com). The **Villa del Rey Villas** are luxury accommodations with a wide range of amenities, including a spa, private garden

retreat, swimming pool and upscale dining (**$$$$**). The **Mansion Suites** is a 15-bedroom hotel, recently renovated, which comes with a 24-hour restaurant, Wi-Fi Internet access, cable TV and more (**$$$**). The **Villa del Rey Cabanas** is a bit more rudimentary, but has its share of mod cons. It is within walking distance of the Camsur Watersports Complex, Skatepark and Bike Trail (**$$**).

Hotel Mirabella
Caceres Street, Dinaga, Naga
Tel: 054-473 9537
Fax: 054-811 1379
Quiet, old, well-kept hotel. Nice garden, pool. Excellent view of Mt Isarog. **$$**

New Crown Hotel
P. Burgos Street, San Francisco, Naga
Tel: 054-473 1845
Conveniently located, fronts Quince Martires Monument and San Francisco Church. Rooms with aircon, cable TV, hot showers. **$$**

Aristocrat Hotel
E. Angeles Street, Dinaga, Naga City
Tel: 054-473 8832
Fax: 054-811 6605
Naga's most imposing structure, tastefully decorated, excellent view of Mt Isarog and Mt Mayon. **$**

Albay

Albay Hotel
88 Penaranda Street, Legaspi City
Tel: 052-480 8660
Fax: 052-214 3642
Discounts for long-staying guests. Airport transfer, pool, parking, daily newspaper. Excellent view of Mt Mayon. **$$$**

Porta Azure
Barangay Padang, Legaspi City
Manila tel: 02-807 8405
www.asialeisureescapes.com
Well-decorated villas set on the black sands of Legaspi Bay, in the shadow of Mt Mayon. Enjoy Bicolano delicacies and a massage on your own private stone cabana. **$$$**

Hotel la Trinidad
Rizal Street, Legaspi
Tel: 052-480 7469, 212 2951–53
Fax: 052-214 3148
Simple rooms with very cold aircon

(no "off" switch) – bring a sweater. Restaurant. A 90-minute drive to Donsol whale sharks. **$$**

Mayon International Hotel
419 Quezon Avenue, Legaspi
Tel: 052-245 5028, 480 1655
e-mail: tesa@globalink.net.ph
On the slopes of Mt Mayon at 762 metres (2,500 ft). Fresh east wind and exhilarating view of the Pacific Ocean. Full trekking packages. At the time of writing, the hotel was closed for renovations. **$$**

Catanduanes

Bosdak Beach Resort
Magnesia del Sur, Virac
Tel: 052-633-1703
Wide range of accommodations, aircon or fan. Sports facilities, disco, restaurant. **$$**

Kosta Alcantara Beach Resort and Restaurant
Marilima, Virac
Tel: 052-811 1459
Clear water good for swimming. **$$**

Puting Baybay Resort
Puraran, Baras
Basic but comfortable, with meals. **$**

Sorsogon

Rizal Beach Resort
Rizal Gubat
Tel: 056-211 1056
Former school turned into a beautiful resort. Spectacular views of Rizal Beach. **$$**

San Mateo Hot and Cold Springs Resort
San Benon, Irosin
Native design in rural setting. Perfect for relaxation. Well-kept rooms, excellent view of San Mateo Springs. **$$**

Fernandos Hotel
Pareja Street, Bitan-o
Tel: 056-211 1573
Fax: 056-211 1357
e-mail: fernandohotel@hotmail.com
Tranquil ambience, classy and elegant. Diving and whale-watching packages, tours of Sorsogon, Bulusan volcano. **$**

Villa Kasanggayahan Pension
Rizal Street, Sorsogon
Tel: 056-211 1275
e-mail: koriksl@hotmail.com
Well-preserved colonial house. Rustic, pleasant and green. **$**

OUTLYING ISLANDS

Mindoro
Coco Beach Resort
Coco Beach, Puerto Galera
Cell tel: 0912-305 0476
www.cocobeach.com
Self-contained, romantic resort:
nipa bungalows on secluded beach.
Tennis, swimming, diving;
restaurants. **$$–$$$**
Blue Water Lodge
White Beach, Puerto Galera
Manila tel: 02-714 6632
Cell tel: 0926-839 4222
www.bluewaterlodge.com.ph
Clean, air-conditioned rooms,
perfect for five or six people, in a
serene and cozy environment.
Rooms come with TV and hot
shower. Located approximately 60
meters (65 yd) from the beach. **$$**
La Gensol Plaza Hotel
95 Natinal Road, Mamburao
Tel: 043-711 1072
Mamburao's best. Antique beds,
nice bath, aircon, cable TV, 24-hr
restaurant. Friendly staff. **$$**
**La Laguna Beach Club & Dive
Center**
Big La Laguna Beach, Puerto Galera
Cell tel: 0917-794 0323
www.llbc.com.ph
Luxurious native-style lodgings with
swimming pool. Excellent diving. **$$**
Pandan Island Resort
Sablayan, Mamburao
Cell tel: 0919-305 7821
www.pandan.com
Respectable, clean, private
bungalows of native materials.
Restaurant, dive center.
Meals included. **$$**

EASTERN VISAYAS

Leyte
Leyte Park Resort Hotel
Magsaysay Boulevard, Tacloban
Tel: 053-325 6000
e-mail: leypark@tac.weblinq.com
15 minute to airport. Originally built
for Imelda Marcos' friends in her
hometown, recently renovated,
overlooks Samar's Mt Danglay.
Tropical gardens, guitar-shaped
pool. Full amenities, restaurants,
bars, disco. **$$$**

MacArthur Park Beach Resort
Government Ctr, Candahug, Palo
Tel: 053-323 4095/96
Manila tel: 02-812 1984
Fax: 053-323 2877
Near MacArthur Memorial Landing
along Red Beach. Well-appointed
rooms, tasteful native decor.
Sailboats, restaurant, pool. **$$$**
Asia Stars Hotel
P. Zamora Street, Tacloban City
Tel: 053-325 5322
Near city center. Nice interiors,
friendly staff. **$$**
Dio Island Beach Resort
San Jose, Tacloban
Tel: 053-323 2389
Seaside tranquility, near airport.
Watersports. **$**

Samar
The Surf Camp
ABCD Beach, Calicoan Island,
Guiuan, Eastern Samar
Cell tel: 0917-530 1828
www.calicoansurfcamp.com
A collection of eight luxuriously
outfitted cottages inspired by Thai,
Balinese, Indonesian and Filipino
architecture. Infinity pool, exquisite
landscaping and instant access to
prime Pacific surfing waves make
this worth the journey to the end of
the archipelago. **$$$$**
Celbalor Lodging House
Basey, Samar
Clean, spacious rooms. Overlooks
Samar's Golden River through a wet
market. **$**
Leyte Park
Marabut, Samar
Tacloban tel: 053-325 6000
Elegant cabins along pristine shore,
near wonderful rock formation. **$**

CENTRAL VISAYAS

Bohol
Alona Palm Beach Resort
Alona Beach, Tawala, Panglao
Tel: 038-502 9141
www.alonapalmbeach.com
Easily the nicest resort in Alona,
with beautifully manicured grounds,
luxurious rooms, and rock-star
swimming pool. **$$$$**
Panglao Nature Resort
Panglao Island

Tel: 038-411 5982
www.panglaoisland.com
Sprawling, beachfront tribute to
nature, beautiful rooms; Jacuzzi,
pool. **$$$$**
Sun Apartelle Luxury Apartment
Alona Beach, Tawala, Panglao
Tel: 038-502 9063
www.sunapartelle.com
Free Wi-Fi internet access, business
centre, kitchenette, DVD player, and
one of the most stunning pools in
the Visayas. Long-term stays
possible. **$$$**
Alona Tropical Beach Resort
Alona Beach, Tawala, Panglao
Tel: 038-502 9024
Filipino-style *nipa* bungalows,
sprawling garden, recent award
winners for environmental
awareness. **$$**

Mactan Island
Plantation Bay
Marigondon, Mactan
Tel: 032-340 5900
Manila tel: 02-844 5024/25
www.plantationbay.com
Luxurious rooms with private
garden, gazebo, whirlpool.
Swimming lagoons, watersports.
Beach-side dining. **$$$$$**
Shangri-La's Mactan Island Resort
Punta Engaño Road, Lapu-Lapu City,
Mactan
Tel: 032-231 0288
www.shangri-la.com
Fine resort located near airport.
Rooms overlook luxurious pool,
beach and sea. International,
Filipino, Chinese cuisines. **$$$$$**
**Waterfront Mactan Island Hotel &
Casino**
Airport Road, Lapu-Lapu City,
Mactan
Tel: 032-340 4888
Fax: 032-340 5862
Several restaurants, casino, cigar
and whisky bar, nightclub. **$$$$**

Cebu City
Marriott Cebu City
Cardinal Rosales Avenue, Cebu
Business Park
Tel: 032-232 6100
www.marriott.com
Centrally located hotel inside Cebu
Business Park, within reach of
Mactan Airport, shopping centers.

Well-staffed with good restaurants and bars. Geared towards business travelers. **$$$$**

Eddie's Hotel
F. Manalo Street corner Queens Road
Tel: 032-254 8570
Fax: 032-254 8578
A comfortable well-run hotel in the heart of town. Excellent in-house steak restaurant. **$$**

Montebello Villa Hotel
Banilad
Tel: 032-2323589
www.montebellovillahotel.com
145 well-appointed guest rooms and suites. Two pools, lush tropical garden area, Spanish-inspired hacienda. **$$**

City Park Inn
Archbishop Reyes Avenue
Tel: 032-232 7311–3
Small tourist inn. **$**

Cebu Island
Cabana Beach Club Resort
Panangsama Beach, Moalboal
Cell tel: 0927-950 9968
www.cabanaresort.com
Classy ocean-view rooms complete with private pier and decks, which are perfect for intimate meals. **$$$**

Malapascua Exotic Island Dive and Beach Resort
Malapascua Island
Tel: 032-437 0983
Cell tel: 0917-327 6689
www.malapascua.net
Good hosts and organises 3- and 4-day "dive safaris" – liveaboard diving expeditions. **$$**

Ravenala Beach Bungalows
White Beach
Tel: 032-232 5452, 474 0075
www.ravenala.net
Ravenala offers quaint bungalows located a few steps from the beautiful White Beach. This is the only dive resort here. **$$**

WESTERN VISAYAS

Negros Oriental
La Planta Hotel
Mabini Street, Bais City
Tel: 035-541 5755
Manila tel: 02-899 8756
Fax: 035-541 5756

Stately white building in Spanish style, bright, airy rooms. For those who like golf, dolphins and inviting ocean waters. **$$$**

La Residencia Al Mar
Rizal Avenue, Dumaguete City
Tel: 035-225 7100–1, 422 8449
All executive rooms have balconies facing sea. Free breakfast. Nearby is Don Atilano Steakhouse. **$$**

Liberty's Lodge/Apo Island
Off Zamboangita/Dauin
Tel: 035-321 1036
Cell tel: 0920-238 5704
www.apoisland.com
The island is home to some of the best coral ecosystems you'll see in the country. Simple but creative lodgings. Package deals can fit every type of diver, snorkeler or explorer. **$$**

South Sea Resort
Bantayan, Dumaguete City
Tel: 035-225 2409
Slightly more upscale than others, with seaside garden setting. Swimming pool and good restaurant – but service is slow. Shuttle van takes guests to city center 10 min. away. Or take tricycle. **$$**

Sta Monica by the Sea
Banilad, Dumaguete City
Tel: 035-225 0704
Seaside cottages, quiet and isolated. Good restaurant by the beach. Reached only by 20-minute tricycle ride from downtown or shuttle van. **$$**

Wuthering Heights Hotel
San Jose
Dumaguete tel: 035-225 0487
Beachfront hotel 16 km (10 miles) north of Dumaguete. Fine terrace restaurant and deck overlook Tañon Strait and surrounding countryside. Aircon, bathtub, cable TV. The hotel is named for site's resemblance to the setting in the movie *Wuthering Heights*. **$$**

Bethel Guest House
Rizal Boulevard, Dumaguete City
Tel: 035-225 2000
Located near downtown area. Elegant lobby, spartan rooms, no drinking or smoking. Fast-food restaurant overlooks sea. **$–$$**

Bahia de Bais Hotel
Dewey Island Hilltop,
Capiñahan, Bais City

Tel: 035-402 8850–1
Garden and terrace with a panoramic view of Bais Bay and surrounding lowlands. Mini-bar and small restaurant. Trips to sandbar, mangrove park and Tañon Strait for whale-and-dolphin spotting. **$**

Negros Occidental
L'Fisher Hotel
14th–15th Lacson Street, Bacolod
Tel: 034-433 3731
Arguably the city's best hotel, modest-looking with a small lobby and atrium, fine restaurant and café around a cozy pool. **$$$**

Sugarland Hotel
Araneta Street, Singcang, Bacolod
Tel: 034-435 2691
Fax: 034-435 2645
Near airport. An old favorite among locals, golfers hang out here. **$$**

Bacolod King's Hotel
San Sebastian corner Gatuslao Street, Bacolod
Tel: 034-433 0572
A popular tourist inn. **$–$$**

Iloilo
Amigo Terrace Hotel
Iznart corner Delgada Street
Tel: 033-335 0908
Fax: 033-337 0144
One of the most popular hotels – especially during Dinagyang festival, when balcony is in great demand as point to view festivities. Restaurant, swimming pool, disco. **$$–$$$**

Harbor Town Hotel
J.M. Besa corner Aldeguer Street
Tel: 033-337 2384
A luxury hotel just 10 minutes from the harbor with traditional Ilonggo hospitality and five-star comfort. **$$–$$$**

Sarabia Manor Hotel
General Luna Street
Tel: 033-335 1021
Iloilo's best value with large pool. Carpeted rooms. **$$**

Guimaras
Nagarao Island Resort
Jordan, Guimaras
Cell tel: 0912-520 0343
A 10-hectare island with sandy beach, good snorkeling. Pool, tennis court, restaurant with lounge, bar, library, business center. 2 hours

from Iloilo by boat and jeep. At the time of writing, the resort was temporarily closed following an oil spill that hit Guimaras. **$$$**

Costa Aguada Island Resort
Inampulugan Island, Sibunag
Tel: 02-890 5333 ext. 615/6
www.costa.com.ph
Pleasant resort with beaches, turtle park, mini-zoo, hilltop jungle park, swimming pool, horseback riding. Located off Guimaras Island; access by pumpboat. Model village on island manufactures soap, copra, bamboo crafts. **$$**

Antique
Barrio House Resort
Madrangca, San Jose
Tel: 036-540 7024
Dining hall, picnic facilities. **$$**

Boracay
Rates are those of peak season November–May. Off-season rates often drop 50 percent. More than 100 budget inns are available, most offering rooms with fans, away from the beach.
Mandala Spa & Villas
Malay, Aklan
Tel: 036-288 5858
www.mandalaspa.com
The Mandala deserves every one of the superlatives it hears. Award-winning spa and stunning villas tucked in landscaped greenery. **$$$$$**

Friday's Boracay Resort
Tel: 036-288 6200
www.fridaysboracay.com
With 34 stylish cottage-style rooms and six luxurious suites. The beachfront restaurant, serving Asian and Filipino cuisines, has a popular barbecue buffet on Friday. **$$$$**

The Panoly Resort
Punta Bunga
Tel: 036-288 3134
Manila tel: 02-536 0682
www.thepanoly.com
Expensive clustered cottages. Restaurants, pools, bar, disco. **$$$$**

Sandcastles Beach Resort
Tel: 036-288 3207
Manila tel: 02-823 2725
www.boracaysandcastles.com
Known for outdoor sporting activities, including kayaking and sailing.

Comfortable, recently refurbished rooms, Thai restaurant. **$$$$**

Cocomangas Beach Resort
White Beach
Tel: 036-288 3409
Renowned for Moondog's Shooters Bar: immortalize your name on the wall after slamming 15 shots of various liquors. **$$$**

PALAWAN

Puerto Princesa
The Legend Palawan
Malvar Street
Manila tel: 02-638 9256
www.legendpalawan.com.ph
A business hotel with the usual mod cons. Organizes island cruises and underground river tours. **$$$**

Casa Linda
Trinidad Road
Tel: 048-433 2606
Comfortable, cozy rooms in a garden setting. **$$**

Northern Palawan
Amanpulo
Pamalican Island
Manila tel: 02-759 4040
www.amanpulo.com
Lush, exclusive island getaway. White sand beach, watersports, cycling, tennis, picnics, massage. **$$$$$**

El Nido Resorts
Miniloc and Lagen Islands,
Bacuit Bay
Manila tel: 02-894 5644
www.elnidoresorts.com
Gorgeous, environment-friendly resorts worth every centavo. **$$$$$**

Club Noah Isabelle
Apulit, Taytay
Manila tel: 02-845 1976
www.clubnoah.com.ph
A beautiful resort with turquoise waters and sparkling beaches. Higher rates include diving. **$$$$–$$$$$**

SOUTHERN & CENTRAL MINDANAO

Davao City
Marco Polo
P.O. Box 81540, C.M. Recto Street
Tel: 082-221 0888
Manila tel: 02-893 0888

www.marcopolohotels.com
Luxurious, business-style rooms with view of Mt Apo or Davao Gulf. Café, lounge and swimming pool. **$$$$**

Royal Mandaya Hotel
J. Palma Gil Street, Davao
Tel: 082-225 8888
www.royalmandaya.com
First-class hotel. Native detailing at an international standard. **$$$**

Waterfront Insular Hotel
J.P. Laurel Avenue, Lanang, Davao
Tel: 082-233 2881–7
Manila tel: 02-687 5970
www.waterfronthotels.net
A Davao Institution, with enviable beachside location, impressive grounds and first-class restaurants. Jogging path, poolside gym, private pier, ethnic weaving center. Close to airport, Lanang Golf Course, casino and Davao Museum. **$$$**

Apo View Hotel
Camus Street, Davao City
Tel: 082-221 6430–40
www.apoview.com
In Davao City's business district, 20 min. from airport. Close to shops, church, entertainment, jogging oval. Full amenities including fitness center, barber, bakery, poolside bar. Free airport shuttle. **$$**

Casa Leticia
J. Camus Street, Davao
Tel: 082-224 0501
www.casaleticia.com
In city center. Small but classy, Spanish style, good service. Studio rooms. **$$**

Hotel Galleria
Gov. Duterte Street, Davao
Tel: 082-221 2480
Fax: 082-221 8162
In financial/entertainment district, 15 min. from airport. A Spanish-Mediterranean-inspired structure, with waterfall-fed swimming pool. **$$**

Villa Margarita Hotel
J.P. Laurel Avenue, Bajada, Davao
Tel: 082-221 5674
e-mail: villamar@interasia.com.ph
Cozy, peaceful. Nice pool, excellent service. **$$**

Samal Island
Pearl Farm Beach Resort
Damosa Complex, Lanang, Davao
Tel: 082-235 0876
Manila tel: 02-750 1896–8

www.pearlfarmresort.com
In secluded cove on Samal Island.
The 11-hectare (27-acre) site once
a pearl farm cultivating white-lipped
oysters from the Sulu Sea for pink,
white and gold pearls. Modern
facilities; native-inspired rooms and
cottages. Arranges transfers from
Davao. **$$$$**
Bluewaters Beach Resort
Tel/Fax: 082-225 4009
Centrally located. White sandy
beachfront with shaded tables and
huts. Mediterranean-style guest-
rooms with terrace and view. **$$**
Paradise Island Park and
Beach Resort
Samal, 1181-Km 9, Sasa, Davao
Tel: 082-233 0251/52
www.paradiseislanddavao.com
Rooms with fan or aircon. Seafood
restaurant near beach. Bar, sports
facilities, mini-zoo and park. **$$**

South Cotabato/Gen. Santos City
Sydney Hotel
Pioneer and Roxas avenues,
General Santos City
Tel: 083-552 5478–81
Excellent service and good
accommodations with views of
the city and the majestic Mt
Matutum or Sarangani Bay. Piano
bar and ballroom. Vancouver Plaza
Restaurant serves good seafood.
$$
Family Country Hotel and
Convention Center
Mateo Road, Lagao,
General Santos City
Tel: 083-552 8895–7
e-mail: fchcc@bayandsl.com
Spread out over two complexes.
Nice, simple, affordable rooms and
cheery staff. **$–$$**
Durian Garden ATBP
Awas, Sulit, Polomolok, South
Cotabato, 24 km (15 miles)
northwest of General Santos City
Humble but one-of-a-kind
accommodations, in the shadow
of Mt Matutum. A perfect stopover
for relaxation, the property is
actually a durian orchard, with
pomelo and other fruit trees, birds
and animals. **$**
Hotel Dolores
Santiago Boulevard, General
Santos City

Tel/Fax: 083-552 4139
e-mail: anchor@gslink.net
Close to public market and financial
center. Aircon rooms, hot showers,
cable TV, business services;
restaurant. **$**

North Cotabato
Highlander Hotel
Osmena Drive, Kidapawan
Tel: 064-288 1445
Fax: 064-288 1321
Conveniently located, yet has
privacy and security; ethnic design.
Well-trained staff. Restaurant
features live bands on Wednesday
and Saturday. **$$**

Maguindanao
Estosan Garden Hotel
Gov. Gutierrez Street, Cotabato City
Tel: 064-421 5488
Wonderfully sprawling hotel with
flower garden. Modern
conveniences with nostalgic
touches, right in the city center. **$$**
Hotel Cerilona
Sinsuat Avenue, Cotabato
Tel: 064-421 7523–24
Fax: 064-421 3583
An unassuming yet elegant hotel,
impressive Muslim-inspired lobby. **$$**
Pacific Heights Hotel
66 Don Juliano Avenue, Cotabato
Tel: 064-421 2249
e-mail: pacific_hotel@hotmail.com
Aircon rooms with cable TV and free
shuttles to airport and downtown.
With steam bath and health spa,
seminar facilities, food and
beverages services and business
center. **$$**
Evie's Gardenville
Don Sero Street, Cotabato
Tel: 064-421 2271
Fax: 064-421 4223
Set in beautiful tropical garden.
Great sunrise view from terrace. **$**

NORTHERN MINDANAO
AND CARAGA

Misamis Oriental
Malasag Resort
Alwana Business Park, Cugman, CDO
Tel: 088-855 2198
e-mail: marco@alwana.com
Full amenities, including ballroom,

fine dining, business center, pool
and jacuzzi. Excellent service, very
nice view, big lawn. **$$$**
Dynasty Court Hotel
Tianno Hayes Street, CDO
Tel: 08822-724516
www.philcom.ph/dynasty
Conveniently located downtown; 25
minute from airport. Impressive
Chinese-inspired interior. Excellent
service. Live band daily. Internet
access. **$$**
Cha-Li Beach Resort
Cugman, CDO
Tel: 08822-732929, 732 840
Fax: 088-855 2108
e-mail: cha-li@cdo.philcom.com.ph
A three-story hotel near Macajalar
Bay, surrounded by cottages,
convention halls. Rooms have
aircon, cable TV, hot showers. **$**
Parkview Hotel
Tirso Neri Street, CDO
Tel: 08822-726 565
Simple, new, centrally located
lodgings. **$**
River View Inn
Vamenta Boulevard, CDO
Tel: 088-858 4245/46
Ideally located along Cagayan River
– a soothing change of scenery, 20
minute from airport and seaport.
International cuisine and open-air
café. Full amenities, Internet. **$**
Southwinds Hotel
Captain Vicente Roa Ext., CDO
Tel: 08822-727 623
Fax: 08822-724 803
This white-washed hotel has nice
hardwood floors, garden and small
lawn, friendly staff. Parking. Daily live
jazz band. Near shopping malls. **$**

Camiguin
Camiguin Beach Club
Yumbing, Mambajao
Tel: 088-387 9028
Fronting White Island. Pool, tree-
lined beach, telephone, parking,
restaurant, pumpboat, bar. **$$**
Casa Grande Hotel and Café
Poblacion Mambajao
Tel: 088-387 2075
Renovated Old Spanish house
opposite municipal building and
grandstand. Ideal for business
meetings. Most guests are
Europeans. Reservations
recommended, especially during

Lanzones Festival (October) and Lenten season. **$$**

Caves Dive Resort
Agoho, Mabajao
Tel: 088-387 9040
Opposite the White Island; scenic view from native-design rooms. Aircon or fan, *nipa* and bamboo cottages. Walking distance to Ardent Spring. **$**

Misamis Occidental
Plaza Beatriz Hotel
Port Road, Ozamis
Tel: 088-521 1394–95
Picture windows give bustling view of city and nearby port area. **$$**

Minerva Tourist Inn
Washington Street, Ozamis City
Tel: 088-521 0065
Clean, busy inn; simple, tasteful designs and furniture. **$**

Royal Garden Hotel
Burgos corner Zamora Street, Ozamis City
Tel: 088-521 2888–9
Fax: 088-521 0008
Newest, biggest hotel with well-appointed rooms, in city center. **$**

Lanao del Norte
Corporate Inn
5 Sparrow Street, Isabel Village, Pala-o, Iligan
Tel: 063-221 4456–8
A reputable, secluded inn at the foothills of Mt Agad-Agad. Lobby bar and dinette looks on mountain. **$$**

Maria Cristina Hotel
Gen. Aguinaldo Street, Iligan
Tel: 063-221 5308, 221 3352
Fax: 063-221 3940
Iligan's oldest hotel, fronts city plaza, fine views. Near mall and transport. Café, live band. **$$**

Caprice Pensionne House
Badelles corner Lluch Street, Iligan
Tel: 063-221 2018
Clean hotel with friendly staff. Close to fast food and public transport. **$**

Bukidnon
Haus Malbu
Bonifacio Drive corner Camisio Street, Malaybalay
Tel: 088-221 5741
Garden setting, clean, comfortable. Fan, cable TV, fridge, phone, hot showers. **$**

Pine Hills Hotel
Fortich Street, Malaybalay
Tel: 088-221 3211
Near DXMB radio station. A wealth of ornamental plants, amenities and café-cum-bistro in the lobby – perfect for lounging. **$**

Agusan del Norte
Almont Hotel
San Jose Street, Butuan City
Tel: 085-342 5263/64
Fax: 085-341 5010
An impressive view of Rizal Park. Caraga's best café in a garden setting with man-made waterfall. **$$$**

Hotel Karaga
Montilla Boulevard, Butuan
Tel: 085-341 5405, 342 8387
www.hotelkaraga.com
Butuan's most popular hotel. Aircon, cable TV, phone, hot showers, restaurants, bar, Internet access. **$–$$**

Agusan del Sur
Diwata Training Center and Resort
Purok 3, San Isidro, San Francisco
Tel: 085-343 8185
Formerly a handicraft training center, now converted into a sprawling resort of native design. Big fishpond on one side, plus a karaoke bar. **$**

Surigao del Sur
Mueco's Resort by the Bay
Mabwa Beach, Tandag
Tel: 086-211 8888
Give yourself a real rural treat and stay in a native-design room with ocean view. Drift off to sleep under sun-dried sheets, wake up to the rooster's crow at dawn. **$**

Royal Christian Hotel
Tandag
Tel: 086-211 3140
Spacious and cozy, with a garden at the back. Homely rooms with beds made of rare Philippine hardwood. **$**

Surigao del Norte
Pansukian Tropical Resort
Gen. Luna, Siargao Island
Cell tel: 0918-903 9055
www.pansukian.com
Manila: 02-813 8718, 817 0169
Cebu: 032-253 4380 or 88
One of the Philippines' nicest resorts. Island getaway style, with tasteful native furnishing (fine bamboo, rattan basketry and wood decoration), plus fine dining, kayaking, open-air massage hut and beachfront hammocks. **$$$$–$$$$$**

Sagana
Cloud 9, Gen. Luna, Siargao
Cell tel: 0919-809 5769
www.cloud9surf.com
Possibly one of the best surf camps in the country. Ambient, well-decorated rooms, with world-famous surf breaks 200 meters' walk away. The best food on the island. **$$–$$$**

Ocean 101
Cell tel: 0910-848 0893
www.ocean101cloud9.com
Cloud 9, Gen. Luna, Siargao
Everything a budget-minded surfer could ask for: good food, clean simple rooms, and cable TV. **$$**

Cabuntog Lodge & Cottages
Takbo, General Luna, Siargao
Cell tel: 0919-363 2507
Basic accommodation on the lagoon, between Gen. Luna and Cloud 9. **$**

Philippine Gateway Hotel
Km. 2 Checkpoint, Surigao
Tel: 086-232 4257
Biggest hotel in city. All rooms with aircon, hot showers, cable TV, phone, parking, flower garden in front, big lobby with nice, rural view. **$**

ZAMBOANGA

Zamboanga del Norte
Dakak Park and Beach Resort
Dakak, Brgy Taguilon, Dapitan
In Dipolog City: Echaves Street corner Quezon Avenue
Cell tel: 0918-595 0713/16
e-mail: philt@world.net
Easily the best resort in this area. Sunny white beach facing Sulu Sea, waterfalls, spring-fed pool, extensive modern facilities and amenities, plus aqua sports center. **$$$**

Camila Hotel
General Luna Street, Dipolog City
Tel: 065-212 3009
Fax: 065-212 3008
Homely ambience with ethnic design. Big lawn with children's playground, babysitting services. **$$**

Top Plaza Hotel
Quezon Avenue, Dipolog
Tel: 065-212 5777
Fax: 065-212 5788
Ideally located near Dipolog's bustling shopping and business center; 10 min. from Dipolog Airport and 30 min. from Pulawan Port in Dapitan City. **$$**

Ramos Hotel
Rizal Avenue corner Magsaysay Street, Dipolog
Tel: 065-212 3504
Fax: 065-212 2436
Garden terrace with excellent view of nearby Sulu Sea. Seafood restaurant. **$**

Zamboanga del Sur

Grand Astoria Hotel
Major Jaldon Street, Zamboanga
Tel: 062-991 2510–15
www.grandastoria.com
Ideally located; 5–10 min. from airport. Mini-bar, cable TV, hot and cold water, restaurant, car rental, café, boutique, laundry, shuttle service, business center. Accepts major credit cards. **$$**

Hotel Guillermo
Rizal Avenue, Pagadian
Tel: 062-214 1471
Spanish-inspired look, touts ballroom dancing facility. Located at center of city but has secluded ambience. **$$**

Lantaka Hotel by the Sea
Mayor Valderrosa Street, Zamboanga
Tel: 062-991 2033
Fax: 062-991 1626
In the city's heart, near tourist destinations. Seafood restaurant with view of wharf, bar, pool. Docked nearby are small boats to ferry tourists to Sta Cruz Island. **$$**

Argamel Hotel
Governor Camins Avenue, Zamboanga City
Tel: 062-991 2023
Nice view of city at night. Rooftop restaurant, piped-in music, cable TV, shuttle service, laundry. **$**

D'laville Orchard Park
Sunrise Village, Pagadian City
Tel: 062-215 2123
A theater-style convention facility with 300-person capacity, piano bar, swimming pool, and floating and non-floating cottages. **$**

Where to Eat

What to Eat

Filipino cuisine is an intriguing blend of Malay, Spanish and Chinese influences. Many visitors are surprised by its mildness after having experienced other more fiery Southeast Asian food such as Thailand's curries.

Most Filipinos eat rice three times a day. At McDonald's, a visitor may sample a Filipino breakfast of fried rice and *longaniza* (native sausage) with an egg done sunny-side up. The meal usually includes salted and dried fish, accompanied by tomatoes and *patis* (fish sauce).

During mealtimes, watch the locals. Before the food arrives, sauce dishes are brought to the table. Filipinos automatically reach for the vinegar bottle with hot chilli, or the soy sauce, which is mixed with *calamansi* (small native limes, which also make a refreshing juice.) Grilled items (*ihaw-ihaw*) are good with crushed garlic, vinegar and chilli. Meals are often prefaced by

Wine and Water

Wine prices have plummeted in recent years, and good South American and Australian wines can be had for around P100–200 a glass. Another good option is to order the local brew, San Miguel, which costs less than P20 in the street, and usually no more than P100 at fine establishments.

A note on drinking water. It is best not to take any chances; stick to bottled water, even for brushing your teeth – especially outside of Manila. In larger cities, major hotels and restaurants serve filtered water.

sinigang, a clear broth slightly soured with green tamarind and prepared with *bangus* (milkfish) or shrimp.

Some typical Philippine dishes worth trying are chicken *tinola* and *pancit molo*, dumplings of pork, chicken and mushrooms cooked in a broth. *Adobo* is pork or chicken in small pieces, simmered in a light vinegar with garlic and spices. Seviche-like *kinilaw* is fish marinated in a garlic and chilli vinaigrette with raw onions.

A typical fiesta dish, *lechon* is suckling pig stuffed with tamarind leaves and roasted on an open spit over heated coals until the skin is crackling and the meat tender; it is generally served with liver sauce. *Sinanglay*, another festive dish, is fish or crab with hot pepper wrapped in Chinese cabbage, and cooked in coconut milk.

Other Filipino favorites include egg-roll-like *lumpia*, a salad of heart-of-palm, pork and shrimp wrapped in a tissue paper-thin crepe and served with garlic and soy sauce; and *kare-kare*, a rich mixture of oxtail, knuckles and tripe, stewed with vegetables in peanut sauce and served with *bagoong*, a fish-based sauce.

Desserts are generally made with coconut milk. *Bibingka* consists of ground rice, sugar and coconut milk, baked in a clay oven and topped with fresh and salted duck egg. *Guinatan* is a coco-pudding, served with lashings of coconut cream. Ice cream comes in a variety of flavors such as *nangka* (jackfruit), *ube*, *macapuno* or *buko* (coconut), mango and even *queso* (cheese).

Restaurant Listings

Restaurants are listed by area in the same order as they appear in the Places section of the book. Unlike in many other cities, hotel restaurants in Manila are among the best. In smaller cities, dining options may be limited, though hotels can point you in the right direction.

Manila restaurants are

categorized by the type of food served; restaurants elsewhere are listed alphabetically.

Price Guide

The following price categories indicate the cost of a standard three-course dinner for one person, without drinks:
$$$$: US$30 and up
$$$: US$20–30
$$: US$10–20
$: Under US$10

MANILA

Filipino

Andok's Lechon Manok
Numerous Andok's outlets are located throughout Manila and beyond – look for the yellow sign with a heart. They serve excellent roasted chicken (*manok*) and *lechon* (roast pig). Carry out; cash only. **$**

The Aristocrat
432 San Andres Street corner Roxas Boulevard, Malate
Tel: 02-524 7671–80
Delicious barbecued chicken and *kare-kare* (oxtail). 24-hour takeout counter. **$**

Casa Xocolat
B. Gonzales Street, off Katipunan, by Ateneo University, Quezon City
Tel: 02-929 4186
A wonderful little place celebrating the Pinoy love for cacao and chocolate in their different forms, from churros to rich hot drinks, to fondues that'll put a smile on your face. Focaccia sandwiches and other creative entrees are on the menu too. There's also Wi-Fi Internet access and a pleasant patio. **$**

Gerry's Grill
25 branches around Manila and the country, including:
20 Jupiter Street corner Antares Bel-Air, Makati
Tel: 02-897 9862
Ultra-cheap Filipino food. Request for a seat outside – it can be noisy inside. The chargrilled (*inihaw*) squid and tuna belly, tuna or traditional *tanigue kinilaw* (marinated raw fish) and *kilawin puso ng saging* (marinated heart of banana) are

recommended. For dessert, try leche flan custard or the refreshing pandan-buko dessert. Reservations recommended. **$**

Guava
1st Level, Piazza Serendra, Bonifacio Global City, Taguig
Tel: 02-856 0489
Try creative Filipino fusion dishes such as *kare-kare* with *bagoong* and *tsokolate* (peanut curry with fish paste and chocolate), *monggonisa* (chickpea sausage), and *Pinoy na foie gras* (local foie gras). **$$$**

Ihaw-Ihaw, Kalde-Kaldero
(Singing Cooks and Waiters)
Roxas Boulevard corner Gil Puyat Avenue (Buendia), Pasay City
Tel: 02-832 0658, 831 5015
J P Rizal corner Makati Avenue, Makati
Tel: 02-899 7528
Quezon Boulevard, Quezon City
Tel: 02-372 3204
The food is Pinoy and the waiters even more so, entertaining you with song while you wait. **$**

Kamayan
47 Arnaiz Avenue (Pasay Road) Makati
Tel: 02-843 3604
Use your fingers to lift rice and meats off the banana leaf. Recommended are the *lechon de leche* (roasted piglet), crispy *pata* (fried ham hocks) and *kare-kare*. The other branches are located at West Avenue (Quezon City), Greenhills, Pasay Road (Makati), Megamall, Glorietta and Robinson's. **$**

Lami Barbecue
South Road corner Parade Street, Luneta Park, Intramuros
Tel: 02-400 7440
Charcoal-roasted Cebuano food is served here. A second, smaller branch (no phone) has recently opened along the Baywalk stretch of Roxas Boulevard, perfect for watching Manila's famous sunsets. Two great locations near the waterfront. **$**

Chinese

Chuan Kee
G/F, 650 Ongpin corner Nueva Street, Binondo
Tel: 02-242 9759
This Chinatown institution has

served home-made soups and special brews for more than 70 years. Cash only. **$**

Gloria Maris
10 branches in the Metro area, including Greenhills Shopping Center, Ortigas Avenue, San Juan, tel: 02-722 5508; G/F, Rockwell Powerplant, tel: 02-897 8310.
Try the fried crab, baked lobster or Peking duck. *Dim sum* all day. **$$**

The Legend (Hong Kong) Seafood Restaurant
Boom na Boom Compound, CCP Complex, Roxas Boulevard, Pasay City
Tel: 02-833 1188, 833 3388
Choose your fish or other seafood from the aquarium, Hong Kong style. Salt and pepper squid and fish lip soup are amongst the most popular here. **$**

North Park
1200 Makati Ave (close to Jp Rizal)
Tel: 02-897 9039
The easiest way to find out the nearest branch of the ever-expanding North Park chain near you is to e-mail and ask. Good, well-priced Chinese food in clean, ambient surroundings make this a favorite until the 3am closing time. **$$**

Pot and Noodle House
Level 4 Building A, SM Megamall EDSA, Mandaluyong
Tel: 02-634 1260/61
Jupiter Place, 136 Jupiter Street, Makati
Tel: 02-899 8999
SM Manila
Tel: 02-522 8840/9159
Delicious hand-pulled noodles in soup, dumplings and claypot meals. Good for business lunches. **$**

Quick Snack
637–639 Carvajal Street, Binondo
Tel: 02-242 9572
A favorite, quick lunchtime spot with Chinatown locals. Extremely delicious *lumpia* (spring rolls) that are fresh, not fried and *kunchay-ah* (pastries filled with meat and vegetables.) **$**

Royal Garden
851 Padilla (Gandara) Street corner Ongpin, Binondo
Tel: 02-733 1122
Perhaps not the best atmosphere, but good *dim sum* and steamed *lapu-lapu* fish. **$$**

Seafood Market Restaurant
1190 Jorge Bocobo, Ermita
Tel: 02-524 5761, 524 5744
Pick and choose your own live
seafood and vegetables, then tell
the chef precisely how you like it,
and voila! Delicious. **$$**

Seafood Wharf Restaurant
Army-Navy Club Compound,
South Drive, Luneta Park
Tel: 02-536 3522
Choose your own fresh ingredients
and let the chef get to work. Relax
on the open-air deck overlooking
Manila Bay, or take a quick dip in
the pool before dinner. Great
sunset view. **$**

Tin Hau
Mandarin Oriental Hotel, Makati
Tel: 02-750 8888
Delicate Chinese food at hotel
prices. Try the steamed or baked
crab and garoupa *(lapu-lapu)*, Peking
duck, and Sichuanese specialties.
Dim sum from 11.30am–2.30pm. **$$**

Japanese and Korean

Furusato Japanese Restaurant
Level 1, Glorietta, Ayala Center
Makati
Tel: 02-892 5115
1712 Roxas Boulevard, Pasay City
Tel: 02-523 0476
Authentic Japanese cuisine. **$$**

Inagiku
Makati Shangri-La Hotel,
Ayala corner Makati Avenue
Tel: 02-813 8888
Order sushi by the set or sit by the
grill. **$$$**

Kaya Korean Restaurant
6 branches, including:
62 Jupiter Street, Bel-Air, Makati
Tel: 02-895 0404
Good Korean barbecue. Try the
bulgogi (roasted beef), *kalbi gui*
(short ribs) and *japchae* (clear
sweet potato noodles). **$$**

Korea Garden
128 Jupiter Street, Makati
Tel: 02-895 5443, 896 4361
Popular Korean restaurant. **$–$$**

Shinjuku Ramen House
7853 Makati Avenue corner
Hercules Street, Makati
Tel: 02-890 6106
Great bowls of ramen; *gyoza*
(dumplings) is a specialty. A favorite
among Japanese residents. **$**

Wasabi Bistro and Sake Bar
7912 Makati Avenue, Makati
Tel: 02-840 4223, 892 1870
Good food in a stylish atmosphere,
updating traditional Japanese
delicacies with a modern twist. Try
signature dishes such as #1 Special
and Dynamite Sushi Rolls. **$$$**

Southeast Asian

Benjarong Royal Thai Restaurant
Mezzanine Level, Dusit Hotel
Nikko, Makati
Tel: 02-867 3333, 867 3888.
Some of the best Thai food in
Makati. Open daily for lunch and
dinner. **$$$$**

Phobac Vietnamese Specialties
Level 1, Robinson's Galleria,
Ortigas Center, Pasig City
Tel: 02-632 9460
Level 2, Glorietta
Tel: 02-894 4308
Level 1, Robinson's Place, Ermita
Tel: 02-586 3176
G/F, Fort Bonifacio, Global City
Tel: 02-815 6529
A popular noodle shop chain with
hearty, exotic meals at good prices. **$**

Soms Thai Noodle House
5921 Alger Street, Makati
Tel: 02-757 8079
Cheap and tasty Thai food. Must-
tries are the Thai milk tea, catfish
salad and the curries. Open daily
9am–11pm. **$**

Spices
The Peninsula Manila, Ayala corner
Makati Avenue, Makati
Tel: 02-810 3456
Mouth-watering Asian selections,
including Thai and Indian. **$$**

Indian and Middle Eastern

Hossein's Persian Kebab
7857 LKV Building, Makati Avenue
(near Jupiter), Makati
Tel: 02-890 5928, 890 8503
Classy Middle Eastern dining.
Sublime kebabs, hummus and
vegetarian entrees. **$$**

Ziggurat Restaurant
Ground Level, Sunette Tower,
Durban Street, Makati
Tel: 02-897 5179
www.zigguratcuisine.com
Impressively varied menu that
offers samplings from the
Mediterranean, India, Africa and the

Middle East. Open 24 hours, this
quiet oasis in the bustling P. Burgos
Street area has an outdoor patio
with comfortable seating. **$$**

Italian

California Pizza Kitchen
Alabang Town Center, 2nd Level,
Alabang Commercial Corporation,
Alabang-Zapote Road, Muntinlupa
Tel: 02-850 5771
Shangri-la Plaza Mall, 2nd Level,
EDSA corner Shaw Boulevard,
Mandaluyong City
Tel: 02-687 7841–2
243 Tomas Morato corner
Fuentabella Street, Quezon City
Tel: 02-372 7371–2
Glorietta, 1st Level, Glorietta 3,
Ayala Center, Makati
Tel: 02-893 9898
Greenhills Promenade,
Ground Level, San Juan
Tel: 02-725 7377
The gourmet pizzas are good, and
their salads are among the best in
town. **$$**

Il Ponticello
2/F, Antel 2000, 121 Valero Street
Makati
Tel: 02-887 7168, 887 4998
Trendy Italian eatery. Try Chef
Romeo Garchitorena's *risotto del
Boscaiolo* and a*i funghi Porcini con
Gorgonzola*. Ponticello turns into a
modern late-night bar. **$$**

L'Opera
26th Street corner 5th Avenue,
Fort Bonifacio, Taguig
Tel: 02-889 3963, 889 2784
www.loperagroup.com
Home-made pizzas and pastas;
good ravioli. Among Manila's best
Italian restaurants. Open daily for
lunch and dinner. **$$**

Mi Piace
The Peninsula Manila, Makati
Tel: 02-810 3456
Exquisite Italian dining with the
focus on seafood. Try the grilled
seabass. **$$$**

Paparazzi
2/F, Shangri-La EDSA Hotel,
Ortigas Center
Tel: 02-633 8888
A popular business lunch
destination featuring northern
Italian specialties. Excellent pasta
and rib-eye steak. **$$–$$$**

Portico 1771
Serenda Piazza, Ground Level,
Fort Bonifacio, Taguig
Tel: 02-856 0581 to 85
Creative Italian food in a fabulous
music bar setting. **$$**

Continental

Barbara's Restaurant
Plaza San Luis, Gen. Luna Street,
Intramuros
Tel: 02-527 3893
Elegantly served Spanish and Filipino
cuisine. Try the seafood bonbon,
wrapped in phyllo pastry and baked
in lemon butter. Closed Sunday. **$$**

Casa Armas
J. Nakpil Street corner Bocobo
Malate
Tel: 02-523 5763
Wonderful Spanish food by owner
Jesus Armas. *Bocarones* (marinated
sardines with garlic), Spanish
sausage, garlic shrimp and olives;
paella, garlic chicken (order in
advance) and unbelievable crab.
Reservations recommended. **$$**

**Casa Armas Tapas Bar and
Restaurant**
132 Jupiter Street, Bel-Air
Makati City
Tel: 02-897 3605, 897 3542
With more space than the original
Malate restaurant, Makati's Casa
Armas offers the same fine
offerings as the original.
Reservations recommended. **$$**

Chateau 1771
El Pueblo Real, ADB Avenue corner
Vargas, Ortigas Center, Pasig City
Tel: 02-631 7340/41
Featuring "no borders" cuisine,
from seafood *jambalaya* and steak
to beef *fondue* and soufflés. **$$$**

El Cirkulo
900 Arnaiz Avenue (Pasay Road)
corner Paseo de Roxas, Makati
Tel: 02-810 8735
Innovative Spanish cuisine with
excellent *tapas.* **$$**

Florabel
G/F, The Podium, 18 ADB Avenue
Ortigas Center, Mandaluyong
Tel: 02-638 7527, 667 3220
Exquisite Continental cuisine in a
low-key but classy environment.
Signature dishes are the Wagyu rib
eye, the crispy prawn salad and the
foie gras burger. **$$$**

Gaudi
Greenbelt 3, 4th Level, Makati
Tel: 02-757 2710, 757 2711
Serenda Piazza, G/F,
Fort Bonifacio, Taguig
Tel: 02-854 0474, 856 0473
Well-regarded Spanish cuisine from
some of the best Castilian chefs
this side of Madrid. **$$$$**

Ilustrado
744 Calle Real del Palacio
Intramuros (formerly Gen. Luna)
Tel: 02-527 3674
Evokes the lifestyle of well-traveled
Filipinos of the Spanish era; the
ilustrados knew how to dine. Closes
Sunday at 6pm. **$$**

Inyo
66 Esteban Abada Street,
Loyola Heights, Quezon City
Tel: 02-928 6459
Tucked away in an inviting
traditional capiz-windowed house
under huge trees, the Asian/
Continental fusion cuisine is
sophisticated and creative. **$$$**

Le Soufflé
The Fort Bonifacio Entertainment
Center, Makati
Tel: 02-887 5109
One of the best choices for Manila
dining. Great seared tuna, steaks
and of course, soufflés.
Reservations recommended. **$$$$**

Mag:net Gallery
ABS-CBN Compound, Quezon City
Tel: 02-410 0995
Paseo de Roxas Avenue, corner
Sedeno Street, Makati
Tel: 02-817 7895
335 Katipunan Avenue, Quezon City
Tel: 02-929 3191
www.magnet.com.ph
With three branches around the
Metro, Mag:net is a great place to
get an idea of the Philippines arts
scene. The flagship Katipunan
branch is a mix of bookstore,
nightspot, gallery and restaurant
offering up tasty, well-priced food. **$**

M Café
Ayala Museum, Greenbelt 4
Ground Level, Makati Avenue corner
Legaspi Street, Makati
Tel: 02-757 3000, 757 6000
With spacious and classy indoors
seating and outdoor patios. Asian
and international cuisines. This is a
bustling weekend nightspot. **$$**

Melo's Steak and Seafood
58 Bohol Avenue, Quezon City
Tel: 02-924 9168
22 Jupiter Street, Makati
Tel: 02-899 9403, 899 2456
The undisputed home of certified
Angus beef in Manila. Reservations
recommended. **$$$**

Mexicali
www.mexicali-phil.com
Baja cuisine the way it should be
done: tasty, served in unpretentious
surroundings, and in hearty
portions. Current branches located
at Greenhills (tel: 02-725 3921);
Glorietta (tel: 02-894 0987);
Robinsons Manila (tel: 02-400
6869); SM Megamall (tel: 02-635
6079) and other areas. **$**

Old Manila
Peninsula Manila, Ayala corner
Makati Avenue
Tel: 02-810 3456
Among the finest of Manila's French
restaurants. Certified Angus beef,
plus exquisite delicacies from
around the world. Sublime *foie gras,*
and casserole of lobster with
homemade egg linguine.
Reservations recommended. **$$$$**

Old Swiss Inn
Olympia Towers, Makati Avenue
Tel: 02-818 8251, 818 0098
Garden Plaza Hotel,
Belen Street Paco
Tel: 02-522 4835
Madrigal, 2/F, BMW Building,
Alabang
Tel: 02-809 2326, 809 2342
Enjoy traditional Swiss pork
knuckles, lamb chops, roesti
potatoes and sauerkraut. **$$**

Patio Guernica
1856 Jorge Bocobo Street
Remedios Circle, Malate
Tel: 02-521 4415, 524 2267
An old Spanish church turned into a
stylish Spanish restaurant. Cozy
and romantic. **$$**

Red Restaurant
Makati Shangri-La Hotel,
Ayala corner Makati Avenue
Tel: 02-813 8888
Refined French and international
cuisine by a Provencal chef. Try the
halibut or lamb. **$$$$**

Sala
610 J Nakpil Street, Malate
Tel: 02-524 6770

The ever-changing menu maintains freshness and quality. Rich desserts include rhubarb crème brulee and homemade ice cream. Reservations are recommended. Sala will move to Greenbelt 3 in the future; call for details. **$$$**

Schwarzwälder German Restaurant
Atrium Center, Makati Avenue, Makati
Tel: 02-893 5179
Authentic German food. **$$**

Top of the Citi/Le Soufflé
34/F CITIBANK Tower, 8741 Paseo de Roxas, Makati
Tel: 02-750 5810/11
Some of the best food in town served at the highest elevation. Open to non-members for dinner, Monday to Friday. A great place for evening drinks, with a commanding view over Makati. **$$$$**

MANILA'S ENVIRONS

Tagaytay
Josephine's Restaurant
Km 58, Gen. E. Aguinaldo Highway, Tagaytay
Tel: 046-413 1801
A tradition of fine Filipino dining, with an excellent view over Lake Taal and volcano. Try the *lechon de leche* (traditional roast piglet) and *pinakbet*, a vegetable stew with fish sauce. **$–$$**

Sonia's Secret Garden
Aguinaldo Highway, west of Tagaytay
Cell tel: 0917-532 9097
Sonia welcomes visitors to her house, where pre-set, home-cooked lunches and dinners are served with fresh fruit juice. Exquisite garden. Call in advance. Lunch from 11am, dinner from 4pm. Cash and cards accepted. **$$**
(To get there: head west along Aguinaldo Highway, beyond Tagaytay. Turn right into Barangay Buck Estate at the archway past Royale Tagaytay. Café Alfonso is too far. Sonia's place is on the left, obscured by overgrown flower bushes. Must call ahead.)

Calamba, Laguna
Various restaurants serve local *binalot* – the original Pinoy fast food

in banana leaf wrappers. Usually includes fried rice, pork or chicken, and an egg. Lift the first layer of banana leaf to uncover the salt with which to dip the egg.

Dura-Fe Restaurant
General Jaina Street, Pagsanjan
Excellent Filipino food. **$**

Exotik Restaurant
National Highway, Longos, Kalayaan (near Paete)
Tel: 049-557 1036
Serves delights such as deer, wild boar, python, turkey, eel and monitor lizard. An interesting diversion on the eastern shore of Laguna de Bay. **$**

Samaral Seafood Restaurant
National Highway, Calamba (near Pansol)
Decent seafood in a pleasant outdoor setting. **$**

Rizal
Balaw-Balaw Restaurant
Doña Justa Village, Angono
Tel: 02-651 0110
Restaurant-cum-art gallery of artist-chef-owner Perdigon Vocalon. Try the game dishes – wild boar, python, monitor lizard and frogs' legs. Nude sketching for artists on Friday. **$$**

Padi's Point
Sumulong Highway, Antipolo
Tel: 02-240 5088/89
A cluster of a bar and several restaurants popular among local and foreigners alike on this mountain ridge. Among the choices Dad's, Nipa Hut Restaurant, The Balcony, Cycling Station, Motoyori Japanese and Leonardo's. **$**

CENTRAL PLAINS

Pampanga
Aling Cely's Carinderia
Nepo Complex, Angeles City
Tel: 045-888 0014
Let *Aling* (Auntie) Cely feed you the best of Kapampangan (local Pampanga) cuisine, with tasty meat dishes. **$**

Aling Lucing's
158 Pineda Street, C.M. Recto, Angeles City
Tel: 045-888 7148

A Pampanga institution serving Angeles diners for almost 50 years. Some of the best *sisig* (pig's ears) in Central Luzon. **$**

Camalig
292 Sto Rosario Street, Angeles City
Tel: 045-888 1077
A restored 1840 barn. Armando's pizza, pasta, barbecue. **$**

Cottage Kitchen Café
582 Don Juico Avenue (Perimeter Road), Clarkview Subdivision, Balibago, Angeles City
Tel: 045-322 3366
Superior cajun and American soul food from a former US Air Force major who is right when he says his barbecue is so good "it'll make you go home and slap your momma." **$**

Ituro Mo Iluto Ko
Olongapo–Gapan Expressway, San Fernando
Tel: 045-961 5417/18
The name translates as "I point it, you cook it," in reference to the restaurant's original set-up. This is the original branch of the Cabelen chain in Manila. Good Filipino food. **$**

Zambales
Golden Dragon
Aguinaldo Street corner Canal Road, Subic Bay
Tel: 047-252 2222
Authentic Chinese food prepared by Hong Kong chefs. **$$**

Sakura
Sta. Rita Road corner Rizal Highway, Subic Bay
Tel: 047-252 2666
Catering to the large number of Japanese businessmen here, Sakura offers authentic Japanese food, taking advantage of the abundant fresh local seafood. **$$**

ILOCOS REGION

Hundred Islands, Pangasinan
Maxine by the Sea
Lucap, Alaminos
Tel: 075-551 2537
Simple cuisine, including fresh seafood. Overlooks the Hundred Islands. Similar to other hotel restaurants in the area. **$**

La Union
Fat's Bar and Grill
Se-Bay Resort, Urbiztondo, San Juan
Tel: 072-888 4075
Typical Filipino food with a great
view of sea and surfers. **$**
S.O.U.L Café
Camp 1, Main Highway, Rosario,
by the Shell Station
Tel: 072-712-0852
Perfectly placed highway stop, right
before (or after) the demanding
zigzags of Kennon Road to that goes
to Baguio. Good pastries and coffee,
including civet cat coffee, the
world's most expensive coffee. **$**

Ilocos Sur
Café Leona
Near plaza, Crisologo Street, Vigan
Tel: 077-722 2212
Thai food festival buffet spills into
the street every Friday and
Saturday, 6pm. Good chicken
barbecue and squid salad. A true
Vigan experience. **$**

Ilocos Norte
Chinese Full Moon
Ft Ilocandia Resort, Barrio
Caylayab, Laoag City
Tel: 077-772 1166–70
Hotel restaurant serving Taiwanese
cuisine. **$$–$$$**
La Preciosa
Rizal Street, Laoag
Tel: 077-773 1162
Fine Ilocano dining, not far from
Texicano Hotel. **$**

CAGAYAN

Cagayan
Bali Leisure Club/The Port
Pallua Road, Tuguegarao City
Tel: 078-844 7808, 846 3283
Japanese and local cuisines,
and *pulutan* (finger food that
accompanies drinks). **$$**
Family Fastfood and Bakeshop
College Avenue, Tuguegarao
Tel: 078-844 2110
Buttered chicken, fish fillet, *adobo*,
pork roll and other dishes in
university area. **$**
Kusina Cagayana
Pengue Ruyu, Tuguegarao City
Tel: 078-844 2880

Down-home Ilocano food, like
pinakbet (meat and vegetable
stew), *inabrao* (vegetable stew),
and *bagnet* (deep-fried pork). **$**
Pampangueña Restaurant
Bonifacio Street, Tuguegarao
Tel: 078-844 1829
Modest, with specialties like
kare-kare and *sinigang*. Open
7am–8pm. **$**

Isabela
Carig Coffee Shop
Mabini, Santiago City
Tel: 078-682 7143
Best coffee in town; bargain
Filipino, American breakfast. Open
5.30am–9pm. **$**
King George Hall
Bonifacio Avenue, Victory Norte
Santiago
Tel: 078-682 8743
Delicious tenderloin and Spanish
omelet. Request the King George
Sunriser special. Open 6am–9pm. **$**
Vanda Café
Paguirigan Street, Ilagan
Tel: 078-624 2050
Serves deer and steak; weekly
exotic specialties. **$**

Nueva Vizcaya
Bread N' Bites
National Highway, Solano
Tel: 078-326 6085
A better version of Jollibee. Very
popular. Open 6.30am–8.30pm.
FTM Fastfood
Bayombong, Nueva Vizcaya
Tel: 078-321 2572
Nueva Vizcaya's most popular
restaurant serves Filipino,
Japanese and Chinese food.
Ballroom, big-screen TV, karaoke. **$**

CENTRAL CORDILLERA

Benguet
Bliss Café
Munsayac Inn, Leonard Wood Road,
(across Teachers Camp), Baguio
Tel: 074-442 2451
Cell tel: 0917-846 4729
www.blissnbaguio.com
Art and music space offering
wholesome lacto-vegetarian and
vegan food, taking advantage of
Baguio's fresh produce. Open

Mon–Fri from 11am, weekends
from 9am. **$**
Café by the Ruins
In front of Baguio City Hall
Tel: 074-442 4010
Don't leave Baguio without trying
this garden café, which takes
advantage of Baguio's fresh
produce. With its own bakery and
an Igorot-style *ato*, this place is
perfect for drinking a mountain tea.
Open daily 7am–9pm. **$$**
Le Fondue Bar and Restaurant
112 Session Road, Baguio
Shares space with food stalls until
dinner, when it has the second-floor
deck all to itself until 9pm, or later
if there is live music. A nice airy
place to hang out at, with
interesting fondue offerings. **$**
OMG (Oh My Gulay)
4th Floor, La Azotea Bldg., Baguio
Vegetarian restaurant ("*gulay*"
means veggies) with artistic
delivery. Fresh, creative, organic
and well-priced, serving salads,
pasta, desserts and a refreshing
drink menu (no alchohol). Worth
going just to see the theme park-
like layout. Open noon–9pm. **$**
PNKY Café
13 Leonard Wood Road, Baguio
Tel: 074-446-7094
www.pnkyhome.com
Part of a bed and breakfast
accommodation, the café offers
all-day Filipino and American
breakfasts as well as a large
selection of dishes from steaks and
burgers to pizzas and pastas. **$**

Mountain Province
Log Cabin
Uphill from the jeep parking plaza,
Sagada
Some of the tastiest food to be
found in the Cordilleras. Order from
the special menu before 4pm for
dinner that later that night. **$**
Yoghurt House
Downhill from the Town Hall
Homemade yoghurt, hearty meals
and great service. **$**

Ifugao
For restaurants in Banaue and
Batad, refer to the *Where To Stay*
section. Independent restaurants
are rare in these parts.

BICOL

Camarines Norte
Louie's Restaurant
Daet, Camarines Norte
Tel: 054-571 2801
Local cuisine served in native setting. Fast service, clean. **$**

Camarines Sur
Aristocrat Restaurant
E. Angeles Street, Dinaga, Naga
Tel: 054-473 8832
Seafood, Bicolaño delicacies, Chinese food. Open 6am–7pm. **$**

Patio Magdelena
Burgos Street, Sta Cruz, Naga
Tel: 054-473 9828
Delicious Filipino cuisine by the poolside in Hotel Mirabella. Open 4pm–midnight. **$**

Plaza Grill
Hernandez Street, Naga City
Tel: 054-473 6534
Local food in an elegant setting. Nightly entertainment. Open 6am–midnight. **$**

Rodson Café
Burgos Street, Sta Cruz, Naga
Tel: 054-473 9828
Short orders, drinks, coffee. Open 24 hours. **$**

Albay
Café Ola
88 Penaranda Street, Legaspi
Tel: 052-214 3640
24-hour seafood restaurant. **$**

Lobby Lounge
Casablanca Hotel
Peñaranda Street, Legaspi
Tel: 052-480 8334–5
Grilled prawns and tenderloin steaks. **$**

Orient Graden
Peñaranda Street, Legaspi
Tel: 052-480 8334
Chinese restaurant serves steamboat dishes. **$**

Sorsogon
Kalunduan Seafood Restaurant
Pareja Street, Bitan-o Sorsogon town
Tel: 056-211 1573
Fresh seafood, native cuisine, Western fare and wholesome entertainment by the sea. **$**

Rizal Beach Restaurant
Rizal Gubat, Sorsogon
Tel: 056-211 1056
Fresh seafood and native dishes; overlooks Rizal Beach. **$**

Mindoro
La Gensol Restaurant
95 National Road, Mamburao
Tel: 043-711 1072
Seafood galore in marine setting; excellent service. Open 24 hours. **$**

Traveler Restaurant
120 National Road
Payompon, Mamburao
Tel: 043-711 1136
Serves chop suey, pork *tapa*, *calderatang usa* (deer) and other local specialties. Open 7am–10pm. **$**

Doña Lina, The Carabao, The Dolphin, The Palmera Café, The Barracuda
Coco Beach, Puerto Galera
Tel: 097-377 2115
These restaurants offer Filipino, French and Indian cuisines, plus seafood. Good style and service with tropical drinks and wines. The resort is French-owned. **$**

EASTERN VISAYAS

Leyte
Giuseppe's Restaurant
Avenida Veteranos, Tacloban
Tel: 053-321 8758
Italian and Filipino cuisine. **$**

Green House
Coca-Cola, Fatima Village, Tacloban
Tel: 053-321 2974
Delicious Filipino dishes served in a garden setting. **$**

San Pedro Bay Restaurant
Magsaysay Boulevard, Tacloban
Tel: 053-325 6000
Wide variety of food. **$$**

CENTRAL VISAYAS

Cebu
Aranus
31 Fairlane Village, Guadalupe
Tel: 032-256 1934
Offering some of the best Spanish dishes in Cebu for over 15 years, with specialties such as paella and *callos* (tripe). It is a little challenging to find, but its food is worth the trouble. Open Mon–Sat 6–9pm.

Café Laguna
Ayala Center, Cebu Business Park
Tel: 032-233 8600
Regional and home-style cooking. Specialties include *puto bumbong* (colored rice flour steamed in bamboo tubes), *pancit palabok* (traditional noodle dish), vegetable rolls and *sinigang* stew. **$**

Cowrie Cove
Shangri-La's Mactan Island Resort
Tel: 032-231 0288
Seawater aquarium is a fitting backdrop for really fine seafood, including chilli crab. **$$$–$$$$**

Formo Restaurant
Banilad Town Centre, Banilad
Tel: 032-416 1990
Serving international (Mexican, Vietnamese, etc) cuisine. Happy hour is 6–10pm, after which it becomes an engaging nightspot with house, acoustic and Latin music, and other themed entertainment. **$$**

Giuseppe Pizzeria and Sicilian Roast
Mancao Compound, Maria Luisa Road, Banilad, Cebu City
Tel: 032-343 9901
Pizza and pasta on the menu here, made with love. **$$**

Golden Cowrie
Salinas Drive, Lahug
Tel: 032-233 4243
Inexpensive seafood. Native setting with pebble floors and bamboo decor. Specialties include baked mussels, lobster, sizzling squid and grilled blue marlin. **$**

Goodah.gud Grill & Seafood
#935-B Salinas Drive, Lahug
Tel: 032-234 2716
24 hour, fresh seafood, barbecue. Where the night owls go when they start getting hungry. **$**

Gustavian
Maria Luisa Road, Banilad
Tel: 032-344 7653
Swedish ambience and mixed Continental fare, with excellent breakfasts and surprises like gravlax. Good set menu. **$$**

Ichiriki Chaya
A.S. Fortuna Street, Banilad
Tel: 032-345 1300
One of the most innovative Japanese dining complexes in

town, with restaurant, sake and sushi bar, Korean-style barbecue and even massage facilities. **$$**

Kaishu
168 Buot Punta Engano,
Lapu Lapu City, Mactan
Tel: 032-495 2888
Kaishu moved from Cebu City to Mactan several years ago; devoted patrons still make the longer trek out to this well-regarded Japanese restaurant with excellent sashimi and sushi. **$$**

La Tegola Cucina Italiana
Banilad tel: 032-345 6080
Mactan tel: 032-340 9070
Upper Busay tel: 032-419 2220
Italian. Several branches around Cebu, including one up on the hilltop park Tops, which has a view of Cebu that makes it worth the extra drive time. **$$**

Red Moon
GQS Building, between Petron and UFC, Banilad
Tel: 032-232 4367
Pinoy-Chinese restaurant. Specialties include honey spring chicken, *kiampong* (fried rice) and oyster omelet. **$**

Spice Fusions
Banilad Town Center
Tel: 032-344 2923
Never empty, this restaurant offers

dishes from around Asia, from Thai curry to Malay *sate*, Singaporean desserts to Hainanese and Filipino offerings. The *roti* (bread) is a scrumptious way to start a meal. **$$**

STK
Near Mactan Island Shangri-La
This assortment of foodstalls overlooking a mangrove swamp serves fresh seafood from the adjacent wet market. S for *sinugba* (grilled food), T for *tinola* (stewed), or K for *kinilaw* (fresh food in vinegar) – or "Shoot To Kill." **$**

Tinderbox
Banilad Road, next to Crossroads Mall
Tel: 032-234 1681
Well-stocked wine and cigar rooms, continental menu and a connected store with one of the best selections of imported meats, veggies and other goods in the city. **$$$**

PALAWAN

Puerto Princesa

KaLui Restaurant
369 Rizal Avenue
Tel: 048-433 2580
Delicious seafood in a *nipa*-hut atmosphere. Remove shoes and lounge on floor cushions. **$$**

SOUTHERN AND CENTRAL MINDANAO

Davao

Ah Fat Seafood Plaza
Victoria Plaza Compound, Bajada, Davao City
Tel: 082-224 0002
Tasty, reasonably priced Chinese food. So popular it opened a second branch next door. **$$**

Banok's Garden Barbikyu
Washington Street, Bonifacio Circle
Tel: 082-227 6529
Fortune Road, Lanang
Tel: 083-235 2338
Outdoor chicken barbecue restaurant. **$**

Claude's Café de Ville
Habana Compound, 29 Rizal Street
Tel: 082-222 4287
French cuisine, excellent steaks, clams and Jambalaya gumbo. **$$**

Colasa's & Marilou's Barbecue
Washington Street, Bonifacio Circle
Tel: 082-221 2959
Barbecue food; *kamayan*-style dining. Stays open late. **$**

Karahay
Victoria Plaza, J.P. Laurel Avenue
Tel: 082-227 1159
Pick fresh food and tell the chef how to cook it. **$**

Mandarin Tea Garden
With locations in Uptown Plaza,

Fresh Juices and Local Brews

What to drink? You will be spoilt for choice. On the healthy side, there are non-alcoholic juices made from fresh tropical fruits. For something a little more exciting, San Miguel beer is a regular fixture throughout the country, and there are some pretty potent local brews in the rural areas. Here's a quick rundown:

Calamansi juice Made from local limes and not unlike lemonade. This is a refreshing drink served hot or cold that almost every visitor loves.

Green mango shake Ripe mango shakes are delicious but green mango shakes introduce a subtler flavor of sour, unripe fruit with just

a hint of sugar. You have to experience it yourself.

Fresh fruit juice Melon, pineapple, papaya and mango in season all make delicious juices to soothe the soul and spirit. Sip one on the beach for an instant pick-me-up.

Buko juice Look for a vendor with a cart full of young green coconuts, and watch him get to work slicing and dicing. Insert a straw and sip away. After drinking the coconut water, the vendor will chop it open for you to eat the tender flesh inside.

San Miguel This one hardly needs an introduction. The country's most famous commercial beer is best enjoyed in the Philippines. Connoisseurs swear that the "San

Mig" in Hong Kong doesn't even compare – blame it on the water...

Tanduay Rum This is perhaps some of the cheapest and tastiest rum-mixes in the world – well with almost anything.

Tuba A favorite home brew in rural areas, it is made from the sap of coconut or palm trees. Despite its relatively low alcohol content, it can knock you out in a hurry.

Basi Made from sugar cane, this wine of the Ilocos region is famous. Find out why.

Lumbanog This Coconut Vodka is most fragrant and potent when fresh, but it is also available in processed form, and in such flavors as green apple and bubble gum.

Dining in Davao

Exotic Davao delicacies include *kinilaw* (raw fish concocted with vinegar, Philippine lemon and spices), *inihaw na panga* (grilled tuna jaw) and *bihod* (fish roe). Fresh seafood such as prawns, crab, lobsters and deep-sea fishes are abundant and available in most restaurants.

Gverro Street, Amgar Plaza, SM Mall and Gaisano Mall, offering affordable *dim sum*. **$**

Tsuru Japanese Restaurant
Don R. Castillo Building, Legaspi Street
Tel: 082-221 0901
Davao's best Japanese food and well worth the price. Great native coffee too. **$$**

South Cotabato

The Garden Grill
Anchor Hotel, Cagampang Ext. Street, General Santos
Tel: 083-552 4660
Grilled and steamed *pompano*, smoked *bangus sinigang*, grilled *bangus* belly. **$**

Nanay Bebeng
Gaisano Mall, J. Catolico Street, General Santos City
Cell tel: 0926-326 1571
Various *viand* (rice toppings) from the Cagayan/Ilocos region. **$**

Orange Café
Pioneer Avenue, General Santos
Tel: 083-301 0992
Great for coffee, lunch and snacks. Tasty handmade cheeseburgers, and the noodle dish *palabok* is a town favorite. **$**

Rooftop Grill
6/F, Sydney Hotel
Pendatun Street, General Santos
Tel: 083-552 5479/80
Sergeant fish: grilled, *kinilaw*, sashimi. Views overlooking bay. **$**

Seafront Restaurant
Tropicana Resort, Tambler
General Santos
Tel: 083-380 7328
Good tuna and grilled chicken. **$**

North Cotabato

Rock Star Café
Osmeña Street, Kidapawan

Tel: 064-288 1445/46
Average food; live band Wednesday and Saturday. **$**

Maguindanao

Casa Blanca
Sinsuat Avenue, Cotabato City
Tel: 064-421 2126
Excellent native cooking in colonial wooden house. **$**

Sunburst
Don Rufino Alonzo Street, Cotabato
Tel: 064-421 2582
Open-air dining. **$**

NORTHERN MINDANAO AND CARAGA

Misamis Oriental

Café Alexandria
Captain Vicente Roa Ext.
Cagayan de Oro City
Tel: 08822-727 623
Red-carpet treatment and good coffee – unexceptional seafood. Open 6am–midnight. **$**

Consuelo Steakhouse
192 Corrales Avenue, CDO
Tel: 08822-725 416
Great buffets and giant dessert. **$**

Dynasty Restaurant
Tianno Hayes Street, CDO
Tel: 08822-724 516, 727 825
Best in town for Chinese, Filipino and European cuisines. Ideal for families; plays classical music. **$**

Kagay-anon Restaurant
Rosario Arcade, Limketkai Center Lapasan, CDO
Tel: 08822-729 003
Healthy food. Recipient of "Kalinisan (Cleanliness) Award of Excellence." Fresh crab, Filipino delicacies: *pinakbet* served inside squash, *kinilaw* in clam shell, *sinagang* rice in bamboo tube. **$**

Live Site
Tianno Hayes Street, CDO
Tel: 08822-726 876
Opposite Picasso RestoBar. Live band, disco, till 2am. **$$**

Mama Iya's Restaurant
Opol
Tel: 08822-735 563
Nestled in a grove of mature *talisay* trees between beach and pool in Lauremar Resort. Innovative Asian cuisine and local delicacies. **$**

Pecan Tree Café
Rosario Arcade, Limketkai Center Lapasan, CDO
Tel: 08822-729 292
Fine Continental cuisine with great exotic food: sizzling ostrich steak, grilled pink Tasmanian salmon. Heavenly pecan pie and gourmet coffee. **$**

Picasso RestoBar
7/F, Dynasty Hotel
Tianno Hayes Street, CDO
Tel: 08822-724 516
Unassuming coffee shop by day, hot disco by night. CDO's finest. Live bands. Open till 2am. **$$**

Sasutukil Seafood Grill
Cugman, CDO
Tel: 08822-732 929
Trademark grilled seafood in a beach setting. **$**

Sea Garden Restaurant
Velez Street, CDO
Tel: 08822-723 551
Seafood in the city center. **$**

Sir Henry's Restaurant
Velez Street, CDO
Tel: 08822-726 080
Henry's the owner – ask about the VIP Noodles: one of a kind. Best green mango shake in town. Open 24 hours. **$**

Tabing Dagat Restaurant
Opol
Tel: 08822-754 488
Wholesome Filipino and American dishes in a panoramic setting. 20 min. from CDO. **$**

Tres Marias
Cugman, CDO
Tel: 08822-732 929
Delicious Filipino and international delicacies. **$**

Camiguin

Casa Grande Hotel and Café
Poblacion Mambajao
Tel: 088-387 2075
Only place here for international cuisine; caters to foreigners. Open 8am–8pm. **$**

RJ Pension and Restaurant
Mabajao
Tel: 088-387 0089
Fast food, seafood. **$**

Misamis Occidental

Café Rosario
Marcelo H. Del Pilar, Dayawan

Oroquieta City
Fax: 088-531 1158
Delicious chop suey, *kinilaw, sinugba, calamares*. Open 24 hours. **$**
Lapyahan Seafoods
Bliss, Sta Cruz, Ozamis
Seafood by the beach. **$**
La Veranda Restaurant
Burgos corner Zamora Street
Ozamis. Tel: 088-521 2888/89
Excellent seafood. **$**

Lanao del Norte
Dear Manok Grilled Chicken House
Quezon Avenue Ext. corner La Salle
Street, Iligan City
Tel: 088-221 9221
Grilled chicken on banana leaf. Also
delicious *kinilaw* and *buko* juice. **$**
Pagoda Fastfood Restaurant
Quezon Avenue, Iligan
Tel: 088-221 3163
Try Iligan's hottest *sepo guisado*, a
fiery mixture of squid, fish, shrimp,
vegetables and chilli. **$**
Patio Alejandra
San Miguel Street, Iligan
Tel: 088-221 2754
Iligan's finest seafood. Grilled
tanigue, prawns, squid, sizzling
shrimp and more. Near Maria
Cristina Falls. **$**
Sunburst Fried Chicken
Badelles Ext., Pala-o, Iligan
Tel: 088-221 2559
Iligan's best fried chicken. Cozy
garden-style eatery. **$**

Lanao del Sur
Marawi Resort Hotel Restaurant
MSU, Marawi
Tel: 063-520 981
Exotic choice of Maranao and non-
Maranao dishes served in
traditional Islamic ware. **$**

Bukidnon
Town Café and Bar
Fortich Street, Malaybalay
Tel: 088-221 3211
Excellent seafood in Chinese-
Filipino style. **$**

Agusan del Norte
Aling Cora's Lutong Bahay
R. Calo Street
Tel: 085-342 5281
Native delicacies. Highly
recommended for food your mom

would cook if she were Cebuana.
Another branch fronting Gaisano
Mall. **$**
Embassy Restaurant
Montilla Boulevard corner Pili Drive
Butuan
Tel: 085-342 8883, 225 2200
Best Filipino dishes in town.
Friendly staff. **$**
True Brew Gourmet Coffee
J.C. Aquino Avenue
Tel: 085-341 5879
Nice sophisticated light sandwiches
and rice meals. **$**
Weegol's Garden
Doongan, City Hall Drive, Butuan
Tel: 085-342 5558
Garden restaurant with *nipa* huts;
serves chicken barbecue on banana
leaf. Also wild boar and deer. **$**

Agusan del Sur
Diwata Restaurant
Purok 3, San Isidro, San Francisco
Tel: 085-343 8185
Sells fresh fish and other seafood,
cooked to order. **$**

Surigao del Sur
Mueco's Restaurant
Mabwa Beach, Tandag
Tel: 086-211 8888
Seafood delights. Fish *kinilaw,
sinugba,* and *tinola;* lobster, prawns
and crabs. **$**
Royal Christian Restaurant
Tandag, Surigao del Sur
Tel: 086-211 3140
Good food. Romantic setting. **$**

Surigao del Norte
Adriano's KTV by the Sea
Port Area, Surigao City
Tel: 086-232 4728
Sing, eat and drink while gazing at
spectacular sunset. Surigao's best
seafood. **$**
Berna & Carol Barbecue
Borromeo Street, Surigao
Tel: 086-231 7300
Offers hot, mouth-watering
barbecued food on banana leaf.
Crowded 6–7pm. Native setting. **$**
Mario's
Next to Town Hall, Surigao City
Tel: 086-826 2003
Garden restaurant with live music at
nights. Great barbecue and grilled
seafood. **$**

ZAMBOANGA

Zamboanga del Norte
Shell Park Remedios Restaurant
Rizal Avenue, Dipolog City
Tel: 065-212 2226
American, Chinese and native
cuisine. Singers, ballroom, live
band entertainment. **$**
Golden Pot Restaurant
Arellano Street, Dipolog
Tel: 065-212 3451
Serves Filipino cuisine and seafood;
homemade ice cream. Ballroom
dancing in the evenings. **$**
Top Diner
Top of Plaza Hotel
Quezon Avenue, Dipolog
Tel: 065-212 5777
A capriciously furnished, rooftop
restaurant with Dipolog's best
seafood and great city view.
Roadside Café
Rizal Avenue corner Magsaysay
Street, Dipolog
Tel: 065-212 3504
Seafood in an excellent setting.
Open 24 hours. **$**

Zamboanga del Sur
Paradise Food Court
Capitol Site, Pagadian
Tel: 062-214 1320
Seafood, swimming pool and
billiards. **$**
Alavar Seafood House
Don Alfaro Street, Tetuan
Tel: 062-991 2483
The most popular seafood
restaurant here, due to the
romantic setting and excellent
sunset view. **$**
Palmeras
Pasonanca, Zamboanga City
Tel: 062-991 3284
Enjoy deliciously cooked seafood
using your fingers. **$**
Café Bianca
34 Barcelona Street, Zamboanga
Tel: 062-991 2514
Delicious coffee and Filipino
cooking; excellent balcony view. **$**

Culture

General

There are a number of free magazines and websites devoted to listing current happenings in Manila and the rest of the Philippines. *Circuit* (tel: 02-896 3028), available monthly at coffee shops, bars and restaurants, covers hot clubs, restaurants, art galleries and contemporary cultural events. *Loud* (www.loudph.com) covers the Pinoy rock scene, and is a good place to get to know the vibrant Manila music scene. *Citiguide* is a comprehensive bimonthly publication, an excellent resource for information with maps, schedules of events and business listings. The website www.bandstand.ph is also a great resource for mostly rock and world music event schedules.

Check the **National Commission for Culture and the Arts** (NCCA) website at www.ncca.gov.ph for events such as the Philippine Arts Festival, held every February in venues nationwide.

When in Cebu, pick up a free copy of *Bite* magazine (tel: 032-344 7047), the pocket-sized monthly guide to music gigs, art exhibitions, live performances, hip events and more. It is available in top hotels, cafés, bars and restaurants.

Buying Tickets

For information about concerts, plays and other events, call **Ticketworld** at 02-891 1000. Tickets can be purchased over the phone with credit cards, then picked up by arrangement at one of their many outlets around the city, such as at National Bookstores or at Glorietta cinemas.

Aside from concerts and plays at the Cultural Center of the Philippines, Ticketworld handles Philippine Basketball Association (PBA) games at Ultra in Pasig City, and Pasay's Cuneta Astrodome.

DANCE

Ballet Philippines is the country's foremost company, followed by the **Philippine Ballet Theater**. The **Bayanihan National Dance Company** and **Ramon Obusan Folkloric Group** excel in cultural and folk dancing. These companies perform regularly at the **Cultural Center of the Philippines** (CCP). More information is available on the CCP website www.culturalcenter.gov.ph.

Cultural Center of the Philippines (CCP)

The sprawling **Cultural Center of the Philippines** complex on Roxas Boulevard houses theaters, museums, a library, restaurants, galleries and exhibition rooms. Most of Manila's plays, ballets and concerts take place here. It was built as the pride and joy of former first lady Imelda Marcos nearly 40 years ago. Tel: 02-832 1125; www.culturalcenter.gov.ph.

THEATER AND CONCERTS

The following venues also host theatrical and musical performances:

GSIS Theater
GSIS Building, CCP Complex, Manila
Tel: 02-891 6161 x 4021

Manila Metropolitan Theater
Liwasang Bonifacio, Manila

Philippine Ballet Theater
Ortigas Avenue, Pasig City
Tel: 02-632 8848
Plays and musicals year-round.

Tanghalang Pilipino
CCP Complex, Roxas Blvd, Manila
Tel: 02-842 0137, 832 3704

William J. Shaw Theater
5/F, Shangri-La Plaza, EDSA corner Shaw Blvd, Mandaluyong
Tel: 02-633 4821 to 25

Performances by Repertory Philippines.

MUSIC

The Philippine Philharmonic Orchestra, **Philippine Madrigal Singers** and UST **Symphony Orchestra** perform regularly at the **Cultural Center of the Philippines** (CCP; tel: 02-832 1125; www.culturalcenter.gov.ph). Various open-air concerts are held in Rizal Park every Sunday at 5pm, and in Paco Park on Friday at 6pm.

MOVIES

Movie-going is as popular as ever, and one of the best entertainment bargains in town: tickets cost P90–150. American films are the most popular.

Tagalog cinema is a big deal for locals, though many of the films are of doubtful merit. The glamour inspires many young Filipinos to dream of becoming film stars.

With the opening of Mall of Asia, the Philippines has its first IMAX movie theatre, and its eight-story screen and bone-shaking sound make for a great family trip out. Ticket prices are about P200–300, depending on the feature. Call 02-556 IMAX.

For information about movies at the various Robinsons Malls around Manila and the country (Galleria, Ermita, etc), check out www.robinsonmovieworld.com.

ShoeMart (SM) Malls around the country, such as Megamall, Mall of Asia and Clark, has SM Dial-a-Movie service at tel: 02-833 9999 for their movie offerings.

Information about Ayala Malls movie tickets (Glorietta, Greenbelt, Alabang Town Center, Ayala Center Cebu, etc) can be found at www.sureseats.com.

ART GALLERIES

Impressive collections of Philippine masters, including Luna, Hidalgo,

Guerrero and Flores, are scattered throughout Manila.

Ateneo Art Gallery
Ateneo de Manila University, Loyola Heights, Quezon City, Metro Manila. Selected works by Philippine contemporary artists
Tel: 02-426 6001 x 4160
Open Monday–Friday 8am–5pm; Saturday 8am–noon.

Lopez Memorial Museum
Benpres Building, Exchange Road corner Meralco Avenue, Pasig City
Tel: 02-631 2417
More than 13,000 rare Filipino books and manuscripts for researchers, plus paintings by National Artists, and archeological finds from Calatagan burial sites. Open Monday–Saturday 8am–5pm; entrance fee.

Mueso ng Sining
GSIS Building, CCP Complex, Manila
Tel: 02-832 3702
Contemporary Filipino art, especially Fernando Amorsolo and Hernanda Ocampo, plus monthly rotating displays. Open Tuesday–Sunday 10–6pm; entrance fee.

UP (University of the Philippines) Vargas Musuem
Roxas Avenue, Diliman, Quezon City
Tel: 02-920 5301 x 7408, 928 1927
Three floors of modern Filipino paintings from collection of Jorge Vargas, former executive secretary to president Manuel Quezon. Open Tuesday–Sunday 9am–4pm; entrance fee.

OTHER MUSEUMS

American Historical Collection
Ateneo de Manila University, Loyola Heights, Quezon City
Tel: 02-426 6001 x 5917
Resource library documenting American presence in Philippines, 1898–1946. Contains historical papers available nowhere else. Open Monday–Friday 8am–5pm, Saturday 8am–noon; entrance fee.

Ayala Museum of Philippine History and Iconographic Archive
Corner Makati Avenue and De la Rosa Street, by Greenbelt Park
Tel: 02-757 7117–21

The Ayala Museum is a must-see for anyone visiting Makati. While still displaying its 60 intricate dioramas portraying key episodes in Philippine history, the museum is now also host to a rotating display of multimedia exhibits and events held at its hip M Café. Open Tuesday–Friday 9am–6pm, Saturday–Sunday 10am–7pm; entrance fee.

Bahay Tsinoy (Chinese House)
Cabildo corner Anda Street, Intramuros
Tel: 02-527 6083
Documents Chinese influence. Open Tuesday–Sunday 1–5pm; entrance fee.

UST (University of Santo Tomas) Museum of Arts and Sciences
Grand Hall, Mezzanine, UST Main Building, España, Metro Manila
Tel: 02-781 1815, 740 9718
Natural history, ethnography, Chinese trade ceramics, paintings by Filipino masters, Philippine religious images. Open Tuesday–Friday 9am–4.30pm; entrance fee.

Cultural Centers

Besides offering tasty French lunches for a good price, **Alliance Francais** (209 Nicanor Garcia Street, Bel-Air II, Makati; tel: 02-895 7585, 895 7441; www.alliance.ph) offers plenty of interesting cultural events, most notably French Spring and Fête de la Musique, both held in June.

Get in touch with the Philippines' Spanish heritage at the **Cervantes Institute** (manila.cervantes.es), a Spanish government program that has helped protect the last vestiges of the 300-year Spanish colonial rule. Check schedules for music, film, lectures and book launches.

For those wanting a more active cultural experience, inquire at the **Clara Ramona Centro de Danza Flamenca** (5917 Alger Street, parallel to Rockwell Drive, tel: 02-890 8030 or cell tel: 0915-434 5789) for dancing instruction in flamenco, sevillana and Andaluzi belly dancing. Classes are offered for kids, teens and adults.

Nightlife

General

Manila by night is a swinging town with a flurry of distinctive colors, flavors, and styles, from nightclubs to ballroom dancing to movies, bars and casinos. Though Quezon City and Malate have their superb corners, the recent opening of Greenbelt and The Fort have made Makati shine brightest under the Manila moonlight. Smokers take note: Makati has a no-smoking ordinance that prohibits smoking in non-designated areas of restaurants and bars. Just ask the staff if you're looking for a puffing place.

Don't make the assumption that your outfit for the beach will also work on a night out in Manila; Filipinos do not entirely embrace casual dress for the evening. Pants and shoes should at very least be worn out if you're not sure of your ports of call for the evening.

MANILA

Bar and Clubs
Absinth
3rd Level, Greenbelt 3
Tel: 02-757 4967
Hip hop, live and house music fueled hip hangout. Always a decent crowd here.

Blue Room
615 Nakpil Street, Malate
Tel: 02-524 6870
Mall of Asia, G/F
Tel: 02-556 0288
A pleasant club for 30-somethings, piped-in jazz music.

Café Havana
1903 Adriatico corner Remedios, Malate
Tel: 02-524 5526
1st Level, Greenbelt, Makati

Tel: 02-757 4370
Cuban music and dancing galore.
Grab a *mojito* and swing, or head
upstairs to Hemingway's for cigars.

Capone's
G/F Frasier Place, Valero Street,
Salcedo Village
Tel: 02-818 1818
Ever changing variety of music,
good ambience and good crowds.

Embassy
Fort Bonifacio Global City
Tel: 02-816 4346
One of the most happening places
in town with house and R&B music.

Fez
Piazza Serendra, Fort Bonifacio,
Taguig
Tel: 02-901 1840
Plays house music, with variations
during the week.

Government
7840 Makati Avenue
Some of the best house music in
town, with a great sound system.
Gay-oriented.

Handlebar
31 Polaris Street, off of Jupiter
Street, Makati
Tel: 02-898 1976
www.handlebar.com.ph
Rock 'n Blues expat hangout with
great ambience. Billiards, and
sporting events on a big screen.

Nuvo
G/F Greenbelt 2
Tel: 02-757 3698
Swank setting and great for people
watching.

Penguin Café and Gallery
604 Remedios Circle, Malate
Tel: 02-521 2088
Alternative artists' bar; changing
exhibits.

Piedra Bar and Restaurant
3rd Floor, Fort Boni Strip, The Fort
Tel: 02-856 0318 to 20
At around 11pm, this restaurant
turns into a nightspot spinning
house, R&B and retro music.

Temple Bar
G/F Greenbelt 2
Tel: 02-757 4813
A must-visit on a Makati night out.
Hip hop or house, with occasional
live music.

Vida de Malate
612 Julio Nakpil Avenue, Malate
Tel: 02-523 4561

Contemporary minimalist ambience,
bands and DJs.

Live Music

Arcadia
542 Remedios Street, Malate
Tel: 02-400 9776
Live rock music.

70's Bistro
46 Anonas Street, Quezon City
Tel: 02-434 3597
Live bands Monday–Saturday after
10pm.

Hobbit House
1801 Mabini Street, Malate
Tel: 02-521 7604
Folk-music bar staffed by midgets.

Ratsky Manila
1663 Bocobo Street, Malate
Tel: 02-523 8608
Just like its cousin in Cebu, this is
where the rockers hang out.

Strumm's
110 Jupiter Street, Bel-Air, Makati
Tel: 02-895 4636, 890 1054
Open Monday–Saturday 6pm–
2.30am. Live retro music after 9pm.

Cabaret

Jools Cabaret
5043 P. Burgos Street, Makati
Tel: 02-897 9061
www.jools.ph
Well-choreographed burlesque shows
almost every night on the hour. A
little naughty, but not over the top.

The Library
1779 Adriatico Street, Malate
Tel: 02-522 2484
Stand-up comedy, usually in
Tagalog. You may be part of the act.

Cafés

Bo's Coffee
www.boscoffee.com
This Cebu favorite has 10 branches
in Manila (part of a nationwide
network of 32 branches) and offers
a local alternative to international
coffee chains. Freshly roasted
coffee in pleasant settings.

Café Bola
2/F, Greenbelt
Tel: 02-757 2652
Contemporary Pinoy diner.

Café Breton
There are now over seven Café
Bretons in various locations,
including Greenbelt, Alabang,

Podium and Mall of Asia. Tasty late-
night eats. Call 02-771 2114 for
the nearest one to you.

ANGELES CITY

The area along Fields Avenue, just
outside the former Clark Air Force
base, remains a major nightlife
district for foreigners and Filipinos
alike. Some of the most popular go-
go bars in the area are **Brown
Sugar** and **King of Diamonds**, while
huge Bangkok-style bars, such as
Blue Nile and **Neros Forum**, have
opened more recently. There are
plenty of other types of bars in
Angeles as well, including
Margarita Station, where you will
find no dancing girls but good Thai
and Mexican food. Filipino pool
personality Bata Reyes sometimes
graces the tables. At **Rick's Café**, a
quiet ambience dominates while
movies are played on a wide screen
television 24 hours a day.

BAGUIO

Baguio has a reputation for
accomplished singer-musicians, and
many a surprise can be found while
strolling up Session Road, or in
other artist nests around the city.

Alberto's
Otek Street, opposite Mt. Crest
Hotel, Baguio
Tel: 074-443 3467
Live bands from Baguio and Manila,
open daily. Packed on weekends.

Nevada Square
2 Loakan Road, Baguio City
Tel: 074-443 5904
Over 10 establishments from
karaoke and acoustic bars to dance
clubs and cafés.

Rumours
Session Road, Baguio
A popular Baguio hangout. One of
a few bars on this strip that offer
acoustic and rock music.

CEBU

Paseo (F. Cabahug Street, in
Mabolo) is the city's first year-round

night market and entertainment center, with over 30 F&B outlets, 100 market stalls, and a big open-air stage with covered seating capacity of up to 2,000 people, which hosts entertainers of different stripes.

Bars and Clubs

After Hours Tapas Lounge
Crossroads Arcade, Banilad
Tel: 032-233 4089
Watch this hair salon by day literally fold up into the walls and transform into a chill-out venue for food, booze and live soul music.

Badgers Sports and Dining Pub
RCBC Building, Gov. M. Cuenco Avenue
Tel: 032-345 2199
Comfortable *Cheers*-like ambience. Meat pies, billiards and draft beer.

The Loft
Skyrise Building, Asia Town I.T. Park
Tel: 032-238 0532
DJs play house, chill-out and R&B music.

Handuraw
460 Gorordo Avenue
Tel: 032-232 6401
Old Coaco Building, Cuenco Avenue, Mabolo
Tel: 032-233 8678
One of the best places in town to hear live ska, rock, acoustic and other genres of music.

Jazz and Blues
F. Cabahug Street
Tel: 032-232 2698
Just as the name says, this establishment offers exactly that – live jazz and blues.

Sunflower City Disco
Salinas Drive, Lahug, Cebu City
Tel: 032-231 8413
Huge cavernous beer hall, live music and dancing.

Theatro
Crossroads Mall, Archbishop Reyes, Banilad
Charming pocket bar, house music on bottom, piano bar with piano player ready to play your requests.

DAVAO

Davao night owls know their bars close at 2am as per city ordinance, so they aim to do it right before closing time. Most nightlife is centered around entertainment complexes with a live performance area surrounded by restaurants, bars and clubs of various description. Smoking ordinances in effect in Davao.

Blue Posts Bar & Billiards
J.P. Laurel Avenue
Tel: 082-224 6349
Enjoy billiards and exotic *pica-pica* with buddies.

Matina Town Square
Matina Highway
Live bands both local and from Manila, sports bars, jazz, cultural shows and stand-up comedy.

Pagasa Piano Bar
G/F, The Apo View, J. Camus Street
Tel: 082-221 6430
Live band entertainment.

Pinoy Republik
Ilustre Street
Good food and cheap drinks.

Rizal Promenade
On Rizal Street by Philamlife Building. Another interesting collection of dance, chill, reggae and live music bars.

Summit Bar
9/F, Royal Mandaya Hotel, Palma Gil corner Reyes Street
Tel: 082-225 8888

The Venue
Jacinto Extension Street
Tel: 082-224 4150
Part of The Compound, a collection of disco and live band venues. Apparently one of the biggest party complexes in the country.

SUBIC

In Subic, there are remnants of the nightlife that once boomed during US Navy days. It is much more low-key than Angeles, with friendly seaside bars in Barrio Barretto like **Islander**, run by a veteran who used to serve on US submarines. At the **Rock Lobster**, expatriates working at the Subic Freeport gather in the evenings. The **Midnight Rambler** is popular with European travelers and features one of the most amazing blues and classic rock and roll CD collections in the Philippines.

Festivals

January

January 1 New Year's Day.
First Sunday Three Kings' Pageant. Santa Cruz and Gasan, Marinduque.
January 9 Feast of the Black Nazarene. Quiapo, Manila.
Third weekend Ati-Atihan (Landing of the 10 Bornean Noblemen): Colorful processions in Kalibo, Aklan; Fiesta de Santo Niño (Feast of the Christ Child), Cebu City (Sinulog).
January 25 Feast of St Paul Vigan.
Fourth weekend Dinagyang: (similar to Ati-Atihan).
Variable Appey (planting festival). Bontoc, Mt Province.

February

February 11 Feast of Our Lady of Lourdes. Quezon City.
Second week Bamboo Organ Festival. Las Piñas; International Hot Air Balloon Fiesta, Clark Field.
February 22–25 People Power at EDSA (celebrates overthrow of Marcos). Metro Manila.
Last weekend Panagbenga Flower Festival. Baguio.
Variable Hari Raya Hadji. Muslims mark pilgrimage to Mecca; Lunar New Year. Chinese celebrate the start of the new lunar year.

March & April

First weekend Paraw Regatta, Race of native sailboats. Iloilo.
March 10–16 Araw ng Dabaw. Town fiesta. Davao City.
April 9 Araw ng Kagitingan (Day of Valor). Commemorates the Death March. Nationwide.
Lenten Week Moriones Festival Boac, Marinduque.
Variable Good Friday and Easter.

May: Fiesta Month

Entire month Santacruzan (procession of Sta Helena of Constantinople); Flores de Mayo (floral parades); Bohol Fiesta: Pilgrimage to the Shrine of Our Lady of Peace and Good Voyage. Antipolo, Rizal.
May 1 Labor Day. Nationwide.
First week Viva Vigan! Town fiesta.
May 14–15 Carabao Festival. Pulilan, Bulacan and Angono, Rizal.
May 15 Pahiyas Festival. Sariaya and Lucban, Quezon.
May 15–17 Kailonawan (fertility rites). Obando, Bulacan.

June

June 12 Independence Day.
June 24 Feast of St John the Baptist. San Juan, Metro Manila.
June 24 Parada ng Lechon (parade of roast pigs). Balayan, Batangas.
June 27 Our Lady of Perpetual Help. Baclaran, Metro Manila.
June 29 Apung Iru Fluvial Parade. Honors St Peter. Apalit, Pampanga.
June 28–30 Pintados Festival. Tacloban, Leyte.
Last Friday Feast of the Sacred Heart. Lucban, Quezon.
Variable Maolod En Nabi. Birthday of Prophet Mohammed; Fête de la Musique, Metro Manila.

July

First Sunday Pagoda sa Wawa (Fluvial Procession). Bocaue, Bulacan.
July 29 Fluvial Festival for St Martha. Pateros, Manila.
Fourth Sunday Abayan Festival for St Anne. Butuan, Agusan del Norte.
Variable Apuy and Pisit (harvest rituals). Ifugao and Mountain provinces.

August

August 19 Gigantes Festival. Town fiesta in Lucban, Quezon.
August 18–31 Kadayawan sa Dabaw (Fruit and Flowers Festival). Davao.
August 27–28 Cagayan de Oro Fiesta. Cagayan de Oro.
Variable Lesles and Fagfagto (planting rites); Sumbali (Aeta Festival). Bayombong, Nueva Vizcaya.

September

Third weekend Peñafrancia Festival (fluvial procession). Naga City, Camarines Sur; T'boli Festival. Lake Sebu, South Cotabato.
September 29 Señor San Miguel. Iligan, Lanao del Norte.
Variable Sunduan. Procession of marriageable lads and ladies. Parañaque, Metro Manila.

October

October 7–8 Halaran Festival. Roxas City, Capiz.
October 7–12 Zamboanga Hermosa. Fiesta with regatta. Zamboanga City.
Second Sunday La Naval de Manila. Quezon City.
Fourth weekend Masskara (Festival of Smiling Masks). Bacolod City; Lanzones Festival. Mambajao, Camiguin.
Last Sunday Feast of Christ the King. Nationwide.

November

November 1 All Saints' Day. Nationwide.
November 23 Gigantes Festival. Angono, Rizal.
November 30 Binabayani. Zambales.
November 30 Bonifacio Day. Nationwide.

December

December 1–14 Fiesta Intramuros. Manila.
December 8 Feast of the Immaculate Conception. Nationwide; fluvial parade in Malabon, Manila.
December 8–9 Feast of Our Lady of Caysaysay. Fluvial parade. Taal, Batangas.
December 16 Misa de Gallo. Start of nine pre-Christmas dawn masses in Catholic regions.
December 16–24 Simbang Gabi. Midnight masses.
Weekend before Christmas Giant Lantern Festival. San Fernando, Pampanga.
December 25 Christmas Day.
December 30 Rizal Day. Nationwide.

Sport

Spectator Sports

COCKFIGHTING

Two roosters enter the ring; only one emerges victorious. Watching their battle is a favorite national pastime, as the audience takes bets. Not for the faint of heart. Places you can catch this in Manila:
Pasay City Cockpit
Tel: 02-843 1890
Roligon Mega Cockpit
Tambo, Parañaque
Tel: 02-833 1638
Araneta Coliseum
Cubao
Tel: 02-911 3101
www.aranetacoliseum.com
No self-respecting small town is without a cockpit; fights usually take place Sunday afternoon.

BASKETBALL

Thanks to American influence, basketball is a well-loved national sport. Metro Manila has three semi-professional leagues, with the **Philippine Basketball Association** (PBA) sometimes traveling across the country in an outreach program. Tel: 02-638 1815 or call Ticketworld.

HORSE RACING

Horse races generally take place on Tuesday, Wednesday, Saturday and Sunday at San Lazaro Leisure Park (tel: 02-914 4838) and Santa Ana Race Track (tel: 02-890 4015) in Manila. Betting on horses is a big-time operation. Major races include the Gran Copa, National Grand Derby, the Founder's Cup and the Presidential Cup.

Participant Sports

GOLF

For many visitors, golf is a big attraction, as the country has some of the finest courses in the world – including championship ones. The attraction includes teeing off amid lush tropical vegetation and water-laced inland resorts.

Perhaps Manila's most accessible course is **Club Intramuros**, which winds round the stone walls of the old Spanish fort. Its 18 holes are open to the public daily; night-time golf is highly recommended. Last tee-off is at 7pm. (Bonifacio Drive corner Aduana Street, Intramuros, tel: 02-527 6613).

To date there are more than 70 golf courses in the archipelago; golf features in locations such as Boracay, Angeles City and Subic Bay. From its low-key start of a few thousand golfers in the 1920s, golf has grown with the advent of international golf tournaments and well-appointed country clubs. Former president Fidel Ramos is a fixture on Manila's courses.

Many golf courses purport to be for "members only," although visiting tourists can often make a case for themselves. Caddies, carts, clubs and "umbrella girls" are available for hire.

DIVING

The Philippines is reputed to have more than 28,000 sq. km (10,808 sq. miles) of coral reefs, making it a perfect site for diving and underwater exploration – despite destructive practices in some areas. Diving promotes ecological awareness of underwater life and in many cases – Anilao being the perfect example – diving has helped bring damaged reefs back from the brink of extinction.

Many divers rent their equipment on site. Although this is generally safe, be sure to check the equipment first, and use caution at all times. For a list of certified

scuba diving organizations, contact the Philippine Commission on Sports Scuba Diving at the Department of Tourism in Manila, tel: 02-524 1703.

Dive operators in Manila include **Aquaventure** (tel: 02-899 2831) and **Scuba World** (Makati tel: 02-895 3551, fax: 02-890 8982; Parañaque tel: 02-807 8134; and San Juan tel: 02-726 0115, 724 8880; www.scubaworld.com.ph, www.explorerfleet.com).

WIND SPORTS

Windsurfing and kite boarding are alive and well in the Philippines. Wind and wave conditions are ideal, plus there is ample rental equipment available, in Boracay, for instance. The island hosts the Boracay Funboard Cup every January or February, which is open to windsurfers of all ages and abilities. Check out www.asianwindsurfingtour.com, and www.kiteboardingboracay.com.

OUTDOOR ACTIVITIES

For something out of the ordinary, check out **Planet Action Adventure** (Cebu tel: (032) 474 0068; planet@action-philippines.com), an outdoor-sports company based in Moalboal. From canyoneering down five-tiered waterfalls, horseback riding, caving and kayaking, to visits to ethnic villages and trekking around Cebu, this company offers a wide range of outdoor activities. Check the website at www.action-philippines.com for more details.

Shopping

What to Buy

The Philippines is an old Asian shopping emporium, dating back to the days when its coastal towns sold pearls, beeswax and tortoise shells to trading vessels from China and Arabia. Today, the emphasis is on handicrafts, woodcarvings and the produce of the sea. Native handicrafts are certainly cheaper in the provinces, but good buys can be found in major cities as well.

BASKETRY

Popular Philippine baskets are found everywhere. Made from natural rattan, *nipa*, bamboo, abaca and palm, the baskets come in a range of sizes and purposes, and are both functional and decorative.

MATS AND HANDBAGS

First cousin to the baskets, Philippine mats are fascinating bits of local color. Many are made of *pandan* or abaca, although Prince Charles orders his in *buri*, an indigenous grass. They may be scarce in Manila, but have a look at the Ilalim ng Tulay (Under the Bridge) market in Quiapo.

Handbags, however, are enjoying a resurgence. Buy yours in Manila before they hit Fifth Avenue.

HANDICRAFTS

Abaca hats, placemats, coasters, bamboo trays, shells and ceramic pots are ubiquitous in airport tourist shops, the Makati commercial center and Ermita tourist belt. Newer developments include lovely handmade paper, picture frames made from coconut husks and bamboo, and capiz-shell Christmas ornaments. Native woven pieces are always popular.

EMBROIDERY

Very few first-time visitors can resist Philippine embroidery. The un-tucked, no-tie-required *barong Tagalog* is beloved by casual tourists and foreign expatriate businessmen. Ask the hotel concierge to suggest a tailor. Choose either the translucent pineapple fiber, *piña,* with the finest hand embroidery, or the cheaper *ramie* or cotton with machine-embroidery. For women, there are the embroidered *terno* dresses, with matching scarves, bags and handkerchiefs.

JEWELRY

Aside from pearls, the most typical Philippine jewelry is made of shell and silver. Mother-of-pearl is perhaps the most popular. Visitors are advised not to purchase items made from coral or tortoise shell, as supporting such unsustainable trade contributes to the degradation of the Philippine seas – which in turn harms the local population. Moreover, trade in some items is illegal.

The best silver jewelry is found in Baguio, where the guild-like training of St Louis University has engendered fine craftsmanship.

You can also find wood and vine jewelry in the specialty shops of Ermita and Makati, as well as beadwork from the tribes, notably the necklaces, earrings and ornamental hair pieces of the T'boli, Mangyan and Ifugao people.

PEARLS

Quality pearls from Mindanao can be found in quantity at Virra Mall in Greenhills, San Juan, Metro Manila. (A few days each month, the merchants travel to the sources to restock). Most of the strands are freshwater pearls in irregular shapes, exotically beautiful and selling for a song. Cultured pearls are available as well, with Mikimoto "seconds" finding many satisfied customers. South Sea black pearls, at bargain prices compared to the international market, are sold too.

Serious pearl shoppers can drop by Jewelmer's showroom in Megamall B. Jewelmer (www. jewelmer.com) is the world's second-largest producer of salt-water pearls.

FURNITURE

Beautiful wicker and rattan furniture is light enough to ship without spending large amounts of money. Angeles City is the shopper's best bet and offers made-to-order items.

Cebu has emerged as the country's main source of export-quality furniture. In Manila, drop by one of Firmas shops to see where the cutting edge in house decor is.

ANTIQUES

Situated on the old Chinese trade route, it is fitting that the Philippines has so many antiques for sale – among them, Chinese trade vessels beloved for the storing of wine, water and vinegar. Spanish religious items (including *santos* – the Christ child) appear with remarkable frequency, as does old Chinese and Indonesian furniture. Good antiques can be had in Manila, the roadside stalls of Laguna and in historic towns like Vigan. Several shops in the provinces offer antiques "made to order."

BRASSWARE

The first smiths of the Philippines are from Mindanao. To this day, Mindanao's craftsmen continue to manufacture gongs, jewel boxes, betel nut boxes, brass beds and cannon replicas. Ermita's tourist belt area hawks a fair amount of brassware, though the true collector will head to Mindanao.

WOOD CARVING

Giant hardwood carvings of the mountain-dwelling Ifugao were among the first local items that the Americans brought home. What they missed were other, more fascinating items, such as carvings of the rice granary god (*bulol*) and the animal totems from Palawan that can now be found in the Ermita tourist belt. Hardwoods become more precious by the day, and the Philippines has its fair share of fine narra and molave. Visit the woodcarving village in Baguio, or make your way through the Central Cordillera, especially Banaue.

Where to Buy

HANDICRAFTS

Balikbayan Handicrafts
290–298 Palanca Street, Quiapo
Tel: 02-734 9040/46
3F Market! Market!
Fort Bonifacio, Taguig
Tel: 02-886 7798, 886 7813
Alabang Town Center Expansion
Tel: 02-842 1661, 842 5376
1010 Arnaiz, Makati
Tel: 02-893 0775 to 77
Kayumanggi Arts and Crafts
Ninoy Aquino Avenue, Parañaque
Tel: 02-820 6916
Narda's
5781 Felipe Street, Makati
Tel: 02-896 7372
Also in NAIA, Baguio, La Trinidad, Cebu, Alabang
Silahis Center
744 General Luna Street, Intramuros
Tel: 02-527 2111, 527 2114
Fax: 02-527 2112
Also at: LRI Plaza N. Garcia Street, Makati
Tel: 02-898 2125
Alabang Town Center
Tel: 02-842 1505
One-stop shopping for handicrafts from around the archipelago.
Tesoro's
1325 Mabini Street, Ermita
Tel: 02-524 3936

Also at: The Landmark, tel: 02-812 1945; Arnaiz Avenue, tel: 02-844 4253; Manila Hotel, tel: 02-527 5341.

ANTIQUES

Jo-Liza Antique Shop
664 Jose Abad Santos, Little Baguio, San Juan
Tel: 02-725 8303, 725 8151
Megamall tel: 02-635 3013
Alabang tel: 02-807 2256
Grandma's Gallery
206 M. Paterno Street, San Juan
Tel: 02-723 3736
Call for appointment.
Goldcrest Village Square and **Glorietta 4**
Ayala Center, Makati. Several antiques vendors.
The Legaspi Collection
2/F, Textron Building, 168 Luna Mencias Street, San Juan
Tel: 02-724 3477
916 L. Mencias Street, Addition Hills Mandaluyong
Tel: 02-717 0900
la O' Center
Makati corner Arnaiz Avenue, Makati
Via Antica
1411 Mabini Street, Ermita
Tel: 02-524 7726
Parañaque tel: 02-852 8776

Shopping Malls

Shopping malls abound in Metro Manila, most offering daily air-conditioned comfort (10am–8pm) and reasonable prices for the foreign visitor. Near the airport, visit the **Duty Free Fiesta Mall** and **Duty Free Philippines** (check-out lines can be exasperating). Just north, in the Malate–Ermita tourist belt, are **Robinson's Place** and **Harrison Plaza**, on Mabini Street. North of the Pasig, check out the flea market-esque **Tutuban Center**, in the heart of **Divisoria market**, or **SM Shoemart Manila** (81 C Palanca Street, Quiapo).

Quezon City's shopping options range from **Araneta Center** – including **Ali Mall** and **SM Shoemart** – in Cubao to **Isetann Shopping**

Mall (C.M. Recto corner Quezon Boulevard). South, in San Juan, the **Greenhills Shopping Center** stands along Ortigas Avenue, with pearls available at **Virra Mall**, and many restaurants nearby. In Mandaluyong City, shoppers can enjoy the Philippines' largest mall, **SM Megamall** on EDSA. Other area malls include the upscale **Shangri-La Plaza Mall**, **Rustan's** and **Crossings Department Store**.

In Makati, **Ayala Center** includes department stores such as **Landmark**, **SM Shoemart** (soon to be relocated to Fort Bonifacio) and **Rustan's**. **Makati Cinema Square** (with its indoor firing range) round out the list of regular malls, while the upscale boutiques of **6750 Ayala Avenue** carry internationally known brands at internationally recognized prices. The **Greenbelt Shopping Complex** has redefined the Manila shopping experience, with its cutting-edge shops.

The **SM Mall of Asia**, built in Pasay at the end of EDSA, is the largest shopping mall in the country and the sixth largest in the world.

Southwards, the residential community of Ayala Alabang in Muntinlupa City offers the **Alabang Town Center**, **Festival Mall** (Corporate Avenue corner Civic Drive, Alabang) and **SM Southmall**.

Have a Cigar

The nation's **Tabacalera** cigars is an outstanding product. A whole range of tastes and sizes are available, from Tabacalera, using tobacco from northern Luzon, to the premier Don Juan Urquijo brand, with tobacco from the Dominican Republic. Visit their showrooms at major hotels. The true aficionado may wish to trek out to the La Flor de la Isabela factory at Km 14 West Service Rd, South Super Highway, Parañaque, tel: 02-823 6266, 821 1881, fax: 02-823 7833.

Language

General

Pilipino and English are national languages. Much of Pilipino is derived from Tagalog, the language of Manila and nearby provinces. Other major languages are Ilocano, Visayan, Cebuano and Maguindanao, although at least 110 languages prevail throughout the archipelago.

Listed below are some useful Tagalog expressions. Tagalog is pronounced phonetically, with no distinct accents on any particular syllables. "Siy" is pronounced "sh;" "ts" becomes "ch," and "ng" takes on a nasal, guttural sound.

GREETINGS

Welcome	*Mabuhay*
How are you?	*Kumusta ka?*
Fine. And you?	*Mabuti. At ikaw?*
Fine also	*Mabuti rin*
Good morning	*Magandang umaga (po)*
Good afternoon	*Magandang hapon (po)*
Good evening	*Magandang gabi (po)*
Goodbye	*Paalam*
Thank you	*Salamat (po)*
You're welcome	*Walang anuman*

SHOPPING

How much is this?	*Magkano ito?*
expensive	*mahal*
cheap	*mura*
I want...	*Gusto ko ng...*
Do you have...?	*Meron ba kayong...?*
How much per meter?	*Magkanong metro?*
How much of a discount?	*Magkanong tawad?*

OK, wrap it up.	*Pakibalot nga.*
Bill, please.	*Ang bill nga.*

USEFUL PHRASES

What is your name?	*Anong pangalan mo?*
My name is...	*Ang pangalan ko ay...*
How old are you?	*ilang taon ka na?*
Just a moment, please.	*Sandali lang.*
May I take a photo?	*Maari po. bakayong kunan ng retrato?*
I don't know.	*Hindi ko alam.*
yes/no	*oo/hindi*
good/bad	*mabait/masama*
many	*marami*
who	*sino*
what	*ano*
when	*kailan*
where	*saan*
delicious	*masarap*
sweet	*matamis*
sour	*maasim*
cold/hot	*malamig/mainit*
water	*tubig*
old/young	*matanda/bata*
new/old	*bago/luma*
big/small	*malaki/maliit*
clean/dirty	*malinis/masama*
man/woman	*lalaki/babae*
father/mother	*tatay/nanay*

NUMBERS

1	*isa*
2	*dalawa*
3	*tatlo*
4	*apat*
5	*lima*
6	*anim*
7	*pito*
8	*walo*
9	*siyam*
10	*sampu*
11	*labin-isa*
12	*labin-dalawa*
20	*dalawampu*
30	*tatlumpu*
40	*apatnapu*
50	*limanapu*
100	*isang daan*
200	*dalawang daan*
500	*limang daan*
1000	*isang libo*

Further Reading

Travel

Insight Pocket Guide: Manila and Environs by Julie Gaw. Apa Publications, 2000. A companion guide to this volume, with focused tours of the Philippine capital.

History & Politics

Bound to Empire: The United States and the Philippines by H.W. Brands. Oxford University Press, 1992. A sweeping narrative that examines the complex history of these two intertwined nations.

America's Boy: The Rise and Fall of Marcos and Other Misadventures of US Colonialism in the Philippines by James Hamilton-Paterson. Henry Holt, 1999. Topical, timely insights into a century of US-Philippine relations.

Comfort Woman: A Filipina's Story of Prostitution and Slavery Under the Japanese Military by Maria Rosa Henson. Rowman & Littlefield, 1999. The powerful autobiography of a teenage girl captured by the Japanese in April 1943 and forced to be a "comfort woman" for countless Japanese soldiers during World War II. A simply-told account of triumph over adversity.

In Our Image: America's Empire in the Philippines by Stanley Karnow. Ballantine Books, 1990. A Pulitzer Prize-winning look at America's sometimes blundering steps in the dance of colonialism. An invaluable perspective on the past.

Developing as a Democracy: Reform and Recovery in the Philippines, 1992–1998 by Fidel V. Ramos. St Martin's Press, 1999. A history of the Philippines under the Ramos administration.

Bataan: Our Last Ditch: The Bataan Campaign, 1942 by John W. Whitman. Hippocrene Books, 1990. A comprehensive history of the Death March.

Corazon Aquino and the Brushfire Revolution. Louisiana State University Press 1995. An unflinching account of the failures of the Aquino administration written by a reporter who covered it in its entirety.

Waltzing with a Dictator: The Marcoses and the Making of American Policy by Raymond Bonner. Vintage Books 1988. Using extensive documentation obtained through the Freedom of Information Act in the United States, this account outlines the tragic folly of the Marcos years as well as any.

Literature & Fiction

Brown River, White Ocean: An Anthology of Twentieth-Century Philippine Literature in English edited by Luis Francis. Rutgers University Press, 1993. Stories and poems that throw light on the flow of Philippine society, greatly influenced by its intervening foreign "big brothers."

Ghosts of Manila by James Hamilton-Paterson. Farrar Straus & Giroux, 1994. A disturbingly dark fictionalization of the Philippine underworld.

Dusk: A Novel by F. Sionil José. Modern Library, 1998. An epic novel set in the late 19th century, following the difficult lives of a tenant family after the expulsion of the Spaniards by American forces.

Noli Me Tangere (Shaps Library of Translation) by Jose P. Rizal. Edited by Raul L. Locsin; translated by Ma Soledad Lacson-Locsin. University of Hawaii Press, 1997. National hero Rizal's semi-autobiographical account of the harshness of life under Spanish rule. Required reading, along with his follow-up, *El Filibusterismo*.

Ghost Soldiers by Hampton Sides. Doubleday 2001. The best-selling book and soon-to-be Hollywood movie tells the story of the Bataan death march and a heroic mission to rescue its survivors. An important part of Philippine history told in riveting detail.

ART & PHOTO CREDITS

APA 344
Dr Christian Adler/PAL 21
Jim Barrome 211
Lito Beltran 9T
Marcus Brooke 231L
Philippe Body/HBL Network 220
Ben Cabrera 29
Franck Camhi/HBL Network 37
Cultural Centre of the Philippines 88
Kathy V. Chua/Adphoto 334
Mark Downey 4/5, 8T, 61, 74/75,
84/85, 87, 122/123, 143, 148,
180, 232T, 233, 236, 256, 263,
264, 295, 297, 299T, 302, 312T,
326, 336, 338, 339, 342
Sonny Evangelista 99, 108, 218T
Alain Evrard 6BL, 26, 30, 32, 44,
55, 70, 78, 118/119, 130, 138,
141, 151, 165, 185, 188, 190,
196R, 230, 275L, 306/307, 324T,
328T, 329T, 331T, 341, 341T
Alain Evrard/APA 200R, 218
Veronica Garbutt 4B, 98, 144R,
152, 163, 184, 193, 214, 232,
252, 271, 275R, 275T, 277, 310,
314T, 320, 332
Kevin Hamdorf 7B, 10/11, 45, 47,
86, 116, 117, 124, 146, 169, 179,
187, 190T, 192, 197, 200L, 201,
223, 226, 227, 234/235, 238, 242,
242T, 244, 245, 247, 249, 249T,
250, 251, 253T, 260, 263T, 268,
268T, 269, 270, 277T, 300, 319T,
327, 330, 333, 335, 343, 343T
Van Der Hilst/HBL Network 43
Hans Höfer/APA 5B, 38/39, 80,
82, 174, 182L, 186, 191, 197T,
209, 210, 221, 239, 272, 311,
317, 323, 325, 331, 340
**Jay Ireland & Georgienne E.
Bradley** 8C, 46, 166T, 173, 178T,
182R, 255, 262, 267, 288, 289,
294, 298, 301, 303, 303T, 313
Catherine Karnow 12/13, 14, 31,
33R, 34, 36, 51, 53, 62, 64,
66/67, 71, 92, 100, 104,
110/111, 147, 153, 161, 176, 248

Max Lawrence/APA 152T, 155
Lyle Lawson 23
Patrick Lucero 1, 2/3, 2B, 7T, 8B,
9CL, 9CR, 42, 50, 56, 60, 63, 68,
72, 76, 79, 81, 83, 96/97, 102,
105, 107, 109, 120/121, 134,
149L, 157L/R, 158, 159R, 160,
162, 166, 167, 168, 172, 175L/R,
175T, 176T, 177, 189, 194, 198,
199, 203, 208, 209T, 215,
217L/R, 219, 221T, 222, 224,
228, 229, 229T, 231R, 243, 246,
253, 254, 258, 259, 261, 265,
266, 273, 274, 276, 284/285,
290, 291, 291T, 292, 293, 293T,
299, 308, 314, 315, 316, 317T,
318, 319, 328, 329, 337
Patrick Lucero/APA 6BR, 7C,
35L/R, 52, 57, 65, 106, 112, 113,
115, 128/129, 137, 137T, 139T,
142, 144L, 144T, 145, 147T,
149R, 149T, 150, 154, 156, 156T,
158T, 164, 164T, 177T, 186T,
189T, 205T, 206L/R, 279, 280,
281, 286, 321, 322, 324, 333T
Leonard Lueras/APA 16/17, 20,
25, 135
**Lester V. Ledesma/Skylight
Images** 6T, 48/49, 139, 140
Mary Evans Picture Library 18, 22,
24, 27, 54, 114
Office of the President 19
PAL TPP 196L, 207
Pierre Alain Petit 225
Private archives 91, 93
G. P. Reichelt/APA 183
Blair Seitz/APA 69, 103, 159L,
202, 205
Lory Tan 101
Arthur Teng 58/59, 77, 89, 278
Topham Picturepoint 90
US Embassy – Manila 28
Andrew Wheeler 178
Noli Yumsuan 33L
Alfred Yuson 73, 181, 195

Picture Spreads

Pages 40/41: Top row from left to right: Lito Beltran, Cox Aban, Lito Beltran, Patrick Lucero. Centre row from left to right: Cox Aban, Mark Downey. Bottom row from left to right: Veronica Garbutt, Patrick Lucero, Aaron M. Favila, Jay Ireland & Georgienne E. Bradley.
Pages 94/95: Top row from left to right: Patrick Lucero, Aaron M. Favila, Rey Dalmacio, Patrick Lucero. Centre row from left to right: Mark Downey, Patrick Lucero, Patrick Lucero. Bottom row from left to right: Lito Beltran, Lito Beltran, Kevin Hamdorf.
Pages 212/213: Top row from left to right: Cox Aban, Boy Samson, Patrick Lucero. Bottom row from left to right: Jim Barrome, Patrick Lucero, Mark Downey, Cox Aban, Patrick Lucero, Mark Downey.
Pages 282/283: Top row from left to right: Lito Beltran, Patrick Lucero, Patrick Lucero, Jay Ireland & Georgienne E. Bradley, Mark Downey. Bottom row from left to right: Veronica Garbutt, Jay Ireland & Georgienne E. Bradley, Aaron M. Favila, Patrick Lucero, Mark Downey.

Map Production Cosmographics
© 2008 Apa Publications GmbH & Co.
Verlag KG (Singapore branch)

Cartographic Editor **Zoë Goodwin**
Production **Carol Low**
Design Consultants
Carlotta Junger, Graham Mitchener
Picture Research **Hilary Genin,
Britta Jaschinski**

Index